UNDERSTANDING AND EVALUATING EDUCATIONAL RESEARCH

THIRD EDITION

James H. McMillan

Virginia Commonwealth University

Jon F. Wergin

Antioch University

PEARSON

Merrill
Prentice Hall

Upper Saddle River, New Jersey
Columbus, Ohio

Library of Congress Cataloging-in-Publication Data

McMillan, James H.
 Understanding and evaluating educational research/James H. McMillan, Jon F.
Wergin.—3rd ed.
  p. cm.
 Includes bibliographical references and index.
 ISBN 0-13-172127-5
 1. Education—Research—Methodology. 2. Education—Research—Evaluation.
3.Action research in education. I. Wergin, Jon F. II. Title.

LB1028.M366 2006
370'.7'2—dc22   2005017472

Vice President and Executive Publisher: Jeffery W. Johnston
Publisher: Kevin M. Davis
Editorial Assistant: Sarah N. Kenoyer
Production Editor: Mary Harlan
Production Coordinator: Stephanie Levy, nSight
Design Coordinator: Diane C. Lorenzo
Text Design and Illustrations: Laserwords
Cover Design: Jason Moore
Cover Image: Corbis
Production Manager: Laura Messerly
Director of Marketing: Ann Castel Davis
Marketing Manager: Autumn Purdy
Marketing Coordinator: Brian Mounts

This book was set in Garamond Book by Laserwords. It was printed and bound by Bind Rite Graphics. The cover was printed by Coral Graphic Services, Inc.

Pearson Education Ltd.
Pearson Education Singapore Pte. Ltd.
Pearson Education Canada, Ltd.
Pearson Education–Japan
Pearson Education Australia Pty. Limited
Pearson Education North Asia Ltd.
Pearson Educación de Mexico, S.A. de C.V.
Pearson Education Malaysia Pte. Ltd.

10 9 8 7 6 5 4 3
ISBN: 0-13-172127-5

PREFACE

The purpose of this book is to help students become better and more informed consumers of published educational research studies. For many students, their only direct exposure to research methods will be in introductory research classes or classes that include a research component. Many students will approach the content with dread or, at best, resignation. Why should I have to learn about research methods if I'm never going to do this kind of work myself? they ask. Our response is simple. Practicing professionals, whether teachers, principals, or counselors, need to be able to read, understand, and evaluate research studies. They need to approach research data with a critical eye—to discriminate sound arguments from specious ones, to discern appropriate uses of statistics from those meant to mislead or obfuscate. As professionals they should not have to depend on others' assessments of the credibility or usefulness of research; they should be able to read, critique, and evaluate research information themselves.

This book provides students with a systematic approach for first identifying whether an article or report should be considered "research," then understanding the type of research, and, finally, utilizing criteria by which studies of each type should be judged. This approach is illustrated with published articles from various journals. With each article we include questions that will help students learn how to apply appropriate criteria, both for the case at hand and for other studies of its type, and provide answers to illustrate the thinking of informed consumers. By the end of the book we hope that students will have developed a way of thinking about published research and a greater sense of confidence in their ability to read it profitably.

Understanding and Evaluating Educational Research is not meant to supplant the main text for an introductory research class, but rather to serve as a supplement to it, especially in classes where a major focus is on understanding research. Research articles have been organized to be consistent with the methodological classification found in most introductory research texts. The writing uses nontechnical language for the research novice. Important terms and concepts are boldfaced.

ORGANIZATION

The organization of the third edition remains unchanged, with one significant addition. In the first chapter we lay out our typology, suggest how the reader might use it to classify research studies, and present criteria by which all educational research should be judged. Succeeding chapters present the research types one at a time, describe their peculiar characteristics, and present criteria by which each type ought to be evaluated. This edition includes a new chapter, on mixed-method designs. In the final chapter we discuss action-oriented research and practitioner research studies that transcend the categories.

NEW TO THIS EDITION

The third edition includes the following enhancements:

- Additions of a new chapter on mixed methods and two mixed-methods studies
- Revised discussion of research typology

- Revised and expanded discussion of qualitative methods and designs
- Eight new articles
- More emphasis on randomized designs

Our criteria for selecting the published articles included the following:

1. *Publication date*. Most articles have been published within the past five years.

2. *Topic*. The articles represent the diversity of topics found in education (e.g., educational administration, counseling, special education, curriculum, adult education, and early childhood education).

3. *Relevance*. The articles are interesting, relevant, and useful.

4. *Level of difficulty*. The articles range from easily understood to moderate levels of difficulty.

5. *Journals*. The articles come from a wide variety of journals.

ACKNOWLEDGMENTS

We are most appreciative of the support and expertise of the Merrill/Prentice Hall staff in preparing and publishing this book. We are also grateful to our students who have provided helpful suggestions on the choice of articles, on the introductory sections to each chapter, and on changes made to the third edition. We also wish to thank our reviewers: W. Sam Adams, University of Wisconsin; James H. Banning, Colorado State University; John E. Bonfadini, George Mason University; Joe Cornett, Texas Tech University; Ayres D. Costa, Ohio State University; Karen Ford, Ball State University; Michael K. Gardner, University of Utah; Andrea Guillaume, California State University; Joseph Maxwell, George Mason University; Carmen Montecinos, Northern Iowa; Tamara B. Murdock, University of Missouri; Karin Sconzert, Loyola University; R. Lee Smith, Indiana University South Bend; and Karen Westburg, University of Connecticut.

CONTENTS

1 INTRODUCTION TO READING EDUCATIONAL RESEARCH

In this introduction we will summarize a series of steps that will help you identify if an article or report is empirical research, determine the type of research, and ask the kinds of questions that will facilitate an understanding of the study. In subsequent chapters we will provide more information about specific types of research designs and the kinds of questions to ask for each type. We refer to the first few steps as a "roadmap" for identifying different types of research (see Fig. 1).

WHAT IS EDUCATIONAL RESEARCH?

Good professional practice is informed in a number of different ways, including, but not limited to, what we are here calling "research." Not all of what is published in a professional journal is research. Many journal materials are in the form of essays, thought pieces, anecdotes, commentaries, or articles with such titles as "The Future of Site-Based Management" or "One School's Experience with High-Stakes Testing." Op-ed pieces like these can be provocative and insightful, but they do not constitute research as we are defining it in this book. We are also choosing to exclude certain forms of scholarship often called research in other contexts, namely integrative literature reviews and presentations of theory. While these approaches represent powerful means of generating new knowledge, they are not, strictly speaking, forms of research. Research has the following three distinguishing features:

- Research is *systematic*. It relies on careful, formal procedures for setting up the investigation, collecting and analyzing data, and interpreting results. These procedures are transparent enough to allow for verification of findings by others.
- Research is *rigorous*. It embodies a certain skepticism about observations and conclusions, and employs procedures designed to reduce and control bias.
- Research is *empirical*. It relies on data that are tangible, that is, accessible to the senses. Empirical data can be in the form of numbers, such as scores or frequencies, or in the form of text, such as interview transcripts.

Given these three criteria it is clear why essays and commentaries, while based on empirical evidence, are not necessarily the result of systematic and rigorous investigation; or why theory development, while based on systematic and rigorous processes, is not necessarily empirical.

In sum, **educational research** is a systematic investigation, involving the analysis of information (data), to answer a question or contribute to our knowledge about an educational theory or practice. As systematic, disciplined inquiry, educational research relies on methods and principles that will produce credible and verifiable results. Defined in this way, research is not simply gathering information about something, such as going to the library and doing a research paper. Rather, information is gathered from individuals, groups, documents, existing data bases, and

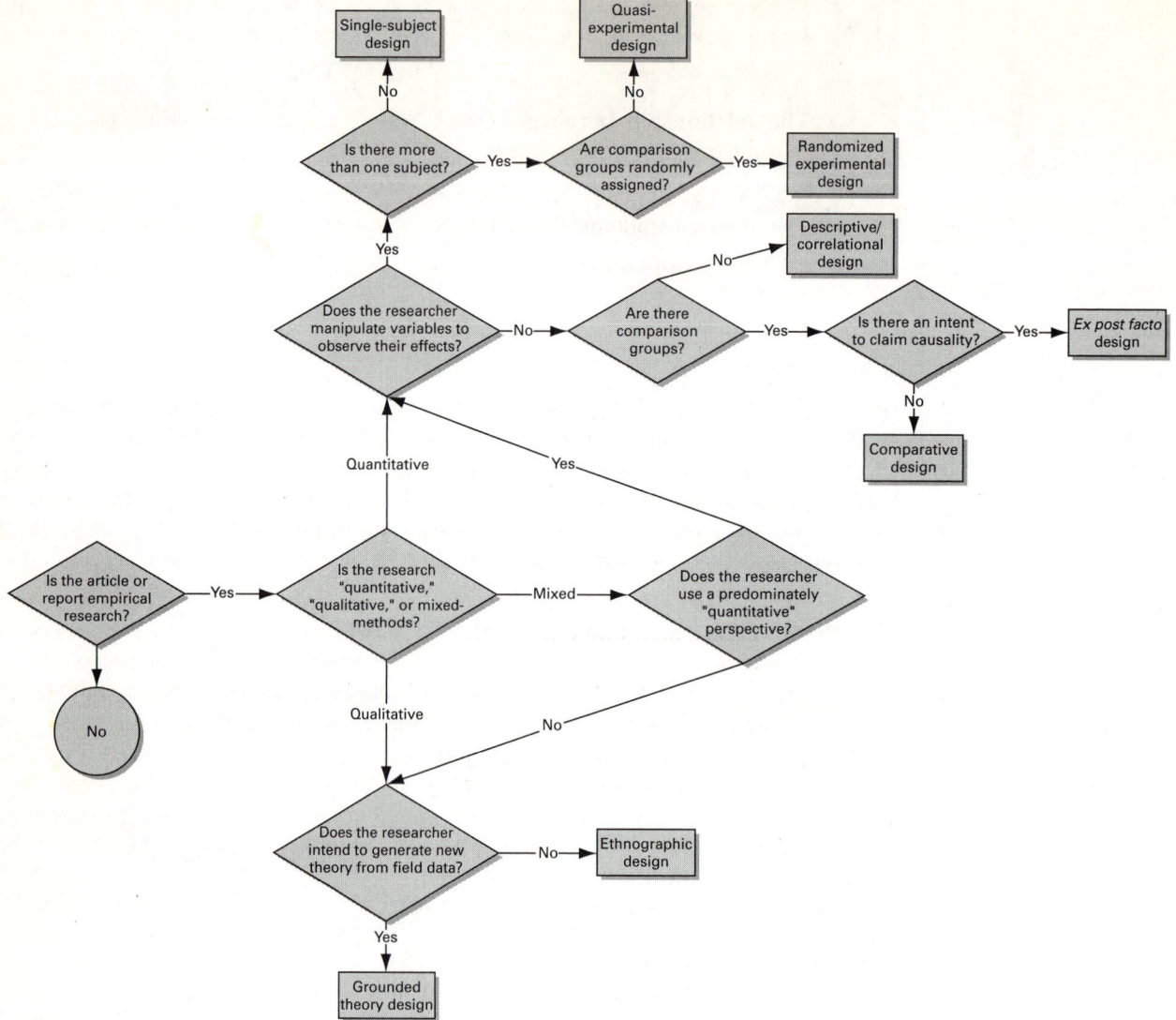

Figure I.   Roadmap for identifying types of educational research.

other sources, then analyzed and interpreted. Typically, research consists of a series of steps such as the following, though the sequence may vary depending on the specific nature of the study:

1. Frame the initial question or problem.
2. Determine what previous research says about the question or problem.
3. Frame a research question, problem, or hypothesis.
4. Design a plan for collecting or obtaining data to address the question, problem, or hypothesis.
5. Analyze the results of gathered data.
6. Generate conclusions.

The first step in understanding research is to be able to recognize that an article or report is, in fact, research. You will need to distinguish between empirical studies (research) and other forms of scholarly writing. Here is a summary of what to look for in making this determination:

1. Does the title suggest that data have been gathered or obtained from existing records? The titles of research articles typically contain language that suggests

the collection and analysis of data. The terms *study* and *investigation* denote research, as would phrases such as "an investigation of," "the relationship between," and "the effect of." Here are some examples.

- The relationship between cognitive style and student effort in learning mathematics problem solving.
- A study of teacher decision making concerning assessment and grading.
- Incentives for students: The effect of varying types of rewards on achievement.
- Effects of cooperative and individualized methods of instruction on student altruism.

The title of an article is one clue as to whether it is research. If the previous words or phrases are used, it is probably research, but some studies might not contain any of these words or phrases.

2. Are new data collected? Most research involves the collection of new information (some research reanalyzes information that has already been collected). This means that there will be reference to a procedure that was followed to collect the data. Usually there is a section that uses terms such as *instruments, measures,* or *data collection.*

3. Is there a methodology or methods section? In a research article or report there will be a methodology or methods section. The purpose of this section is to summarize the manner in which subjects or participants were obtained, the instrumentation utilized, procedures for collecting information, and any direct interventions on the subjects. This is usually a major heading.

4. Is there a findings or results section? Since the purpose of research is to analyze information to answer a question, there will usually be some kind of results or findings section that summarizes what the data show. This section often includes tables or graphs to summarize the information.

WHAT ARE THE VARIOUS TYPES OF EDUCATIONAL RESEARCH?

While all educational research shares such attributes as a focus on empiricism and disciplined inquiry, there are many different ways or methods by which the research is carried out. Each of these methods has distinct purposes, advantages, and disadvantages. The second step toward becoming an intelligent consumer of educational research, then, is to recognize which method has been used. The third step is to assess the quality of the research according to criteria appropriate for that method.

For example, you would analyze a study of parental attitudes toward AIDS education very differently from a study reporting the results of an experimental curriculum. In the first case you would probably be most interested in questions like these: How were the parents chosen for this study, and how many participated? What method was used to collect data from parents, and how appropriate were the questions the researchers asked? What inferences were drawn from the results, and how valid were they? For the second case, in contrast, you would probably be most interested in questions like these: What precisely was different about the "experimental" curriculum? How was it implemented? What effects was it supposed to have, and how did the researchers choose to measure these effects? Did the researchers use a *control* group? How was it selected? Did the researchers find the effects they were looking for? Were these effects significant?

Types of educational research are categorized in Figure 1.1. It may be read, from left to right, as a decision tree. (Action/participant research is a unique type of study that is discussed in Chapter 6.) Here are the major distinctions to keep in mind as you work your way through it.

QUANTITATIVE/QUALITATIVE/MIXED-METHODS RESEARCH

The most fundamental difference in methodology of research is whether it is *quantitative, qualitative,* or *mixed-method* (some combination of the two). **Quantitative** research involves the use of numerical indices to summarize, describe, and explore relationships among traits. There is a reliance on control, statistics, measurement, and experiments. In **qualitative** research, the emphasis is on conducting studies in natural settings using mostly verbal descriptions, resulting in stories and case studies rather than statistical reports. Research employing mixed methods has qualities of both quantitative and qualitative designs. All three approaches are viable in education. Until recently, almost all educational research was quantitative. Today, qualitative and mixed-method studies are reported with increasing frequency.

Quantitative Research: Experimental/Nonexperimental

Once you have determined that a study is quantitative, it is helpful to determine if it is an experiment. An **experimental** study is one in which the researcher has control over one or more factors (variables) that may influence the responses of the subjects. There is *manipulation* of factors that may affect subjects' behavior. The purpose of this control is to determine whether one factor causes a change in another one. A **nonexperimental** study is one in which there is no control over what may influence subjects' responses. The investigator is interested in studying what occurred or occurs *naturally.* Nonexperimental studies are generally used to describe phenomena and uncover relationships. For example, suppose that you were interested in looking at the relationship between students' participation in class discussion and teachers' verbal reinforcement of their comments. You could conduct a nonexperimental study by observing teacher and student behavior and noting when certain behaviors appear to occur together. If, however, you were interested in isolating more specific cause-and-effect relationships—that is, whether teacher reinforcement actually causes more student participation—you could conduct a more experimental-type study by systematically manipulating teacher behavior and noting its apparent effect on students. While this latter kind of study may appear more precise, it also introduces other kinds of problems, as we will see in Chapter 3. Experimental-type studies can be further broken down into three categories: randomized-experimental, quasi-experimental, and single-subject.

Experimental Research: Randomized-Experimental/Quasi-Experimental/Single-Subject. Randomized experimental research involves something very specific, namely, the use of comparison groups that have been **randomly assigned.** Random assignment means what it says: assignment of subjects to comparison groups has been done completely at random, like flipping a coin or drawing names out of a hat. Random assignment strengthens the argument that any apparent effect of the treatment is not due to other factors, such as inherent differences among the groups. **Quasi-experimental** research is that which manipulates treatments but does not use randomly assigned treatment groups. If, for example, you were interested in assessing the impact of a new science curriculum on fifth graders, you might want to implement the new curriculum with one sample of students and then see how they do compared to another sample exposed to the traditional approach. Ideally you'd want to assign students to these two groups at random; practically, this may be impossible, however, and so you use two intact fifth-grade classes instead, implementing the new curriculum with one and the traditional with the other. As you might imagine, what quasi experiments gain in feasibility, they give up in explanatory power. **Single-subject** research is much like an experiment in that a condition is actively manipulated by the investigator to examine its impact on behavior. In single-subject studies, however, there is only one person (or just a few people) in the study. This kind of research is common in situations in which it is difficult or impossible to identify large groups of subjects, such as with children with learning disabilities. Careful observation of targeted behavior is the most common method of collecting data.

Nonexperimental Research: Descriptive/Comparative/Correlational/*Ex Post Facto*. Once you determine that the study is nonexperimental, you will need to further classify it as descriptive, comparative, correlational, or *ex post facto*.

Descriptive research that is quantitative simply describes a phenomenon with statistics such as frequencies, percentages, averages, and sometimes a measure of variability, such as the range, and with visual images such as frequency polygons, pie charts, and bar graphs. There are no comparisons made or relationships examined. For example, a descriptive study could investigate the nature of teacher opinions about the use of high-stakes standardized testing. A survey could be prepared and a sample of teachers could respond to such questions as: Have high-stakes standardized tests affected what you teach or how you teach? Have these tests had an impact on the types of classroom assessments used? How have the tests affected your morale? Percentages could be used to summarize the results, for example, 20 percent of the teachers indicated that the high-stakes tests have had a significant effect on what they teach, or 60 percent of the teachers indicated that the tests have had a negative impact on teacher morale.

Comparative research investigates the relationship between two or more variables by examining the differences that exist between two or more groups of subjects. That is, the groups are compared to one another. For example, suppose a researcher is interested in whether a relationship exists between grade level and self-concept. Samples of subjects are obtained from several different grades, and the mean self-concept scores for the sample from each grade are calculated. The average scores from each grade are compared. For instance, if grades 4 through 10 are compared and the average self-concept scores for grades 8, 9, and 10 are higher than the scores for grades 4, 5, and 6, then a positive relationship exists between grade level and self-concept. Unlike *ex post facto* studies, comparative research makes no claim of causality.

Correlational designs investigate relationships among variables by calculating correlation coefficients, rather than looking at differences. To calculate a correlation, each subject presents scores from two variables. The correlation coefficient is calculated using these sets of scores to indicate the direction and strength of the relationship. The direction is either positive or negative; the strength varies from little or no relationship to moderate to strong. Here are some questions that would be investigated using a correlational design: How is teacher satisfaction related to the degree of autonomy on the job? Does a relationship exist between the degree of parental involvement with the school and socioeconomic status? How well do SAT scores predict college grades? Correlational studies are common in education and generally use survey methods as a means of collecting data.

Ex post facto research, also called causal-comparative research, is a nonexperiment dressed up to look like an experiment. Ex post facto studies examine a phenomenon that has already occurred and attempt to infer cause-and-effect relationships. These are examples of questions leading to ex post facto studies: Do children who have attended day care programs do better in kindergarten? Do couples who seek out marriage counselors have more stable marriages? Do people who smoke have higher rates of lung cancer than those who don't? In each case a treatment variable is identified—day care, marriage counselors, cigarette smoking—and those who have been exposed to it are compared to those who have not some variable of interest—in these examples, academic performance, marital happiness, cancer incidence. Teasing out whether in fact any differences are due to the treatment variable is very difficult in *ex post facto* studies, as we will see later.

Qualitative Research: Ethnography/Grounded Theory

All qualitative research is based on a philosophy called *phenomenology,* a perspective that holds that knowledge is gained by understanding the direct experience of others. Research based on phenomenology is descriptive in nature, relying primarily on narrative and story. Thus the term *qualitative* is used to distinguish this type of research from that which is based primarily on measurements and numbers.

Once you have determined that the study is qualitative, examine it further to determine whether it is an ethnographic design or a grounded theory design. An **ethnographic** study involves direct engagement with the participants and environments to obtain an in-depth description and interpretation of behavior within a culture or social group. Since the intent is to understand in depth the phenomena being studied, the observations and interviews typically take place in naturally occurring settings and tend to be prolonged. Ethnographies collect observational and/or interview data and then summarize and analyze the data. Conclusions are based on a synthesis of the data collected, and the results are generally presented in the form of a case study.

In a **grounded theory** investigation the researcher's intent is to discover or generate a theory that pertains to a specific entity or phenomenon. The theory is "grounded" in data that are collected in the field. Grounded theory studies usually begin with a few very general "foreshadowed" questions. As data are collected—through interviews, observation, and analysis of documents—themes begin to emerge that are tested and refined until the thematic categories hold up under scrutiny. Results of a grounded theory study are generally presented in the form of new constructs, which can then be tested in other settings.

Mixed-Methods.   More and more often, research in education is employing so-called *mixed-methods* approaches. As you'll see in the articles included in this chapter, mixed-methods research uses narrative in designs generally associated with quantitative research, numbers in designs associated with qualitative research, or both quantitative and designs in the same study. The reasoning is logical: why not design studies that capture the best of what both quantitative and qualitative methods have to offer? At least on the surface the reasoning makes sense: add some flesh-and-blood interest to an otherwise lifeless quantitative study by including some in-depth case studies, or cut through the verbiage of a qualitative text by including some hard data.

As reasonable as this argument may seem, mixed-methods studies have serious issues all their own. First and most obviously, they can flummox the novice consumer. Just when you think you're able to classify research articles according to the decision tree in Chapter 1, along comes an article that defies classification. What set of criteria am I supposed to use now?, you ask. Both? Neither? Some amalgam of the two?

The second issue is a more serious epistemological question. As we've noted elsewhere in this book, the choice of whether to undertake a quantitative or qualitative study isn't just about the nature of the research question or the preferences individual researchers may have for certain types of data. Choice of designs also depends on the assumptions the researcher has about the nature of truth and how to arrive at it. Researchers with a quantitative bent are relatively more concerned about matters of prediction and control: isolating relationships among variables, discerning effects of educational interventions, preserving objectivity, and finding results that can be generalized beyond the study sample. Researchers with a qualitative bent, on the other hand, are relatively more concerned about matters of description and understanding: perceiving the multiple realities of a program or classroom, being careful to respect the particularities and nuances of the individual case, or worrying more about how well the research report provides a vicarious experience for the reader than about any generalizable truths it may contain. These are substantial differences, and they are not easily negotiated.

As a consequence, mixed *paradigm* studies continue to be quite rare. While researchers may increasingly use mixed methods in their designs, with few exceptions they continue to operate from a dominant worldview. The challenge for the informed research consumer is to discern what that worldview is, and then to apply the appropriate criteria accordingly. Here are some questions to apply when making that judgment.

- Do the researchers begin the study with some clear hypotheses they want to test?
- Do they set up comparison groups?
- Do they express concern about the representativeness of samples, or the generalizability of results?

If the answer to any of the above questions is yes, then it is likely that the researchers are operating from a dominant quantitative paradigm, and the study should be evaluated accordingly. If the answer to all of the above is no, then it's likely that the researchers are using a qualitative paradigm, and the study should be evaluated using qualitative criteria.

WHAT CRITERIA ARE USEFUL FOR UNDERSTANDING AND EVALUATING RESEARCH ARTICLES?

As we have already noted, each type of research study has certain criteria for excellence that are indigenous to it, and we will focus on these criteria in exploring further each major type of research in subsequent chapters. Some criteria, however, pertain to all educational research, regardless of type; we present these criteria here. Ultimately, it is important to meet these criteria for the research to be credible and useful.

Credibility is the extent to which the information is understandable, trustworthy, valid, and logical. If the article is well written, complete, and meets most of the criteria summarized below, then it is more likely to be credible and useful. You may find what could be called fatal flaws in some studies–deficiencies so serious that the conclusions are uninterpretable. More commonly, though, you will find that while the study may have some limitations, the information is helpful. Consequently, our intent is to help you become a critical reader, but not hypercritical.

In the following sections, different parts of research articles are summarized, and questions are formulated for each part that you can ask as a guide to understanding and evaluating that part of the article. While the major sections presented apply to most research articles and reports, there is published research that will not have these parts as we have labeled them. Many qualitative studies, in particular, will use different language or have different sections.

Introduction

The purpose of the introduction is to set the context of the study and to indicate the research problem. This part of the article is usually one to several paragraphs long. It may provide background to the study and indicate why it is significant to conduct the research. This is often accomplished with quotes or references to other studies that set a historical context. Most introductory sections will contain a general statement of the problem that will be investigated; in some studies the specific research questions will replace a general statement of purpose.

Questions to ask

1. Is the general purpose of the study clear?
2. Is the study significant? Will it make a practical or theoretical contribution?
3. Is the introduction well organized and clear?

Review of Literature

Quantitative. The review of literature for quantitative studies is one to several paragraphs in which previous studies of the same or similar problems are summarized and analyzed. The purpose of the review is to show how the current study is related to other studies. A good review is selective and goes beyond simply reporting what others have found. It is best if the review includes a critical analysis of previous studies and indicates implications of the analysis for the present study. The articles in the review should be closely related to the problem under investigation so that the problem is logically connected to what else has been done in the area. The review should use as many current articles as possible, but relevance is more important than recency. It is organized by topic and not by date. The review should concentrate on other studies that are closely related to the current one and should only mention briefly minor studies that are not very relevant.

Questions to ask

1. Does the review contain up-to-date, relevant studies?
2. Is there an emphasis on primary sources (i.e., actual studies, rather than other review articles)?
3. Is there a critical review or a summary of findings?
4. Is the review well organized?
5. Does the review clearly relate previous studies to the current research problem?
6. Does the review help establish the importance of the research?

Qualitative. In qualitative studies the review of literature has a somewhat different function and form. Qualitative researchers use a *preliminary literature review* to present conceptual frameworks, broad areas of study, and scholarly concepts; this provides a foundation for phrasing foreshadowed questions. Once the study has begun, a continued search of the literature is integrated with the methodology and tentative findings and interpretations. The *continuous literature review* is needed to connect previous studies with ongoing changes in the focus and methodology of the study. By the end of the study there is a complete review of related literature that contains, like quantitative studies, a critique and analysis of the works. Thus, while in quantitative studies a clear literature review section almost always precedes the methodology, in qualitative studies the review is interspersed throughout the document.

Research Problem, Question, or Hypothesis

While a general problem statement is usually included in the introductory section, in quantitative studies it is necessary to indicate a specific research problem statement, question, and/or research hypothesis. Sometimes the specific problem statement or question is located at the end of the introduction, before the review of literature. More commonly, a specific research question or hypothesis follows the review. In fact, the review helps to establish the specific questions or hypotheses. (A **research hypothesis** is a statement that indicates the expected or predicted relationship between two or more variables.) The specific problem can be formulated as either a statement or a question. Regardless of the form, it is important for the specific problem to be clear, succinct, and researchable. It should give you an indication of the type of research method being used (e.g., experimental or nonexperimental), the independent and dependent variables, and the subjects.

In a qualitative study the research problem is formulated as the **foreshadowed problem** or **question.** It is more general than specific questions or hypotheses found in quantitative studies. The foreshadowed problem or question provides a broad framework for beginning the study and is reformulated as data are collected. The emphasis is on what, where, and why, rather than on relationship among variables.

Questions to ask

1. Is the problem or hypothesis clear and concise?
2. If there is a hypothesis, is it consistent with the review of literature?
3. If quantitative, does the problem or hypothesis communicate the variables, type of research, and population?
4. If qualitative, is the initial problem reformulated?

Methodology: Subjects, Participants, or Sources of Information

A **subject** or **participant** is a person from whom information is gathered to answer the research question. **Sources of information** refers to the documents, people, or settings from which data are collected. In most articles you will find a section of the methodology that will be labeled *subjects, sample, participants,* or *population.* In this section, the individuals from whom the data are collected will be described. It is important to know about the subjects since their backgrounds and characteristics may influence the results. Some qualitative studies use documents, artifacts, pictures, and other sources of data that are not directly from people. Often, qualitative investigations will select a **purposeful sample** to meet a specific need.

Questions to ask

1. Is the population described adequately?
2. Is the sample of subjects, participants, or other sources of information clearly described?
3. Is the method of selecting the sample clear?
4. Could the method of selection affect the results?
5. Are subjects likely to be motivated to give biased responses?

Methodology: Instruments

Credibility of research depends on the quality of the measurement of the variables and procedures for collecting the data. If the measurement and procedures are weak, then so too are the results. **Instruments,** or **measures,** are devices that are used to gather information from subjects. Instruments can take a wide variety of forms, including tests, oral or written surveys, ratings, observation, and various archival and unobtrusive measures.

For quantitative studies the credibility of the information gathered with these techniques depends on two kinds of evidence: validity and reliability. **Validity** refers to the appropriateness of the inferences made from the data collected. These are examples of validity questions: How useful are SAT scores as a measure of academic achievement in high school? How useful are they as a measure of likely academic achievement in college? To what extent do student responses on a survey that is meant to measure self-esteem really reflect self-esteem, and not some other variable such as verbal skill or social desirability?

Evidence for validity should thus be presented in the context of how the results are to be used. Just because an instrument is established or standardized does not mean that it is valid; for example, it wouldn't make sense to use an intelligence test to measure musical ability. Validity is often established during a pilot test of the instrument.

Reliability refers to the degree of error that exists when obtaining a measure of a variable. No measure or instrument is perfect; each will contain some degree of error. The error may be due to the individual (general skills, attitudes, illness, motivation, etc.) or because of the way the instrument is designed and administered.

Reliability is the estimate of the error in the assessment. Generally you will look for evidence of the instrument's consistency, whether across time or across raters, or within the instrument itself.

In a qualitative study the technical features of instrument validity and reliability are not used. Nevertheless, the more general ideas of appropriateness of the inferences (validity) and error in collecting information (reliability) are still important. When observing in a qualitative study, for example, the extent of the observation and background of the observer are key elements in determining quality. Typically, for example, observers are in the field for an extended period of time, often several months. Detailed field notes become evidence that what is reported is what actually occurred.

It will also be helpful to examine the procedures used to collect the information. Who administered the instrument or who were the observers? Would they be biased? Were the observers trained? Did the subjects have sufficient time to answer the questions? If the instrument concerned attitudes, was it anonymous? Would the respondents want to give socially desirable answers?

The purpose of any data collection instrument is to provide accurate information about the variables being studied. Thus, each variable is actually defined by how it is measured and reported, as well as how it is labeled or defined conceptually by the researcher. There are advantages and disadvantages to using different procedures to collect information, but each should provide evidence of validity and reliability. Look for anything in the procedures or the instrument itself that could bias the results.

Questions to ask

1. Is evidence for validity and reliability clearly presented and adequate?
2. Is there a clear description of the instrument and how it was used?
3. Is there a clear description of the procedures for collecting the information?
4. Is it likely that the subjects would fake their responses?
5. Are interviewers and observers trained?
6. If appropriate, what are the norms used to report percentile rank and other results?

Methodology: Procedures

The procedures subsection will indicate, depending on the study and journal, how subjects or participants were selected, how instruments were developed and administered, and how experimental treatments, if any, were conducted. A qualitative study will describe procedures the researcher used to gain entry into the field, the nature and length of observations and interviews, and how participants were approached. In this section you will want to look for characteristics of the study design that might lead to erroneous interpretations of the data. For example, could the researcher's own biases and desires affect the results? Could the participants' awareness of being in a study affect their behavior when an observer is present?

Questions to ask

1. Are there any clear weaknesses in the design of the study?
2. Are the procedures for collecting information described fully?
3. Is it likely that the researcher is biased?

Results

The results, or findings, section of the article presents a summary of the data analysis. This section is usually organized by the research question or hypothesis. It is helpful if the researcher first presents the findings without interpreting them. This will often involve the use of tables and charts. Basically the researcher is saying, this is what I found.

With advances in computer technology, statistical analyses are usually done without mathematical error. It is another matter, however, to know whether the appropriate statistical methods have been used and whether the results are interpreted correctly. While it is beyond the scope of this book to cover different analysis techniques, some basic principles will help you to understand these sections.

In quantitative studies, researchers often use **inferential statistics** to make probability statements about what is likely to be true. That is, how certain can we be that a statistical finding reflects reality? The degree of probability or certainty depends most on the amount of measurement and sampling error in the study. For example, when we select a sample from a population, inferential statistics tell us what is probably true about the population even though we only use a portion of the population in the study. Statistical significance is not the same as practical significance, importance of the finding, or whether the study has a strong design. Some studies that use a very large number of subjects can report statistically significant results that are of little practical importance. Conversely, studies using a very small number of subjects may not be able even to establish statistical significance due to the small sample size.

In qualitative research there is a need to document a systematic process of analyzing the data. Often qualitative researchers will code transcripts and rearrange examples of different kinds of evidence in an effort to identify trends or conclusions. **Triangulation** is used often, in which different sources of data pertaining to the same question are used to verify consistency of findings. The results are typically presented as they flow from the data, rather than in predetermined categories, and quotes from participants and specific events from observations are used to illustrate the findings.

Questions to ask

1. Are the findings presented clearly?
2. Is there appropriate use of tables, charts, and figures?
3. Is the number of subjects taken into consideration when presenting the results?
4. Is there sufficient descriptive information to interpret the results?
5. Are the results presented in relation to the research question, or does the study seem more like a "fishing expedition" to find something, anything, that is "statistically significant"?
6. If qualitative, are the results accompanied by illustrative quotes and specific instances?

Discussion and Conclusions

Once the results have been summarized, the researcher will present a discussion of their meaning. This interpretation is helpful in understanding why certain results were obtained. Usually the researcher evaluates the findings in light of the methodology to explain what the results mean and how they can be used. The researcher uses the research question and review of literature in this analysis. Essentially this is a statement of the judgment of the researcher given the research problem, review of literature, methodology, and results. Often limitations are summarized, due to subject selection, the nature of the instrument used, or a weakness in the procedures.

The final section of the article will present **conclusions**—summary statements of the findings and how the researcher interprets them. Conclusions should be supported by the data and logical analysis. It is helpful for the researcher to indicate limitations to the conclusions based on subject characteristics, the context of the research, when the research was conducted, the nature of the treatments, and instruments used to collect information. An important research concept related to limitations is **generalizability** of the findings. **External validity** is a term that is used to refer to the extent to which the findings can be generalized to be true for other individuals, settings, times, treatments, and measures. That is, what is true for sixth graders who were involved in a study may not be true for ninth graders, or true for other sixth graders across town, and results demonstrated by one measure of creativity may not be replicated if a different measure of creativity is used. In qualitative studies generalizability is determined by the **translatability** and **comparability** of the findings. The emphasis is on how well the data, categories, procedures, and patterns are described, and how well other researchers can understand the findings so that they can be used in other settings. While it is possible to be overly strict in judging external validity, it is best to use reasonable professional judgment.

Questions to ask

1. Is the discussion based on the research problem and results, or is there a tendency to discuss unrelated material or ideas?
2. Is there an adequate interpretation of the findings?
3. Is the interpretation separate from the results?
4. Are the results discussed in relation to previous studies?
5. Are limitations due to methodology included in the discussion?
6. Are the conclusions clearly stated and based on the results and discussion?
7. Are the conclusions reasonable? Do they go beyond the interpretation of the findings?
8. What is the generalizability of the findings? What factors would affect generalizability?

2 | QUANTITATIVE NONEXPERIMENTAL DESIGNS

Quantitative nonexperimental research is conducted to describe phenomena or to investigate relationships among variables. **Descriptive** nonexperimental research uses frequencies, percentages, averages, and other simple statistics to provide a description of the data collected. In a descriptive study the nature of the sample and instrumentation are key to understanding the results. While descriptive investigations are particularly valuable when something is first researched, most nonexperimental studies go beyond mere description to examine comparisons and relationships among variables.

A relationship is expressed as either a correlation or a comparison. A **correlational** study is one in which there are at least two measured variables for each subject. These variables are related by using one or more correlational analyses. A correlation is computed to show the direction and magnitude of the relationship. A **simple (bivariate)** correlation relates one variable to another one. It results in a number between -1 and $+1$. If the correlation is positive, then the relationship is positive (not necessarily good), which means that as the value of one variable increases, so does the value of the other variable. A negative, or inverse, relationship is designated by a negative correlation and means that increases in one variable are associated with decreases in the other variable. The size of the correlation is important for interpreting the results. As the correlation approaches either -1 or $+1$ (depending on whether it is positive or negative), it becomes stronger. A correlation of .75 or above would be considered high, around .5 moderate, and below .3 low. A correlation of $-.86$ is stronger than a correlation of .78.

Another common type of correlational analysis is called a **multiple correlation** or **multiple regression.** In this type of study several independent variables are combined to see how well they predict one or more dependent variables. The resulting relationship shows how well the combined independent variables predict. For example, a researcher may want to see how well several variables from a sample of high school students, such as socioeconomic status, family structure, and aptitude test scores, predict college grades. The analysis will tell the researcher how these three independent variables, together, predict grades, and also how much each of the three contributes to the overall correlation.

Another type of quantitative nonexperimental study that investigates relationships is comparative. The purpose of **comparative** research is to provide an accurate description of how two or more groups differ on some phenomenon (dependent variable). The variable that differentiates the groups is the independent variable. Thus, if a study compares the achievement of male students to female students, gender is the independent variable and achievement is the dependent variable. Comparative studies can examine the differences over time of the same or similar group of subjects, or can investigate how groups that are not the same compare. A **developmental** study investigates changes in subjects over time. If the same subjects are investigated, the study is **longitudinal.** If different groups of subjects who do not have the same age are studied at one time, the study is **cross-sectional.**

While longitudinal developmental studies are stronger and more credible, they are more difficult to complete and require more time and resources. In a cross-sectional study, the researcher needs to be careful that differences among the subjects in different age categories in characteristics such as ability, motivation, background, and attitudes do not account for the results.

If groups that are different on the independent variable are compared, it is usually a straightforward study. For instance, the following questions suggest a comparative study: Do teachers with tenure have different attitudes about merit salary increases than untenured teachers? How does the self-concept of high achieving students compare with the self-concept of low-achieving students? What is the difference in attitudes toward parking of commuter and noncommuter students? In each case there is a clearly defined independent variable with two or more levels.

In both correlational and comparative studies, the results rely heavily on the quality of the instrument, the nature of the sample, and the manner in which different groups have been identified. Thus, it is important to pay particular attention to these aspects of the study (e.g., Was the sample comprised of volunteers? Who administered the instrument? What were the circumstances of instrument administration? Were the scores from the instrument valid and reliable? What were the criteria for identifying subjects as being in different groups? How were subjects placed in each group?).

As with most nonexperimental designs, you need to be careful not to infer causation from correlations or comparative differences. A correlational study may show that students who have larger biceps are better readers, but that doesn't imply that students will read better if they are put on weight training! (Older students, with larger biceps, are better readers. This is a good example of the need to examine the nature of the sample carefully.)

Criteria for Evaluating Quantitative Nonexperimental Studies

1. Is the general purpose of the study clear? Will the study provide a significant contribution?
2. Does the review of literature establish the relationship between previous studies and the current one? Is the review well organized and up to date?
3. Is the specific research hypothesis or question clearly and concisely stated?
4. Is the method of sampling clearly presented? Could the way the sample was obtained influence the results?
5. Is there anything in the procedures for collecting information, or in the instruments themselves, that could bias the results or weaken the study?
6. Is the magnitude of the correlation or difference between/among groups large enough to suggest practical significance or importance?
7. Do graphic presentations of the data distort the findings?
8. Do the conclusions and interpretations follow logically from the results presented? Are unwarranted causal conclusions made from correlational or comparison data? Are limitations indicated?

Another type of nonexperimental design is called *ex post facto* (or **causal-comparative**). In this type of study the researcher is able to identify past experiences of subjects that are consistent with a treatment, and compares those subjects with others who have had a different treatment or no treatment. The goal of an *ex post facto* design is to establish a cause-and-effect relationship between the independent and dependent variables, much like an experiment. However, in an *ex post facto* study the independent variable has already occurred; it is not directly manipulated by the researcher. Since there is no manipulation of the independent variable, this design is technically nonexperimental, even though in all other respects it looks like an experiment—there is a treatment group, control or comparison group, a posttest, and sometimes a pretest. Since the treatment has already occurred, there can be no random assignment of subjects unless it was instituted prior to the treatment.

A good example of this design would be a study of the effect of attending a small or large high school on student achievement. While it is possible to conduct an experiment by identifying students starting high school and measuring their achievement three years later, an *ex post facto* study can investigate the question without waiting three years by identifying graduating students who have attended small high schools and comparing their achievements with those of students who have attended large high schools. Since the students would not have been randomly assigned to type of high school, it is important to see if the groups that are compared differ on variables that would affect the results. Also, there may be other factors that differentially influence achievement at each school. For example, small schools could differ from large ones in the type of curriculum offered, qualifications of teachers, or socioeconomic status of the community. Each of these factors could affect achievement, in addition to size. Thus, when conducting an *ex post facto* study, it is important to think about whether differences other than the independent variable could affect the results.

Criteria for Evaluating *Ex Post Facto* Studies

1. Is the general purpose of the study clear? Will the study provide a significant contribution?

2. Does the review of literature establish the relationship between previous studies and the current one? Is the review well organized and up to date?

3. Is the specific research hypothesis or question clearly and concisely stated?

4. Is the method of sampling clearly presented? Could the way the sample was obtained influence the results?

5. Is there anything in the procedures for collecting information, or in the instruments themselves, that could bias the results or weaken the study?

6. Has the presumed treatment already occurred? Is the treatment well defined?

7. Are subjects in different groups similar except for the treatment?

8. Do the conclusions and interpretations follow logically from the results presented? Are casual conclusions made with caution? Are limitations indicated?

The Impact of Alternate Assessments: A Statewide Teacher Survey

Harold L. Kleinert   Sarah Kennedy   Jacqueline Farmer Kearns
University of Kentucky

ABSTRACT

The Individuals with Disabilities Education Act (IDEA) Amendments of 1997 require that all states, by July 2000, will have developed and implemented alternate assessment methods for those students with disabilities who cannot be included within regular state and local district educational assessment and accountability measures. A statewide survey of teachers involved in the nation's first alternate assessment and accountability system for students with moderate and severe disabilities was conducted to determine the extent to which these teachers perceived benefits of including their students in state and school accountability measures, as well as their perceptions of the instructional impact of the alternate system upon student outcomes. The results of this survey indicated that teachers did realize such benefits, and perceived positive changes in both instructional programming (e.g., students' learning to follow their own individualized schedules, students' learning to assess their own performance) and enhanced student outcomes (an increased percentage of students having functional augmentative communication systems). However, teachers also expressed frustration with the amount of time required to complete student assessment portfolios, and concern over scoring reliability and the extent to which the alternate assessment was more of a teacher assessment than a student assessment.

With the passage of the Individuals with Disabilities Education Act (IDEA) Amendments of 1997, all states were required to ensure that students with disabilities become fully included in state and local district measures of educational accountability. Specifically, IDEA requires that "children with disabilities be included in general State and district-wide assessment programs, with appropriate accommodations, where necessary" (612(a)(17)(A)) and "as appropriate, the State or local educational agency: (i) develops guidelines for the participation of children with disabilities in alternate assessments for those children who cannot participate in state and district-wide assessment programs; and (ii) develops and, beginning not later than July 1, 2000, conducts those alternate assessments" (612(a)(17)(A)(i-ii)).

Driving these federal requirements for the participation of students with disabilities in educational assessments, which entails developing alternate assessments for students who cannot participate in regular assessments, are several critical concerns: (a) Students with disabilities are, as often as not, excluded from state and local measures of educational accountability and thus are not held to the same high learning expectations as other students ("CEC Fights," 1995; United States Department of Education, 1995); (b) students with more severe disabilities are nearly universally excluded from such measures (Elliott, 1997; Thurlow, Ysseldyke, & Silverstein, 1993); and (c) school effectiveness measures are truly meaningful only if we account for the learning of all students (Kleinert, Kearns, & Kennedy, 1997). Although many authorities endorse this direction toward inclusive assessment and accountability (Elliott, 1997; Kleinert et al., 1997; Sailor, 1997; United States Department of Education, 1995; Ysseldyke et al., 1996), sorting out, on a national scale, all of the conceptual and logistical issues involved in making instructionally valid accommodations to regular assessments, and designing appropriate alternate assessments for students with more severe disabilities, represent a task of immense proportions.

Moreover, educational assessment is itself undergoing profound changes. Given the perceived limitations of more traditional, standardized multiple-choice tests (Earl & LeMahieu, 1997), assessment specialists are increasingly looking to performance-based assessment, including collections of students' works (portfolios), open-ended response questions requiring students to apply critical thinking skills, and student exhibitions and culminating projects (Earl & LeMahieu, 1997; Wolf, LeMahieu, & Eresh, 1992). The goal of these newer assessments is to more accurately depict what students can do, in more authentic or real-life contexts, and to focus classroom instruction on the development of problem-solving and higher order thinking and writing skills. The thoughtful inclusion of students with disabilities in large-scale, performance-based assessments, it is hoped, will result in improved instructional practices and enhanced learning outcomes for these students, though that result is far from certain (Langenfeld, Thurlow, & Scott, 1997).

Indeed, research is limited on whether performance-based assessments translate into significant positive changes in instructional practice for students without disabilities. When writing portfolios were included as a part of large-scale assessments for students in Vermont and Pittsburgh, teachers reported that they liked the portfolios and that they integrated the new assessment activities into their daily classroom instruction (Gearhart & Herman, 1995; Langenfeld et al., 1997; LeMahieu, Gitomer, & Eresh, 1995). However, teachers in Great Britain were far less enthusiastic about a national performance-based assessment (based on that nation's Core Curriculum); they viewed the assessment tasks as increased work and time taken from teaching and as wholly separate from their daily instructional routine (Torrance, 1993).

The relationship between performance assessment and changes in instruction becomes even further complicated when those assessments are conducted in the context of high-stakes accountability (i.e., rewards for schools that improve performance and sanctions for schools that fail to meet their improvement targets). One result of using performance-based assessments in high-stakes accountability environments is that the field is developing its knowledge base even as the assessments are being implemented (Earl & LeMahieu, 1997). Several authors have noted that basing school rewards and sanctions on the results of performance-based assessment measures might well "[trivialize] both the skills measured and the instructional strategies" (Miller & Legg, 1993, p. 14) and "[compromise] the very nature of performance assessment" as a tool for improving student learning (Jones & Whitford, 1997, p. 280).

Guskey (1994), in reporting a study conducted by one of his doctoral students (Vitali, 1993), noted that teachers had not made changes in basic lessons or instructional practices as a result of Kentucky's high-stakes, performance-based assessment and accountability system, with the exception that additional writing tasks were assigned for the writing portfolio. Vitali's findings were based on extensive teacher interviews, questionnaires, and classroom observations. Vitali's study was conducted in the early implementation phases of Kentucky's assessment; Guskey hypothesized that the lack of change in instructional practice was related to teachers' not knowing how to make those changes and not having sufficient time to implement them. Petrosko (1997), in a comprehensive research review on the instructional impact of Kentucky's assessment and accountability system, found that although teachers did report making

instructional changes and saw those changes as beneficial for students, they had very negative attitudes about the "high-stakes" pressures of the accountability system itself. However, none of the above studies considered the instructional impact of an alternate assessment for students with disabilities who were unable to participate in the state or district's regular assessment program (even with appropriate adaptations); IDEA's new mandate for the implementation of such alternate assessments for students with disabilities makes such research imperative.

Kentucky's Inclusive Assessment and Accountability System

There are few existing models from which we can draw lessons and guidance for the development of alternate assessments, or about how such assessments might impact instructional practice. One current statewide model for an assessment program that includes all students is the one found in Kentucky. Kentucky has included all students, even those with severe disabilities, in its mandated statewide assessment and accountability system since 1992 (Ysseldyke et al., 1996). In that state's system, developed under the landmark Kentucky Education Reform Act of 1990 (KERA), most students with disabilities participate in the regular assessment system, which to date has included writing portfolios; on-demand achievement tasks in math, social studies, reading, science, practical living, and arts and humanities; as well as more traditional achievement test items. Students with disabilities may have accommodations within the regular system, provided that the accommodations (a) are part of regular instruction for that student, (b) are identified on the student's Individualized Education Program (IEP), and (c) do not invalidate the test's purpose (e.g., orally reading to a student an item that is intended to measure reading comprehension of printed material). Students with more severe disabilities (moderate, severe, and profound cognitive disabilities) participate in the state's alternate system, the Alternate Portfolio. Approximately .5% of all students in Kentucky are in the state's alternate assessment system; although their numbers are small, each student in the alternate system carries a weight proportional to the effect of any student in the regular system in determining the school's accountability index or score.

Each school's accountability score is derived from a combination of cognitive indicators (the combined averaged scores for all students in both the regular and alternate assessments) and noncognitive indicators (e.g., attendance rates, dropout and retention rates, and postschool outcomes). The initial accountability score for a school is its threshold, or baseline, measure. It is from that initial index that all subsequent improvements are calculated.

Moreover, Kentucky's accountability system is "high stakes" (Steffy, 1993). Depending on a school's overall improvement or decline from one 2-year accountability cycle to the next, it receives rewards (including recognition and monetary awards) or penalties (including the dismissal of the principal and the staff, in extreme cases of decline). Thus, schools have strong incentives for ensuring that students do well in the assessments. As noted above, these incentives extend to all students, as every student contributes equally to the school's accountability score.

Components of the Alternate Portfolio

The Alternate Portfolio is structured to reflect "best programming practices" for students with moderate and severe disabilities (Kleinert et al., 1997). Individual entries in the Alternate Portfolio are constructed so as to provide evidence that a student has acquired critical skills in the context of school, home, and community settings; natural supports (e.g., peers and/or co-workers); interactions and friendships with typical peers; functional life domains (e.g., a resume is required for all 12th-grade students); and the state's academic expectations for all students. Critical components of the Alternate Portfolio include:

- *The student's primary mode of communication.* This is essential in that a considerable number of students who meet the eligibility criteria for the Alternate Portfolio cannot communicate verbally and thus need an alternative or augmentative way of communicating, such as picture communication systems or signing/gesturing.
- *The student's daily/weekly schedule.* This schedule must be presented in the form in which the student is learning to use it (e.g., a printed schedule for a student who can read, a picture or object schedule for a nonreader), along with a description of how the student uses that individualized schedule to initiate his or her own activities throughout the day.
- *A student letter to the reviewer.* This letter must indicate why each portfolio entry has been chosen. It can be written as a collaborative effort with typical peers, as long as the amount of assistance provided is described.
- *Projects and investigations.* To the maximum extent possible, each project or entry should involve nondisabled peers and focus on one or more of the learner outcomes identified for all students.

(For a complete description of Alternate Portfolio content and scoring standards, see Kleinert et al., 1997.)

Students in the alternate system are scored on the same four-level scale as are all other students. Those levels, from lowest to highest, are Novice, Apprentice, Proficient, and Distinguished. Most important for accountability purposes, even students with the most significant disabilities can score at the higher levels (Proficient and Distinguished) if the learning reflected in their portfolio entries is evidenced in multiple settings, with natural supports, and in the context of extensive peer interactions, and demonstrates enhanced functional life skills.

Essential to the inclusion of all students in state and local measures of accountability are two fundamental assumptions: (a) Including all students in measures of school accountability will ensure that schools give due attention to everyone's learning needs, via appropriate learning opportunities; and (b) how and what we measure drives our instructional practices; that is, if we construct our assessments carefully, we will see positive changes in how schools are educating students (Ysseldyke et al., 1996).

The purpose of the present study was to ascertain teachers' perceptions about the accuracy of these two assumptions in the context of Kentucky's statewide alternate assessment and accountability process for students with moderate and severe disabilities. More specifically, our statewide survey of all teachers with students in the alternate assessment was designed to gauge their perceptions about the benefits of including students with severe disabilities in state and district accountability measures, as well as their perceptions about the changes in instructional programming that have resulted for these students as a function of their participation in Kentucky's performance-based assessment and accountability process. These issues are important to our field, given that by the year 2000, all states must develop and implement similar alternate assessments. Their importance is further accentuated by the lack of research on the instructional impact of performance-based assessment measures on students with disabilities (Coutinho & Malouf, 1993). At this point, Kentucky represents the only comprehensive, fully inclusive statewide pilot of what such a system might look like and what its impact might be (Kleinert et al., 1997; Ysseldyke et al., 1996).

Given the lack of basic communication skills of many students with the most significant disabilities, we were especially interested in the potential impact of the Alternate Portfolio's requirement of direct evidence of the student's primary mode of communication. Although deficits in basic communication skills for these students have been reported throughout the literature (Coots & Falvey, 1989; Orelove & Sobsey, 1996), of specific interest to our research was a statewide survey (Wheatley, 1993) of teachers of students with moderate, severe, and multiple cognitive disabilities conducted in Kentucky during the baseline year of the state's alternate assessment. Wheatley found that of the students eligible for participation in the alternate system (*n* = 3,125), 49% did *not* have intelligible speech (i.e., were rated as nonverbal). Moreover, of those students *without* intelligible speech (*n* = 1,536), only 42% (643) had functional augmentative communication systems. We hoped to compare these findings with similar teacher ratings of the communicative status of nonverbal students in the alternate assessment 4 years after its initial implementation; specifically, was there a change in the teacher-reported percentage of nonverbal students who now had augmentative communications systems? Given that evidence of the student's communication system is an essential component of the alternate assessment, this is an area in which one might expect to see a positive change.

METHOD

Teacher Survey

A one-page teacher survey was designed to assess (a) the extent to which teachers serving students with moderate and severe disabilities believed that their students should be a part of the accountability process; (b) whether any benefits to teachers or students had accrued from the participation of these students in Kentucky's assessment program; (c) the extent to which the accountability process had increased their students' participation in general education classes, in typical school activities, and in community-referenced instruction; (d) the extent to which portfolios were a part of the daily classroom routine (as opposed to being separate or isolated "events"); and (e) the extent to which students were using their own individualized schedules and assessing their own progress (two instructional elements of the Alternate Portfolio). Each item was constructed along a simple 5-point Likert scale (*strongly agree* to *strongly disagree*).

In addition, teachers were asked to identify whether their students who were placed in the alternate assessment system (a) had intelligible speech, (b) used an augmentative communication system, or (c) had no formal means of communication. To compare the results of this study with those of Wheatley (1993), we worded the communication questions on the present survey identically to those in the Wheatley study.

Students in the Alternate Portfolio, like all students in Kentucky, are assessed for accountability in the 4th, 8th, and 12th grades. Thus, for all students in the state, there are three accountability points in their school careers. To ensure that the teacher survey was sent to only those teachers who presently had or recently had had students completing their Alternate Portfolios, surveys were sent to teachers who had attended one of the required scoring trainings in either the 1995–1996 or the 1996–1997 school year. A total of 508 teachers were identified. Each teacher was mailed a survey, a brief cover letter explaining confidentiality of all responses and inviting written comments, and a bag of gourmet tea in appreciation for responding. A self-addressed return envelope was enclosed. Teachers' school addresses were used for mailing purposes.

RESULTS

Item Analysis

Of the 508 surveys mailed, 331 were returned (a response rate of 65.2%). Two factors that probably prevented a higher response rate were that (a) the surveys were mailed late in the school year (mid to late April), when teachers are typically involved in end-of-the-year activities, and (b) potential respondents were culled from attendees at scoring-training sessions conducted over a 2-year period. Undoubtedly, a number of teachers would have transferred positions or changed schools during that time and thus would not have received the survey. This second response factor is especially significant, given the documented rate of turnover in special education (see Boe, Cook, Bobbitt, & Terhanian, 1998). Although precise data for yearly turnover among special educators in Kentucky are not available, one indication of this turnover rate in the state is the presence of 57 emergency and probationary certified teachers in the area of moderate and severe cognitive disabilities for the 1996–1997 school year (Kentucky Office of Educational Accountability, 1998).

Teachers were not required to provide any identifying information on the survey. An ad hoc analysis of postmarks on returned surveys indicated that all areas of the state (both urban and rural) were clearly represented. Although teachers did not indicate their years of experience on the survey form itself, several teachers offered that information in their written comments. The range of experience for teachers who did indicate this information ranged from 1st year to more than 20 years in the classroom.

Table 1 presents the cumulative responses and average response for each item. First, teachers as an overall group did believe it was important for all students, including students with severe disabilities, to be a part of school accountability measures. Of the 329 teachers responding to this question, 180 (54.8%) agreed or strongly agreed with this statement, whereas only 28.5% disagreed or strongly disagreed with it (the remaining respondents rated themselves

Table 1 Alternate Portfolio Teacher Survey Results (Percentage of Respondents by Category)

Item	Strongly Agree 5	4	3	2	Strongly Disagree 1	Average Response
1. It is important that all students be included as a part of Kentucky's school assessment and accountability process.	35.0	19.8	16.7	11.2	17.3	3.44
2. I see benefits to having my students included in the accountability process for my school.	29.8	23.1	20.1	10.9	15.8	3.40
3. Portfolios are a part of our everyday classroom routine.	24.7	37.5	21.0	10.4	5.5	3.66
4. As a result of the inclusion of my students in the accountability process, it has been easier to						
Include my students in school activities	13.3	21.7	23.5	19.5	22.0	2.85
Include my students in regular age-appropriate classrooms	11.8	18.9	22.0	25.1	22.3	2.73
Provide needed community-based instruction	22.5	21.0	21.9	14.5	20.1	3.11
5. My students check their schedules before changing activities throughout the day.	24.8	29.1	27.2	10.1	8.9	3.51
6. My students use adapted checklists to record their progress on at least two instructional activities.	25.5	31.1	23.4	11.1	8.9	3.53
7. My students regularly participate in academic activities in a general education classroom with age-appropriate peers.	28.7	19.8	20.1	17.6	13.9	3.32

Note: Item 8. Number of students currently enrolled in your class who are eligible for the Alternate Portfolio (including those students not presently in their accountability year) = 2,036; Item 9. How many of the above students do not have intelligible speech (*defined as speech readily understandable by people who do not know the student*)? = 820 (40.2% of total in #8); Item 10. Of the students who do not have intelligible speech (Question 9), how many of these students have alternative or augmentative communication systems? = 515 (62.8% of total in #9).

as neutral). As to the statement that these teachers actually saw benefits from their students' being included in Kentucky's assessment and accountability process, 52.9% agreed or strongly agreed, and 26.7% disagreed or strongly disagreed. Important from the standpoint of instructional impact, the majority of teachers (62.2%) indicated that they had incorporated the portfolio assessment process into their daily classroom routines; only 15.9% of those responding disagreed with this statement.

However, respondents were considerably less positive about the impact of the alternate assessment on helping them leverage access to general education classes and typical school routines. This is important, in that a key assumption of inclusive assessment systems is that schools will be motivated to attend to the learning needs of all students by

providing them with appropriate learning opportunities and access to the school's general curriculum. For example, only 35% of respondents agreed or strongly agreed that the Alternate Portfolio had made it easier to include their students in typical school activities, even though performance across multiple settings, the use of natural supports, and extensive interactions with typical age-peers are required elements of the Alternate Portfolio. This pattern also held for the teachers' perceptions of the impact of the Alternate Portfolio on enabling them to include their students in general education classes (only 30.7% agreed or strongly agreed with that statement). Teachers rated slightly more positively the impact of the Alternate Portfolio on implementing needed community-based instruction (43.5% in agreement vs. 34.6% in disagreement).

However, these data should not be interpreted to mean that teachers were not *already* implementing these practices. In response to Question 7, about the extent to which their students regularly participated in academic activities in general education classrooms, 48.5% of the teachers agreed or strongly agreed with this statement, even though only 30.7% of respondents believed that the Alternate Portfolio had made such access easier. Indeed, a number of teachers added written comments at the end of their surveys indicating that they were already implementing these practices before the advent of the Alternate Portfolio.

Items 5 and 6 directly addressed the impact of the Alternate Portfolio on two specific instructional practices required as evidence in the alternate assessment: students' own use of their individualized daily schedules (Item 5) and students' use of adapted checklists to record or evaluate their own progress on at least two instructional activities (Item 6). Of those responding, 53.9% agreed or strongly agreed with Item 5 (with only 19% disagreeing or strongly disagreeing with this statement), and 56.6% agreed with Item 6 (with only 20.0% disagreeing).

For the tabular information required on students' communication systems teachers indicated that they had a total of 2,036 students eligible for the Alternate Portfolio, with 40.3% ($n = 820$) of those students not having intelligible speech. Of those students without intelligible speech (i.e., rated as nonverbal), teachers reported that 62.8% had functional communication systems.

Additional Teacher Comments

A number of teachers ($n = 101$, or 30.5%) chose to add their own comments to the survey. To categorize teachers' comments (which generally took the form of concerns, suggestions, difficulties, or frustrations), the first and second author each read a preselected set of 27 written comments to develop an initial set of categories. As the lead author then analyzed all of the comments, he expanded the list of "comment categories" as new ideas or thoughts surfaced. It should be noted that many teachers had comments in multiple categories. The most commonly voiced concerns and frustrations were as follows:

- Completing portfolios takes time away from teaching (19 respondents or 5.7% of the total indicated this);
- The Alternate Portfolio process seems more focused on an assessment of the teacher (and his or her classroom practices) than on the student (18 respondents, or 5.4%);
- For students with the most severe cognitive disabilities, certain elements of the alternate assessment are not appropriate (e.g., using individualized daily schedules, using adapted checklists to chart one's own progress) (14 respondents, or 4.2%);
- Teacher creativity/work is a greater factor in determining the ultimate score than is student learning (13 respondents, or 3.9%);
- Portfolio scoring is too subjective (12 responses, or 3.6%); is done on one's own time (5 responses, or 1.5%); and is rushed or stressful (3 responses, or 0.9%);
- Some of the documentation required as evidence of the learning standards is not natural to typical learning environments (e.g., taking photos of student activities, obtaining peer notes that indicate participation in cooperative learning activities or mutual friendships, students' checking off their daily schedule as activities are completed) (11 respondents, or 3.3%);
- More scoring training is needed, as well as more timely training, so that teachers can better understand the scoring requirements or have more time to ensure that the standards are embedded within their students' portfolios (10 responses, or 3.0%); and
- No benefits are seen for students (9 responses, or 2.7%), though of the responses in this category, one teacher did indicate that she had seen improvement in her own teaching, and another indicated that though she had seen no changes in her students, "they are proud of their work and accomplishments and are overwhelmed with pride when it is all put together."

Eleven teachers (3.3%), though not disagreeing with the concept of alternate assessment and the inclusion of their students in state and local accountability, commented about the possibility of other methods of assessing student accountability. Their suggestions included unannounced school site visits by state department personnel, analyses of learning outcomes across a student's IEP objectives for the current year, and even the development of a single *teacher* portfolio across students (as opposed to individual student portfolios).

Positive comments, with each category indicated at least twice, included statements that the Alternate Portfolio process

- is an excellent framework or structure for instruction and individual student planning (5 respondents);
- increases administrative support for community-based instruction and regular class opportunities (2 responses);
- fosters joint ownership of students and awareness of importance of inclusion among regular educators (2 responses);

- helps to capture student progress (2 responses); and
- increases students' pride or satisfaction in their own work (2 responses).

DISCUSSION

The results reported in this survey were consistent with those of a number of other studies on the impact of performance-based assessment on student achievement and teacher practices (Gearhart & Herman, 1995; Guskey, 1994; Petrosko, 1997). At the same time, these findings, especially in the written teacher comments, indicated some serious issues that must be addressed as local districts and whole states strive to develop alternate assessment systems for students who are unable to participate in the regular assessment process.

First, teachers of students with moderate and severe disabilities, despite frustration at the increased work involved with the alternate assessment process, were generally favorable about the inclusion of their students in school and state accountability measures, and they did see benefits for students in this process. Second, these teachers reported that, on the whole, they had incorporated specific instructional practices into their daily routines—including teaching students to use their own individualized schedules and to chart or evaluate their own progress within regularly occurring instructional activities. These results were similar to those of a limited set of more in-depth, on-site teacher interviews (Kleinert et al., 1997) that also indicated increased use of individualized schedules (28% of teacher interviews), as well as more opportunities for student choice making as a result of the assessment process (53% of those interviewed). Moreover, the present results were also consistent with observations that larger instructional effects (e.g., more extensive opportunities in general education classrooms, increased opportunities for community-referenced instruction) are more difficult to document, and that these broader instructional effects tend to lag behind (or in some cases even precede) changes in assessment of learning (Guskey, 1994). For example, in this study, although 48.5% of the teachers indicated that their students with moderate and severe disabilities regularly participated in academic instruction with their age-peers in general education classrooms, only 30.7% attributed this to, at least in part, the alternate assessment. Given the two "fundamental assumptions" that we have cited about the purpose of inclusive educational assessments, it would seem that the results of this survey provide limited evidence for changes in instructional practices, but our results are inconclusive as to whether students are receiving increased learning opportunities and access to the general curriculum as a direct outcome of their participation in Kentucky's statewide assessment.

One area in which positive changes were clearly indicated was in teacher perceptions of the communicative abilities of their nonverbal students. As noted earlier, in a similar statewide study conducted by Wheatley (1993) during the baseline year for the Alternate Portfolio, teachers reported that only 42% of their students without intelligible speech had other functional augmentative or alternative communication systems. Identically worded questions in the present survey indicated that approximately 63% of nonverbal students now had functional communication systems. Given that the Alternate Portfolio requires clear documentation of the student's mode or system of communication, these data indicated that this is one area in which the alternate system may have already had considerable instructional impact. Still, these data must be interpreted with caution: Despite the confidentiality of the surveys (they were neither coded nor numbered), teachers may have felt uncomfortable indicating that one or more of their students did not have a functional system for communicating. Also, because this survey went to all teachers who had attended the scoring trainings, it included a small number of teachers of students with more mild disabilities who may have had one or more students in the alternate assessment system (during the 1996–1997 school year, 14.5% of all students participating in the Alternate Portfolio system were identified as having mild disabilities). It is possible that the magnitude of this change in augmentative/alternative systems resulted from these teachers' participation. On the other hand, of the students with mild disabilities in the alternate system, very few would require augmentative systems, and therefore their inclusion in the data would not appreciably affect the percentage of nonverbal students who had functional augmentative communication systems.

Perhaps the results that deserve the greatest attention are the teacher comments. The cover letter to the survey invited teacher comments; 30.5% of all respondents took advantage of that opportunity. Although the teachers did have positive comments to make, their written comments, for the most part, were negative. It is possible that teachers who had long felt frustration with the process (and who had not been given the opportunity, or never felt that they had "permission," to tell anyone) responded with written comments proportionately much more than those who were generally satisfied or were neutral about the alternate assessment. It is also true that the timing of the survey may have had something to do with the level of concern expressed in the comments. The surveys were sent immediately after portfolios had been completed and scored; teachers whose students had scored more poorly than they had expected may have felt unfairly penalized by the assessment process.

It should also be noted that Kentucky's assessment system is very much a high-stakes accountability environment. Both general and special educators (as well as their principals) regularly express high levels of stress, concern, and frustration at meeting their threshold levels (the school performance level required for rewards), as well as fear of becoming a school "in decline" or "in crisis" ("A Test of Trust," 1997; Winograd et al., cited in McIntyre & Kyle, 1997). Accountability indices and threshold values for individual schools are determined down to a tenth of a point (on a scale of 0 to a maximum of 140), and individual student scores do make a very real difference. The concerns expressed by the respondents in the present survey in respect to the amount of teacher time required, increased paperwork, detraction from teaching responsibilities, and subjectivity of portfolio scoring are consistent with continuing frustrations with portfolio assessment in general (Baker & Linn, 1993; Cronbach, Linn, Brennan, & Haertel, 1995; Dietel, 1992), as well as Kentucky's assessment system in particular (see Jones & Whitford, 1997; Pankratz, 1997; Petrosko, 1997). The question is whether apparent gains in student learning and changes in instructional practice are worth the added efforts, frustrations, and technical threats to reliability (Dietel, 1992; Gearhart & Herman, 1995) that come with both regular and alternate performance-based assessments. Indeed, as this issue goes to press, the Kentucky Department of Education is redesigning its regular assessment and accountability system (e.g., more multiple choice questions to allow for a more precise national comparison, streamlining other components) to address some of these same concerns.

Of interest in these results was the perception, expressed in the written comments of 5.4% of all respondents, that the Alternate Portfolio is more a measure of teacher accountability than it is one of student accountability. That is, in Kentucky's alternate assessment system, it is the teacher more than the student who is being assessed. Kleinert et al. (1997, 1998) have noted elsewhere that, especially for students with the most severe disabilities, measures of school accountability should reflect the extent to which students are given high-quality, supportive learning experiences. These authors (1998) specifically noted that

accountability systems for these students should ideally capture not only learned skills, but also the range of environments in which the student currently participates and evidences those skills, as well as the social networks and quality of supports provided to enable the student to be a valued member of his/her school community.

Gearhart and Herman (1995) similarly argued that portfolio assessment provides a picture of students' best performance with the support of effective instruction; and LeMahieu et al. (1995) noted that "portfolios help to discriminate among the learning experiences and opportunities that students have across classrooms" (p. 27). Yet, from the results of this survey, it is clear that not all classroom teachers share these views; rather, a significant number perceive this focus on the evidence of learning opportunities (e.g., the documentation of targeted skills across multiple settings in the context of natural supports from peers) as an unfair expectation of Kentucky's alternate assessment.

Moreover, a number of teachers reported that the effort to document these opportunities took time away from teaching, added greatly to their already heavy paperwork loads, and did not really benefit their students. On the other hand, it has been the experience of one of the authors, whose role it is to provide professional development statewide on alternate assessment, that a number of teachers have noted that the issue is not so much one of finding the time to do this extra work but of learning to integrate portfolio assessment into the context of ongoing regular instruction. More research must be done to document successful strategies for integrating portfolio assessment into daily instruction for students with moderate and severe disabilities, so that important outcomes can be reliably measured without adding to teachers' already heavy paperwork requirements.

Perhaps an even more fundamental question is whether newly developed, more authentic performance-based measures should, in the current state of their development, be used in situations of high-stakes accountability, in which teachers and administrators often operate in a context of fear of low scores (Cronbach et al., 1995; Gearhart & Herman, 1995; Jones & Whitford, 1997; Miller & Legg, 1993). This limited teacher survey suggests that some positive changes in classroom practices (e.g., student use of their own individualized schedules, student self-charting and evaluation of performance) are occurring, as are positive teacher reports of important student outcomes (a reported statewide increase in the percentage of nonverbal students who had a functional augmentative means of communication). Yet it also reveals a significant level of teacher frustration in still another requirement for which they must take the primary responsibility and for which they may very well receive a negative evaluation that detracts from the overall performance of their school. For teachers of students in the alternate assessment, this pressure to do well may be even more acute, in that a student in the alternate system receives a single score for his or her portfolio that is the equivalent of a general education student's combined math, writing, and content area test scores.

Kentucky's alternate assessment system represents only one route that local districts and states might take in the development of alternate assessments under IDEA. Many of the concerns expressed in this survey may be unique to Kentucky's alternate assessment system. They also may echo the difficulties the state is having in sustaining the practices for all students (e.g., new performance-based assessments as the foundation for high-stakes accountability in all schools) that were put in place by the landmark Kentucky Education Reform Act (KERA), recognized nationally as the most sweeping statewide restructuring effort yet attempted (Petrosko, 1997). Still, a number of implications from Kentucky's experience are of direct relevance to all states.

Limitations

Several limitations to this study should be noted. First, we did not attempt to measure changes in classroom practices and student outcomes directly, but relied wholly on teacher self-report data. Second, we were not able to correlate actual student scores in the alternate assessment with teacher perceptions of changes in instructional practices and student benefits. We suspect that we would have found a relationship between Alternate Portfolio scores and teacher perceptions of student benefits and changes in instructional practices, but we had no way to test that relationship within the limits of this study. Third, we have no information as to the compatibility or equivalence of the responding (65.2%) and nonresponding (34.8%) teachers; thus, we cannot state with confidence that the responses of these teachers are representative of all teachers in Kentucky who have students in the Alternate Portfolio. Fourth, we were unable to analyze the extent to which teacher experience, scope and recency of teacher training, or other salient teacher characteristics were related to reported adoption of instructional practices and teacher perceptions of the benefits of the alternate assessment to their students. These limitations should be addressed in future research on the impact of alternate assessments.

Implications

Essential areas that require further research if all students, including students with severe disabilities, are to be meaningfully included in district- and state-level assessment and accountability systems include the following:

- *Development of performance-based measures for students with significant disabilities that meet the rigorous technical requirements of interrater scoring reliability necessary for high-stakes accountability.* In this study, 11 teachers

(3.3% of the respondents) commented that they felt the scoring on Kentucky's alternate assessment was too subjective. Their perceptions were consistent with state-level difficulties in interrater reliability for the Alternate Portfolio reported elsewhere (Kleinert et al., 1997). Extremely heterogeneous populations of students, as well as more open-ended formats for performance-based tasks, exacerbate the difficulties with reliability typically associated with more authentic assessments (Baker & Linn, 1993; Linn & Baker, 1992). If teachers are to score students' portfolios, then frequent scoring training is essential. State or local districts must also ensure that training is continuous throughout the life of the assessment system.

- *Parent perceptions of the benefits that do or do not accrue to their son or daughter with a severe disability as a result of participation in state and district assessments.* Despite the importance of parent involvement in enhancing student outcomes (Guskey & Sparks, 1996), we know of no studies in this vital area. Whereas the present study dealt with teacher perceptions of the impact of one state's alternate assessment and accountability system, parent perceptions of this impact might be especially insightful, given the emphasis in the 1997 Amendments to IDEA on increased parent involvement in determining life outcomes for students with disabilities.

- *The relationship of student scores in alternate assessments to long-term postschool outcomes (e.g., vocational status, community living and participation).* This is especially relevant given the historically poor outcomes documented in the transition literature for students with significant disabilities (Blackorby & Wagner, 1996). Moreover, if we were able to find evidence of increased student learning in the context of typical classroom, school, and community activities, we would expect to find commensurate gains in postschool outcomes for these students, as well.

- *The relationship of alternate assessments for students with severe disabilities to these students' IEPs.* Several teachers in our survey commented that the alternate assessment should be more closely tied to demonstrated progress on IEP objectives. On the other hand, others have noted that educational assessment systems, be they regular, accommodated, or alternate, should reflect a set of standards common to all students (Jorgensen, Fischer, & Roach, 1997), as well as increased access to the general curriculum (1997 Amendments to IDEA).

- *More extensive evidence of changes in both classroom practices and student outcomes as a result of student participation in state-and district-level assessments.* The present study provided some tentative insights into teacher perceptions but did not offer conclusive evidence of actual changes in either classroom practices or student outcomes. Ideally, more authentic assessments, such as student portfolios, should drive instruction, ensuring that students are engaged in more meaningful learning tasks with enhanced outcomes. We clearly need more research in this area to establish that this is the case.

- *Specific strategies for embedding performance-based assessment systems (e.g., student portfolios, performance-based events) in normal school and classroom routines.* The comment that teachers most frequently made was that the assessment process takes time away from classroom instruction. Given the increased work associated with performance-based and portfolio assessment (see Wesson & King, 1996), documented strategies for integrating assessment into daily instruction and routines should prove very helpful for practitioners.

It is clear that as we attempt to include all students in state and local measures of accountability, and as we attempt to develop alternate assessments for students who cannot participate in regular assessments even with accommodations, we need to listen to teachers carefully and not create any more new burdens or frustrations than are absolutely necessary to achieve this laudable goal. The rewards of including all students in measures of our schools' effectiveness can be great, but, as this brief survey has indicated, the challenges to achieving this goal are no less significant.

AUTHORS' NOTE

Preparation of this article was supported, in part, by the U.S. Department of Education Office of Special Education and Rehabilitation Services (Grant No. H086J20007). However, the opinions expressed do not necessarily reflect the position or policy of the U.S. Department of Education, and no official endorsement should be inferred.

REFERENCES

A test of trust. (1997, July 27). *The Lexington Herald Leader,* p. E1.

Baker, E., & Linn, R. (1993, Spring). The technical merit of performance assessment. *The CRESST Line: Newsletter of the National Center for Research on Evaluation, Standards, and Student Testing,* p. 1-2.

Blackorby, J., & Wagner, M. (1996). Longitudinal post-school outcomes of youth with disabilities: Findings from the National Longitudinal Transition Study. *Exceptional Children, 62,* 399-414.

Boe, E., Cook, L., Bobbitt, S., & Terhanian, G. (1998). The shortage of fully certified teachers in special and general education. *Teacher Education and Special Education, 21*(1), 1-15.

CEC fights to include special education in assessment. (1995). *CEC Today, 1*(9), $$$pp. 1, 10.

Coots, J., & Falvey, M. (1989). Communication skills. In M. Falvey (Ed.), *Community-based curriculum: Instructional strategies for students with severe handicaps* (pp. 255-284). Baltimore: Brookes.

Coutinho, M., & Malouf, D. (1993). Performance assessment and children with disabilities: Issues and possibilities. *Teaching Exceptional Children, 25*(4), 62-67.

Cronbach, L., Linn, R., Brennan, R., & Haertel, E. (1995, Summer). Generalizability analysis for educational assessments. *Evaluation Comment,* pp. 1-28.

Dietel, R. (1992, Fall). Portfolios as worthwhile burdens? *The CRESST Line: Newsletter of the National Center for Research on Evaluation, Standards, and Student Testing,* 3-5.

Earl, L., & LeMahieu, P. (1997). Rethinking assessment and accountability. In A. Hargreaves (Ed.), *1997 ASCD Year Book: Rethinking educational change with heart and mind* (pp. 149-168). Alexandria, VA: Association for Supervision and Curriculum Development.

Elliott, J. (1997). Invited commentary. *Journal of the Association for Persons with Severe Handicaps, 22,* 104-106.

Gearhart, M., & Herman, J. (1995, Winter). Portfolio assessment: Whose work is it? *Evaluation Comment,* pp. 1-16.

Guskey, T. (1994). What you assess may not be what you get. *Educational Leadership, 51*(6), 51-54.

Guskey, T., & Sparks, D. (1996). Exploring the relationship between staff development and improvements in student learning. *Journal of Staff Development, 17*(4), 34-38.

Herman, J., & Winters, L. (1994). Portfolio research: A slim collection. *Educational Leadership, 52*(2), 48-55.

Individuals with Disabilities Education Act Amendments of 1997, 20 U.S.C. § 1400 et seq.

Jones, K., & Whitford, B. (1997). Kentucky's conflicting reform principles: High-stakes accountability and student performance assessment. *Phi Delta Kappan, 79,* 276-281.

Jorgensen, C., Fisher, D., & Roach, V. (1997, July). Curriculum and its impact on inclusion and the achievement of students with disabilities. *Issue Brief* (Vol. 2, pp. 1-15). Pittsburgh: Allegheny University of the Health Sciences, Consortium on Inclusive Schooling Practices.

Kentucky Office of Educational Accountability. (1998). *Special education resolution study.* Frankfort: Author.

Kleinert, H., Kearns, J., & Kennedy, S. (1997). Accountability for all students: Kentucky's Alternate Portfolio system for students with moderate and severe cognitive disabilities. *Journal of the Association for Persons with Severe Handicaps, 22,* 88-101.

Kleinert, H., Kearns, J., & Kennedy, S. (1998). *Including all students in educational assessment and accountability.* Manuscript submitted for publication.

Langenfeld, K., Thurlow, M., & Scott, D. (1997). *High stakes testing for students: Unanswered questions and implications for students with disabilities* (Synthesis Report 26). Minneapolis: University of Minnesota, National Center on Educational Outcomes.

LeMahieu, P., Gitomer, D., & Eresh, J. (1995). Portfolios in large-scale assessments: Difficult but not impossible. *Educational Measurement: Issues and Practice, 14*(3), 11-28.

Linn, R., & Baker, E. (1992, Fall). Portfolios and accountability. *The CRESST Line: Newsletter of the National Center for Research on Evaluation, Standards, and Student Testing,* 1-19.

McIntyre, E., & Kyle, D. (1997). Primary program. In J. Clark, J. Petrosko, & R. Pankratz (Eds.), *1996 review of research on the Kentucky Education Reform Act* (pp. 119-142). Frankfort: The Kentucky Institute for Educational Research.

Miller, M., & Legg, S. (1993). Alternative assessments in a high stakes environment. *Educational Measurement: Issues and Practice, 12*(2), 9-15.

Orelove, F., & Sobsey, D. (1996). *Educating children with multiple disabilities: A transdisciplinary approach* (3rd ed.). Baltimore: Brookes.

Pankratz, R. (1997). What we have learned about school reform in Kentucky from statewide surveys. In J. Clark, J. Petrosko, & R. Pankratz (Eds.), *1996 review of research on the Kentucky Education Reform Act* (pp. 289-313). Frankfort: The Kentucky Institute for Educational Research.

Petrosko, J. (1997). Assessment and accountability. In J. Clark, J. Petrosko, & R. Pankratz (Eds.), *1996 review of research on the Kentucky Education Reform Act* (pp. 3-50). Frankfort: The Kentucky Institute for Educational Research.

Sailor, W. (1997). Invited commentary. *Journal of the Association for Persons with Severe Handicaps, 22,* 102-103.

Steffy, B. (1993). Top-down-bottom-up: Systemic change in Kentucky. *Educational Leadership, 51*(1), 42-44.

Thurlow, M., Ysseldyke, J., & Silverstein, B. (1993). *Testing accommodations for students with disabilities: A review of the literature* (Synthesis Report No. 4). Minneapolis: University of Minnesota, National Center on Educational Outcomes.

Torrance, H. (1993). Combining measurement-driven instruction with authentic assessment: Some initial observations of national assessment in England and Wales. *Educational Evaluation and Policy Analysis, 15*(1), 81-90.

U.S. Department of Education. (1995). *Individuals with Disabilities Education Act Amendments of 1995: Reauthorization of the Individuals with Disabilities Education Act.* Washington, DC: Author.

Vitali, G. (1993). *Factors influencing teachers' assessment and instructional practices in an assessment-driven educational reform.* Unpublished doctoral dissertation, University of Kentucky, Lexington.

Wesson, C., & King, R. (1996). Portfolio assessment and special education students. *Teaching Exceptional Children, 28*(2), 44-49.

Wheatley, S. (1993). *Communication systems for students with intellectual disabilities: A statewide survey.* Unpublished manuscript, University of Kentucky at Lexington.

Wolf, D., LeMahieu, P., & Eresh, J. (1992). Good measure: Assessment as a tool for educational reform. *Educational Leadership, 49*(8), 8-13.

Ysseldyke, J., Thurlow, M., Erickson, R., Gabrys, R., Haigh, J., Trimble, S., & Gong, B. (1996). *A comparison of state assessment systems in Kentucky and Maryland.* Minneapolis: University of Minnesota, National Center on Educational Outcomes.

Evaluation Criteria	**Discussion Questions**
1. Is the general purpose of the study clear? Will the study provide a significant contribution?	**1.** How could the introduction be reduced without adversely affecting the case for significance?
The general purpose of the study is clear, as stated in the second paragraph before the Method section. It would be helpful to state this purpose in the first paragraph or two. There is much introductory material in this article to provide reasons for significance. While the topic is clearly an important one, a better case could be made for the need for teachers' perceptions.	
2. Does the review of literature establish the relationship between previous studies and the current one? Is the review well organized and up to date?	**2.** Which of the sources cited would be considered directly related to the purpose of the study, and which would be considered background or context?
There is very little directly related literature reviewed; most of the citations are for ideas, theory, and best practice. More analysis and depth could be reported on the Wheatley study since, as a survey of teachers, it is most similar to this study.	
3. Is the specific research hypothesis or question clearly and concisely stated?	**3.** What is an example of a specific research question that would be appropriate for this study?
There are no specific research questions stated, nor are there any research hypotheses (though research hypotheses would not be needed).	
4. Is the method of sampling clearly presented? Could the way the sample was obtained influence the results?	**4.** What type of sampling is represented? Is this a random sample? Is the sample potentially so biased that the results are not helpful?
Since teachers contacted had received training for the alternative portfolio, it could be argued that this group would be more favorable than teachers not receiving the training. The response rate is actually not too poor for this kind of study, though a higher rate would be much better. Unfortunately, there is little demographic information about those responding (e.g., grade level and type of school), so a biased sample is possible.	
5. Is there anything in the procedures for collecting the information, or in the instruments themselves, that could bias the results or weaken the study?	**5.** How could validity and reliability be established for this kind of survey?
Anonymity is a strength. While the instrument had been used previously, there is no reference to validity or reliability. This is potentially a major weakness of the study.	

6. Is the magnitude of the correlation or difference among the groups large enough to suggest practical significance or importance?

The wide range of percentages of teachers agreeing and disagreeing to the questions makes it difficult to establish findings that have practical value. Clearly the teacher comments that the authors thoughts were very significant are too few to suggest practical value.

7. Do graphic presentations of the data distort the findings?

No graphics are presented in this study.

8. Do the conclusions and interpretations follow logically from the results presented? Are unwarranted causal conclusions made from correlations or comparisons? Are limitations indicated?

The relatively extensive conclusions and interpretations are appropriately integrated with results of previous studies, though tend to be based on general literature as much as the specific results of this study. Limitations are appropriate. Teacher comments should not receive the most attention. No unwarranted correlational or causal conclusions are made.

6. What could the authors do, if anything, with the percentages presented to make a stronger case for practical significance?

7. What kind of graphic could be used to present the results?

8. Which of the specific implications follows directly from the data presented?

Credibility Scorecard
The Impact of Alternate Assessments: A Statewide Teacher Survey

	Excellent	Very Good	Adequate	Marginal	Poor
General purpose	5	4	3	2	1
Contribution/ significance	5	4	3	2	1
Review of literature	5	4	3	2	1
Research questions or hypotheses	5	4	3	2	1
Subjects or participants	5	4	3	2	1
Instrumentation	5	4	3	2	1
Procedures	5	4	3	2	1
Results	5	4	3	2	1
Practical significance	5	4	3	2	1
Graphics	5	4	3	2	1
Conclusions	5	4	3	2	1
Any fatal flaws?					

Factors That Influence Self-Efficacy of Counseling Students: An Exploratory Study

Mei Tang   Kathleen D. Addison   Danielle LaSure-Bryant   Rhonda Norman
William O'Connell   Joseph A. Stewart-Sicking

The study examined whether age, prior work experience, number of courses taken, and number of internship hours have a positive relationship with counseling self-efficacy. Participants were 116 counselor education students. The results from correlation and multivariate analyses of covariance revealed that the length of internship hours and prior related work experience were positively correlated with counseling self-efficacy. The differences in counseling anxiety, affection adjustment, and assessment found between the students in programs accredited by the Council for Accreditation of Counseling and Related Educational Programs (CACREP) and those in non-CACREP-accredited programs disappeared when the background variables were controlled as covariates.

Training counselors to be good practitioners is a primary mission of most graduate counselor education programs. Discussion in the literature regarding ideal pedagogy for counselors suggests that counselor competency is developed in settings wherein counselor trainees can develop critical thinking skills that are related to real-world activities (Kaczmarek, Barclay, & Smith, 1996; Nelson & Neufeldt, 1998; Spruill & Benshoff, 2000). The ability of counselors to identify their counseling skills and to be confident in their ability to use these skills in real-life settings has a direct influence on the quality of counseling services they provide (Bradley & Florini, 1999). Hence, the curricula of counseling programs often have two components—theoretical foundations, and clinical instruction and experiences. In fact, counselor education programs strive to bridge the gap between theory and praxis (Fong, Borders, Ethington, & Pitts, 1997; Nelson & Neufeldt, 1998; Woodard & Lin. 1999). One of the common clinical experiences for students is internship. The expectation of counselor educators is that internship experiences will provide students with learning opportunities that

will help them develop competence in practicing counseling. These internship experiences function as the vicarious learning and task performance discussed by Bandura (1986) as the sources for individuals' self-efficacy.

SELF-EFFICACY

Perceived self-efficacy is defined as the judgment of what one can do with whatever skill one possesses (Bandura, 1977, 1986). As counselors enter the field, self-efficacy is an important determinant of their ability to assume their roles as professionals with success and confidence. Bandura (1977, 1986) asserted that an individual's task performances are the most significant factor influencing his or her self-efficacy. In other words, if an individual has successfully completed a task in the past, he or she expects that the specific task or a similar one can be performed again equally successfully. Perceived self-efficacy includes skill performance, assessment, and evaluation by self and others. It is important for individuals to have an accurate assessment of their abilities to function successfully (Bandura, 1986).

Melchert, Hays, Wiljanen, and Kolocek (1996) found that a student's level of training and clinical experience contributed to higher self-efficacy for counselor skills. Research has indicated that counselor training can have a positive influence on perceived self-efficacy over time (Melchert et al., 1996). However, a meta-analysis based on 14 studies about the relationship between counselor self-efficacy and levels of training yielded mixed findings. Some studies found a positive relationship between students' levels of training and their counseling self-efficacy, whereas others found no linear relationship (Larson & Daniels, 1998). Watson (as cited in Larson & Daniels, 1998) reported that counseling course work and related work experience accounted for 43% of the variance in counselor self-efficacy. Internship experience was found to have a positive impact on a

From *Counselor Education and Supervision*, Vol. 44, 71–80, 2004 ACA. Reprinted with permission. No further reproduction authorized without written permission from the American Counseling Association.

Mei Tang, College of Education, University of Cincinnat; Kathleen D. Addison, St. Aloysius Orphanage, Cincinnatt, Ohio; Danielle LaSure-Bryant. Pastoral Counseling Department, Loyola College in Maryland; Rhonda Norman and William O'Connell, Graduate Program in Counseling. Xavier University; Joseph A. Stewart-Sicking, Virginia Theological Seminary. Correspondence concerning this article should be addressed to Mei Tang, Counseling Program, College of Education, University of Cincinnati, M. L. 0002, Cincinnati, OH 45221 (e-mail: mei.tang@uc.edu).

student's self-efficacy in practicing counseling (Heidel, 1999). Students who had regular clinical supervision had higher levels of self-efficacy than students who had little or no clinical supervision (Cashwell & Dooley, 2001).

CACREP VERSUS NON-CACREP PROGRAMS

Since 1981, the Council for Accreditation of Counseling and Related Educational Programs (CACREP) has come to be regarded as the commonly accepted standard in counselor training programs (Schmidt, 1999). Counselor educators from both CACREP and non-CACREP programs are in agreement regarding the relevancy of CACREP standards and counselor training curricula to counselor practice (Vacc, 1992). In addition, counseling students from both CACREP and non-CACREP programs have positive attitudes about CACREP accreditation standards (Wilcoxon, Cecil, & Comas, 1987).

CACREP programs have a minimum number of required courses, distribution requirements, and content requirements for courses and internship hours, whereas non-CACREP programs may or may not meet the minimum standards. Thus, it becomes interesting to know whether the length of course work in both content areas and clinical training that students are required to take in a CACREP program will lead students to have a higher self-efficacy level compared with students who may not necessarily have the same amount of training. Few empirical studies have investigated the result of students' participation in a counselor training program on their self-efficacy when assessed as part of their overall counseling effectiveness.

This study was designed to investigate counseling self-efficacy of graduate students in counselor education programs to determine whether Bandura's (1986) self-efficacy theory applies. Specifically, we investigated the relationship between the training background of graduate counseling students and counselor self-efficacy. We also investigated demographic variables to determine if age, prior work experience, and gender made a difference in individuals' confidence about their counseling competency. Another purpose of the study was to explore whether the variation in training experiences because of the CACREP- and non-CACREP-accredited status affected students' self-efficacy regarding their performance of counseling tasks. In other words, we examined whether students from CACREP-accredited and non-CACREP-accredited counselor training programs would demonstrate differences in counseling self-efficacy and, further, whether the CACREP accreditation status or the amount of training experience would account for differences.

METHOD

Participants

One hundred sixteen participants were recruited from six different counselor education programs in the midwestern area of the United States. Three programs had CACREP accreditation, and three did not have CACREP accreditation. Among students who participated in the study, approximately 83% were women and 17% were men. Students from CACREP-accredited programs accounted for 48% of the total number of participants. Regarding student race and ethnicity, 83% were Caucasian American, 13% were African American, and the remaining 4% reported other racial/ethnic identities. Almost half (45%) of the participants were part-time students. The average age of the sample was 32.17 years with a standard deviation of 8.6. The amount of prior work experience related to human services was 2.19 years on average for CACREP students and 3.48 years on average for non-CACREP students. The detailed demographics of participants compared by CACREP accreditation status are presented in Table 1. Table 1 also shows the summary of actual courses and internship hours that participants had completed. In this study, both CACREP-accredited programs and non-CACREP-accredited programs require 60 semester credits with 600 clock hours of internship.

Instruments

A demographic questionnaire was developed to capture data about participants' age, gender, race, years of work experience in human services, and student status (part-time or full-time). The questionnaire was also designed to elicit from students the number of courses they had taken at the time of the study in the areas recommended by CACREP standards. The list of courses included counseling theories, career development, human growth and development, professional identity and issues, social and cultural diversity, helping relationships, group work, assessment, research and program evaluation, psychopathology/abnormal behavior, diagnosis of mental and emotional disorder, evaluation of mental and emotional status, methods of intervention, supervision, and specialized areas (e.g., family counseling and chemical dependency counseling). The total number of courses was calculated from these two sets of information. In addition, the same questionnaire also elicited information on clinical instruction and internship clock hours that participants had completed. Clinical instruction referred to the areas of essential counseling skills training courses, practicum, and internship. Participants indicated how many credits they had obtained in each of the above clinical instruction areas. Internship credits

Table 1 Demographic Information of Participants Compared by CACREP Status

Demographic	CACREP		Non-CACREP		Total	
	n	%	n	%	N	%
Sex						
Men	4	4	16	14	20	17
Women	52	49	44	38	98	83
Status						
Part-time	25	22	27	23	52	45
Full-time	31	27	33	28	64	55
Academic courses						
1–3	14	12	10	9	24	21
4–7	3	3	29	26	32	28
8–12	18	16	14	12	32	28
13–15	19	17	6	5	25	21
Clinical instruction						
None	5	4	22	19	27	23
One course	17	15	11	10	28	24
Two courses	11	10	4	3	15	13
Three courses	23	20	23	20	46	40
Internship clock hours						
None	23	21	40	36	63	57
0–100	5	5	9	8	14	13
101–300	5	5	5	5	10	10
301–600	15	14	4	4	19	17
600+	4	4	0	0	4	4
Work experience						
None	26	23	26	23	52	47
1–5 years	20	18	21	19	41	36
6–10 years	6	5	8	7	14	12
11+ years	1	1	5	4	6	5

Note. CACREP = Council for Accreditation of Counselling and Related Educational Programs. Percentages do not total 100 because of rounding.

were considered different from internship clock hours, which were the actual clock hours students had worked as a counselor-in-training at an internship site. For instance, programs with CACREP accreditation require 600 hours of internship.

To measure general self-efficacy for counseling, the Self-Efficacy Inventory (S-EI; Friedlander & Snyder, 1983) was used. This instrument measures participants' self-efficacy for counseling by asking respondents to rate their confidence in their ability to perform tasks in five domains of counseling: academics, assessment, individual counseling, group and family intervention, and case management (Friedlander & Snyder, 1983). The range of possible scores is from 0 to 9, with 0 indicating *no confidence* and 9 indicating *very confident.* The Total score is the mean of all 20 items. The mean scores of each subscale mentioned above indicate the confidence level in the five domains. Each individual score measures the perceived self-efficacy in a specific counseling task, for instance, making appropriate referrals

and providing counseling for personality disorders. The instrument has shown high internal reliability, with Cronbach's alpha of 0.93 (Friedlander & Snyder, 1983). The S-EI also has high face and content validity. The items in the S-EI were chosen from a list of desired practice-based competencies developed by a committee of counseling supervisors. The randomly chosen counselor educators then examined the items and rated them to be "appropriate" and "important" for final item selection.

Procedure

A list of counseling programs from one state in the Midwest region was obtained. These programs were sorted into two categories: CACREP and non-CACREP. Three programs from each category in close proximity to the researchers' campus were selected for initial contact to request assistance in collecting data. If the particular program declined the request, another one from the same category was solicited until six institutions were selected. Classes with students nearing completion of core courses (e.g., foundation courses such as counseling theories, group work) and starting or finishing field placement courses were sampled. Counselor educators at the respective research sites were contacted to determine an appropriate time for us to administer the instrument to the class.

We administered the demographic questionnaire and the S-EI to the selected classes in the counseling programs. All students were briefed about the purpose of the study and their rights to withdraw from the study. Students who agreed to participate completed the questionnaire and the inventory in class. No names or identifying information were collected, and participants placed their completed questionnaires in anonymous collection envelopes.

Data Analysis

Two analyses were completed on the data. First, the data were grouped according to CACREP accreditation, and a two-group multivariate analysis of variance (MANOVA) was conducted to examine any demographic differences between the two groups and self-efficacy for counseling—the Total score as well as the individual items of S-EI—because each item references a specific counseling task (Friedlander & Snyder, 1983). Second, a multivariate analysis of covariance (MANCOVA) was performed to control for demographic variables such as age, courses taken, hours of internship, and work experience. The purpose of performing a MANCOVA was to determine whether the differences (if found) between the two groups would remain when all the above variables were controlled.

RESULTS

To explore demographic differences, a two-group MANOVA was conducted, with CACREP status as the grouping variable and with five dependent variables: age, clock hours of internship, years of work experience, total course work completed, and clinical course work completed. This analysis found a significant difference between the CACREP and non-CACREP participants on the demographic variables taken together, Hotelling's Trace = .193, $F(5, 99)$ = 3.820, $p < .01$. Following this test with univariate t tests and controlling overall alpha, using a Bonferroni correction for the number of tests conducted (α = .05/5 = .01), significant differences were found between the two groups on clock hours of internship and total courses (see Table 2).

To investigate any significant difference in self-efficacy between CACREP and non-CACREP students, a two-group MANOVA was conducted, using CACREP status as the grouping variable and the 20 items of the S-EI as dependent variables. This analysis indicated a significant difference, Hotelling's Trace = .683, $F(20, 93) = 2.159, p < .007$, between the groups when all the counseling self-efficacy variables were considered simultaneously. However, no significant difference was found between the two groups on total counseling self-efficacy, $t(114) = 1.850, p < .067$. This apparent discrepancy indicates that although the two groups had different response patterns on the individual items of the S-EI, these differences in several items did not yield a difference of the Total score.

Because of the number of items on the S-EI, investigating differences between the groups on individual items would result in either spurious significant results (due to accumulated Type I error) or insufficient power (if Bonferroni corrections to Type I error were made, even a liberal test would be small: e.g., α = .10/20 tests = .005). However, moderate effect sizes were seen in these data that are worthy of further study. Because the medium effect size is conventionally set at close to .50 (Stevens, 1996), the CACREP students showed more self-efficacy than the non-CACREP students on the items measuring counseling

Table 2 Univariate Test for Differences on Demographic Variables

Variable	CACREP			Non-CACREP			
	n	M	SD	n	M	SD	t
Age	55	30.40	7.48	60	33.97	9.38	−2.212
Internship hours	52	239.00	1.49	58	68.00	0.92	4.170**
Work experience	54	2.19	3.29	60	3.48	5.01	−1.628
Total course work	54	9.30	4.84	59	6.66	3.69	3.259**
Clinical course work	56	1.93	1.04	60	1.46	1.34	2.086
Counseling self-efficacy	56	5.70	1.76	60	5.13	1.78	1.700

Note. CACREP = Council for Accreditation of Counseling and Related Educational Programs; Internship hours = clock hours; Work experience = number of years. *t* was computed not assuming equal variances between the groups.
*$p < 01$.
**$p < .001$.

anxiety reactions (d = .54), assessing using a clinical interview (d = .49), counseling adjustment reactions (d = .49), and counseling affective disorders (d = .48).

Bandura's (1986) theory would indicate that differences on demographic variables between the two groups could be responsible for the differences in self-efficacy. To test this prediction, a MANCOVA was conducted with the 20 items of the S-EI as dependent variables; CACREP status as the grouping factor; and age, work experience, clock hours internship, total course work, and clinical course work as covariates. Although not able to equate the two groups (Stevens, 1996), this procedure can eliminate any systematic bias due to differences between the groups on the covariates. After verifying the assumptions of MANCOVA (Stevens 1996), the effect of CACREP status was calculated, resulting in no statistically significant differences between the groups after adjusting for the covariates, Wilks's lambda = .804, $F(20, 74)$ = .903, p < .585.

An overall examination of the relationships among the demographic variables and total counselor self-efficacy revealed that self-efficacy was most strongly linked with course work (r = .59, p < .01), internship hours (r = .47, p < .01), and clinical instruction (r = .40, p < .01); Pearson r values ranged from .40 to .59, indicating moderate to strong association of these variables with self-efficacy. These results provide further corroboration of Bandura's (1977, 1986) theory of the development of self-efficacy.

DISCUSSION

The findings of this study indicate that there were no differences in Total scores of self-efficacy between graduate students from CACREP and non-CACREP-accredited programs when amount of course work, hours of internship, and prior work experience were controlled; there was also a significant difference in several specific areas of counseling self-efficacy between students in CACREP programs and those in non-CACREP programs. Although we were not able to determine the statistical significance of Total scores of self-efficacy, our analysis also suggested that students from CACREP-accredited programs may have higher self-efficacy in counseling anxiety reactions, assessing using a clinical interview, counseling adjustment reactions, and counseling affective disorders than students from non-CACREP programs. Perhaps future research should focus on differences in self-efficacy and training in these areas, especially given that they are part of the specialization requirements mandated by CACREP and often bypassed by non-CACREP programs, particularly those that require fewer than 60 semester credits.

The results suggest that differences found in some counseling tasks were not due to CACREP accreditation. When background variables were controlled for (i.e., work experience, clock hours internship, and total amount of course work), there were no significant differences between the two groups of students on total self-efficacy. The CACREP accreditation label itself made no difference in students' self-efficacy; the results suggest that the primary source of variation in students' self-evaluation of their counseling skills was the number of training hours and prior related work experience they had. In other words, the finding may imply that the higher number of required courses and hours of field experiences of CACREP-accredited programs could account for variances in the counseling self-efficacy of the participants.

This finding provides empirical evidence for Bandura's (1986) theory of self-efficacy, which states that past experience and actual involvement in related tasks help individuals to develop more confidence in accomplishing a task. In this study, students who had more course work, more internship hours, and more related work experience perceived that they were more competent in performing the counseling skills in some specific domains. A closer examination of the data illustrates that the areas in which students from CACREP programs appear to be moderately more self-efficacious are, in fact, those associated with clinical endorsement, such as working with anxiety disorders, affective disorders, and clinical assessment and diagnosis. It is logical that students in these areas need more clinical training so that individuals can develop a high confidence level. It is worth noting that CACREP accreditation does require specific courses, particularly specific internship hours, that can provide counseling student interns opportunities to be exposed to a variety of counseling services.

The additional course work required by the practitioner standards (e.g., community counseling, school counseling) is likely to increase students' overall self-efficacy for counseling as well as specific self-efficacy for performing clinical tasks. Yet, although the number of accredited programs is increasing, many programs still remain unaccredited. Although the barriers for seeking accreditation may be varied for different programs, many studies have found that the extended hours of internship (i.e., 600 clock hours) have been identified as an obstacle to accreditation (Bobby & Kandor, 1992; Smaby & D'Andrea, 1995). Ironically, this study indicates that it is exactly the increased course work and internship hours that make the difference in self-efficacy.

There are limitations to this study that must be addressed. The results are limited due to the relatively small sample size in a restricted region. Moreover, in this study, the measurement about training is based on the self-reported courses and internship hours that participants have completed. The training experience should also be examined from a quality point of view. Future researchers should be cautious and attempt to distinguish the difference between the quantity and quality of training. Developing reliable and valid measures of training experiences and internship experiences will be vital for further investigation of the relationship between counselor training and counseling students' self-efficacy and proficiency. Similarly, developing appropriate assessment of self-efficacy regarding specific counseling tasks would be helpful. Future research might investigate those areas where moderate effect sizes (but not statistical significance) were observed: counseling anxiety reactions, completing assessments using a clinical interview, counseling adjustment reactions, and counseling affective disorders.

As many state counseling licensure laws begin to reflect the CACREP model of 60 semester hours, 100 hours of practicum, and 600 hours of internship, it is likely that unaccredited programs will either consider accreditation or create "CACREP-like" programs, in which the curriculum is modeled after the CACREP standards, but the expense and requirements of the accreditation process are avoided. However, the accreditation status does not necessarily shape the differences. The quality and intensity of course work and practical experiences are important for students to develop their self-efficacy. Another important caveat remains: Self-efficacy is not equivalent to competence, nor are the domains of counselor self-efficacy identical to being a competent counselor.

In summary, this study indicates that in the realm of self-efficacy, the length of internship hours and prior related experiences to counseling would increase students' self-efficacy as Bandura's (1977, 1986) theory asserts. The CACREP standards, which require 600 clock hours of internship, give students the needed experiences for developing self-efficacy in counseling. Programs that do not plan to consider the additional hours and field experiences should take this under advisement. However, self-efficacy alone, although an important predictor of career satisfaction and success, cannot be the only area of investigation into the effects of accreditation on counselor education outcomes. Studies of the effect of accreditation status on successful licensure, National Counselor Examination scores, and ratings of counseling graduates would provide important information in conjunction with this study, especially if significant differences were found on these more objective variables but few were to be seen on subjective ones.

REFERENCES

Bandura, A. (1977). Self-efficacy: Toward a unifying theory of behavior change. *Psychological Review, 84,* 191-215.

Bandura, A. (1986). The explanatory and predictive score of self-efficacy theory. *Journal of Social and Clinical Psychology, 4,* 359-373.

Bobby, C. L., & Kandor, J. R. (1992). Assessment of selected CACREP standards by accredited and non-accredited programs. *Journal of Counseling & Development, 70,* 677-684.

Bradley, C., & Fiorini, J. (1999). Evaluation of counseling practicum: National study of programs accredited by CACREP. *Counselor Education and Supervision, 39,* 111-119.

Cashwell, T. H., & Dooley, K. (2001). The impact of supervision on counselor self-efficacy. *Clinical Supervision, 20,* 39-47.

Fong, M. L., Borders, L. D., Ethington, C. A., & Pitts, J. H. (1997). Becoming a counselor: A longitudinal study of student cognitive development. *Counselor Education and Supervision, 37,* 100-114.

Friedlander, M. L., & Snyder, J. (1983). Trainees' expectations for the supervisory process: Testing a developmental model. *Counselor Education and Supervision, 22,* 342-348.

Heidel, L. S. (1999). One stage of therapist development: A longitudinal study of interns. (Doctoral dissertation. University of Illinois at Urbana-Champaign, 1999). *Dissertation Abstracts International, 59,* 4067.

Kaczmarek, P., Barclay, D., & Smith, M. (1996). Systematic training in client documentation: Strategies of counselor educators. *Counselor Education and Supervision, 36,* 77-84.

Larson, L. M., & Daniels, J. A. (1998). Review of counseling self-efficacy literature. *The Counseling Psychologist, 26,* 179-218.

Melchert, T. P., Hays, V. L., Wiljanen, L. M., & Kolocek, A. K. (1996). Testing models of counselor development with a measure of counseling self-efficacy. *Journal of Counseling & Development, 74,* 640-644.

Nelson, M. L., & Neufeldt, A. S. (1998). The pedagogy of counseling: A critical examination. *Counselor Education and Supervision, 38,* 70-88.

Schmidt, J. (1999). Two decades of CACREP and what do we know? *Counselor Education and Supervision, 39,* 35-45.

Smaby, M. H., & D'Andrea, L. M. (1995). 1994 CACREP standards: Will we make the grade? *Journal of Counseling & Development, 74,* 105-109.

Sprutif, D. A., & Benahoff, J. M. (2000). Helping beginning counselors develop a personal theory of counseling. *Counselor Education and Supervision, 40,* 70-80.

Stevens, J. (1996). *Applied multivariate statistics for the social sciences.* Mahwah, NJ: Erlbaum.

Vacc, N. (1992). An assessment of the perceived relevance of the CACREP standards. *Journal of Counseling & Development, 70,* 685-687.

Wilcoxon, S. A., Cecil, J. H., & Comas, R. (1987). Student perceptions of accreditation programs in counseling. *Counselor Education and Supervision, 27,* 184-189.

Woodard, V. S., & Lin, Y. (1999). Designing a prepracticum for counselor education programs. *Counselor Education and Supervision, 39,* 134-144.

Evaluation Criteria	Discussion Questions

1. Is the general purpose of the study clear? Will the study provide a significant contribution?

The purposes of the study are summarized in the sixth paragraph. These purposes are somewhat clear; it is difficult to understand all of the purposes as written with so much repetition. It would be helpful to list the purposes separately. It would also be helpful to state the more general purposes earlier in the introduction. A fairly good case is made for overall significance, though the lack of study in an area does not mean it would be significant to research it (last sentence in fifth paragraph).

1. Write a sentence that summarizes the general purpose of this study that could be inserted at the end of the first paragraph. What additional information could be provided to make a stronger case for significance?

2. Does the review of literature establish the relationship between previous studies and the current one? Is the review well organized and up-to-date?

The review of literature is contained in the third paragraph, under the Self-Efficacy heading. Additional literature is cited as background information and provides a theoretical basis for the study. The short review is up-to-date and well organized, though only a very brief summary of the research is provided. Much more detail could be given about these studies and how they specifically relate to the present study. The meta analysis is a statistical summary of many primary studies.

2. What kinds of information would be helpful to report related to the studies summarized in the third paragraph? Consider, for example, designs, samples and instruments.

3. Is the specific research hypothesis or question clearly and concisely stated?

There are no specific research hypotheses or questions. Implied research hypotheses would be that there are positive relationships between extent of training and self-efficacy, and that students in CACREP programs would have higher self-efficacy scores than students in non-CACREP programs.

3. There are three main purposes to this study. What are examples of specific research questions and/or research hypotheses for each of these purposes?

4. Is the method of sampling clearly presented? Could the way the sample was obtained influence the results?

While it is clear that students in six institutions constituted the convenient sample, it is not clear how specific classes were selected, and how many institutions and students refused to participate. If the CACREP students differed in ability or self-efficacy at the time of admissions these differences could account for the findings. Also, differences in professors could account for findings.

4. What kind of sampling procedure would improve the credibility of the study?

5. Is there anything in the procedures for collecting information, or in the instruments themselves, that could bias the results or weaken the study?

The explanation of the purpose of the study that is given to students by the researchers could influence the results (e.g., was CACREP versus non-CACREP mentioned?). A specific protocol that would be the same for both groups of institutions should be presented. The self-efficacy instrument has established technical merit (e.g., reliability and validity), though this is only for the total score, not for individual items. It would be helpful to include the specific items.

5. What would be an example of a protocol that could be used by the researchers when explaining to students the purpose of the study? Validity is limited to evidence based on the content of the items. What additional kind of evidence would be helpful?

6. Is the magnitude of the correlation or difference among the groups large enough to suggest practical significance or importance?

This study uses effect size appropriately as an indicator of practical significance. In both the correlations and mean differences the magnitude of the findings does support practical significance.

6. What additional information about effect sizes would be helpful to the reader to understand how this concept is related to the conclusions?

7. Do graphic presentations of the data distort the findings?

No graphics are presented in this study.

7. What kinds of graphics could be used to present the results? Would a scatterplot of the correlations be helpful?

8. Do the conclusions and interpretations follow logically from the results? Are unwarranted causal conclusions made from correlations or comparisons? Are limitations indicated?

Generally, the discussion follows from the results and, for the most part, there are appropriate interpretations. However, the emphasis on the findings related to individual items is at best exploratory. Appropriate limitations are addressed, though additional limitations concerning the nature of the samples and measure of self-efficacy could be addressed. An inappropriate causal statement is made in the first sentence of the last paragraph.

8. What are some conclusions that could be drawn from the results of this study given the limitations?

Credibility Scorecard
Factors that Influence Self-Efficacy of Counseling Students: An Exploratory Study

	Excellent	Very Good	Adequate	Marginal	Poor
General purpose	5	4	3	2	1
Contribution/significance	5	4	3	2	1
Review of literature	5	4	3	2	1
Research questions or hypotheses	5	4	3	2	1
Subjects or participants	5	4	3	2	1
Instrumentation	5	4	3	2	1
Procedures	5	4	3	2	1
Results	5	4	3	2	1
Practical Significance	5	4	3	2	1
Graphics	5	4	3	2	1
Conclusions	5	4	3	2	1
Any fatal flaws?					

Relationship between Parents, Peers, Morality, and Theft in an Adolescent Sample

Beth Judy
University of South Carolina

Eileen S. Nelson
James Madison University

ABSTRACT

Relationships between attachment to parents, morality, peer theft, and self-reported theft were examined in a sample of 83 male and 91 female high school students. Measures of care and overprotection from the Parental Bonding Instrument contributed to the parental attachment scores. A score for morality was obtained with Rest's Defining Issues Test-Short Form, and measures of theft and peer theft were established through the use of an adapted portion of the National Youth Survey. Adolescents reporting involvement in burglary had significantly lower morality scores than those who reported no involvement in burglary in the past year. Also in support of the hypotheses, peer involvement in theft prevailed as the strongest correlate of adolescent theft. No significant relationships were found between attachment to parents and theft. Implications for school counseling were discussed in relation to this study's findings.

In recent years, the behavior of adolescents has become increasingly problematic and threatening to the well-being of our nation. In the adolescent subculture of the 1950s, characteristic "delinquent" behavior consisted of smoking, swearing, and wearing blue jeans (Kett, 1977). Teenagers of the 1960s and 1970s were responsible for an increase in drug use and promiscuity (Mirel, 1991; Uhlenberg & Eggebeen, 1986). Between 1960 and 1980, delinquency in adolescence became more serious and much more pronounced. For ten- to seventeen-year olds the delinquency rate actually increased by 131% (Mirel, 1991). The growth in the delinquency rate has continued into this decade. According to the Statistical Abstract of the United States, in 1993, individuals under the age of 18 made up 29.3% of all arrests for serious crimes. For crimes such as arson, motor vehicle theft, and vandalism, juveniles were responsible for a higher percentage of arrests than any other age group (U.S. Department of Commerce, 1995). To some extent, adolescent involvement in problem behaviors can be explained by factors inherent in developmental progression toward adulthood. According to Kennedy (1991), in other societies as well as our own, the adolescent participation rate in delinquent behaviors increases during this turbulent developmental period and decreases as adulthood is achieved. Why is it that most individuals make the transition from childhood to adulthood without participating in criminal activity while increasing numbers fall into a pattern of delinquent behavior? This question has been the focus of a vast amount of research attempting to identify the specific causes of adolescent delinquency (Dishion, Patterson, Stoolmiller, & Skinner, 1991; Kandel, 1996; Warr, 1993a; Warr, 1993b).

When considering the reasons why an adolescent would commit a crime, it may be equally important to examine factors that prevent others from committing the same crime. Theorists from the cognitive-developmental tradition argue that a person's level of moral development affects the ability to resist the temptation to behave immorally (Ward, 1991). While the concept of morality is vague, Schulman (1989) and others agree that behavior can be considered moral if it adheres to the normative standards of the situation at hand and follows an intention to act fairly and considerately (Hogan, 1973; Villegas de Posada, 1994). On the other hand, an immoral act is committed when another person is harmed or put at a disadvantage because of someone else's intentional behavior.

INFLUENCE OF MORALITY

Piaget and Kohlberg extensively studied the development of moral reasoning and proposed processes by which they believe moral decisions are made. Lawrence Kohlberg (1984) described three levels (preconventional, conventional, and postconventional) through which an individual is said to progress as a result of her or his cognitive development. These were based upon Piaget's stages of moral realism and moral relativism. Each of Kohlberg's three levels is made up of two stages. Progression is determined by the criterion upon which a person bases her or his moral decisions. The criteria for each of the stages are fear of punishment (stage 1), personal gain (stage 2), consideration of society's needs (stage 3), respect for authority and law (stage 4), universal moral principals (stage 5), and human rights (stage 6) (Conger & Galambos, 1997). Since the progression from one stage to the next represents a step towards more mature reasoning, researchers examined the existence of a possible connection between moral reasoning level and moral behavior (Villegas de Posada, 1994).

The hypothesized existence of a positive relationship between moral reasoning and moral action was supported in a study by Richards, Bear, Stewart, and Norman (1992). They found that conduct problems in fourth and eighth graders decreased as their moral development level increased from stage 2 to stage 3. This connection was supported by other research (Richards et al., 1992; Turiel and Rothman, 1972). Jurkovic (1980) reviewed literature that addressed the relationship between moral reasoning and moral action. One of the first was an early study by Kohlberg that compared the moral development levels of delinquent and nondelinquent boys. In this research, Kohlberg found the delinquent boys reasoned largely at the preconventional level (stages 1 and 2), while the nondelinquent boys reasoned at conventional levels (stages 3 and 4), thus providing support for the direct connection between moral development level and behavior (Kohlberg, as cited in Jurkovic, 1980). Hudgins and Prentice (1973) who found evidence for delinquent adolescents functioning at conventional levels further examined this relationship. These findings suggest that a person who reasons at relatively high levels of moral reasoning may still exhibit delinquent behaviors. Jurkovic concluded that the argument that lower levels of moral maturity are to blame for the delinquent behavior of adolescents is not strong. It may, then, be necessary to look outside the individual at other variables that may override moral maturity and result in delinquent behavior. In the past, these variables have been largely overlooked with respect to the moral reasoning moral action controversy (Villegas de Posada, 1994).

PEER INFLUENCE

When examining the adolescent's environment for factors involved in facilitating delinquent behavior, the peer group emerges as a potential focus. In the transitional period from childhood to adulthood, adolescents become more dependent upon their peers (Camarena, 1991; Conger & Galambos, 1997; Foster-Clark & Blyth, 1991; Ward, 1991). Some have proposed that peers become more influential than

parents during adolescence (Windle, 1991). In peer relationships, the pressure to conform to the standards of the group strongly influences the behavior of teens, especially in early adolescence (Coleman, 1980; Foster-Clark & Blyth; Warr, 1993a). Much research has focused on the effect that delinquent peers can have on an adolescent's behavior. The majority of this research has supported a connection between adolescent delinquency and peer group deviance showing a tendency for increased conformity through middle adolescence with a decline into adulthood (Foster-Clark & Blyth). Brownfield and Thompson (1991) measured the relationship between self-reported delinquency and peer delinquency in a sample of white males with either juvenile or police records. They found a significant positive relationship between the two, congruent with prior research on this subject (Cox, Cox, & Moschis, 1990; Kaplan, Martin, & Robins, 1984).

PARENTAL INFLUENCE

Warr (1993b) examined the ability of parents to counteract pressure from peers to engage in delinquent behaviors. Based both on his disbelief that adolescents enter their peer groups leaving behind everything they have learned from their parents and on information incorporated from theorists in the field, Warr identified three ways in which parents may extend their influence past the front door. Warr's study showed that one of the greatest predictors of low delinquency rates was the amount of time parents spent with their children. Those adolescents who spent more time with their parents participated in less delinquent behavior than adolescents who spent less time with parents.

Warr also found that the more attached a child was to her or his parent, the less likely she or he was to become involved with delinquent peers (Warr, 1993b). In this way, attachment to parents proved to be a factor in reducing delinquency in adolescents (Aseltine, 1995; Warr, 1993b). Other researchers have shown that parental attachment is directly related to delinquency in adolescence (Patterson & Dishion, 1985).

The concept of attachment began to develop into its present form with the early theories of Bowlby (1969, 1973). Bowlby (1977) provided the link between attachment, based on the behavior of parents, and the mental health of the child. In this article, Bowlby outlined many of the disorders believed to stem from early attachment problems. Emotional detachment, one of the many, typically results from a lack of maternal care during the early years coupled with either the threat or reality of rejection. Emotional detachment frequently leads to delinquency (Bowlby, 1977).

Since Bowlby, many others in the field of psychology have focused on attachment to parents as an important factor in adolescent and adult disorders. More and more, however, the term *attachment* has become synonymous with one's perceived relationship with her or his parents. Parker pioneered most of the recent research on the effects of what he refers to as attachment on later neurosis when he, along with his colleagues, developed the Parental Bonding Instrument (PBI) (Parker, Tupling, & Brown, 1979). Through factor analysis, Parker et al., isolated two factors most important in healthy attachment to parents, "care" and "over-protection." Care refers to whether or not a warm, understanding, secure environment, was provided for the child, whereas overprotection refers to the implementation of unwarranted control and encouragement of dependency.

Once the care and overprotection dimensions were isolated, Parker et al. (1979) defined four attachment types: *optimal bonding,* high care/low overprotection; *affectionate constraint,* high care/high overprotection; *weak bonding,* low care/low overprotection; and *affectionless control,* low care/high overprotection. While Parker's research generally dealt with the link between attachment and depression and anxiety later in life (Parker, 1983), others have followed suit with studies examining the effect of the care and overprotection dimensions on homelessness and neuroses. (Burbach, Kashani, & Rosenberg, 1989; Dadds, Braddock, Cuers, Elliott, & Kelly, 1993; Rey & Plapp, 1990; Zemore & Rinholm, 1989). Each of these studies supports the hypothesis that lack of maternal care is detrimental to the child.

Parker's care and overprotection dimensions as measured by the PBI have only recently been applied to psychological research on delinquency. Pedersen (1994) analyzed the relationships between care and overprotection and anxiety, depression, and delinquency. He found that both dimensions were clearly related to the three variables with low care being the strongest predictor of both delinquency and anxiety/depression (Pedersen). A similar study by Mak (1994) focused on the effects of attachment on delinquent behaviors in adolescence. Her findings supported past research in that higher measures of maternal and paternal care and lower measures of maternal and paternal overprotection were associated with lower levels of delinquency for both males and females. As was also expected, the group falling into the optimal bonding category reported significantly less delinquency than the affectionless control group (Mak).

In summary, studies consistently suggest the existence of a relationship between delinquent behavior and (a) moral development level, (b) peer involvement in delinquent behavior, and (c) adolescent attachment to parents. The focus on theft follows from its relatively frequent occurrence in adolescent populations in comparison to other crimes. According to the U.S. Department of Commerce (1995), in the year 1993, individuals in the 15–17 age bracket represented 20% more arrests for robbery, burglary, and theft crimes than did the under 15 age group. This represents the greatest increase between any two consecutive age groups for these crimes. In that same year, juveniles represented over 30% of the arrests for each of burglary, larceny, and motor vehicle theft. The purpose of this study was to examine the relationships between the delinquent behavior of theft (including petty larceny, burglary, and robbery) and each of the following variables: moral development level, peer involvement in theft behavior, and attachment to parents as indicated by the participants' perception of care and overprotection. The predicted relationships are as follows:

1. Participants who respond "never" to all items within each of the theft subgroups (low petty, high petty, burglary, and robbery) will have significantly higher P scores (percent of principled morality as measured by the Defining Issues Test) than those who admit involvement, to any degree, in the respective behaviors.

2. Peer theft scores will show a stronger correlation with self-reported theft scores than will Defining Issues Test measures of morality (P scores) or measures of care and overprotection obtained for each parent with the Parental Bonding Instrument.

3. Adolescents with high peer theft scores and low self-reported theft scores will have significantly higher parental care scores, as measured by the Parental Bonding Instrument, than those with high peer theft scores and high self-reported theft scores.

4. Those participants indicating on the Parental Bonding Instrument that their parents implement a high care/low overprotection parenting style (optimal bonding) will report significantly less involvement in theft than will participants reporting parental low care/high overprotection (affectionless control), high care/high overprotection (affectionate constraint), or low care/low overprotection (weak bonding).

METHOD

Participants

Eighty-three male and 91 female students from a midsize, predominantly middle-class Southeastern Virginia high school participated in this study. The participants were in grades 9–12 and ranged in age from 14–18 (M = 15.85, SD = 1.25). Of the original sample of 176 participants, there were 61 participants from ninth-grade English classes, 37 from tenth-grade English classes (20 of whom came from an accelerated class), 42 from eleventh-grade English classes, and 36 from twelfth-grade English classes (16 of whom came from an accelerated class). English classes were selected for data collection because they were required for all students at all grade levels.

Further demographics taken on the sample indicated that 63% of the participants were Caucasian, 17% were black, 5% were Hispanic, 6% were Asian, and 7% reported themselves of "other" ethnic origin. While 84% of all participants indicated that both their mother and their father had raised them, 7% were raised by one biological parent and a stepparent, 9% by just their mother, and 1% by just their father.

Materials

Parental Bonding Instrument. The Parental Bonding Instrument (PBI), developed by Parker et al. (1979) is a 25-item questionnaire designed to measure the amount of care and overprotection adults remember receiving from their parents up until they were 16 years old. In the scale's development, factor analysis of a large pool of items resulted in the 25-item form used in this study. Twelve of the 25 items contribute to the overall care score (i.e., "spoke to me in a warm and friendly voice," "made me feel I wasn't wanted"). Thirteen items are concerned with overprotection (i.e., "tried to control everything I did," "gave me as much freedom as I wanted"). Each item has four possible responses, *very like, moderately like, moderately unlike,* and *unlike.*

The scale's test-retest reliability was determined in a study where a Pearson correlation coefficient of .76, $p < .001$, for care and .63, $p < 0.001$ for overprotection were obtained. A test of split-half reliability produced a Pearson correlation coefficient of .88, $p < .001$ for care and .74, $p < .001$ for overprotection. Concurrent validity was assessed by correlating raters' scores of parents on the two dimensions with the scores provided by their children on the PBI. The correlations for this measure ranged from .78 for the care scale to .48 for overprotection. The low correlation found for overprotection is thought to stem from the ambiguity of the factor and the fact that it is so closely related to a lack of care (Parker et al., 1979). A study assessing the validity of five measures of adolescent attachment to parents established the convergent and construct validity of the PBI (Heiss, Berman, & Sperling, 1996).

Theft Inventory. The participants' involvement in theft was measured by a self-report questionnaire modified from an instrument developed by Elliott and Ageton (1980). The inventory from which this questionnaire was extracted was originally used as a measure of delinquent behavior and drug use in the National Youth Survey.

Of the 47 items included in the original inventory, the 10 that measured theft behavior were selected for use in this study. Participants were asked questions such as, "How many times in the last year have you stolen (or tried to steal) things worth $5 or less?" and, "How many times in the last year have you used force to get money or things from other students?" Instead of the open-ended response style used in the National Youth Survey, multiple choice responses were provided ranging from *never,* to *more than seven times.*

For scoring purposes, the 10 items of the theft questionnaire were divided into four categories by a panel of experts with law degrees. The objective of this division was to group items of similar severity together so they could be considered simultaneously. The first of these categories we called *low petty* and consists of two items. *High petty,* the second group, consists of three items. The third group, *burglary,* consists of one item assessing theft involving breaking and entering, and one with an established equivalence with regard to severity. The last and most severe subgroup, *robbery,* is comprised of three items relating to motor vehicle theft and rated as the most severe category because the items within it deal with the use of force against other humans.

Peer Theft Inventory. Peer theft was measured by a set of four questions. The instructions proceeding the four items asked the participant to think of his/her friends. The participant was then instructed to think of these friends when responding to questions about their behavior, such as, "How many of your friends have stolen anything worth more than $50?" Responses provided were *none of them, one of them, some of them,* and *all of them.* This style of question was based on the questionnaire used to measure peer delinquency in the National Youth Survey.

Defining Issues Test—Short Form. The Defining Issues Test (DIT) was developed by Rest in 1979 to function as an objective alternative to the highly subjective and time-consuming Moral Judgment Interview. Both were designed to measure moral development level of the participant according to Kohlberg's theory of moral development. The short form of the DIT is composed of three dilemmas, each followed by twelve questions that the participant must rank in order of importance to the moral decision-making process.

Stage scores and principled morality scores are obtained for each participant. The principled morality score (P score) represents the amount of postconventional thinking (stages 5A, 5B, and 6) preferred by the participant. This is the score used to distinguish those making a high percentage of principled morality decisions from those thinking mostly at preconventional and conventional levels (stages 2, 3, and 4). Since the P score was used as the moral development variable in this study, reliability and validity of the DIT will be discussed in terms of that score alone. A study of test-retest reliability by Davison and Robbins (1978) showed the P score to have a reliability of generally .80. A Cronbach's Alpha measure of internal consistency provided an alpha in the .70s for the P score of both the 6-story version and the short form. The three stories making up the short form used in this study (Heinz and the Drug, Escaped Prisoner, and Newspaper) were chosen for their high P score correlation (R = .93) with the P score of the original 6-story version (Rest, 1990).

Design and Procedure

Participants were first given an informed consent form to sign. On this informed consent form, and also in the instructions of the experimenter, it was clearly stated that individual responses would be completely anonymous and confidential. Confidentiality was assured by instructing the participants to refrain from putting their names or any identifying information on any of the forms and to insert their completed answer sheets into the empty manila envelope at the front of the room. Then, a questionnaire packet consisting of the PBI, the Theft Inventory, the Peer Theft Inventory, and Demographic Questionnaire was administered to the consenting participants. One student, of the original sample of 177, chose not to participate for an unknown reason. The 25-item PBI was completed twice by each participant who reported having been raised by both her or his mother (or stepmother) and father (or stepfather)—answering one with regard to her or his mother and one with regard to her or his father. Participants indicating that they had been raised by solely their mother (or female guardian) or their father (or male guardian) answered the appropriate 25 questions

only. Once the entire class of participants had finished the first group of questionnaires and placed them in the envelope, the DIT-short form was administered. The DIT-short form was administered after the other questionnaires intentionally so that its moral content would not enhance the social desirability effect that may already have been present on the self-reported theft questionnaire. After completion of the DIT-short form, a debriefing statement was distributed that disclosed the purpose of the study and thanked the participants for their involvement.

RESULTS

Scores for each of the theft subgroups defined previously (low petty, high petty, burglary, and robbery) were assigned by giving a 0, to any participant for a category if it was indicated that she or he had never (in the past year) committed any of the acts making up that particular category. These groups will be referred to as the NO groups of each theft category. A 1 was assigned to a participant for a category if she or he admitted having participated in one or more of the behaviors falling into that category at least once in the past year. These groups will be referred to as the YES groups of each category. Low petty was the only exception to this rule. In this case, a response of "once" to the item "How many times in the past year have you stolen (or tried to steal) something worth $5 or less?" was considered equivalent to a NO group response. This was done to differentiate between those who habitually steal and those who may have stolen something small once, but never again. See Table 1 for rates of involvement in each category.

For analysis of the first hypothesis, which predicted higher P scores for those in the NO group of each subgroup discussed above, a general linear model was created at alpha level .05. With P score as the dependent variable, each of the subgroups (low petty, high petty, etc.) and all possible two-way interactions were entered into the model and systematically removed if they were not statistically significant. Although the P score means for the NO group were higher than the YES group for each of the subgroups, the resulting model showed a significant

Table 1   Percent Admitting Involvement in Different Types of Theft, by Age Group

Theft Subgroup	Age					
	14 n = 32	15 n = 40	16 n = 39	17 n = 48	18 n = 15	ALL n = 176
Low petty	21.9%	27.5%	25.6%	29.9%	26.7%	26.7%
High petty	50.0%	55.0%	41.0%	39.6%	40.0%	45.5%
Burglary	12.5%	10.0%	17.9%	16.7%	26.7%	15.3%
Robbery	15.6%	10.0%	10.3%	12.5%	20.0%	12.5%

Table 2   Comparison of P Score Means for the NO and YES Groups of Each of the Theft Subgroups

	Group					
	NO			YES		
Theft Subgroup	M	SD	n	M	SD	n
Low petty	26.28	14.70	94	22.53	16.14	33
High petty	25.63	14.24	71	24.88	16.27	56
Burglary*	26.64	15.41	107	18.17	11.21	20
Robbery	26.28	15.57	113	17.38	6.94	14

*means are significantly different, $p < .05$

main effect for burglary, alone, $F(1, 125) = 5.48$, $p = .02$ (see Table 2 for group means).

A separate theft score was computed for the second hypothesis, which predicted peer theft to correlate most highly with total theft. The total theft score was developed by adding together the values (either zero or one) of the four subgroups (low petty, high petty, etc.) for each participant while taking into account the differences in severity between the categories. Severity was accounted for by multiplying the score for low petty by one, high petty by two, burglary by four, and robbery by eight. The weighted subgroup scores were then added together to create one theft score for each participant ($M = 2.67$, $SD = 3.60$).

In order to compute the peer theft score, the four items of the peer theft inventory were ordered according to severity. From least to greatest severity, the items are 1, 2, 4, 3. The responses to each of these items ($a = 0$, $b = 1$, $c = 2$, $d = 3$) were multiplied by 1, 2, 3, or 4, according to the item's severity ranking. The sum of the resulting values became the peer theft score ($M = 6.85$, $SD = 6.80$). Since the mean self-reported theft scores for males ($M = 3.70$) and females ($M = 1.75$) were significantly different $F(1, 123) = 13.54$, $p < .001$, relationships were analyzed for males and females separately. In support of the second hypothesis, peer theft was not only the

variable most highly correlated with participant theft, but it was the only variable (of peer theft, P score, and mother care, father care, mother overprotection, and father overprotection) that was significantly correlated with participant theft. Peer theft scores were significantly correlated with participant theft scores for both males and females (see Table 3).

It was then hypothesized that those reporting high peer theft and low self-reported theft would have significantly higher parental care scores than those reporting both high peer theft and high self-reported theft. For analysis of this hypothesis, high and low groups were formed for both peer theft and self-reported theft by splitting each of the variables at their respective means. Participants were then put in one group if they had been classified as high in peer theft and low in self-reported theft and the other group if they were classified as high in peer theft and high in self-reported theft. An analysis of variance was performed to analyze the differences between these groups in terms of mother and father care scores as measured by the PBI. No significant differences were found between the two groups for mother care scores $F(1, 64) = 0.15$, $p = .70$ or father care scores $F(1, 60) = 3.89$, $p = .053$.

For analysis of the association between attachment and theft, care and overprotection scores for

Table 3   Pearson Correlations between P Score, Peer Theft, Attachment Measures, and Self-Reported Theft

Measure	1	2	3	4	5	6	7
1. P score	—	−.01	.03	−.09	.01	−.16	−.08
2. Peer theft	−.18	—	−.47**	.21	−.12	.15	.28**
3. Mother care	−.09	−.14	—	−.45**	.13	−.01	−.13
4. Mother overprotection	.11	.15	−.57**	—	.09	.20	−.03
5. Father care	−.19	−.18	.43**	−.19	—	−.46**	−.14
6. Father overprotection	.32*	.20	−.20	.30**	−.50**	—	.07
7. Self-report theft score	−.17	.52**	−.02	−.08	−.14	.11	—

Note: Correlations for females are located in the top triangle, while those for males are displayed on the bottom.

*$p < .05$

**$p < .01$

both mother and father were used to classify each participant under one of the four attachment types described by Parker et al. (1979). As suggested in past research, the four groups were formed by splitting each of the measures (mother care [M = 27.16, SD = 7.16], father care [M = 22.92, SD = 9.31], mother overprotection [M = 14.49, SD = 7.26], and father overprotection [M = 12.27, SD = 7.19]) at its mean and forming groups from the appropriate combinations of these groups. The combination of care and overprotection making up each attachment style are as follows: high care/low overprotection, optimal bonding; high care/high overprotection, affectionate constraint; low care/low overprotection, weak bonding; and low care/high overprotection, affectionless control. The number of participants falling within each attachment group and the mean theft scores of these groups can be found in Table 4. Using an alpha level of .05, a general linear model was created taking into account gender, each of the attachment types for both parents, and possible interactions between them. This method produced no evidence for significant theft score differences between any of the attachment types, regardless of gender and interaction effects.

Because of the large standard deviation of theft scores compared to the mean shown in Table 4, a post-hoc exploratory analysis was conducted that repeated the above procedure including just those cases in which total theft scores were greater than zero. Participants excluded from this analysis reported no theft of any kind (n = 76). This procedure resulted in a slightly improved mean/standard deviation ratio (M = 4.69, SD = 3.66), but also failed to find significant differences between the attachment types.

DISCUSSION

Although the means for the NO group were higher than the means for the YES group for all theft subgroups, only the means for burglary turned out to be significantly different from one another. It is surprising that a significant difference between the two P score means was not found for robbery, the crime

rated as the most severe. The inequality of sample size of the compared groups is one reason that the test could have failed to detect the difference that existed between the means for robbery. The NO group was seven times larger than the YES group for this variable, making significance very hard to achieve. In addition, some problems developed in the administration of the DIT. Twenty-seven percent of all P score measures (DIT-short forms) were invalid. This lowered sample sizes even more, and in all cases except burglary, a higher percentage of the already low YES group was invalid. In the case of robbery, invalid P score measures lowered the sample sizes from a comparison between n = 154 and n = 22, to a comparison between n = 113 and n = 14.

In the case of the large percentage of invalid P score measures, future attempts at measuring moral development with the DIT, especially in adolescents, should be made with extreme care. It may be helpful to repeat instructions more than one time and work through an example with the group of participants. The instructions printed in the DIT manual include an example, but just talking about the example did not prove effective. Perhaps instructions would be better understood if the experimenter completed an example, step-by-step, with the group.

Support for the second hypothesis was found. These results, showing peer theft to be the only significant correlate of male and female theft, indicate that, as expected, there is a powerful association between peer theft and adolescent theft. Although the results for the first hypothesis are contrary to Kohlberg's cognitive-developmental explanation of behavior, a consideration of the results of the first two hypotheses in conjunction with one another provides support for certain other psychological and sociological ideas. For instance, this study's findings support Bandura's (1990) explanation for deviant behavior. According to Bandura, intense external pressures to behave contrary to one's own standards of behavior tend to lead individuals to gradually relinquish these standards. Perhaps the partial lack of support for Kohlberg's theory that capacity for principled moral thinking determines behavior can be explained by the dramatic increase in external pressures (peer relationships) associated with this age

Table 4 Theft Means for Each of the Attachment Styles

| Attachment | Mother | | | Father | | |
Style	M	SD	n	M	SD	n
Optimal bonding	2.30	3.54	69	2.06	3.28	66
Affectionless control	2.91	3.21	53	2.64	3.57	42
Affectionate constraint	2.63	3.98	24	2.35	3.05	26
Weak bonding	3.04	3.55	24	3.30	4.08	23

group. It could be that external pressures exist for certain types of crime and not others. Perhaps peer pressures to commit burglary are not as salient in adolescence as the pressures to engage in the other types of theft studied here.

The strong association found between peer theft and self-reported theft also lends support to the subculture theory of sociology. According to the subculture theory, association with delinquent peers leads to acceptance of deviant activities and, in turn, results in participation in the behaviors as a means of gaining approval from the group (Segrave & Hastad, 1985).

The intent of the third hypothesis was to look to parental care scores as a possible moderator of peer theft. It could be that those who have friends who steal quite frequently, but do not steal themselves, feel more cared for by their parents than those who give in to peer pressure. The failure of this study to support this hypothesis may be explained by Warr's (1993b) research conclusions. Attachment to parents was shown to have an indirect influence on delinquency by inhibiting the formation of relationships with deviant peers. Attachment to parents, however proved to have no moderating effects on delinquency when adolescents had already formed deviant peer relationships. The hypothesis for the present study considered only those reporting high peer involvement in theft, therefore, attachment to parents, according to Warr's study, was understandably ineffective at curbing theft. Although no significance was found between the groups for either maternal or paternal care, it is interesting to note how close the difference came to being significant for father care scores.

Tests for the fourth hypothesis showed no difference between the theft scores of adolescents with different types of attachments to their parents. These findings support neither a direct (hypothesized by Patterson and Dishion, 1985 to exist) nor an indirect (hypothesized by Warr, 1993b to exist) theory of parental attachment influence. The results indicate that the attachment styles set forth by Parker et al. (1979) may not capture the individual effects of the care and overprotection dimensions more often shown to be involved in the formation of delinquent behavior.

Based on the findings of the present study interventions attempting to prevent adolescents from engaging in theft crimes should focus on the quality of adolescent peer relationships. Instead of dealing with the individual committing the delinquent behaviors separately, it is important to consider her or his behavior as representative of the behavior of her or his group of friends. Explaining to the adolescent why certain behaviors are immoral or unjust may seem to have an effect, but pressures elicited by her or his environment will most likely overcome an understanding of right and wrong.

The idea of incorporating peers into the counseling process has been taken on by many school systems who have developed peer helping groups and group counseling programs. It is the *positive peer culture* (PPC) tradition, however, most often used in more extreme cases such as institutional settings, that seems to most effectively utilize the peer group as a counseling tool (Brendtro & Ness, 1991). The PPC tradition is based on empowering youth to provide behavior management assistance and support to their peer group. One way in which youth are empowered is by allowing them to be involved in planning the rules and expectations of the program. Feedback from the youths and their peer group is so important when considering what type of intervention will work for them. The importance of peers in the lives of youths has been indicated in this study as well as many others.

The relationship among the youths involved in the program is developed through group counseling sessions. When an appropriate trusting relationship is developed within the counseling group, the support can extend past the session and into each individual's environment.

Future research on the topic of adolescent delinquency should attempt to isolate the effects of peers on behavior. Although certain other factors seem to contribute somewhat to the formation of these behaviors, it is evident that the strongest of these influences is that of the peer group.

REFERENCES

Aseltine, R. (1995). A reconsideration of parental and peer influences on adolescent deviance. *Journal of Health and Social Behavior, 36,* 103–121.

Bandura, A. (1990). Selective activation and disengagement of moral control. *Journal of Social Issues, 46*(1), 27–46.

Bowlby, J. (1969). *Attachment and loss, volume 1: Attachment.* London: Hogarth Press.

Bowlby, J. (1973). *Attachment and loss, volume 2: Separation.* London: Hogarth Press.

Bowlby, J. (1977). The making and breaking of affectional bonds: I. Aetiology and psychopathology in the light of attachment theory. *British Journal of Psychiatry, 130,* 201–210.

Brendtro, L. K., & Ness, A. E. (1991). Extreme interventions for extreme behavior: Peer-assisted behavior management in group treatment programs. *Child and Youth Care Forum, 20*(3), 171–181.

Brownfield, D., & Thompson, K. (1991). Attachment to peers and delinquent behaviour. *Canadian Journal of Criminology, 33*(1), 45–60.

Burbach, D. J., Kashani, J. H., & Rosenberg, T. K. (1989). Parental bonding and depressive disorders in adolescents. *Journal of Child Psychology and Psychiatry, 30*(3), 417–429.

Camarena, P. M. (1991). Conformity in adolescence. In the *Encyclopedia of adolescence* (Vol. I, pp. 172–174). New York & London: Garland Publishing, Inc.

Coleman, J. C. (1980). Friendship and the peer group in adolescence. In Adelson, J. (Ed.), *Handbook of Adolescent Psychology* (pp. 408-431) New York: John Wiley & Sons.

Conger, J. J., & Galambos, N. L. (1997). *Adolescence and youth: Psychological development in a changing world* (5th ed.). New York: Addison Wesley Longman, Inc.

Cox, D., Cox, A. D., & Moschis, G. P. (1990). When consumer behavior goes bad: An investigation of adolescent shoplifting. *Journal of Consumer Research. 17*(2), 149-159.

Dadds, M. R., Braddock, D., Cuers, S., Elliott, A., & Kelly, A. (1993). Personal and family distress in homeless adolescents. *Community Mental Health Journal, 29*(5), 413-422.

Davison, M., & Robbins, S. (1978). The reliability and validity of objective indices of moral development. *Applied Psychological Measurement, 2*(3), 391-403.

Dishion, T. J., Patterson, G. R., Stoolmiller, M., & Skinner, M. L. (1991). Family, school, and behavioral antecedents to early adolescent involvement with antisocial peers. *Developmental Psychology, 27*(1), 172-180.

Elliott, D. S., & Ageton, S. S. (1980). Reconciling race and class differences in self-reported and official estimates of delinquency. *American Sociological Review, 45,* 95-100.

Foster-Clark, F. S., & Blyth, D. A. (1991). Peer relations and influences. In the *Encyclopedia of adolescence* (Vol. II, pp. 767-771). New York & London: Garland Publishing, Inc.

Heiss, G. E., Berman, W. H., & Sperling, M. B. (1996). Five scales in search of a construct: Exploring continued attachment to parents in college students. *Journal of Personality Assessment, 67*(1), 102-115.

Hogan, R. (1973). Moral conduct and moral character: A psychological perspective. *Psychological Bulletin, 79,* 217-232.

Hudgins, W., & Prentice, N. M. (1973). Moral judgment in delinquent and nondelinquent adolescents and their mothers. *Journal of Abnormal Psychology, 82,* 145-152.

Jurkovic, G. J. (1980). The juvenile delinquent as a moral philosopher: A structural-developmental perspective. *Psychological Bulletin, 88*(3), 709-727.

Kandel, D. B. (1996). The parental and peer contexts of adolescent deviance: An algebra of interpersonal influences. *Journal of Drug Issues, 26*(2), 289-315.

Kaplan, H. B., Martin, S. S., & Robbins, C. (1984). Pathways to adolescent drug use: Self-derogation, peer influence, weakening of social controls, and early substance use. *Journal of Health and Social Behavior, 25,* 270-289.

Kennedy, R. E. (1991). Delinquency. In the *Encyclopedia of adolescence* (Vol. I, pp. 199-206). New York & London: Garland Publishing, Inc.

Kett, J. (1977). *Rites of passage: Adolescence in America 1790 to the present.* New York: Basic Books.

Kohlberg, L. (1984). *Essays on moral development: Vol. 2. The psychology of moral development: The nature and validity of moral stages.* San Francisco: Harper & Row.

Mak, A. S. (1994). Parental neglect and overprotection as risk factors in delinquency. *Australian Journal of Psychology, 46*(2), 107-111.

Mirel, J. E. (1991). Adolescence in twentieth-century America. In *The encyclopedia of adolescence* (Vol. II, pp. 1153-1167). New York & London: Garland Publishing, Inc.

Parker, G. (1983). Parental 'affectionless control' as an antecedent to adult depression; A risk factor delineated. *Archives of General Psychiatry, 40,* 956-960.

Parker, G., Tupling, H., & Brown, L. B. (1979). A parental bonding instrument. *British Journal of Medical Psychology, 52,* 1-10.

Patterson, G. R., & Dishion, T. J. (1985). Contributions of families and peers to delinquency. *Criminology, 23,* 63-79.

Pedersen, W. (1994). Parental relations, mental health, and delinquency in adolescents. *Adolescence, 29*(116), 975-990.

Rest, J. (1979). *Development in judging moral issues.* Minneapolis: University of Minnesota Press.

Rest, J. (1990). *Manual for the defining issues test, 3rd Edition.* Minneapolis: Center for the Study of Ethical Development, University of Minnesota.

Rey, J. M., & Plapp, J. M. (1990). Quality of perceived parenting in oppositional and conduct disordered adolescents. *Journal of the American Academy of Child and Adolescent Psychiatry, 29*(3), 382-385.

Richards, H. C., Bear, G. C., Stewart, A. L., & Norman, A. D. (1992). Moral reasoning and classroom conduct: Evidence of a curvilinear relationship. *Merrill-Palmer Quarterly, 38*(2), 176-190.

Schulman, M. (1989). The prevention of antisocial behavior through moral motivation training: Or, why isn't there more street crime? *Prevention in Human Services, 7*(1), 255-263.

Segrave, J. O., & Hastad, D. N. (1985). Evaluating three models of delinquency causation for males and females: Strain theory, subculture theory, and control theory. *Sociological Focus, 18*(1), 1-17.

Turiel, E., & Rothman, G. R. (1972). The influence of reasoning on behavioral choices at different stages of moral development. *Child Development, 43,* 741-756.

Uhlenberg, P., & Eggebeen, D. (1986). The declining well-being of American adolescents. *Public Interest, 82,* 25-38.

U.S. Department of Commerce: Bureau of the Census (1995). *Statistical Abstract of the United States* [CD-ROM]. Washington, DC: Administrative and customer services division.

Villegas de Posada, C. (1994). A motivational model for understanding moral action and moral development. *Psychological Reports, 74,* 951-959.

Ward, S. L. (1991). Moral development in adolescence. In the *Encyclopedia of adolescence* (Vol. II, pp. 663-668). New York & London: Garland Publishing, Inc.

Warr, M. (1993a). Age, peers, and delinquency. *Criminology, 31*(1), 17-40.

Warr, M. (1993b). Parents, peers, and delinquency. *Social Forces, 72*(1), 247-264.

Windle, M. (1991). Problem behavior in adolescence. In the *encyclopedia of adolescence* (Vol. II, pp. 839-844). New York & London: Garland Publishing, Inc.

Zemore, R., & Rinholm, J. (1989). Vulnerability to depression as a function of parental rejection and control. *Canadian Journal of Behavioral Sciences, 21*(4), 364-376.

Evaluation Criteria	**Discussion Questions**
1. Is the general purpose of the study clear? Will the study provide a significant contribution?	**1.** From reading the introduction and research hypotheses, what are the independent and dependent variables in this study? Do the variables change when the results are presented?
The general purpose is very clear, as stated in the first sentence in the abstract and again just prior to the research hypotheses. Significance is well established with the excellent discussion of theories of adolescent delinquency.	
2. Does the review of literature establish the relationship between previous studies and the current one? Is the review well organized and up to date?	**2.** If the review establishes a relationship between delinquent behavior and variables of interest, why do this study? How is this study related to previous studies of the same thing?
The review is nicely organized by major headings. The emphasis is on theory, with only a few primary studies mentioned. The summary is excellent and provides a good transition to the predicted relationships.	
3. Is the specific research hypothesis or question clearly and concisely stated?	**3.** What could be deleted from the statements of "expected relationships" to make them more concise without losing much information?
The research hypotheses are clearly stated just prior to the Method section.	
4. Is the method of sampling clearly presented? Could the way the sample was obtained influence the results?	**4.** Is it clear what the "predominantly middle class" means when describing the nature of the sample? What difference could socioeconomic status have on the results?
The sample is very well described. It is a convenience nonprobability sample. It is not clear whether all students in the school were sampled or only those from selected classes were used.	
5. Is there anything in the procedures for collecting the information, or in the instruments themselves, that could bias the results or weaken the study?	**5.** Who administered and collected the questionnaires? What difference would it make if it was the teacher or the researcher? How honest do you think adolescents would be?
There are excellent descriptions of the instruments with appropriate information about both validity and reliability. Sound procedures are used with needed confidentiality, especially given this subject. The order of completing the instruments should have been counterbalanced. Also, it is unclear if parental approval was obtained.	
6. Is the magnitude of the correlation or difference among the groups large enough to suggest practical significance or importance?	**6.** Examine Table 3, which presents correlations. What narrative statements are based directly on the correlations? Is it clear what the correlations mean? Examine Table 4. What is suggested by the fact that standard deviations are larger than the means?
Statistically significant differences are large and probably represent practical significance, as do correlations around .45 or higher. Non-significant differences and correlations are problematic due to the relatively small sample size.	

7. Do graphic presentations of the data distort the findings?

No graphic presentations are used.

8. Do the conclusions and interpretations follow logically from the results? Are unwarranted causal conclusions made from correlations or comparisons? Are limitations indicated?

The discussion is well organized by each of the research hypotheses. Appropriate limitations are discussed, and the results are examined in light of previous literature. Unwarranted causal conclusions are not made.

7. What would a bar graph look like for the data in Table 2? Would such a graph add much to understanding the data?

8. What would be two or three reasonable conclusions from this study?

Credibility Scorecard
Relationship between Parents, Peers, Morality, and Theft in an Adolescent Sample

	Excellent	Very Good	Adequate	Marginal	Poor
General purpose	5	4	3	2	1
Contribution/ significance	5	4	3	2	1
Review of literature	5	4	3	2	1
Research questions or hypotheses	5	4	3	2	1
Subjects or participants	5	4	3	2	1
Instrumentation	5	4	3	2	1
Procedures	5	4	3	2	1
Results	5	4	3	2	1
Practical significance	5	4	3	2	1
Graphics	5	4	3	2	1
Conclusions	5	4	3	2	1
Any fatal flaws?					

College Success of Students from Three High School Settings

Joe P. Sutton   Rhonda S. Galloway
Bob Jones University

ABSTRACT

Widely publicized reports have documented problems in our public schools since the mid-1980s. But profound issues also plague private and home schools. Taken collectively, the problems that persist in our nation's schools, particularly high schools, raise questions about the quality of education and the effects these shortcomings are having on our nation's students and their future success. While many students enter the work force or the armed forces after graduation from high school, a large number go on to college. This study focused on investigating the undergraduate success of a sample of college graduates from three high school settings: home school (n = 21); private school (n = 26); and public school (n = 17). Subjects represented all four major regions of the United States and several foreign countries. Data included 40 indicators of college success reflecting five domains of learning outcome: achievement, leadership, professional aptitude, social behavior, and physical activity. There were no significant differences among the three groups in 33 of the 40 variables. However, results from multivariate analysis of variance showed college graduates from home schools held significantly more leadership posts for significantly greater periods of time than did the private school group. The public school group remained unaffected.

With increasing scrutiny, parents and national leaders are questioning the quality of instruction in our nation's schools and the many ill-prepared students who graduate each year. Concerns over the effectiveness of education are not new, however. The widely publicized report, *A Nation at Risk* (1983), along with other noteworthy exposés in the 1980s (e.g., *Tomorrow's Teachers,* 1986; *A Nation Prepared: Teachers for the 21st Century,* 1986), were frank in their disclosures of the shortcomings of public schools and teachers. During this same period,

renowned scholars, including Boyer (1981) and Levine (1984), leveled serious indictments against schools, notably high schools, for their poor quality of education. Unfortunately, concerns about public education in general (e.g., *Education Week,* 1997) and high schools in particular (e.g., Oliver, 1992; Schlafly, 1990) persist today, despite ongoing national efforts to improve education in America (e.g., *Goals 2000*).

But problems in the education of children and youth are not limited to public schools. Some private schools, for example, appear to be experiencing their own unique set of struggles, which include unqualified teachers (Deuink, 1989, 1991; P. Smith, 1989; Sutton & Watson, 1992), poor leadership and administration (Mills, 1992; Salter, 1988; Stronks, 1991), low teacher salaries (Deuink, 1989; Fremont, 1990; P. Smith, 1989; Sutton & Watson, 1995; White, 1998), and failure to educate disabled and at-risk students (I. Smith, 1988; J. Sutton, 1992, 1994; J. Sutton, Everett, & C. Sutton, 1993; Van Dyk, 1991; Vaughn, 1991). Undoubtedly these problems raise serious questions about the quality of education in some private schools.

Home schools are not without criticism either. Characterized by some educators as "not quite legitimate" (p. 510), according to Lines (1987), and by spokespersons of the National School Boards Association as "a giant step backward into the 17th century" (Esch, 1991, p. 12), the major concerns with home schools are twofold: equivalent education and socialization (Kilgore, 1987). Academically speaking, Gorder (1990) notes that professionals worry about home-schooled students' ability to maintain grade-level performance, to experience similar academic opportunities using comparable curricula, to demonstrate mastery on standardized achievement tests, to learn in adequate facilities, and to receive instruction from qualified teachers. As for the socialization issue, Gahr (1991) explains that some psychiatrists are fearful that sheltered home-schooled students, compared to their public-school counterparts, may not

From "College Success of Students from Three High School Settings", by Joe P. Sutton and Rhonda S. Galloway, 2000, *Journal of Research and Development in Education 33*(3), 137–146. Reprinted with permission of The University of Georgia.

This research was supported in part by a grant from the National Center for Home Education (NCHE), Purcellville, VA, Christopher Klicka, Esq., executive director to Drs. Galloway and Sutton. The views expressed by the investigators do not necessarily reflect the policy of NCHE, and no official endorsement of NCHE should be inferred.

be able to deal properly with potentially unwholesome situations they will inevitably have to face in the future.

The profound issues that plague public, private, and home schools alike raise at least one critically important question: To what extent are the shortcomings of our nation's schools affecting our nation's students and their future success, particularly, success in college? While many students enter the work force or the armed forces upon graduation, a large number go on to college (Johnson, Collins, Dupuis, & Johansen, 1988). Not surprisingly so, the literature is clear that one of the major purposes of the American high school historically has been preparation of students for college (Farris, 1999; Finn, 1986; Van Til, 1974). But it is success in, not just admission to, college that indicates in part the effectiveness of students' high school preparation.

The purpose of the present study, then, was to investigate the undergraduate success of a sample of college graduates who were educated in different high school settings. Research has shown that educational setting may affect teacher behaviors (e.g., Sutton, McKinney, & Hallahan, 1992), student learning outcomes (e.g., Howe & Disinger, 1988), and test scores (e.g., Kleinfield, 1991). Therefore, examining the effects of high school setting on the performance of college students represents a logical and legitimate line of inquiry.

A study of this nature should necessarily include students from the three high school options available today, viz., public schools, private schools, and home schools. While the overwhelming majority of students in America are educated in public schools, data from the U.S. Department of Education (1991) indicate that almost one-fourth of all elementary and secondary schools are privately funded, and approximately one-eighth of all school children are currently enrolled in private schools. National surveys also suggest that from 1 to 2 million students are presently being home schooled in America (Kantrowitz & Wingert, 1998).

Investigating the undergraduate success of college students educated in different high school settings will provide the basic empirical evidence needed to begin determining the effectiveness of our educational system. Moreover, the results, if positive, may serve as a catalyst in rebuilding the public's diminishing confidence in its teachers and schools.

METHOD

Subjects

The students in our sample were matriculated at a private, 67-year-old liberal arts university in the Southeast during the 1992 and 1993 academic years (Galloway & Sutton, 1995). At that time, the university offered 100 undergraduate (i.e., associate and bachelor) and 76 graduate (i.e., master, specialist, and doctoral) degree programs, with a faculty-student ratio of 1:11. Total student enrollment for 1993 was approximately 3,740 students (49% male; 51% female), representing virtually all 50 states and 48 foreign countries. Most of the students were full-time (91%) and resided on campus (76%).

The initial sample included 180 students, divided equally into three groups based on high school educational background: (a) home school; (b) private school; and (c) public school. To qualify for participation in the study, students had to be first-time freshmen who had completed their entire high school program in one setting. For the home school group ($n = 60$), we used all available students. To each qualifying student from conventional private ($n = 600$) and public ($n = 200$) schools, we assigned a three-digit consecutive number. Using a table of random numbers (Gay, 1987), we selected 60 private school students and 60 public school students to match the home school group in gender, race, age, and geographic region.

Only students in the initial sample who had graduated with a baccalaureate degree by May of 1997 comprised the final sample for this study, which included 21 home-school graduates, 26 private-school graduates, and 17 public-school graduates (see Figure 1). The remaining students from the original subject pool had either withdrawn or were still in the process of completing their degrees at the time of data collection. Chi-square analyses revealed no significant differences among the three groups for most of the demographic variables (see Table 1). The private-school group had significantly greater representation of students from the Southern region of the country ($X^2 = 7.75$, $p = .005$), however, and there were significantly more foreign students in the home school group ($X^2 = 4.66$, $p = .03$).

Since this study included multiple groups of students from varying backgrounds and cultures, we

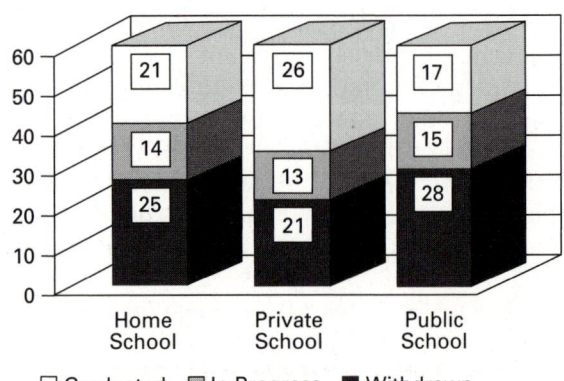

Figure 1.   Number of students in sample who graduated from college by high school background.

Table 1 Sample Description

	High School Setting		
	Home School $n = 21$	Private School $n = 26$	Public School $n = 17$
Gender			
Male	9	13	10
Female	12	13	7
Total	21	26	17
Mean age (in years)	21.97	21.84	22.28
U.S. region of residence			
Northcentral	5	7	10
Northeast	1	4	3
South	9	13	2
West	0	1	0
Foreign	6	1	2
Total	21	26	17
Mean family income	$27,159.67[a]	$36,185.86[b]	$36,025.85[c]
College degree focus			
Arts & science	10	10	8
Business	2	6	2
Education	2	1	1
Fine arts	4	5	2
Religion	3	4	4
Total	21	26	17
Number of semesters	7.76	7.88	8.06

Note. [a]Data available for 15 Ss; [b]Data available for 14 Ss.; [c]Data available for 13 Ss.

were especially concerned about the potential impact of socioeconomic status (SES) on the student learning outcome data collected. Research has established a link between SES and school achievement (Schaie & Roberts, 1971) as well as SES and intelligence (Burt, 1959; Roberts, 1971). Therefore, using parental income as an indicator of SES, we gathered data on the salaries of parents represented by the students in our sample. While the mean income of the home school group was observably lower than that of the two other groups (see Table 1), results from analysis of variance of the three group means revealed no significant differences ($F = 2.94$; $df = 2.39$; $p = .06$).

Procedures

We gathered student data on 40 indicators of college success (see Table 2) which centered on five major domains of learning outcome: (a) achievement; (b) leadership; (c) professional aptitude; (d) social behavior; and (e) physical activity. Sources of data included university transcripts, academic files, general files, discipline records, work scholarship records, extracurricular activities records, intern records, community service records, fine arts records, and student activity records. We designed a data sheet for the purpose of recording all student information prior to

computer input. All data were gathered and recorded by one of the coinvestigators of this project and one research assistant.

Of the 10 achievement indicators of college success, four were typical of most colleges and universities: (a) rank in senior class; (b) total GPA; (c) GPA in major course work; and (d) academic awards. The remaining six variables centered on percentages of A, A−, and B+ final grades earned by students in their overall degree programs and major course work. We included actual final grades as indicators of academic success because the university's system of awarding quality points (QPs) and calculating GPAs tended to mask students' true final grades. For example, the number of QPs per unit of credit for a final course grade of A was the same as that of an A−, viz., 4.0 quality points. Similarly, final course grades of B+, B, and B− all received quality points of 3.0 per unit of credit. Counting actual final grades, then, was a more accurate way of measuring students' true academic success than GPA alone.

We identified 16 *leadership* indicators of college success. Offices held by students during their college years was the proxy variable for leadership. Included were academic offices (e.g., secretary of the German club), appointed offices (e.g., dormitory hall leader), elected offices (e.g., secretary, treasurer),

Table 2 Indicators of College Success

ACHIEVEMENT (10)

- A grades, total
- A grades, major
- Academic awards
- Rank, senior class

- A^- grades, total
- A^- grades, major
- GPA, total

- B^+ grades, total
- B^+ grades, major
- GPA, major

LEADERSHIP (16)

- Academic offices, sem.
- Appointed offices, pos.
- Extracurr. offices, sem.
- High offices, pos.
- Work offices, pos.
- Total offices, pos.

- Academic offices, pos.
- Elected offices, sem.
- Extracurr. offices, pos.
- Religious offices, sem.
- Work offices, sem.

- Appointed offices, sem.
- Elected offices, pos.
- High offices, sem.
- Religious offices, pos.
- Total offices, sem.

PROFESSIONAL APTITUDE (3)

- GRE verbal score

- GRE quantitative score

- GRE analytical score

SOCIAL BEHAVIOR (6)

- Demerit-free, sem.
- Extracurr. total, sem.

- Extracurr. music, sem.
- Elected offices, sem.

- Extracurr. drama, sem.
- Elected offices, pos.

PHYSICAL ACTIVITY (5)

- Athletic sports, sem.
- Extracurr. office, sem.

- Athletic cheerleading, sem.
- Extracurr. drama, sem.

- Athletics total, sem.

Note. pos. = positions; sem. = semesters.

extracurricular offices (e.g., athletic director), high offices (e.g., president, vice president), religious offices (e.g., chaplain), and work offices (e.g., job supervisor).

Three indicators of college success revolved around *professional aptitude*. The Graduate Record Exam (verbal, quantitative, and analytical scores), required of all graduating seniors at the university where we drew the sample, served as the sole source of data for this domain of student outcome.

We identified six *social behavior* indicators of college success. Three of the variables centered on extracurricular activities (e.g., the number of semesters membership in a musical or dramatic group). Two of the variables were the number of semesters students served in an elected office and the different types of elected offices held by students. The number of semesters that students maintained a zero-demerit record, a clear indication of the ability to conform to the university behavior code, concluded the variable set.

Finally, we identified five *physical activity* indicators of college success. Four of the variables had to do with involvement in athletics, specifically, the number of semesters students held the office of athletic director, participated in sports, participated in cheerleading, and total athletic activities. The remaining variable was semesters involvement in dramatic productions.

Data Analysis

Since each of the five domains of student outcome represented a conceptually similar and meaningful set of college success indicators (i.e., achievement, leadership, professional aptitude, social behavior, and physical activity), we tested for differences among group means by conducting five multivariate analysis of variance (MANOVA) tests. A series of MANOVAs on smaller groups of variables also permitted a more favorable subject-variable ratio for analyses. The *SPSS* statistical program allowed us to assess multivariate effects by the Wilks' lambda criterion and prompted univariate and Bonferonni statistics to determine the specific source of variance among the multiple sets of dependent variables and the pairs of groups that were affected. An alpha of .05 was adopted as a minimum level of significance for all statistical tests.

RESULTS

Table 3 gives the means and standard deviations of the 40 college success indicators. Table 4 provides the results of the MANOVA tests. The first MANOVA tested for differences among the three groups on the 10 achievement indicators. The resulting Wilks' lambda was significant ($F = 1.872, df = 20, p = .022$). Follow-up univariate statistics (see Table 5) revealed

Table 3 Means and Standard Deviations of College Success Variables by Group

College Success Variable	Home School n = 21		Private School n = 26		Public School n = 17	
	M	SD	M	SD	M	SD
ACHIEVEMENT						
A grades, total[a]	24.93	(9.50)	20.40	(21.91)	21.47	(17.78)
A⁻ grades, total[a]	22.95	(9.53)	15.82	(9.94)	16.70	(10.85)
B⁺ grades, total[a]	11.14	(4.70)	10.48	(6.65)	12.10	(8.92)
A grades, major[a]	22.82	(17.58)	21.09	(25.27)	20.96	(21.11)
A⁻ grades, major[a]	21.32	(12.57)	14.30	(13.17)	16.55	(10.29)
B⁺ grades, major[a]	16.90	(11.08)	10.04	(11.60)	9.00	(12.69)
Academic awards[b]	0.14	(0.35)	0.23	(0.71)	0.24	(0.44)
GPA, total[c]	3.27	(0.28)	3.16	(0.42)	3.12	(0.48)
GPA, major[c]	3.27	(0.41)	3.24	(0.48)	3.08	(0.58)
Rank, Senior class[d]	64.35	(20.25)	54.82	(26.70)	50.43	(30.23)
LEADERSHIP[b]						
Academic offices, sem.	0.67	(1.56)	0.07	(0.39)	0.00	(0.00)
Academic offices, type	0.38	(0.86)	0.03	(0.20)	0.00	(0.00)
Appointed offices, sem.	6.05	(3.71)	1.88	(3.71)	4.59	(3.87)
Appointed offices, type	2.29	(1.55)	0.62	(1.13)	1.47	(1.12)
Elected offices, sem.	2.48	(2.54)	1.27	(1.97)	1.24	(1.60)
Elected offices, type	1.76	(1.89)	0.81	(1.23)	1.00	(1.32)
Extracurr. offices, sem.	1.62	(1.63)	1.27	(1.97)	1.24	(1.60)
Extracurr. offices, type	1.24	(1.30)	0.81	(1.23)	1.00	(1.32)
High offices, sem.	6.95	(4.36)	2.11	(3.78)	4.88	(3.74)
High offices, type	2.71	(1.98)	0.81	(1.20)	1.71	(1.10)
Religious offices, sem.	5.14	(2.52)	1.00	(2.15)	3.71	(2.66)
Religious offices, type	2.09	(1.61)	0.38	(0.75)	1.41	(1.00)
Work offices, sem.	1.52	(2.93)	0.88	(1.86)	1.18	(2.43)
Work offices, type	0.57	(0.95)	0.23	(0.51)	0.29	(0.59)
Total offices, sem.	8.71	(4.62)	3.15	(3.97)	5.82	(3.70)
Total offices, type	4.00	(2.76)	1.42	(1.53)	2.47	(1.55)
PROFESSIONAL APTITUDE[d]						
GRE verbal score	38.79	(23.98)	40.92	(25.04)	48.06	(19.10)
GRE quantitative score	28.63	(16.63)	34.80	(23.70)	43.13	(24.77)
GRE analytical score	39.74	(17.95)	47.60	(22.29)	57.88	(27.73)
SOCIAL BEHAVIOR[b]						
Demerit-free, sem.	5.38	(2.31)	5.69	(2.31)	5.59	(2.87)
Extracurr. music, sem.	1.86	(4.08)	0.46	(1.42)	3.06	(7.68)
Extracurr. drama, sem.	0.95	(2.25)	0.46	(1.63)	0.12	(0.49)
Extracurr. total, sem.	2.81	(5.65)	1.00	(2.06)	3.18	(7.65)
Elected offices, sem.	1.62	(1.63)	1.27	(0.81)	1.24	(1.00)
Elected offices, types	1.76	(1.89)	0.81	(1.23)	1.00	(1.32)
PHYSICAL ACTIVITY[b]						
Athletic sports, sem.	1.43	(2.62)	3.23	(3.55)	1.76	(2.91)
Athletic cheerleading, sem.	0.00	(0.00)	0.30	(0.93)	0.24	(0.97)
Athletics total, sem.	1.43	(2.62)	3.54	(3.36)	2.00	(3.24)
Extracurr. office, sem.	0.00	(0.00)	0.04	(0.20)	0.06	(0.96)
Extracurr. drama, sem.	0.95	(2.25)	0.46	(1.63)	0.12	(0.49)

Note. GRE = Graduate Record Exam; sem. = semesters; [a]percentage; [b]frequencies; [c]four-point scale; [d]percentile.

Table 4 Multivariate Analysis of Variance Results

College Success Domain	Wilks' λ	df	F	Significance
Achievement	.541	20	1.87	.022*
Leadership	.376	32	1.81	.015*
Professional aptitude	.896	6	1.04	.406
Social behavior	.788	12	1.18	.304
Physical activity	.849	8	1.23	.286

*$p < .05$ and univariate and Bonferonni tests follow.

Table 5 Univariate and Bonferonni Results for Achievement and Leadership Domain Variables

College Success Variable	F	Univariate p	Bonferonni p	Signif.	Result
ACHIEVEMENT					
A grades, total	0.40	.670	—	ns	—
A⁻ grades, total	3.25	.046*	.056	ns	—
B⁺ grades, total	0.29	.750	—	ns	—
A grades, major	0.05	.954	—	ns	—
A⁻ grades, major	1.93	.154	—	ns	—
B⁺ grades, major	2.75	.072	—	ns	—
Academic awards	0.19	.827	—	ns	—
GPA, total	1.18	.314	—	ns	—
GPA, major	0.50	.610	—	ns	—
Rank, senior class	1.50	.233	—	ns	—
LEADERSHIP					
Academic offices, sem.	3.19	.048*	.094	ns	—
Academic offices, type	3.49	.037*	.077	ns	—
Appointed offices, sem.	7.46	.001**	.001**	s	H > Pr
Appointed offices, type	9.86	.000**	.000**	s	H > Pr
Elected offices, sem.	2.40	.099	—	ns	—
Elected offices, type	2.49	.091	—	ns	—
Extracurr. offices, sem.	0.30	.743	—	ns	—
Extracurr. offices, type	0.66	.522	—	ns	—
High offices, sem.	8.75	.000**	.000**	s	H > Pr
High offices, type	9.63	.000**	.000**	s	H > Pr
Religious offices, sem.	17.86	.000**	.000**	s	H > Pr
Religious offices, type	12.95	.000**	.000**	s	H > Pr
Work offices, sem.	0.41	.665	—	ns	—
Work offices, type	1.50	.230	—	ns	—
Total offices, sem.	10.57	.000**	.000**	s	H > Pr
Total offices, type	9.48	.000**	.000**	s	H > Pr

*$p < .05$; **$p < .001$; H = home school; Pr = private school.

a significant difference among the groups for one variable: A⁻ grades, total. But Bonferroni analysis for pair-wise contrasts showed that the difference between the higher number of total A⁻ grades earned by the home school group over the private school group fell short of significance ($p = .056$).

The second MANOVA tested for differences among the three groups on the 16 leadership indicators. Once more, the resulting Wilks' lambda was significant ($F = 1.814, d = 32, p = .015$). Follow-up univariate statistics revealed a significant difference among the groups for the following variables: academic offices, semesters; academic offices, positions; religious offices, semesters; religious offices, positions; appointed offices, semesters; appointed offices, positions; high offices, semesters; high offices, positions; total offices, semesters; and total offices, positions.

Bonferonni analyses revealed that the home school group held significantly more semesters of the following offices than the private school group: religious offices ($p = .000$); appointed offices ($p = .001$); high offices ($p = .000$); and total offices ($p = .000$). Similarly, Bonferonni analyses also showed that the home school group held significantly more types of offices than the private school group in religious offices ($p = .000$), appointed offices ($p = .000$), high offices ($p = .000$), and total offices ($p = .000$).

The third, fourth, and fifth MANOVAs tested for differences among the groups on professional aptitude, social behavior, and physical activity indicators, respectively. All resulting Wilks' lambdas for these tests were statistically nonsignificant.

DISCUSSION

This study examined the effects of high school setting on the undergraduate success of college graduates who had been formerly educated in either home, private, or public schools. Forty indicators of college success reflecting five domains of learning outcome were identified. In 33 of the 40 variables, analyses revealed no significant differences among the student groups. One chief conclusion, then, is that regardless of high school setting, all college-bound students sampled received essentially equivalent education. Furthermore, we can surmise from the results of this study that home schools, private schools, and public schools are preparing students for college who are able to compete comparably and can succeed on par with each other in the areas of achievement, professional aptitude, social behavior, and physical activity.

The preponderance of nonsignificant results are generally positive for students educated in the public school setting. However, the results of this study seriously challenge the purported claim that some private schools are more effective and, in some cases, far superior to other forms of education. For example, Stoker and Splawn (1980) have contended that students in some Accelerated Christian Education (ACE) schools achieve academically at a level "'two to four years' ahead of the public school students" (p. 22). While this may be true for some students in selected private schools at the K–12 level, their elevated academic performance does not appear to transfer to the postsecondary level in some situations. In this study, we found no statistical difference between the private school and public school college groups in any of the 10 achievement indicators.

Implications from the nonsignificant results are mixed for home schools. First and foremost, the fact that neither the public school nor the private school groups significantly outperformed the home school group is noteworthy. While this finding may be troublesome for public and private school proponents, it is encouraging for home educators who "are routinely harassed by their local school district or law enforcement officials" (Klicka, 1993, p. 230) and who continue to be criticized and harangued for their nonconventional approach to education. Furthermore, these results offer some validation that home education is an increasingly viable educational option.

Conversely, however, the inability of the home school group to outperform their private and public school counterparts academically suggests that home school students are not generalizing their exceedingly high K–12 achievement scores to the college level. Some published studies are showing that grade school and high school students in home schools perform as well as, if not better than, their conventionally educated counterparts (Delahooke, 1986; Lines, 1987; McAvoy, 1986; Ray, 1990, 1992, 1993; Schmidt, 1989; Wartes, 1990). Even more incredibly, results from the two largest home school studies to date (i.e., Ray, 1997; Rudner, 1998) have concluded that the average home-schooled student scores around the 80th percentile in all subjects on standardized tests, while the typical public school student scores around the 50th percentile.

The nonsignificant findings notwithstanding, this study found significant results in the leadership domain, with the home school group holding significantly more types of offices and serving significantly more semesters in office than their private school counterparts. One possible explanation for the home school group's success in this area may have to do with the social ability of most office-holders in getting along well with others and winning peer respect and favor. Paradoxically, it is with this learning outcome that home educators probably receive the most criticism (e.g., Kilgore, 1987). Critics of home education typically charge that the isolated home school environment stifles socialization.

But some research on the social skill attainment of home-schooled students provides evidence to the contrary. For example, Delahooke (1986) showed that home-schooled students did not differ significantly from private school students in virtually all psychosocial areas. Smedley (1992) found that home-schooled students' socialization scores ranked in the top 27th percentile as opposed to the top 75th percentile for public school students. He concluded that "children kept at home are more mature and better socialized than those who are sent to [conventional] school" (p. 12). Shyers (1992), in a large study of 140 students, evenly divided between home and public school settings, found no significant differences between the groups in their assertiveness and self-concept. More importantly, he found that home-schooled students had significantly fewer problem behaviors than their public school counterparts.

This study focused on the effects of high school setting on the postsecondary success of three groups of college graduates. The failure of college graduates from private schools, traditionally recognized as a more effective form of education, to outperform either the public or home school group, coupled with the surprising showing of the home school over the private school group in leadership, clearly suggests the need for more research. But a number of obstacles will likely hamper similar studies in the near future. For example, the low numbers of college students who graduate from home school settings may force researchers to use depressed sample numbers and samples of convenience rather than randomized samples. Only a handful of colleges presently matriculate large numbers of home-schooled graduates each year; many, if not most, colleges admit fewer than a dozen or so home school students annually.

Another related drawback is that additional college success studies of this kind may be limited to student samples drawn from private, religiously affiliated colleges (e.g., Bob Jones University, Brigham Young University) where larger numbers of home school graduates are congregated. Consequently, critics may question whether results, if in favor of home-schooled students, are more attributable to similarities in educational philosophy (i.e., the religious persuasion) shared by the college students themselves and their respective institutions than to high school setting per se.

Future research should also focus on the impact that high school curriculum may have on college success among students coming out of home schools, private schools, and public schools. In a rare 10-year longitudinal study, Adelman (cited in Bracey, 1999) discovered that curriculum intensity and quality was the best predictor of college success, not the more traditional predictors of senior class rank, grade point average, aptitude tests, or even socioeconomic status. Controlling for variance in curriculum used by students coming from home school settings, as opposed to more standardized curricula found in public and private school settings, may be problematic for investigators, however.

In sum, replication studies on high school setting effects among college graduates should concentrate on larger sample sizes and include graduates from state-supported rather than private colleges. Possibly more important than educational setting is the effect that high school curriculum rigor may have on college success among students from different high school backgrounds. Finally, post high-school success is not limited to the college experience. Research that identifies high school graduates who go directly into the work force and examines the quality of their job performances as a function of high school setting is also warranted.

REFERENCES

Boyer, E. L. (1981). Schools and universities need each other. *Educational Leadership, 38,* 556.

Bracey, G. W. (1999). Getting that sheepskin. *Phi Delta Kappan, 81*(2), 169–170.

Burt, C. (1959). Class differences in general intelligence III. *British Journal of Statistical Psychology, 12,* 15–33.

Delahooke, M. (1986). Home educated children's social/emotional adjustment and academic achievement: A comparative study. (Doctoral dissertation, California School of Professional Psychology, 1986). *Dissertation Abstracts International, 47*(2), 475.

Deuink, J. D. (1989). Crucial issues Christian schools must face in the 1990s. *Balance, 10*(1), 1–3.

Deuink, J. D. (1991). Building your professional staff. *Balance, 11*(7), 1–3.

Esch, M. (1991, June 29). Home education increasingly popular as U.S. schools continue to plummet. *WORLD,* 12.

Farris, P. J. (1999). *Teaching, bearing the torch* (2nd ed.). Boston: McGraw-Hill College.

Finn, C. E. (1986). A fresh option for the non-college-bound. *Phi Delta Kappan, 68,* 234–238.

Fremont, W. G. (1990). Providing for professionals in Christian schools. *Balance, 11*(10), 1–2, 4.

Gahr, E. (1991, December 2). Home and not alone. *Insight,* 11–13, 36.

Gay, L. R. (1987). *Educational research: Competencies for analysis and application* (3rd ed.). Columbus, OH: Merrill.

Galloway, R. S., & Sutton, J. P. (1995). Home and conventionally educated students: Aptitude for and achievement in college level English. *Home School Researcher, 11*(1), 1–9.

Gorder, C. (1990). *Home schools: An alternative.* Tempe, AZ: Blue Bird Publishing.

Howe, R. W., & Disinger, J. F. (1988). *Teaching environment education using out-of-school settings and mass media.* Columbis, OH: ERIC Clearing House for Science, Mathematics, and Environment Education. (ERIC Document Reproduction Service No. ED 309 720).

Johnson, J. A., Collins, H. W., Dupuis, V. L., & Johansen, J. H. (1988). *Introduction to the foundations of American education* (2nd ed.). Boston: Allyn & Bacon.

Kantrowitz, B., & Wingert, P. (1998, October 5). Learning at home: Does it pass the test? *Newsweek, 132,* 64–70.

Kilgore, P. (1987, January). *Profile of families who home school in Maine.* (ERIC Document Reproduction Service No. ED 295 280).

Kleinfield, J. (1991). *The Alaska statewide student testing program: Are the tests biased?* Anchorage Alaska Educational Research Association. (ERIC Document Reproduction Service No. ED 335 183)

Klicka, C. (1993). *The right choice: The incredible failure of public education and the rising hope of home school—an academic, historical, practical, and legal perspective.* Gresham, OR: Noble Publishing.

Levine, S. (1984). College admission requirements and the high school program. NASSP *Bulletin, 68,* 19–25.

Lines, P. M. (1987, March). An overview of home instruction. *Phi Delta Kappan, 68*(7), 510–517.

McAvoy, R. (1986, October). Home-bound students: An alternative for rural areas. Paper presented at the Annual

Conference of the National Rural and Small Schools Consortium, Bellingham, WA. (ERIC Document Reproduction Service No. ED 280 633).

Mills, D. W. (1992). Essential competencies for Christian school administrators. *Journal of Research on Christian Education, 1*(1), 35-47.

A nation at risk: The imperative for educational reform. (1983). A report to the nation and the Secretary of Education by the National Commission on Excellence in Education, Washington, DC.

A nation prepared: Teachers for the 21st century. (1986). A report by the Task Force on Teaching as a Profession of the Carnegie Forum on Education and the Economy, New York.

Oliver, C. I. (1992). The problem with college-track high schools. *Education, 113,* 236-239.

Ray, B. D. (1990, November 16). *A nationwide study of home education: Family characteristics, legal matters, and student achievement.* Paeonian Springs, VA: National Center for Home Education.

Ray, B. D. (1992). *Home education in Oklahoma: Family characteristics, student achievement, and policy matters.* Salem, OR: National Home Education Research Institute.

Ray, B. D. (1993). Learning at home in North Dakota: Family attributes and student achievement. Salem, OR: National Home Education Research Institute.

Ray, B. D. (1997). *Strengths of their own—home schoolers across America: Academic achievement, family characteristics, and longitudinal traits.* Salem, OR: National Home Education Research Institute.

Roberts, J. (1971). Intellectual development of children by demographic and socioeconomic factors. (DHEW Publication No. HSM 72-1012). Washington, DC: U.S. Government Printing Office.

Rudner, L. M. (1998). The scholastic achievement and demographic characteristics of home school students in 1998. *Educational Policy Analysis Archives* at http://epaa.asu.edu/apaa/v7n8/.

Salter, G. (1988). The problem with Christian education: Ideational or implementational insufficiency. *Balance, 9*(1), 1-3.

Schaie, K. W., & Roberts, J. (1971). *School achievement of children by demographic and socio-economic factors.* (DHEW Publication No. HSM 72-1011). Washington, DC: U.S. Government Printing Office.

Schlafly, P. (August, 1990). *The reading report* [radio commentary]. Alton, IL: Eagle Forum Radio.

Schmidt, S. J. (1989). *A report of North Carolina home school parents on certain variables associated with social studies instruction.* Unpublished masters thesis, Wake Forest University. (ERIC Document Reproduction Service No. ED 320 798).

Shyers, L. E. (1992). A comparison of social adjustment between home and traditionally schooled students. *Home School Researcher, 8*(3), 1-8.

Smedley, R. C. (1992). Socialization of home school children. *Home School Researcher, 8*(3), 9-16.

Smith, I. J. (1988). Special education in the Christian school. *Balance, 8*(9), 1-2.

Smith, P. D. (1989). The future of Christian education. *Balance, 9*(9), 1-3.

The state of the states. (Editors). (1997, January 22). *Education Week, 3.*

Stoker, W. M., & Splawn, R. (1980). *A study of Accelerated Christian Education schools in Northwest Texas.* (ERIC Document Reproduction Service No. ED 206 095).

Stronks, G. G. (1991). Are these the schools we wanted? *Christian Educators Journal, 31*(2), 22-23.

Sutton, J. P. (1992). Educating students with disabilities: A new item on the Christian school agenda. *Journal for Christian Educators, 9*(3), 7-8.

Sutton, J. P. (1994). Room for growth in Christian education? Pleas from mothers of children with disabilities. *Christian Educators Journal, 34*(1), 16-18.

Sutton, J. P., Everett, E. G., & Sutton, C. J. (1993). Special education in Christian/fundamentalist schools: A commitment to all the children? *Journal of Research on Christian Education, 2*(1), 65-79.

Sutton, J. P., McKinney, J. D., & Hallahan, D. P. (1992). Effects of grade level and educational setting on behaviors of beginning learning disabilities teachers. *Learning Disabilities Research and Practice, 7*(1), 16-24.

Sutton, J. P., & Watson, T. G. (1992). National profile of the Christian school teacher: Cause for contentment or concern? *Christian Educators Journal, 32*(2), 17-20.

Sutton, J. P., & Watson, T. G. (1995). Barriers to excellence: A national survey of teachers from the American Association of Christian Schools. *Journal of Research on Christian Education, 4*(1), 21-33.

Tomorrow's teachers. (1986). A report of the Holmes Group, East Lansing.

U.S. Department of Education. (1991). *National Center for Education Statistics: Digest of Education Statistics 1991.* Washington, DC: U.S. Government Printing Office.

Van Dyk, J. (1991). Johnny at risk. *Christian Educators Journal, 30*(3), 4-5.

Van Til, W. (1974). *Education: A beginning* (2nd ed.). Boston: Houghton Mifflin.

Vaughn, J. (1991). God's hidden treasures. *Frontline, 1*(4), 9-11.

Wartes, J. (1990). Recent results from the Washington home school research project. *Home School Researcher, 6*(4), 1-7.

White, M. R. (1998). *An analysis of the compensation and human resource policies of AACS schools: A multiregional study.* Unpublished doctoral dissertation, Bob Jones University, Greenville.

Evaluation Criteria	Discussion Questions
1. Is the general purpose of the study clear? Will the study provide a significant contribution?	**1.** From the introduction, what reasons are used to suggest that this study will make a significant contribution? Does the funding agency for the study (see the footnote on the first page) suggest potential bias in what was reported and concluded?
The general purpose is clear but not stated until the fourth paragraph. There is some rationale for the significance of the study. Certainly issues of home and private schooling are more relevant given pressures on public schools. This is an *ex post facto* study.	
2. Does the review of literature establish the relationship between previous studies and the current one? Is the review well organized and up to date?	**2.** Which of the sources cited in the review of literature are critical to understanding how this study contributes to existing knowledge about the effect of different kinds of schooling on college success?
The "review" is more an introduction than a review of literature related specifically to this study. It is up-to-date, but more emphasis is needed on studies that investigate the same or similar research questions.	
3. Is the specific research hypothesis or question clearly and concisely stated?	**3.** What are appropriate research questions or hypotheses for this study?
No specific research questions or hypotheses are stated.	
4. Is the method of sampling clearly presented? Could the way the sample was obtained influence the results?	**4.** Home-schooled students clearly had much lower family incomes than either private school or public school students, the possible effects of which are not mitigated by the nonsignificant statistical test. How could such a difference affect the results?
The sampling procedure was clearly presented. Only students from this particular university are used, and in the end the sample size is quite small. Samples from other postsecondary institutions could easily produce different results.	
5. Is there anything in the procedures for collecting the information, or in the instruments themselves, that could bias the results or weaken the study?	**5.** What other ways of operationalizing dependent variables such as physical activity, leadership behavior, or social behavior are possible, and would this affect the results?
Data for the analyses were gathered from existing records, and it is unlikely that such procedures would weaken the study.	
6. Is the magnitude of the correlation or difference among the groups large enough to suggest practical significance or importance?	**6.** What differences among the three groups, besides where they obtained their high school education, could account for the leadership differences noted?
Given the small number of subjects in the study, none of the results have practical significance or importance. This is particularly true for nonsignificant statistical results.	

7. Do graphic presentations of the data distort the findings?

Figure 1 does not distort the findings, but it is also not helpful.

8. Do the conclusions and interpretations follow logically from the results? Are unwarranted causal conclusions made from correlations or comparisons? Are limitations indicated?

Conclusions related to statistically nonsignificant findings are not warranted (e.g., their chief conclusion). Comparisons among the groups suggest some causality, but other differences among the groups not reported could account for the actual reasons. There is a good discussion with good integration of additional literature (which could have been part of the review of literature). The limitation of using students from one kind of college is appropriately noted.

7. What would be a more concise way of presenting the information found in Figure 1?

8. What additional limitations should be noted by the authors? How could a study be designed to provide better data to answer the research questions?

Credibility Scorecard
College Success of Students from Three High School Settings

	Excellent	Very Good	Adequate	Marginal	Poor
General purpose	5	4	3	2	1
Contribution/ significance	5	4	3	2	1
Review of literature	5	4	3	2	1
Research questions or hypotheses	5	4	3	2	1
Subjects or participants	5	4	3	2	1
Instrumentation	5	4	3	2	1
Procedures	5	4	3	2	1
Results	5	4	3	2	1
Practical significance	5	4	3	2	1
Graphics	5	4	3	2	1
Conclusions	5	4	3	2	1
Any fatal flaws?					

3 | EXPERIMENTAL DESIGNS

Experiments are what most people think of as "real science," probably because they create images of laboratories, white coats, and tightly controlled studies. Only part of this image holds for experiments in education. Broadly speaking, an experiment is used to investigate cause-and-effect relationships by determining whether a manipulated independent variable influences the dependent variable. The manipulated independent variable is controlled by the researcher, who deliberately arranges interventions that the subjects will experience. Thus, the investigator has direct control over what the subjects experience and when they experience it. In education, subjects that have different interventions are compared. For example, a researcher interested in the effect of different types of homework assignments on student achievement may decide to do an experiment by giving some students one type of assignment and other students a different type of assignment and then seeing if the achievement of the two groups of students is different.

Beginning in 2003 the U.S. Department of Education supported initiatives that emphasize the increased use of experiments to evaluate educational interventions. The department stressed that *randomized control group* designs are the "gold standard" for determining the worth of the research. As a result, there is a renewed interest in conducting experiments in educational research.

There are three types of experimental designs: *randomized experimental*, *quasi-experimental*, and *pre-experimental*. A **randomized experiment** is one in which there is random assignment of subjects to different interventions, or to an intervention and a control condition. Random assignment is a procedure that helps ensure that the groups being compared do not differ on characteristics that effect the dependent variable, such as ability, background, attitudes, and self-concept. With random assignment each subject has the same probability of being in each group; it is essentially a matter of chance. When researchers use this procedure for enough subjects (minimum of 15 in each group), then it is highly likely that the groups, overall, are not different. Random assignment of one of two classes to intervention A with the other class receiving intervention B would not be considered a randomized experiment.

A **quasi-experimental** study is an experiment in which there is no random assignment of subjects. Other aspects of the design, as well as the research questions, may be the same as found in randomized experiments. Typically, a quasi-experiment will have a pretest and a posttest. For example, a researcher may want to compare two methods of instruction, and has two intact classrooms that have volunteered to participate. Students were not randomly assigned to the classrooms. The researcher gives the students in each class a pretest, selects one class for each method, and then gives the students a posttest (dependent variable).

Some other types of experimental designs do not use random assignment of subjects. These are not always called quasi-experimental, but essentially they constitute investigations that have more potential weaknesses because there is no random assignment and, in some cases, no pretest or comparison group. Sometimes these designs are called **pre-experimental** because they are even weaker than quasi-experimental designs.

The simplest type of pre-experimental design involves a treatment and measurement of the dependent variable, without any comparison group. This type of study is weak because there is no basis of comparison with either a pretest or a comparison group. If the researcher can be relatively sure of the status of the subjects prior to implementing the treatment, and if nothing else is likely to affect the subjects (extraneous events), then the study could be valid. If a pretest is added, then at least there is a basis for statistical comparison. Another type of pre-experimental design contains a comparison group but no random assignment or pretest.

Experimental designs can take many forms. Particularly common are designs that try to answer more than one research question. For example, a study might ask, "Do two new science books produce different scores on a standardized achievement test?" and also ask, Does this achievement also depend on the student's ability level? Such experiments have more than one independent variable, and the design is called a *factorial design*. **Factorial designs** are useful because they can test the effect of the independent variables separately, and also test whether the independent variables together have a unique effect on the dependent variable. This is called an **interaction**, in which the effect of one independent variable depends on the value of another. In our example, the study would find an interaction if high-ability students achieved best with one textbook and low-ability students achieved best with the other.

An important consideration in evaluating experimental designs is whether the procedures have been implemented such that accurate cause-and-effect conclusions can be made. Thus, in the procedures section you will want to look for characteristics of the study design that might lead to erroneous interpretations of the data. Researchers use the term **internal validity** to indicate the extent to which the study is free of so-called "extraneous" or confounding variables or factors that might account for the results. The apparent effectiveness of a new curriculum, for example, might be due primarily to the enthusiasm of the teacher, not to the curriculum itself. If the study is carefully conducted and it is clear that few extraneous or confounding variables could affect the results, then the study is strong in internal validity. If the study is conducted with the potential for extraneous or confounding variables to influence the results, then it is weak in internal validity. How do you know, then, that a study has established adequate internal validity? Depending on the design of the study, the following threats to internal validity should be considered:

Extraneous events (history)—Uncontrolled or unplanned events that occur during the study and affect the values reported for the dependent variable.

Selection—Inherent differences among comparison groups (such as ability, motivation, background) that influence results.

Maturation—Natural changes in subjects because they get older, stronger, tired, etc.

Subject attrition (mortality)—Systematic loss of subjects during the study.

Pretesting (testing)—Taking a pretest or responding to a questionnaire may affect the subjects.

Statistical regression—Groups of subjects who score very high or very low on a pretest will, because of measurement error, score closer to the mean on the posttest.

Diffusion of treatment—Changes in subjects because they learn about what is occurring with subjects in another group (the effect of the treatment is diffused to others).

Experimenter effects—Results that are affected by what the experimenter says or does, deliberately or unintentionally.

Treatment replications—If the number of times the treatment is implemented is smaller than the number of individuals in the study, factors confounded with the treatment may affect the results.

Treatment fidelity—The way the treatment is implemented is not the same each time.

Subject effects—Changes because individuals are aware of being a "subject" in a study.

Instrumentation—Unreliability or changes in instruments or observers may affect the results.

By keeping these threats in mind, you will be able to make judgments about the internal validity of the study. Essentially you ask yourself whether it is likely that each threat could affect the results more for one group than another group.

Criteria for Evaluating Experimental Studies

1. Is the general purpose of the study clear? Will the study provide a significant contribution?

2. Does the review of literature establish the relationship between previous studies and the current one? Is the review well organized and up-to-date?

3. Is the specific research hypothesis or question clearly and concisely stated?

4. Is the method of sampling clearly presented? Was there random assignment of subjects? If there was no random assignment, was there anything in the way the groups were formed that might have influenced the reaction of the group to the treatment?

5. What was manipulated as the independent variable or variables?

6. Are the procedures for collecting information described fully?

7. Are there any threats to internal validity that seem plausible?

8. Do the conclusions and interpretations follow logically from the results presented? Are limitations indicated?

9. Is the experiment so contrived and artificial that the findings have little generalizability?

The Effects of an Early Reading Curriculum on Language and Literacy Development of Head Start Children

Lucy Hart Paulson   Karen L. Kelly   Stacia Jepson   Rick van den Pol
Rhea Ashmore   Merle Farrier   Shannon Guilfoyle
The University of Montana–Missoula

ABSTRACT

This study examined the effectiveness of the Montana Early Literacy Project (MELP) curriculum on literacy and language skills of preschool-age children in Head Start. The MELP model utilizes everyday events and existing routines of classroom and home environments to build literacy and language directly into children's daily experiences. Using a control group design, the researchers analyzed skill development in preschool children participating in a classroom, using the MELP model as a supplement to the traditional Head Start curriculum (n = 14). Results were compared to children who participated in the traditional Head Start curriculum (n = 15). Assessments used were the Emerging Literacy Screening from Building Early Literacy and Language Skills *(Paulson, Noble, Jepson, & van den Pol, 2001) and language sampling. Analyses indicated an important difference in the literacy and language skills gained by children in the MELP classroom, particularly in the areas of narrative discourse, vocabulary, phonological awareness, and print development. Due to the limited sample size, generalization of the data should be interpreted with caution. Nevertheless, findings support the use of the Montana Early Literacy Project curriculum in developing the early literacy and language skills in children who may be at risk of experiencing challenges in learning to read and write.*

Literacy is defined as the ability to read and write and is usually acquired in a relatively predictable manner, beginning at birth and continuing throughout life, assuming that the appropriate exposure and instruction are present (Snow, Burns, & Griffin, 1998).

Early literacy refers to behaviors seen in very young children, typically 2- to 3-year-olds, as they attempt reading and writing acts without the awareness or understanding of letter-sound relationships. Emerging literacy refers to behaviors observed in 4- to 5-year-old children when an awareness and understanding of letter-sound relationships begins to develop. This process builds as children develop their oral language structures, gain an awareness of the sound structure of language, and find meaning in the symbols around them (Braunger, Lewis, & Hagans, 1997; Lonigan, Bloomfield, Anthony, Bacon, Phillips, & Samwel, 1999).

Children use strategies from learning oral language to help them make sense of environmental print. In this way, language-competent children are able to grasp the processes of reading and writing in a timely manner (Katims & Pierce, 1995). More than two decades of research on early and emerging literacy emphatically demonstrates that children can, and do, learn a great deal about reading during the preschool years in preparation for reading independently (Adams, 1990; Lonigan et al., 1999; Snow et al., 1998; van Kleeck, 1998). The likelihood that a child will succeed in 1st grade depends most of all on how much she or he has already learned about reading before getting there (Adams, 1990).

In order to facilitate the development of young learners who exhibit a wide range of needs and abilities the question of preschool curriculum must be addressed. Goffin (2000) acknowledges the dilemma currently faced by early childhood programs as she notes:

> Driven by public demands for positive child outcomes, the sense of urgency surrounding school reform, and the prevalence of poor-quality child care, early childhood curriculum models are being promoted as a way of ensuring that public dollars are wisely spent and that children enter school ready to learn. (http://askeric.org/plweb-cgi/obtain.pl. para 14, retrieved 9-18-02)

A number of early childhood curriculum models, generally based on theories of child development, have been in use for several decades. However, previous investigations of the most commonly used

Funding for this study was provided by Grant HO24B60034, from the Office of Special Education Programs and the Office of Special Education and Rehabilitative Services of the United States Department of Education. Special acknowledgments to Ann Minckler. Mary Bunce, Marcy Otten, Gail Goodner, Amy Foster Wolferman, Clark Schlegel, Joan Kuehn, Chris Lande. Gale Bertoglio, Scot Anderson, Rebecca Anderson, and Jock Schorger for their assistance.

models are generally outdated and fall short of providing a clear picture of the actual practices that are used to link assessment to the curriculum (Pretti-Frontczak, Kowalski, & Brown, 2002). Given that our current national agenda presents a compelling argument for early childhood programs to establish a strong language and literacy environment, research-based teaching/learning models that support early reading principles across the curriculum are necessary. In particular, the demand for curriculum models that provide guidance for the development of print-rich learning environments, oral language activities, and phonological awareness has received considerable attention in response to recent recommendations by the National Reading Panel (2000) and the National Research Council (Snow, Burns, & Griffin, 1998) for evidence-based approaches to early reading instruction.

Early and Emerging Literacy

Three major areas found to be critically important in the development of early and emerging literacy skills (Braunger, Lewis, Hagans, 1997; Lonigan et al., 1999; Snow et al., 1998; Whitehurst & Lonigan, 1998) are: 1) a strong foundation in oral language skills, 2) an awareness of the sound structure of language, and 3) much exposure and experience with print. A strong foundation in oral language skills develops as children gain an understanding of the structures and meaning of language. When children begin to realize that the words they say not only have meanings but also have structures that can be manipulated, they are developing phonological awareness, which is the explicit awareness of word structure—syllables, sounds, etc.—that can be changed depending on the context. As children see and play with written symbols, they develop an awareness of print.

Clearly, a strong connection exists between language and literacy development (Braunger et al., 1997), particularly during the early childhood years of birth through age 8 (Schickedanz, 1999). Families, caregivers, and early childhood educators all have a significant impact on children's language and emerging literacy skills. Those who work with young children have a critical window of opportunity to offer support in helping them acquire rich language and emerging literacy skills (Moats, 2000). A child's literacy development is affected by the language and literacy experiences shared by family members and teachers, the books and written materials found in the home and at school, and the attitudes of the family and school toward literacy. Children who are provided with numerous and varied opportunities to talk, tell stories, read storybooks, draw, and write are generally successful in learning to read and write (Braunger et al., 1997).

Early Identification of At-Risk Readers

Children who exhibit difficulty learning oral language are at significant risk for having problems learning to read (Adams, 1990), as are children growing up in poverty (Rush, 1999). Academic success is highly correlated to economic status (Brint, 1998; de Marrais & LeCompte, 1999). Hodgkinson (2001) claims that poverty is a universal handicap and states that 20 percent of the children in the United States live in poverty. Hart and Risley (1995, 1999) determined that family economics was a significant factor in children's language development, finding that children in low-income families heard less language and said fewer words.

Children who are at risk for reading disabilities can be identified before experiencing reading failure in elementary school by providing the assessment, curricular strategies, and teacher knowledge that are responsive to early recognition. Catts, Fey, Zhang, and Tomblin (2001) investigated kindergarten predictors of 2nd-grade reading outcomes and identified five key variables in their longitudinal study. They concluded that children in 2nd grade who were struggling with reading had difficulty with letter identification, sentence structure, phonological awareness, and word recall when they were in kindergarten. Each of these skills related directly to oral language, phonological awareness, and print awareness. Another predictive variable was the education level achieved by the children's mothers.

Bishop and Adams (1990) developed a *critical age* hypothesis, suggesting that young children who experience difficulty acquiring language and who are able to develop age-appropriate language skills before the age of 5 to 5-1/2 have a much greater chance of learning to read and write without experiencing difficulty. Children whose delays in language development persist after the age of 5 to 5-1/2, however, tend to have a much greater chance of also experiencing similar difficulties learning literacy skills. Unfortunately, many early childhood centers may not provide the learning experiences and teaching strategies that empirical evidence suggests clearly supports early literacy development. In a study of 4-year-olds in Head Starts, Title I kindergartens, and child care centers, Layzer, Goodson, and Moss (1993) noted that more than 25 percent of the classrooms did not have a story time and only 10 percent of the teacher's time was spent in individual language interaction.

The development of emerging literacy skills in young children is too important to allow a wait and see approach. To facilitate the development of literacy skills, children need to acquire oral language skills, develop phonological awareness skills, and have many, varied exposures and experiences with print. Identifying children's strengths and needs in language and emerging literacy skill development allows educators to plan early and appropriate interventions (Marvin & Wright, 1997). Current research overwhelmingly supports the importance of facilitating early and emerging literacy skills in preschool-age children as a critical foundation for literacy development.

Montana Early Literacy Project

The Montana Early Literacy Project (MELP) offers a curricular approach or model that emphasizes early reading activities for preschool children. The purpose of the model is to build early literacy and language skills in young children, especially those with disabilities, by developing partnerships with families, schools, and community members and by using developmentally appropriate services that are individually and culturally sensitive. The model recognizes and expands upon everyday events and existing routines of classroom and home environments to build literacy and language directly into children's daily experiences. Additionally, the model provides teaching and support staff with the knowledge necessary to implement these comprehensive services.

The MELP model incorporates five key components: Component 1 identifies procedures using developmentally appropriate thematic units with specific strategies, interventions, and activities that embed literacy and language throughout children's existing routines during the school day. Component 2 provides a method to identify early literacy and language needs of individual students and to design Individualized Education Program (IEP) goals and objectives that meet children's needs. Component 3 provides strategies to foster family participation in literacy and language activities, both at home and at school. Component 4 addresses means of providing inclusive, respectful, and culturally responsive literacy services that celebrate individual differences of children and their families. It also focuses on the understanding and appreciation of the cultural practices, beliefs, and traditions of Native Americans in Montana. Component 5 provides teachers, support staff, and families with the knowledge and skills necessary to implement the model.

The MELP model was developed for fostering emerging literacy and language skills in young children with diverse abilities at two demonstration sites: CO-TEACH Preschool, located on the University of Montana-Missoula campus, and Cherry Valley Elementary School, located on the Flathead Indian Reservation. The MELP model also was replicated at four sites in Montana: Head Start, Missoula; Awesome Discoveries Daycare, Polson; Missoula County Public School (MCPS) Preschool Program, Missoula; and Smart Start Preschool, Polson.

The purpose of this study was to investigate the impact of the MELP model on improving the early and emerging literacy skills of young children who are at risk of developing reading difficulties. The primary research question was: What effect does the Montana Early Literacy Project curriculum have on the language and literacy development of children in Head Start?

METHOD

Participants

Children, randomly assigned to three Head Start classrooms, participated in this study in either a combined Montana Early Literacy Project and traditional curriculum classroom or a traditional curriculum only classroom. All children in the study were reported to be at risk for developing challenges with academic success, given the low social economic status criteria for participation in the Head Start program. The MELP curriculum group began with 18 children participating in the Head Start classroom and concluded with 14 children. One child moved during the middle of the study, and three children did not complete all of the testing. This group was composed of seven girls and seven boys, and the average chronological age was four years, two months during the pretest and four years, nine months during the posttest. Two children in the group received special education services under the Individuals with Disabilities Education Act (IDEA) (1990). Three of the children in this sample were learning English as a second language.

The traditional curriculum group began with 32 children enrolled in the two Head Start classrooms using the standard curriculum at the beginning of the study. Eleven children moved during the middle of the study, and six children were unable to complete the testing. Fifteen children were included at the end of the study. Of this group, eight were girls and seven were boys, with an average chronological age of four years, three months during the pretest and four years, ten months during the posttest. Two children were receiving special education services under IDEA (1990), and one child was learning English as a second language. Table 1 presents the sample characteristics for the children participating in the study.

Procedure and Measures

The study included the collection of assessment data on early and emerging literacy and language skill development using a pretest/posttest experimental-control group design (Campbell & Stanley, 1963). The children were randomly assigned to each classroom before the beginning of the school year. For the purposes of this research, the education coordinator for

Table 1 Participant Characteristics

	MELP Curriculum (*n* = 14)	Traditional Curriculum (*n* = 15)
Gender	7 girls, 7 boys	7 girls, 8 boys
Chronological Age: Pretest	4 years, 2 months (50 mo.)	4 years, 3 months (51 mo.)
Posttest	4 years, 9 months (57 mo.)	4 years, 10 months (58 mo.)
Children with Disabilities	2	2
English Language Learners	3	1

the area Head Start selected three classrooms of equal size and session length, within the same center under her supervision to participate in the study. The three teachers each had college backgrounds in early childhood education, had been teaching in Head Start for more than seven years, and had participated in required on-site Head Start early literacy trainings. Two classrooms, located in the main Head Start building and using the traditional Head Start curriculum, served as the control group. One classroom, located on the premises of a local elementary school and using the MELP model curriculum in addition to the traditional curriculum, served as the comparison group. High Scope was the traditional curriculum used in each classroom and all the teachers were trained in its implementation.

The control classroom teachers each had Associate of Arts (A.A.) degrees in Early Childhood Education. The comparison classroom (MELP) teacher held a B.A. in Elementary Education and was also trained in the MELP model. Although the subjects were randomly assigned to the three classrooms, giving some control over subject differences, results of this study should be considered with caution, as the individual teachers' educational backgrounds indicate variations in classroom management and social climate that also may be attributed to students' gains.

Pretest data were obtained in September at the beginning of the school year, and posttest data were gathered in May at the end of the school year. The Emerging Literacy Screening in *Building Early Literacy and Language Skills* (Paulson et al., 2001) was used to measure early literacy and language skill development. Assessments were conducted individually in a quiet room near the Head Start classrooms by project staff who were specifically trained in measurement administration.

The Emerging Literacy Screening (Paulson et al., 2001) includes developmentally sequenced skills in three foundation areas of literacy development: language use, phonological awareness, and print development. Skills measured in the Language Use section include basic concepts, narratives, speech intelligibility, sentence structure, and use of rhythmic language. The Phonological Awareness section measured rhyme matching and production, blending of syllables and sounds from words, and segmenting words

into syllables and sounds. The Print Development section measured book and symbol awareness, written name and letter recognition, writing development, and knowledge of the alphabet song. The results provide a raw score and a percent correct score for each of the three sections as well as a total composite raw score and percent correct score.

In order to further evaluate the impact of the MELP curriculum on children's expressive language development, individual spontaneous language samples were collected from each of the participants. Sampling occurred in October, prior to the introduction of the MELP curriculum, and again in April. Language samples were obtained using a set of softbound wordless picture books by Mercer and Marianna Mayer (1967, 1971, 1974, 1975). Individual children were seated at a small table in their classroom, and the researcher prompted them to "Look at the book and tell me what is happening." Children were encouraged to describe the activities in two of the books for the fall sample and two similar books for the spring sample. The researchers prompted children to "Look at that!" and "Tell me what else is going on." However, the children were allowed to guide the speed and duration of each session. Sessions ranged from 10 to 20 minutes, and all utterances were audiotaped for transcription and further analysis.

Language samples from each child were transcribed and entered into the Systematic Analysis of Language Transcripts, Research Version 7.0 (SALT) computer program. SALT is a software package developed by the Language Analysis Laboratory at the University of Wisconsin-Madison (Miller & Chapman, 1992). Using SALT and guided by a specific transcription protocol, researchers obtained an analysis of language performance at the word, morpheme, utterance, and discourse level for each child. Data from fall and spring were grouped into three categories for analysis of expressive language growth: 1) Total Utterances, 2) Mean Length of Utterance (MLU), and 3) Different Word Roots (vocabulary growth). MLU in morphemes corresponds to chronological age as well as to stages of linguistic development and is considered to be a valid index of language development when the MLU is between 1.0 and 4.5 morphemes (Bailey & Wolery, 1989).

The null hypothesis of this study assumed there would be no important or statistically reliable difference between the adjusted average posttest scores of the Head Start classes using the traditional curriculum and the classroom using the MELP model curriculum. An important difference was defined as 10 percentage points on the adjusted mean scores of the Emerging Literacy Screening. Statistical reliability was set at = .05. An expected developmental increase in MLU from pretest to posttest was predicted to be approximately .6, using the following equation: age (in months) + MLU (Miller, 1981). An analysis of covariance (ANCOVA), used to account for initial differences between samples, was calculated for the Emerging Literacy Screening and each of the language sample categories.

RESULTS

At the conclusion of the study, 14 children participated in the Head Start classroom, using the MELP model and the traditional curriculum. Fifteen children in the two Head Start classrooms using the traditional curriculum only served as the control group ($n = 29$).

For the results of the Emerging Literacy Screening, homogeneity of variance was established between the sample groups, which were relatively the same size. The F-test conducted for the homogeneity of regression resulted in an F-value of .36 and a p-value o f .55, indicating that the two samples had common slopes. Therefore, an analysis of covariance (ANCOVA) was run. The ANCOVA resulted in an F-ratio of 20.85 and a p-value of <0.0001, indicating a statistically reliable difference between the groups for this experiment.

Table 2 Pre- and Posttest Mean Scores for the Emerging Literacy Screening and Language Sampling

	MELP Group			Traditional Group		
	Pretest	Posttest		Pretest	Posttest	
		Unadjusted	Adjusted		Unadjusted	Adjusted
Emerging Literacy Screening						
Mean % Correct Scores	41.4%	71.7%	68.2%	33.7%	48.8%	52.0%
Language Sampling						
Mean Total Utterances	42.0	79.6	81.8	51.0	57.3	55.3
Mean Length of Utterance	3.5	3.9	3.9	3.4	3.7	3.7
Total Different Root Words	67.0	121.2	123.6	73.0	91.3	89.1

Table 3 ANCOVA Summary of Adjusted Means

Emerging Literacy Screening

Source	Sum of Squares	df	Mean Squares	F-Ratio	Probability
Between	1838.41	1	1838.41	20.86	<0.0001
Error	2291.73	26	88.14		
Total	4130.14	27			

Language Sampling
Total Utterances

Source	Sum of Squares	df	Mean Squares	F-Ratio	Probability
Between	4730.84	1	4730.84	13.06	.001
Error	9420.88	26	362.34		
Total	14151.72	27			

Mean Length of Utterance

Source	Sum of Squares	df	Mean Squares	F-Ratio	Probability
Between	.34	1	.34	.37	.546
Error	23.51	26	.90		
Total	23.85	27			

Different Root Words

Source	Sum of Squares	df	Mean Squares	F-Ratio	Probability
Between	8518.46	1	8518.46	19.00	.0002
Error	11653.80	26	448.22		
Total	20172.27	27			

On the Emerging Literacy Screening, the MELP group received a pretest mean percent correct score of 41.4%, an unadjusted posttest mean score of 71.7%, and an adjusted posttest mean score of 68.2%. This resulted in an adjusted increase of 26.8 percentage points. The traditional group received a mean score of 33.7% on the pretest score, an unadjusted mean score of 48.8%, and an adjusted mean score of 52.0% on the posttest, an adjusted increase of 18.3 percentage points.

An important difference was set at 10 percentage points a priori for the results of the Emerging Literacy Screening. The class using the MELP model curriculum displayed an adjusted gain of 27.0 percentage points. The traditional group displayed an adjusted increase of 18.3 points. The MELP group outscored the class using the traditional curriculum by 22.2 (unadjusted) and 16.2 (adjusted) percentage points.

Homogeneity of variance again was established between the sample groups for the results of each of the three language sample categories. The F-test conducted for the homogeneity of regression resulted in an F-value of 1.73 and a p-value of .20 for the Total Utterance category, an F-value of .02 and a p-value of .89 for the Mean Length of Utterance category, and an F-value of 2.0 and a p-value of .17 for Different Root Words, indicating that the two samples had common slopes. An analysis of covariance (ANCOVA) resulted in an F-ratio of 13.0 and a p-value of <0.001 for Total Utterances, an F-ratio of .37 and a p-value of .55 for Mean Length of Utterance, and a F-Ratio of 19.0 and a p-value of .0002 for Different Root Words.

An important difference was established between the traditional and comparison groups for the Total Utterance and Different Root Word categories, but not for the Mean Length of Utterance category. The class using the MELP model curriculum demonstrated higher levels of language use in each of the three categories than the class using the traditional curriculum in Total Utterances by 22.3 (unadjusted) and 26.5 (adjusted), in Mean Length of Utterance by .3 (unadjusted) and .2 (adjusted), and for Different Root Words by 29.9 (unadjusted) and 34.5 (adjusted).

In all three of the language sample areas, the children in the MELP curriculum classroom made greater gains than those using the traditional curriculum.

Children in the MELP classroom demonstrated an adjusted increase of 38.8 total utterances compared to the traditional group with an adjusted increase of 5.3. Adjusted growth in MLU for the MELP classroom was .4 words per utterance and .3 for the traditional group, indicating slower growth in linguistic development, particularly in the development of grammatical rules. The mean length of utterance on the pretest for both groups was determined to be within Brown's Early Stage IV, which corresponds to the 42–46 month age range, indicating an average range delay approximating four to nine months. This mild to moderate delay in language skills is typical among Head Start classrooms nationwide, and clearly emphasizes the need for a literacy-rich curriculum.

The adjusted vocabulary growth, as indicated by children's gains in Different Root Words, increased by 56.6 words for the MELP group and by 16.1 words for the traditional group. Individual children in the traditional group evidenced substantial decreases in 14 instances across all three language areas, an alarming outcome considering these children already evidenced language delays. When reviewing individual children's growth in the MELP classroom, minimal decreases were noted in four instances and only in the area of MLU.

The results from each section of the Emerging Literacy Screening provided an interesting comparison. Pretest levels between the MELP and traditional groups were fairly consistent across all assessment measures, including language sampling. The test total score averages were similar. The pretest scores of the language use section had a higher level of skill attainment than the print development and phonological awareness scores. The results of the posttest indicated growth for both groups in language development. The MELP group increased by 21 percentage points, and the traditional group increased by 12 percentage points. The MELP group showed an increase in the mean score of 40 percentage points, while the traditional group showed an increase of 24 points in print development. For phonological awareness, the MELP group began at 29 and rose to 63, an increase of 34 points. The traditional group began at 18 points and gained 11 percentage points. Table 4 presents the subtest scores of the Emerging Literacy Screening for both groups.

Table 4 Subtest Scores of the Emerging Literacy Screening

	MELP Group		Traditional Group	
	Pretest	Posttest	Pretest	Posttest
Print Development	31	71	26	50
Language Use	66	87	59	71
Phonological Awareness	29	63	18	29
Total	41	72	34	49

DISCUSSION

The Montana Early Literacy Project developed a model that provides early childhood educators with the needed supports to expand upon everyday events in existing routines in classrooms and homes to build language, literacy, and early reading activities directly into children's daily experiences, thereby creating language- and print-rich environments. The results of this study determined that the model was successful in developing language and literacy skills in young children who are at risk of experiencing challenges learning to read and write.

Children who participated in the classroom using the model demonstrated important increases in the foundation skills of language, phonological awareness, and print development. At the conclusion of the study, they used more spontaneous language with richer vocabulary. They were developing a sense of the structure of language by rhyming, blending, and segmenting words. They learned many print conventions, and they were writers.

The results of this study determined that each member of the class using the MELP model curriculum gained an average of 30 percentage points on the Emerging Literacy Screening in eight months during the Head Start preschool program. Each member of the class using the standard curriculum gained an average of 15 percentage points during the same time period. The children using the MELP model curriculum outscored the other class by 23 unadjusted and 16 adjusted percentage points on posttest scores of early literacy tasks. Statistical reliability was determined to be <.0001, exceeding the established level of reliability at .05. A statistically reliable and important difference was indicated in that the children in Head Start who participated in the MELP model curriculum had higher levels of early literacy skill development than those participating in the traditional curriculum.

The children who experienced the MELP curriculum made significant gains in narrative discourse development, as evidenced by the 89 percent increase in Total Utterances from the fall to the spring language sampling. They not only had more to say about the topics presented, they also used a broader vocabulary—a critical precursor to reading comprehension. Certainly, some of this gain can be attributed to expected developmental growth over the time period between language samplings. However, when compared to the gains made by the children using the traditional curriculum (23 percent), these data indicate a significant curriculum impact.

This study demonstrated that young children who participated in a Head Start classroom using the MELP model had higher levels of learning in early and emerging literacy skill development compared to young children who participated in the traditional Head Start curriculum. It should be noted that the generalizability of the study results must be interpreted with caution due to the limited sample size, the amount of student attrition, and differences within the classrooms. Clearly, a larger sample size and a broader range of classroom settings are recommended for future studies in order to determine the full efficacy of the MELP model. The researchers also recommend that additional studies be conducted to determine which specific MELP strategies and activities are most effective in developing early literacy skills in preschool-age children.

IMPLICATIONS FOR PRACTICE

The results obtained from this study suggested that children from low-income families and those at risk for early reading failure were able to make considerable gains in their early literacy and language skills by participating in a language- and print-rich environment wherein literacy activities were intentionally embedded into existing classroom routines and events. These critical skills provide the foundation for learning to read and write. Curricula such as that included in the MELP model and similar efforts in Head Start classrooms are vital for providing optimal opportunities for children who are most at risk for developing challenges with literacy.

As early childhood professionals continue to adopt practices that promote early reading skills among young children, it is imperative that evidence-based practices be considered in curriculum design. Children need teachers who will offer a variety of literacy opportunities throughout the day, using curriculum that is meaningful, engaging, and cognitively challenging for a range of abilities and interests. The Montana Early Literacy Project appears to be a viable curricular option for Head Starts and other early childhood centers where early reading skills are facilitated through developmentally appropriate language and literacy activities.

For more information on the Montana Early Literacy Project, see www.soe.umt.edu/ders/MELP/index.htm.

REFERENCES

Adams, M. J. (1990). *Beginning to read, thinking and learning about print*. Cambridge, MA: MIT Press.

Bailey, D., & Wolery, M. (1989). *Assessing infants and preschoolers with handicaps*. Columbus, OH: Merrill Publishing.

Bishop, D. V. M., & Adams, C. (1990). A prospective study of the relationship between specific language impairment, phonological disorders, and reading retardation. *Journal of Child Psychology and Psychiatry, 31*(7), 1027–1050.

Braunger, J., Lewis, J. P., & Hugans, R. (1997). *Building a knowledge base in reading*. Portland, OR: Northwest Regional Educational Laboratory.

Brint, S. (1998). *Schools and societies*. Thousand Oaks, CA: Pine Forge Press.

Campbell, D. T., & Stanley, J. C. (1963). *Experimental and quasi-experimental designs for research*. Chicago: McNally.

Catts, H. W., Fey, M. E., Zhang, X., & Tomblin, J. (2001). Estimating the risk of future reading difficulties in kindergarten children: A research-based model and its clinical implementation. *Language, Speech, and Hearing Services in Schools, 32*(1), 38–50.

de Marrais, K. B., & LeCompte, M. D. (1999). *The way schools work: A sociological analysis of education* (3rd ed.). New York: Addison Wesley Longman.

Goffin, S. (2000). *The role of curriculum models in early childhood education*. ERIC Digest #443597 http://askeric.org/plweb-cgi/obtain.pl. Retrieved September 18, 2002.

Hart, B., & Risley, T. R. (1995). *Meaningful differences in the everyday experience of young American children*. Baltimore: Paul H. Brookes.

Hart, B., & Risley, T. R. (1999). *The social world of children learning to talk*. Baltimore: Paul H. Brookes.

Hodgkinson, H. (2000/01). Educational demographics: What teachers should know. *Educational Leadership, 58*(4), 6–11.

Individuals with Disabilities Education Act, Public Law 100–476 (1990).

Katims, D., & Pierce, P. (1995). Literacy-rich environments and the transition of young children with special needs. *Topics in Early Childhood Special Education, 15*(2), 219–234.

Layzer, J., Goodson, B., & Moss, M. (1993). *Life in preschool: Volume one of an observational study of early childhood programs for disadvantaged four year olds*. Cambridge, MA: ABT Associates.

Lonigan, C. J., Bloomfield, B. G., Anthony, J. L., Bacon, K. D., Phillips, B. M., & Samwel, C. S. (1999). Relations among emergent literacy skills, behavior problems, and social competence in preschool children from low- and middle-income backgrounds. *Topics in Early Childhood Special Education, 19*(1), 40–53.

Marvin, C., & Wright, D. (1997). Literacy socialization in the homes of preschool children. *Language, Speech, and Hearing Services in Schools, 28*(2), 154–163.

Mayer, M. (1967). *A boy, a dog and a frog*. New York: Dial Press.

Mayer, M. (1974). *Frog goes to dinner*. New York: Dial Press.

Mayer, M., & Mayer, M. (1971). *A boy, a dog, a frog and a friend*. New York: Dial Press.

Mayer, M., & Mayer, M. (1975). *One frog too many*. New York: Dial Press.

Miller, J., & Chapman, R. (1992). *SALT: Systematic analysis of language transcripts* (computer program). Madison, WI: Language Analysis Laboratory, Waisman Center, University of Wisconsin, Madison.

Miller, J. (1981). *Assessing language production in children*. Baltimore: University Park Press.

Moats, L. C. (2000). *Speech to print*. Baltimore: Paul H. Brookes.

National Reading Panel. (2000). *Teaching children to read: An evidence-based assessment of the scientific research literature on reading and its implications for reading instruction*. NIH Publication No. 00-4769. Washington, DC: National Institute of Child Health & Human Development, National Institutes of Health.

Paulson, L. H., Noble, L. A., Jepson, S., & van den Pol (2001). *Building early literacy and language skills*. Longmont, CO: Sopris West.

Pretti-Frontczak, K., Kowalski, K., & Brown, R. (2002). Preschool teachers' use of assessments and curricula: A statewide examination. *Exceptional Children, 69*(1), 109–123.

Rush, K. I. (1999). Caregiver-child interactions and early literacy development of preschool children from low-income environments. *Topics in Early Childhood Special Education, 19*(1), 3–14.

Schickedanz, J. (1999). *Much more than the ABCs: The early stages of reading and writing*. Washington, DC: National Association for the Education of Young Children.

Snow, C. E., Burns, M., & Griffin, P. (1998). *Preventing reading difficulties in young children*. Washington, DC: National Academy Press.

van Kleeck, A. (1998). Preliteracy domains and stages: Laying the foundations for beginning reading. *Journal of Children's Communicative Development, 20*(1), 33–51.

Whitehurst, G. J., & Lonigan, C. J. (1998). Child development and emergent literacy. *Child Development, 69*(3), 848–872.

Evaluation Criteria	**Discussion Questions**
1. Is the general purpose of the study clear? Will the study provide a significant contribution?	**1.** How could the first paragraph be changed to incorporate a sentence that describes the purpose of the study?
The general purpose of the study is very clearly stated in the abstract, first sentence, and in the paragraph just before the Method section. The extensive literature cited about the need for early literacy makes a strong case for the significance of the study.	
2. Does the review of literature establish the relationship between previous studies and the current one? Is the review well organized and up-to-date?	**2.** How could the review be written to separate studies that support the significance of the research from studies that investigate the variables targeted by the MELP approach?
Although there are no studies on the effectiveness of the MELP program, several studies investigating similar variables are presented. These studies are summarized though not critically analyzed, beginning with the fifth paragraph. The review is fairly well organized with appropriate subheadings, though research supporting the significance of the study is mixed with results from empirical investigations. The review is up-to-date.	
3. Is the specific research hypothesis or question clearly and concisely stated?	**3.** What would be an appropriate research hypothesis for this study?
The research question is clearly and concisely stated. No research hypothesis is stated, though it would be appropriate in this case.	
4. Is the method of sampling clearly presented? Was there random assignment of subjects? If there was no random assignment, was there anything in the way the groups were formed that might have influenced the reaction of the group to the treatment?	**4.** What additional information about either the students or the teachers would be helpful in interpreting the results?
The overall group of children in the study were clearly described, and were randomly assigned to three head start classrooms at the beginning of the study. Since students met as a group, with different teachers, group differences beyond the curriculum used were created.	
5. What was manipulated as the independent variable or variables?	**5.** What additional variables could be used in this study to further refine the effectiveness of the MELP curriculum?
Type of curriculum was manipulated, with two levels—MELP and traditional.	

6. Are the procedures for collecting information described fully?

There is a good description of how data were collected, though it would be helpful to be assured that the project staff did not have knowledge about which students were in the MELP curriculum group and which students were in the traditional curriculum group.

7. Are there any threats to internal validity that seem plausible?

Yes, several threats are plausible, most related to the design in which groups of subjects were engaged in the treatments. Random assignment controls several threats, including extraneous events, maturation, pretesting, and statistical regression. Selection is a possible threat due to the higher MELP pretest Emerging Literacy Screening score. Experimenter effects are possible since the treatments are only replicated once in each classroom (treatment replications). Treatment fidelity is a threat to the extent that either the traditional or MELP curriculum was not implemented as intended. Instrumentation is a threat without further information about the staff collecting information. Attrition is also a possible threat, though this is controlled to some extent by having pretest data.

8. Do the conclusions and interpretations follow logically from the results presented? Are limitations indicated?

The first part of the discussion section essentially repeats the findings presented in the results section. It is confusing to present percentages increased along with differences between the groups. Limitations are appropriately indicated.

9. Is the experiment so contrived and artificial that the findings have little generalizability?

The fact that this study is conducted in actual head start classrooms with actual curriculums is laudable and good for generalization. On the other hand, the experimental treatment is only replicated once, with fewer than 20 children, which severely limits generalizability. Also, MELP appears to be an add-on program, and any kind of additional emphasis could improve literacy scores.

6. What additional detail could be provided about the staff doing the data collection?

7. What could the researchers have done to limit the potential impact of some of these threats to internal validity?

8. What additional limitations could be emphasized?

9. What could be done to increase generalizability so that it becomes clear that the MELP approach is what makes the difference, not specific aspects of what is done in one setting?

Credibility Scorecard
The Effects of an Early Reading Curriculum on Language and Literary Development of Head Start Children

	Excellent	Very Good	Adequate	Marginal	Poor
General purpose	5	4	3	2	1
Contribution/ significance	5	4	3	2	1
Review of literature	5	4	3	2	1
Research questions or hypotheses	5	4	3	2	1
Subjects or participants	5	4	3	2	1
Instrumentation	5	4	3	2	1
Procedures	5	4	3	2	1
Results	5	4	3	2	1
Practical significance	5	4	3	2	1
Graphics	5	4	3	2	1
Conclusions	5	4	3	2	1
Any fatal flaws?					

The Influence of Concept Mapping on Achievement, Self-regulation, and Self-efficacy in Students of English as a Second Language

Pasana Chularut[1] and Teresa K. DeBacker*

Department of Educational Psychology,
University of Oklahoma, 820 Van Vleet Oval,
Norman, OK 73019-2041, USA

Available online 21 November 2003

ABSTRACT

This study investigated the effectiveness of concept mapping used as a learning strategy with students in English as a Second Language classrooms. Seventy-nine ESL students participated in the study. Variables of interest were students' achievement when learning from English-language text, students' reported use of self-regulation strategies (self-monitoring and knowledge acquisition strategies), and students' self-efficacy for learning from English-language text. A randomized pretest–posttest control group design was employed. The findings showed a statistically significant interaction of time, method of instruction, and level of English proficiency for self-monitoring, self-efficacy, and achievement. For all four outcome variables, the concept mapping group showed significantly greater gains from pretest to posttest than the individual study group. The findings have implications for both practice and research. ©2003 Elsevier Inc. All rights reserved.

Keywords: Concept mapping; Motivation; Self-regulation; Self-efficacy

INTRODUCTION

This study investigated the influence of a particular learning strategy, concept mapping, on learning from text among students for whom English is not a first language. It was anticipated that concept mapping would not only have a positive impact on students' achievement, but would impact self-regulation and self-efficacy as well.

Park (1995) defines learning strategies as the "mental activities that people use when they study to help themselves acquire, organize, or remember incoming knowledge more efficiently" (p. 35). There are a number of learning strategies that can help students to become more sophisticated learners, and thus better able to learn and to achieve in the classroom over the long run. These strategies include meaningful learning, organizing, note-taking, identifying important information, and summarizing (Pressley, 1982; Weinstein, 1988).

Meaningful learning, according to Ausubel (1963), results when a person consciously and explicitly ties new knowledge to relevant concepts or propositions that she or he already possesses. We learn information meaningfully by storing it in long-term memory in association with similar, related pieces of information. With rote learning, on the other hand, there is little or no attempt to make the information meaningful or to understand it in terms of things one already knows. If such information is stored in long-term memory at all, it is stored unconnected to, and isolated from, other related information. The information stored in this unconnected fashion becomes difficult to retrieve (Okebukola, 1990). Novak and his colleagues (Novak, 1981; Novak, Gowin, & Johansen, 1983) were particularly interested in differences between rote and meaningful learning, and in the role of prior knowledge in learning. Their research led to the development of concept mapping.

Concept Mapping

Concept mapping is a tool for representing the interrelationships among concepts in an integrated,

---

Reprinted from *Contemporary Educational Psychology*, Vol. 29, Pasana Chularut and Teresa K. Debacker, "The Influence of Concept Mapping on Achievement, Self-regulation, and Self-efficacy in Students of English as a Second Language", 248–263, Copyright 2004, with permission from Elsevier.

*Corresponding author. Fax: 1-405-325-6655.
[1]Present address: Srinakharinwirot University, Bangkok, Thailand
E-mail address: debacker@ou.edu (T. K. DeBacker).

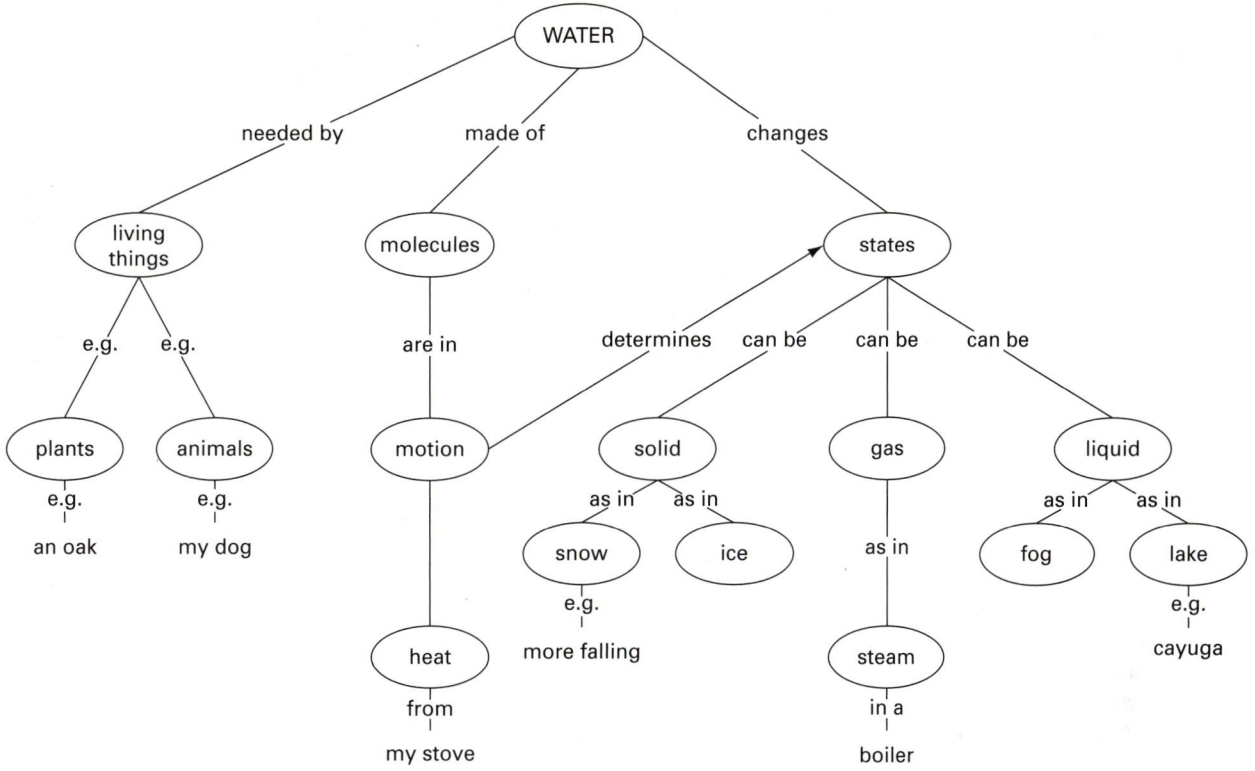

Figure I. Example of a well-constructed concept map.

hierarchical manner (see Fig. 1). Concept maps should not simply list information from text randomly, or even in a linear fashion. Rather, concept maps should depict the structure of knowledge in propositional statements that illustrate the relationships among the concepts in a map (Novak, 1981).

Research indicates that concept mapping is an effective learning strategy that precipitates meaningful learning in child (Roth & Roychoudhury, 1993; Stice & Alvarez, 1987) and adult (McClure & Bell, 1990; Novak & Gowin, 1984) learners, and in a variety of domains, such as genetics and ecology (Okebukola, 1990; Okebukola & Jegede, 1988), physics (Moreira, 1979; Pankratius, 1990), chemistry (Novak & Gowin, 1984; Schreiber & Abegg, 1991), and reading comprehension (Armbruster & Anderson, 1980; Briscoe & LaMaster, 1991; Peresich, Meadows, & Sinatra, 1990; Reutzel, 1985; Ruddell & Boyle, 1989; Sheldon, 1984; Weinstein & Mayer, 1986). Additionally, there is some evidence that concept mapping is a useful strategy for ESL (English as a second language) students (Block, 1986; Carrell, Pharis, & Liberto, 1989; Kamhi-Stein, 1993; Knight, Padron, & Waxman, 1985; Koumy & Salam, 1999). Heinze-Fry and Novak (1990) suggest that meaningful learning is facilitated because concepts are seen not as isolated entities, but as existing in a network of relationships. Furthermore, we propose that the benefits of concept mapping may extend beyond achievement gains to include positive effects on achievement-related variables such as academic self-regulation and self-efficacy.

Self-regulation

Theory suggests that instruction in concept mapping may foster self-regulation. Self-regulation refers to the degree to which individuals become metacognitively, motivationally, and behaviorally active participants in their own learning processes (Zimmerman, 1986). Instruction in strategy use is an effective means of promoting self-regulation (Corno & Mandinach, 1983; Schunk, 1986). Strategies such as concept mapping help students attend to tasks, focus on important features, organize material, and maintain a productive psychological climate for learning (Weinstein & Mayer, 1986).

In social cognitive theory, self-regulation is viewed as entailing at least four components; goal setting, self-observation, self-judgment, and self-reaction (Bandura, 1986; Schunk, 1989). Goal setting is essential to self-regulation. Self-regulated learning processes involve goal-directed cognitive activities that students instigate, modify, and sustain (Zimmerman, 1986). Goals provide standards against which people compare their present performance (Bandura, 1986).

The other three components of self-regulation (self-observation, self-judgment, and self-reaction) are not mutually exclusive but, rather, interact with one another in the service of goal pursuit (Bandura, 1986).

The first of these is the act of self-observation. Self-observation lets the student know if a goal has been achieved, and if not, what is yet to be done (Schunk, 1990). During work on concept maps, students have very concrete evidence of whether and how well their concept map is developing in the direction of their goal.

Another component of self-regulation is self-judgment. Self-judgment, like self-observation, can serve as a point of reference from which to continue progress toward the chosen goal (Bandura, 1986). Upon self-observation, students will evaluate their concept maps in regard to the standards or the goals they hold for themselves. If their performance is judged acceptable, the students will continue with their work. In contrast, if some aspect of the map is judged as unacceptable, the student will make revisions as necessary.

The third component, self-reaction, also plays an important role in the self-regulation process (Bandura, 1986). Following self-observation and self-judgment, the students experience either satisfaction or dissatisfaction in regard to their progress or completed map. Students who judge their map as inadequate may react by seeking further information or asking for assistance. On the other hand, the students who feel satisfied/gratified with their learning progress may be motivated to use concept mapping as a learning strategy in other settings. Schunk (1994) noted that the belief that one is making progress, along with the anticipated satisfaction of goal accomplishment, enhances self-efficacy and sustains motivation.

Self-efficacy

Self-efficacy is a major construct in Bandura's (1986) social cognitive theory, and a key factor in self-regulatory mechanisms governing individuals' motivation and action. Self-efficacy is defined as personal beliefs concerning one's capability to learn or perform skills at designated levels (Bandura, 1986, 1989; Schunk, 1991). According to social cognitive theory (Bandura, 1977; Schunk, 1989), people's feelings of self-efficacy affect several aspects of their behavior, including their choice of activities, their effort and persistence, and ultimately, their learning and achievement.

Research has shown that use of strategies relates positively to both self-efficacy and achievement (Borkowski, Carr, Rellinger, & Pressley, 1990; Pintrich & DeGroot, 1990; Zimmerman & Marinez-Pons, 1992). Students with high self-efficacy have higher achievement (Schunk, 1989; Schunk & Swartz, 1993). Students who believed they were capable of performing tasks used more learning strategies and persisted longer at those tasks than those who did not (Schunk & Rice, 1991; Zimmerman & Marinez-Pons, 1992).

Given the theoretical and empirical support for the benefits of concept mapping as a learning strategy

in a first-language setting, we thought it might be a beneficial strategy for students attending high school or college in the United States, for whom English is not the first language. Large numbers of students for whom English is not the first language need, or wish, to pursue their education in English-language settings. Moreover, large numbers of educators in US schools face the challenge of helping students for whom English is not the first language be academically successful. We wondered if concept mapping would be a beneficial learning strategy for these learners. This study explored the effectiveness of the concept mapping strategy in enabling ESL high school and college students to study in English with improved comprehension. We also wondered if experience with the concept mapping strategy would effect the self-regulation of these learners or increase their self-efficacy for learning in English.

We anticipated that students would enter the mapping activities with the goal of illustrating interrelationships among concepts on the map. This proximal and challenging goal would support students in organizing their efforts as they completed their concept maps. Furthermore, as the students worked on their concept maps, they would employ self-regulatory strategies to acquire information needed to complete the map, and to monitor their progress in completing the concept map. Through self-monitoring students would know which parts of their concept maps were working well and which parts needed improvement. In the course of the mapping activity, students would clarify their understanding and be alerted to confusion or gaps in their comprehension. Finally, as students gained proficiency in concept mapping, they would perceive that they were making progress toward their goal of learning from English-language text, and their self-efficacy for learning from English-language text would increase.

Current Study

The purpose of this study was to investigate the effectiveness of concept mapping as a strategy for learning in English among students in English as a Second Language (ESL) classrooms. Specifically, this study compared ESL students in a concept mapping condition to ESL students in an individual study plus discussion condition, taking level of English proficiency into account, on three variables: achievement when learning from English-language text, self-regulation, and self-efficacy for learning from English-language text.

METHOD

Design

This study took place during the second of two seven-week fall sessions at an English as a second language learning center in the Midwestern United States. A randomized pretest-posttest control group design with (a) a concept mapping group and (b) an individual study plus discussion group was employed. Prior to the intervention, the concept mapping group and the individual study plus discussion group were administered pretests in achievement, self-regulation, and self-efficacy. At the conclusion of the intervention, all participants again completed the achievement test and measures of self-regulation and self-efficacy.

Participants

Seventy-nine students attending a Center for English as a second language located on the campus of a major university in the Midwest volunteered to participate in the study. Participants ranged in age from 15 to 22 years, and included 47 males and 32 females. Fifty-five participants were college undergraduates, while 24 were high school students. Participants represented four levels of English proficiency: 19 students from the beginner level, and 20 students each from the intermediate, advanced, and expert levels. Level of English proficiency was determined by students' scores on the Michigan Test of English Language Proficiency (Corrigan, 1979). Typically, 95% of students attending the center are enrolled in college, or go on to enroll in college, with 50% of students enrolling in the flagship state university.

Instructors

A native speaker of English with many years of experience teaching English at the Center for English as a Second Language was trained in the use of the concept mapping strategy. This instructor conducted formal presentations and lessons for both experimental groups. Both the first author and the trained instructor worked together with each group to provide individual feedback. All sessions were conducted outside of regular class time.

Instructional Materials

Five reading passages constituted the instructional materials for the intervention. The first three passages were selected from TOEFL model tests (Sharpe, 1996). These were three to four paragraphs in length and addressed the following topics: Horace Mann and educational reform, the Wright Brothers and their aircraft, and characteristics of the acacia tree. These passages were described as easy to moderate in difficulty (Sharpe, 1996). The last two reading passages, which were somewhat lengthier and more difficult, were drawn from "Wild Life" magazine (June, 1999). One passage addressed the seasonal activities of Picas, the other was about British corals. Students were accustomed to reading and discussing a wide variety of material in their courses at the Center for

English as a Second Language; therefore, the reading tasks used in this study would not have been unfamiliar to the participants.

Handouts containing definitions of targeted vocabulary were prepared to accompany each reading passage.

The concept mapping group was also provided with handouts that included an introduction to concept mapping, a list of characteristics of concept maps, and examples of well-constructed (see Fig. 1) and poorly constructed concept maps.

Instruments

Survey of Learning Behaviors. This instrument was modified from the "Attitude Toward Mathematics Survey" that was used in two studies conducted by Miller, Green, Montalvo, Ravindran, and Nichols (1996). The survey used in this study consisted of three subscales: (a) self-regulation; self-monitoring subscale, (b) self-regulation: knowledge acquisition subscale, scale and (c) self-efficacy scale. There were 13 items measuring self-regulation: 9 items on the self-monitoring subscale and 4 on the knowledge acquisition subscale. There were 7 items measuring self-efficacy. Participants were asked to indicate the degree to which they agreed with given statements using a five-point scale (1 = never; 5 = always). Cronbach's α coefficients for the current sample were .89 for self-monitoring, .78 for knowledge acquisition, and .61 for self-efficacy.

Achievement Test. The achievement test was used to measure the students' understanding of the reading passages that were studied during the experiment. The test included information from each of the five reading passages used in the study sessions, and consisted of knowledge, comprehension, and application level items (Bloom, 1956). The achievement test employed a multiple-choice format with four response options for each item.

A 52-item achievement test was originally developed to assess understanding of the five reading passages. The content validity of this test was evaluated by a professor of educational psychology and the director of the Center for English as a Second Language. Both agreed that the language used on the test was accurate and appropriate for the test takers, and that the content of the reading passages was adequately sampled. This achievement test was pilot tested on an equivalent sample of students from a different ESL learning center. Item difficulty was assessed and the achievement test was revised to eliminate those items which pilot data suggested were overly easy or overly difficult. The revised instrument consisted of 33 items and was of moderate overall difficulty. The Kuder-Richard (KR20) measure of internal consistency for the current sample was 84.

Groups

Stratified random assignment was employed to assign students to two experimental groups. To form the concept mapping group, the researcher randomly selected 50% of the students from each of the four levels of English proficiency ($n = 40$). The remaining students ($n = 39$) comprised the individual study plus discussion group.

Procedure

Before the intervention began, the researcher collected informed consent letters from the director of the ESL learning center and study participants.

The four-week study consisted of three phases: (a) pretesting, (b) five study sessions devoted to studying the five reading passages assessed on the achievement test (using either concept mapping or individual study plus discussion), and (c) posttesting (see Table 1).

Pretesting. Before students received any instruction, all participants were given the Achievement Test and the Survey of Learning Behaviors as pretests. Due to the length of the achievement test, pretesting was divided across two sessions. In the first session, students read the first three passages described above and responded to 19 multiple-choice items. In the second session, students read the final two reading passages described above and responded to 14 multiple-choice items. They also completed the Survey of Learning Behaviors.

Following pretesting all students participated in five 60-minute study sessions. Each session was devoted to the study of one of the passages included in the achievement test. As described below, either concept mapping or individual study plus discussion was employed in these study sessions. All students were encouraged to study each passage in order to understand both stated and implied information in the passage.

Reading passage study sessions: Concept mapping group. For the concept mapping group, the first study session began with a 30-minute introduction to the concept mapping strategy. Students received handouts that included an introduction to concept mapping, a list of characteristics of concept maps, and examples of well-constructed and poorly constructed concept maps. Participants were asked to complete their concepts maps using the following procedure (quoted from the handout):

1. Select major concepts to be included in the map.
2. Rank or organize the list of concepts from the most inclusive to the most concrete and specific. In general, there will be fewer abstract concepts than concrete ones.
3. Cluster the concepts according to two criteria: concepts that function at a similar level of abstraction (horizontally related) and concepts that interrelate closely (hierarchically related).
4. Arrange the concepts in a configuration to depict relationships among the concepts. This can be the most intense stage requiring rearranging, rethinking, reclustering, adding prior knowledge, and searching for input.
5. Link related concepts with lines and label each line with a logical connective.

On the same day, students were given the first reading passage, definitions of difficult vocabulary from the passage, and a blank sheet of paper so they could spend the remaining 30 minutes studying and mapping the passage. During this period, the instructors monitored student progress and provided feedback. The students' concept maps were collected at the end of the session and feedback was provided in the subsequent session.

Table 1 Treatment Phases in the Study

	Concept Mapping		Individual Study Plus Discussion	
Pretesting				
Week 1: Thursday	Part 1		Week 1: Thursday	Part 1
Week 1: Friday	Part 2		Week 1: Friday	Part 2
Treatment				
Week 2: Monday	CM training; Map "Acacia"		Week 2: Tuesday	Discuss "Acacia"
Week 2: Wednesday	Map "Horace Mann"		Week 2: Thursday	Discuss "Horace Mann"
Week 2: Friday	Map "Wright Brothers"		Week 3: Monday	Discuss "Wright Brothers"
Week 3: Tuesday	Map "Pica Cycle"		Week 3: Wednesday	Discuss "Pica Cycle"
Week 3: Thursday	Map "British Corals"		Week 3: Friday	Discuss "British Corals"
Posttesting				
Week 4: Monday	Part 1		Week 4: Monday	Part 1
Week 4: Tuesday	Part 2		Week 4: Tuesday	Part 2

In four subsequent 60-minute sessions students used the concept mapping strategy as they studied the four remaining reading passages. Each session included the same sequence of events: (a) concept maps from the previous session were returned to students with feedback regarding clarity and accuracy, (b) students were provided with a new reading passage and encouraged to create concept maps of the passage while instructors monitored student progress and provided feedback, and (c) the newly created concept maps were collected for subsequent feedback. During these sessions, instructors did not employ other formal teaching techniques. That is, instructors did not lead class discussions of the meaning of the reading passages, nor did they formally assist students in interpreting the reading passages. Students were aware that they would be retested on their knowledge of the reading passages at the conclusion of the study.

Reading passage study sessions: Individual study plus discussion group. The individual study plus discussion group studied the same five reading passages in the same sequence as the concept mapping group; however, these sessions were conducted using an approach students commonly encountered at the ESL school. That is, students were provided with the reading passage of the day and a handout containing definitions of difficult vocabulary from the passage, and were encouraged to study the passage individually for 30 minutes asking the instructors for assistance as needed. In these sessions, students were free to use any study strategies with which they were familiar; however, no specific suggestions regarding use of a particular strategy, or use of strategies in general, were given.[2] At the conclusion of the individual study period, the instructor led a 30-minute whole-group discussion of the meaning and implications of the reading passage. Students were encouraged to ask questions and offer personal interpretations during the discussion period. Students were aware that they would be retested on their knowledge of the reading passages at the conclusion of the study.

Posttesting. At the conclusion of the treatment period all participants again completed the Achievement Test and the Survey of Learning Behaviors. Like pretesting, posttesting was divided across two sessions.

RESULTS

Split-plot analyses of variance were performed on each of the four dependent variables: achievement, self-monitoring, knowledge acquisition, and self-efficacy. The repeated measure was time (pretest and posttest). The independent variables were method of instruction (concept mapping or individual study plus discussion) and English proficiency level (low or high). Although students represented four different levels of English proficiency as determined by the ESL learning center, these had to be collapsed into two levels (lower and higher) to maintain adequate cell sizes in the tests of three-way interactions (time by method of instruction by English proficiency level). Main effects, two-way interactions, and three-way interactions were tested. An α level of .05 was applied to all statistical tests in this study.

Means and standard deviations for achievement, self-monitoring, knowledge acquisition, and self-efficacy by method of instruction and level of English proficiency are presented in Table 2. To confirm that the two groups were initially equivalent, t tests were performed comparing the two groups on all pretest measures. No significant differences were found.

Achievement

Results indicated a significant main effect of time $[F(1, 75) = 1555.89, p < .001, \text{Partial } \eta^2 = .95]$, a significant main effect of method of instruction $[F(1, 75) = 20.61, p < .001, \text{Partial } \eta^2 = .22]$, and a significant main effect for level of English proficiency $[F(1, 75) = 183.87, p < .001, \text{Partial } \eta^2 = .71]$. Posttest scores were higher than pretest scores, the scores of the concept mapping group were higher than those of the individual study plus discussion group, and the scores of higher English-proficiency students were higher than the scores of lower English proficient students. There were significant two-way interactions between time and method of instruction $[F(1, 75) = 123.85, p < .001, \text{Partial } \eta^2 = .62]$ and between time and level of English proficiency $[F(1, 75) = 80.09, p < .001, \text{Partial } \eta^2 = .52]$. The concept mapping group showed greater gains over time (35 percentage points) than the individual study plus discussion group (20 percentage points), and the lower English-proficiency group showed greater gains over time (34 percentage points) than the higher English-proficiency group (22 percentage points). Finally, there was a significant three-way interaction $[F(1, 75) = 8.10, p < .01, \text{Partial } \eta^2 = .10]$. The differences in gains over time between the concept mapping group and the individual study group were greater for the higher English-proficiency group (20 percentage points) compared to the lower English-proficiency group (12 percentage points).

---

[2] Instructors reported that no students in the independent study plus discussion group spontaneously engaged in content mapping during the individual study period.

Table 2 Means and standard deviations of pretest and posttest scores on achievement, self-monitoring, knowledge acquisition strategies, and self-efficacy by method of instruction and English proficiency level

	Achievement	Self-monitoring	Knowledge acquisition	Self-efficacy
Pretests				
Individual study				
Low proficiency	.29 (.11)	2.31 (.25)	2.02 (.44)	2.41 (.30)
High proficiency	.60 (.08)	2.60 (.26)	2.35 (.44)	2.86 (.26)
Concept mapping				
Low proficiency	.30 (.12)	2.33 (.20)	2.10 (.42)	2.42 (.34)
High proficiency	.60 (.08)	2.44 (.19)	2.35 (.44)	2.62 (.26)
Posttests				
Individual study				
Low proficiency	.57 (.08)	3.18 (.24)	2.90 (.24)	3.51 (.21)
High proficiency	.71 (.04)	3.08 (.29)	2.98 (.38)	3.81 (.21)
Concept mapping				
Low proficiency	.69 (.10)	4.11 (.34)	4.00 (.48)	3.64 (.20)
High proficiency	.91 (.06)	4.52 (.19)	4.42 (.30)	4.11 (.25)

Self-monitoring

Results indicated a significant main effect of time [$F(1, 75) = 1039.52, p < .001$, Partial $\eta^2 = .93$], a significant main effect of method of instruction [$F(1, 75) = 237.56, p < .001$, Partial $\eta^2 = .76$], and a significant main effect for level of English proficiency [$F(1, 75) = 209.62, p < .001$, Partial $\eta^2 = .74$]. Posttest scores were higher than pretest scores, the scores of the concept mapping group were higher than those of the individual study group, and the scores of higher English-proficient students were higher than the scores of lower English-proficient students. There was a significant two-way interaction between time and method of instruction [$F(1, 75) = 237.56, p < .001$, Partial $\eta^2 = .76$]. The concept mapping group showed greater gains over time (difference of 1.92 points) than the individual study group (difference of .69 points). Finally, there was a significant three-way interaction [$F(1, 75) = 18.12, p < .001$, Partial $\eta^2 = .20$]. The differences in gains over time between the concept mapping group and the individual study group were greater for the higher English-proficient group (difference of 1.59 points) compared to the lower English-proficient group (difference of .91 points).

Knowledge Acquisition

Results indicated a significant main effect of time [$F(1, 75) = 410.66, p < .001$, Partial $\eta^2 = .85$], a significant main effect of method of instruction [$F(1, 75) = 121.22, p < .001$, Partial $\eta^2 = .62$], and a significant main effect for level of English proficiency [$F(1, 75) = 20.78, p < .001$, Partial $\eta^2 = .22$]. Posttest scores were higher than pretest scores, scores of the concept mapping group were higher than those of the individual study group, and the scores of lower

English-proficient students were higher than the scores of higher English-proficient students. There was a significant two-way interaction between time and method of instruction [$F(1, 75) = 82.15, p < .001$, Partial $\eta^2 = .52$]. The concept mapping group showed greater gains over time (difference of 1.98 points) than the individual study group (difference of .76 points).

Self-efficacy

Results indicated a significant main effect of time [$F(1, 75) = 954.89, p < .001$, Partial $\eta^2 = .93$] and a significant main effect for level of English proficiency [$F(1, 75) = 66.73, p < .001$, Partial $\eta^2 = .47$]. Posttest scores were higher than pretest scores, and the scores of higher English-proficient students were higher than the scores of lower English-proficient students. There was a significant two-way interaction between time and method of instruction [$F(1, 75) = 19.50, p < .001$, Partial $\eta^2 = .20$]. The concept mapping group showed greater gains over time (difference of 1.35 points) than the individual study group (difference of 1.03 points). Finally, there was a significant three-way interaction [$F(1, 75) = 7.39, p < .01$, Partial $\eta^2 = .09$]. The differences in gains over time between the concept mapping group and the individual study group were greater for the higher English-proficient group (difference of .54 points) compared to the lower English-proficient group (difference of .12 points).

DISCUSSION

The major question addressed in this study was whether the use of concept mapping would improve

ESL students' learning from English text. Students in both groups had significantly higher achievement scores at posttest compared to pretest, but the concept mapping group was found to have significantly greater achievement gains than the individual study plus discussion group. That is, the opportunity to study the passages individually benefited all students; but, when students were given both an opportunity to study, and a particular strategy to employ during their study time, achievement was enhanced. These findings are consistent with the findings of previous studies of native English speakers (Ault, 1985; Fraser & Edwards, 1987; Lehman, Carter, & Kahle, 1985; Okebukola, 1990; Williams, 1997), which provided evidence that concept mapping is an effective tool for learning. Furthermore, these findings are noteworthy in light of the fact that all students in the study had chosen to attend tuition-supported English language classes. This choice implies a group of participants of relatively privileged back-grounds who were academically able and personally motivated to achieve. Yet, even under these circumstances, the concept mapping strategy was related to greater achievement gains compared to the students' typical method of individual study.

There are several possible explanations for the beneficial effects of concept mapping. The construction of concept maps may have helped students to build more complex cognitive structures in regard to information in the passages than they were able to construct on the basis of individual study and in-class discussions. Through the act of mapping, students may have come to understand not only the ideas in the passage, but the relationships among those ideas, leading to a more complete understanding of the passages. In addition, construction of concept maps may have spurred students to make more explicit links to prior knowledge compared to students in the individual study plus discussion group. This could account for their greater ability to recall information from the passages. Finally, it is likely that the act of creating the concept map served to focus students' attention on relevant information in the reading passages (Lipson, 1995; Reutzel, 1985) to a greater extent than did individual study or discussion.

It is interesting that concept mapping was of particular benefit to students of relatively high levels of English proficiency. All students with lower English proficiency made substantial gains in achievement, although those in the concept mapping group improved more than the individual study plus discussion group. Among students with higher English proficiency, those in the concept mapping group made substantial gains in achievement, while those in the individual study group made only modest gains. This could illustrate a ceiling effect among relatively proficient students such that, in the absence of

the opportunity to learn and practice a particular learning strategy, the time spent in individual study of the passages did relatively little to enhance achievement.

In addition to achievement benefits, engaging in concept mapping increased students' self-regulation and self-efficacy relative to the individual study plus discussion condition. In regard to self-regulation, concept mapping requires students to visually represent their understanding of a text. This creates much more tangible evidence of the quality of both the learning process and concept understanding compared to the on-line monitoring of comprehension that students employ during class discussions.

Increased self-regulation would be expected to lead not only to higher achievement (as reflected in the findings), but also to increased self-efficacy. And, in fact, while all students showed increased self-efficacy for learning from English text over the course of the experiment, the gains made by the concept mapping group were significantly greater than those made by the control group. This is consistent with findings by Schunk (1989) that students who believed they were learning a useful strategy were apt to feel efficacious about improving their writing. Barnhardt (1997) also reported a relationship between strategy use and confidence in language learning. Moreover, among those students with higher levels of English proficiency, students in the individual study plus discussion group had the smallest increases in self-efficacy, while those in the concept mapping group had the greatest increases in self-efficacy. This, again, suggests a ceiling effect whereas students at higher levels of English proficiency changed little in level of self-efficacy as a result of further study of English text except when they were introduced to a new learning strategy. Learning a new strategy led to substantial gains in self-efficacy.

CONCLUSION AND IMPLICATIONS

The findings clearly demonstrate that concept mapping can benefit ESL students across a range of levels of English proficiency, including those who were most advanced in English acquisition. This has important implications for both students and educators. Students may optimize their learning by adopting concept mapping as a learning strategy. Because concept mapping is a student-directed strategy that does not rely on teacher involvement or other formal or complex technological supports, it is easily adopted by users. Furthermore, concept mapping is flexible enough to be useful in a variety of learning settings. Educators may enhance the achievement as well as the self-efficacy of their ESL students by familiarizing them with the concept mapping strategy. It appears that the act of concept mapping helps ESL students to tie information from the text at hand to prior knowledge, to organize and summarize their thoughts during reading, and to organize recall of specific text details and difficult vocabulary. In addition to these benefits, concept mapping appears to promote the use of self-monitoring and knowledge acquisition strategies and to increase self-efficacy for learning from English text.

Although evidence is accumulating to suggest that the strategy of concept mapping is beneficial to all learners, including those for whom English is not the first language, there are questions that remain to answered. In regard to ESL students, it remains to be seen whether the benefits of concept mapping would be as pronounced, or present at all, in younger learners of English as a second language. Also, it remains to be seen whether concept mapping would lead to equally large gains in achievement among a less select group of students for whom English is not the first language. Presumably, students who choose to invest their time and money in the study of English are highly motivated to make use of whatever tools are made available to them. Replicating this study with ESL students attending public schools would further illuminate the benefits that can accrue from the use of concept mapping.

REFERENCES

Armbruster, B. B., & Anderson, T. H. (1980). The effect of mapping on the free recall of expository text (Technical Report No. 160). Washington, D.C.: National Institute of Education. (ERIC Document Reproduction Service No. ED 182 735)

Ault, C. R. (1985). Concept mapping as a study strategy in earth science. *Journal of College Science Teaching, 15*(1), 38-44.

Ausubel, D. P. (1963). *The psychology of meaningful verbal learning*. New York: Grune and Stratton.

Bandura, A. (1977). Self-efficacy: Toward a unifying theory of behavioral change. *Psychological Review, 84*, 191-215.

Bandura, A. (1986). *Social foundations of thought and action: A social cognitive theory*. Englewood Cliffs, NJ: Prentice-Hall.

Bandura, A. (1989). Human agency in social cognitive theory. *American Psychologist, 44*, 1175-1184.

Barnhardt, S. (1997). Self-efficacy and second language learning. *The NCLRC Language Resource, 1*(5).

Borkowski, J. G., Carr, M., Rellinger, E. A., & Pressley, M. (1990). Self-regulated strategy use: Interdependence of metacognition, attributions, and self-esteem. In B. F. Jones (Ed.), *Dimensions of thinking: Review of research* (pp. 53-92). Hillsdale, NJ: Erlbaum.

Block, E. (1986). The comprehension strategies of second language readers. *TESOL Quarterly, 20*, 463-494.

Bloom, B. S. (1956). *Taxonomy of educational objectives: The classification of educational goals. Handbook I: Cognitive domain*, New York: McKay.

Briscoe, C., & LaMaster, S. U. (1991). Meaningful learning in college biology through concept mapping. *The American Biology Teacher, 53*, 214-219.

Carrell, P., Pharis, B. G., & Liberto, J. C. (1989). Metacognitive strategy training for ESL reading. *TESOL Quarterly, 23*(4), 647-673.

Corrigan, A. (1979). *The Michigan test of English language proficiency*. Ann Arbor: English Language Institute, University of Michigan.

Corno, L, & Mandinach, E. B. (1983). The role of cognitive engagement in classroom learning and motivation, *Educational Psychologist, 18*, 88-108.

Fraser, K., & Edwards, J. (1987). The effects of training in concept mapping on student achievement in traditional tests. *Research in Science Education, 15*, 158-165.

Heinze-Fry, J. A., & Novak, J. D. (1990). Concept mapping brings long-term movement toward meaningful learning. *Science Education, 74*, 461-472.

Kamhi-Stein, L. (1993). Summarization, notetaking, and mapping techniques: Lessons for L2 reading instruction. (ERIC Document Reproduction Service No. ED 306 816)

Knight, S. I., Padron, Y. N., & Waxman, H. C. (1985). The cognitive reading strategies of ESL students *TESOL Quarterly, 19*, 789-792.

Koumy, E., & Salam, A. (1999). Effects of three semantic mapping strategies on EFL students' reading comprehension. (ERIC Document Reproduction Service No. ED 435 193)

Lehman, J. D., Carter, C. C., & Kahle. J. B. (1985). Concept mapping. Vee mapping, and achievement Results of a field study with black high school students. *Journal of Research in Science Teaching, 22*(7), 663-673.

Lipson, M. (1995). The effect of semantic mapping instruction on prose comprehension of below-level college readers. *Reading Research and Instruction, 34*(4), 367-378.

McClure, J. R., & Bell, P. E. (1990). *Effects of an environmental education-related STS approach instruction on cognitive structures of preservice science teachers*. (ERIC Document Reproduction Service No. ED 341-582)

Miller, R. B., Green, B. A., Montalvo, G. P., Ravindran, B., & Nichols, J. D. (1996). Engagement in academic work: The role of learning goals, future consequences, pleasing others, and perceived ability *Contemporary Educational Psychology, 21*, 388-422.

Moreira, M. A. (1979). Concept maps as tools for teaching, *Journal of College Science Teaching, 8*(5), 283-286.

Novak, J. D. (1981). Applying learning psychology and philosophy of science to biology teaching. *The American Biology Teacher, 43*(1), 12-20.

Novak, J. D., & Gowin, D. B. (1984). *Concept mapping for meaningful learning*. Cambridge: Cumbridge University Press.

Novak, J. D., Gowin, B., & Johansen, G. T. (1983). The use of concept mapping and knowledge Vee mapping with junior high school science students. *Science Education, 67*(5), 625-645.

Okebukola, P. A. (1990), Attaining meaningful learning of concepts in genetics and ecology. An examination of the potency of the concept-mapping technique. *Journal of Research in Science Teaching, 27*(5), 493-504.

Okebukola, P. A., & Jegede, O. J. (1988). Cognitive preference and learning mode as determinants of meaningful learning through concept mapping. *Science Education, 72*(4), 489-500.

Pankratius, W. J. (1990). Building an organized knowledge base: Concept mapping and achievement in secondary school physics. *Journal of Research in Science Teaching, 27*, 315-333.

Park, S. (1995). Implications of learning strategy research for designing computer-assisted instruction. *Journal of Research on Computing in Education, 25*(4), 435-456.

Peresich, M., Meadows, J., & Sinatra, R. (1990). Content area mapping for reading and writing proficiency. *Journal of Reading, 33*(6), 424-432.

Pintrich, P. R., & DeGroot, E. V. (1990). Motivational and self-regulated components of classroom academic performance, *Journal of Educational Psychology, 82*(1), 33-40.

Pressley, M. (1982). Elaboration and memory development. *Child Development, 53*, 296-309.

Reutzel, D. (1985). Story maps improve comprehension. *Reading Teacher, 38*(4), 400-411.

Roth, W., & Roychoudhury, A. (1993). Using Vee and concept maps in collaborative settings: Elementary education majors construct meaning in physical science courses. *Social Science and Mathematics, 93*, 237-244.

Ruddell, R. B., & Boyle, O. F. (1989). A study of cognitive mapping as a means to improve summarization and comprehension of expository text. *Reading Research and Instruction, 29*(1), 12-22.

Schreiber, D. A., & Abegg, G. L. (1991). Scoring student-generated concept maps in introductory college chemistry. Paper presented for the National Association for Research in Science Teaching 1991 Annual Meeting.

Schunk, D. H. (1986). Verbalization and children's self-regulated learning. *Contemporary Educational Psychology, 11*, 347-369.

Schunk, D. H. (1989). Self-efficacy and achievement behaviors. *Educational Psychology Review, 1*, 173-208.

Schunk, D. H. (1990). Goal setting and self-efficacy during self-regulated learning. *Educational Psychologist, 25*, 71-86.

Schunk, D. H. (1991). Self-efficacy and academic motivation. *Educational Psychology Review, 26*, 207-231.

Schunk, D. H. (1994). Self-regulation of self-efficacy and attributions in academic settings. In D. H. Schunk & B. J. Zimmerman (Eds.), *Self-regulation of learning and performance: Issues and educational applications* (pp. 75-99). Hillsdale, NJ: Erlbaum.

Schunk, D. H., & Swartz, C. W. (1993). Goals and progress feedback: Effects on self-efficacy and writing achievement. *Contemporary Educational Psychology, 18*(3), 337-354.

Schunk, D. H., & Rice, J. M. (1991). Learning goals and progress feedback during reading comprehension instruction. *Journal of Reading Behavior, 23*(3), 351-364.

Sharpe, P. J. (1996). *How to prepare for the TOEFL test: Test of English as a foreign language* (8 ed.), New York: Barron's Educational Services Inc.

Sheldon, S. (1984). Comparison of two teaching methods for reading comprehension. *Journal of Research in Reading, 7*(1), 41-52.

Stice, C. F., & Alvarez, M. C. (1987). Hierarchical concept mapping in the early grades. *Childhood Education, 64*(2), 86-96.

Weinstein, C. E., (1988). *Elaboration skills as a learning strategy*. New York: Academic Press.

Weinstein, C. E., & Mayer, R. E. (1986). The teaching of learning strategies. In M. Wittrock (Ed.), *The handbook of research on teaching* (pp. 315-327). New York: Macmillan.

Williams, J. (1997). The relation between efficacy for self-regulated learning and domain-specific academic performance, controlling for test anxiety. *Journal of Research and Development in Education, 29*(2), 77-80.

Zimmerman, B. J. (1986). Development of self-regulated learning: Which are the key subprocesses? *Contemporary Educational Psychology, 16*, 307-313.

Zimmerman. B. J., & Marinez-Pons, M. (1992). Student differences in self-regulated learning: Relating grade, sex, and giftedness to self-efficacy and strategy use, *Journal of Educational Psychology, 82*, 51-59.

Evaluation Criteria	**Discussion Questions**

Evaluation Criteria

1. Is the general purpose of the study clear? Will the study provide a significant contribution?

The general purpose of the study is very clearly stated in the first two sentences, providing a very helpful orientation to the study. A solid case is made for making a significant contribution, summarized in the third paragraph in the Self-efficacy section (1.3).

2. Does the review of literature establish the relationship between previous studies and the current one? Is the review well organized and up-to-date?

There is an impressive amount of literature cited, most of which refers to theories related to the variables. Some studies are cited that investigate the effect of concept mapping on ESL students, though these studies are not detailed, analyzed, or related to the present study. The review is well organized with appropriate subheadings, and is up-to-date.

3. Is the specific research hypothesis or question clearly and concisely stated?

Although no research questions or hypotheses are stated, the research problem is clearly and concisely stated in section 1.4, Current study.

4. Is the method of sampling clearly presented? Was there random assignment of subjects? If there was no random assignment, was there anything in the way the groups were formed that might have influenced the reaction of the group to the treatment?

The subjects were adequately described. It would be helpful to know what percentage of contacted students volunteered. There was random assignment, using a matching procedure to assure that each group had approximately the same level of English proficiency.

5. What was manipulated as the independent variable or variables?

Type of instruction was manipulated with two levels—concept mapping group and individual study plus discussion group. Level of English proficiency, with two levels, is a second, non-manipulated independent variable. What difference would this make in relation to the effectiveness of the type of instruction?

Discussion Questions

1. The presentation of related theoretical literature is quite lengthy. What could be rewritten to be more succinct?

2. What kinds of information about the studies on the effect of concept mapping on ESL students would be helpful to include in the review of literature? How can these studies be related to the present study?

3. What would be an appropriate research hypothesis for this study?

4. What additional information could be provided to show that the random assignment procedure resulted in groups that were essentially the same on characteristics that could influence the results?

5. Was the manipulated variable applied to students individually or in groups?

6. Are the procedures for collecting information described fully?

The procedures are fairly well described so that others could replicate the study.

7. Are there any threats to internal validity that seem plausible?

While several threats are possible, only two are plausible. Random assignment controls several threats, including selection, extraneous events, maturation, pretesting, and statistical regression. Instrumentation is a possible threat due to the lack of information about validity and reliability. Subject effects are possible given the volunteer nature of subject participation. Experimenter effects are plausible since the instructor was informed about the nature of the experiment and presumably the expected results. Treatment replications are plausible since instruction was provided to groups of students.

8. Do the conclusions and interpretations follow logically from the results presented? Are limitations indicated?

Yes, conclusions and interpretations follow logically from the results, with the results section (3) appropriately summarizing the findings without discussion. No limitations are indicated.

9. Is the experiment so contrived and artificial that the findings have little generalizability?

This study has good generalizability from the standpoint of being conducted in a setting that is typically used for teaching. However, generalizability is limited because of the instruments used and the nature of the population of subjects.

6. What additional detail could be provided about how the pre and posttest were administered?

7. What information could be provided to address the possible and plausible threats to internal validity?

8. What limitations to this study could be emphasized?

9. What steps could be taken for the researchers to increase generalizability?

Credibility Scorecard
The Influence of Concept Mapping on Achievement Self-Regulation and Self-Efficacy in students of English as a Second Language.

	Excellent	Very Good	Adequate	Marginal	Poor
General purpose	5	4	3	2	1
Contribution/ significance	5	4	3	2	1
Review of literature	5	4	3	2	1
Research questions or hypotheses	5	4	3	2	1
Subjects or participants	5	4	3	2	1
Instrumentation	5	4	3	2	1
Procedures	5	4	3	2	1
Results	5	4	3	2	1
Practical significance	5	4	3	2	1
Graphics	5	4	3	2	1
Conclusions	5	4	3	2	1
Any fatal flaws?					

Grade Distributions, Grading Procedures, and Students' Evaluations of Instructors: A Justice Perspective

Jasmine Tata

Department of Management, Loyola University

ABSTRACT

This scenario-based experimental study was an examination of the connections between the fairness of grade distributions, the fairness of grading procedures, and evaluations of the instructor. The results showed that the fairness of both the grade distributions and the grading procedures influenced students' evaluations of instructors. Fair grading procedures, however, influenced evaluations of the instructor only when the grade distributions were perceived as unfair—that is, when the grades did not meet expectations. When grade distributions were perceived as fair, there was no significant difference in evaluations of the instructor among participants exposed to fair and unfair procedures. Implications of this study for instructors, administrators, and students are discussed.

Grades are the basic currency of our educational system. Instructors in universities and colleges assign grades to students on a regular basis. High grades result in both immediate benefits to students (e.g., intrinsic motivation, approval of family) and long-term consequences (e.g., admission to graduate school, preferred employment). Students who perceive their grades as unfair are more likely to react negatively toward the instructor, and these negative reactions may influence students' ratings of teaching effectiveness.

A number of researchers have examined the connection between students' grades and their evaluations of instructors. The literature is equivocal on this issue; some researchers (Chacko, 1983; Marlin & Gaynor, 1989; Perkins, Guerin, & Sciileii, 1990; Snyder & Clair, 1976) suggested that student grades and grading standards may bias teaching evaluations because students who receive higher grades tend to rate the instructor more positively than students who receive lower grades. Results of other studies did not find consistent effects of grades on evaluations of teaching (Abram, Dickens, Perry, & Leventhal, 1980; Holmes, 1972).

This inconsistency in the literature concerning the connection between grades and students' evaluations of instructors can be clarified by examining the fairness of grades. It is possible that the connection between low grades and unfavorable evaluations of instructors exists not because of the level of the outcome (the grade) received by the student, but because the low grade is perceived to be unfair. The literature on distributive justice (Adams, 1965; Crosby, 1984; Folger, 1986) indicates that people receiving outcomes that are lower than expected are more likely to perceive the distribution as unfair, and perceptions of unfairness may lead to negative evaluations of distributors. In the context of grade allocations, a student who spends a number of hours preparing for an examination may expect to receive an A. If the student receives a lower grade, the grade may be perceived as unfair, especially if other students who spent fewer hours preparing for the examination received higher grades.

In addition to the grade distribution, grading procedures can also influence students' perceptions of fairness and evaluations of instructors. The literature on procedural justice states that procedures that are consistent and impartial are perceived as fairer than those that are inconsistent and biased (Leventhal, 1980). In the context of the classroom, instructors are expected to apply grading standards (procedures) consistently to all students. If an instructor lowers the standards for a few students, this is likely to be perceived as procedurally unfair. Students who believe that the grade allocation procedures are unfair may be more likely to evaluate the instructor unfavorably.

For this study, I examined the connections between students' evaluations of instructors, the fairness of grade distributions, and the fairness of grading procedures. I also investigated the relative influence of procedural and distributive fairness on evaluations of instructors. Examining these relationships can be of importance to instructors, administrators, and students. Instructors may use the findings to identify how best to allocate grades and the appropriate procedures associated with grade distribution. Administrators and students may understand the extent to which evaluations are influenced by

The Journal of Psychology, Vol. 133, No. 3, pp. 263–271, 1999. Reprinted with permission of the Helen Dwight Reid Educational Foundation. Published by Heldref Publications, 1319 Eighteenth St., N. W., Washington, DC 20036-1802. Copyright © 1999.

students' perceptions of procedural and distributive fairness, and the judgment processes involved in evaluations of instructors (Carkenord & Stephens, 1994).

The Fairness of Grade Distributions

Justice theory and research have dealt with both distributive and procedural justice. *Distributive justice* is concerned with the fairness of decisions about the distribution of resources, whereas *procedural justice* is concerned with the fairness of the procedures used to reach those decisions (Greenberg, 1990). Distributive justice refers to the extent to which the outcomes received in an allocation decision are perceived as fair; this type of fairness has been considered implicitly within the contexts of equity theory (Adams, 1965), relative deprivation theory (Crosby, 1984), and referent cognitions theory (Folger, 1986). These theories suggest that individuals use standards of distributive justice such as equality (outcomes allocated equally to all participants regardless of inputs) and equity (outcomes allocated based on inputs such as productivity) to establish the fairness or unfairness of the outcome (Adams, 1965; Sampson, 1980). Thus, the experience of injustice involves the realization that outcomes do not correspond to expectations determined by standards of distributive justice.

In the context of the classroom, grades are the outcomes allocated to students. Students receiving lower grades than expected are likely to perceive the grades as distributively unfair, whereas students receiving expected grades are likely to perceive the grades as fair; this phenomenon can be explained by relative deprivation and the egocentric bias. Relative deprivation theory (Crosby, 1984) posits that the fundamental source of feelings of injustice is the realization that one's outcomes fall short of expectations. The egocentric bias in distributive justice suggests that individuals' expectations of their own performance and outcomes are higher than their expectations of others' outcomes; hence, people who receive higher outcomes are more likely to perceive those outcomes as fair than people who receive lower outcomes (Greenberg, 1987). Empirical support for this phenomenon has been found in the work of Lind and Tyler (1988) and Tyler (1986), who found connections between outcomes (relative to expectations) and perceptions of distributive justice.

The Fairness of Grading Procedures

Procedural justice refers to the extent to which the processes used in making allocation decisions are perceived as fair (Greenberg, 1990; Leventhal, 1980; Lind & Tyler, 1988; Thibaut & Walker, 1975; Tyler, 1986). Research on procedural justice has evolved from two conceptual models—Thibaut and Walker's (1975) dispute resolution procedures and Leventhal's (1980) principles of resource allocation procedures. These researchers suggested that procedural justice involves the realization that procedures correspond to those determined by certain standards (e.g., consistency, suppression of personal bias, use of accurate information, voice, and congruity with prevailing standards or ethics). In the classroom context, the procedures used to allocate grades could influence students' perceptions of procedural fairness and evaluations of the instructor.

Results of research in organizational contexts (Alexander & Ruderman, 1987; Folger & Konovsky, 1989) have shown that distributive fairness and procedural fairness influence employees' reactions. Folger and Konovsky (1989) found that perceived fairness was related to satisfaction, trust in supervisors, and organizational commitment. Alexander and Ruderman (1987) determined that employees' perceptions of fairness influenced their approval of supervisors.

Extrapolating to the classroom context, the fairness of grade distributions and grading procedures should influence student reactions, such as their evaluations of instructors. Therefore, my first hypothesis was that evaluations of the instructor would be higher for students who received expected grades (fair grade distributions) than for students receiving grades lower than expected (unfair grade distributions). My second hypothesis was that students' evaluations of the instructor would be higher for consistent (fair) grade allocation procedures than for inconsistent (unfair) procedures.

It is possible that procedural and distributive justice are predictive of different types of outcomes. Sweeney and McFarlin's (1993) two-factor model suggests that distributive justice primarily influences attitudes toward the outcome in question, whereas procedural justice influences attitudes toward the system. For example, Sweeney and McFarlin (1993) found that employees who believed their pay was lower than expected (distributively unfair) demonstrated lower levels of pay satisfaction, an attitude specifically directed toward the outcome (pay). In contrast, when pay distributions were made using fair procedures, employees showed higher levels of trust in management and commitment toward the organization (attitudes directed toward the system).

In the classroom context, students' evaluations of instructors can be considered attitudes toward the university system; such attitudes are more likely to be influenced by procedural justice than by distributive justice. Based on Sweeney and McFarlin's (1993) model, my third hypothesis was that consistency (fairness) of grading procedures would influence students' evaluations of the instructor to a greater extent than grade distributions.

METHOD

Participants and Design

Based on a definition of *fairness* as meeting expectations and being consistent, I used a 2 (grade distribution: met expectations vs. did not meet expectations) 2 (grading procedure: consistent vs. inconsistent) between-subjects, scenario-based experimental design. Undergraduate students (51 men and 46 women) participated in the study. Most were sophomores (32%) or juniors (41%), and the rest were seniors. The average age of the students was 20.10 years.

Materials

The participants were asked to respond to one of four different scenarios. Each scenario described a classroom situation and an instructor. Participants were given contextual information about the situation and were asked to place themselves in the position of a student in the class who had worked hard on a term paper by conducting research, writing, and rewriting the paper. On the basis of the grading criteria described in the syllabus, the student expected to receive a grade of A on the paper.

The grade distribution was manipulated by informing the participants that the student received a grade that either met expectations (A = fair grade distribution) or did not meet expectations (B = unfair grade distribution). The grading procedure was manipulated by stating that the instructor used the grading scheme specified in the syllabus to grade the paper (consistent/fair grading procedure) or that the instructor changed the grading scheme after the paper was turned in (inconsistent/unfair grading procedure).

Procedure

Participants were randomly assigned to one of the four manipulation conditions. After reading the scenario, they were asked to complete measures of the dependent variable (students' evaluations of the instructor) and two manipulation checks (distributive justice and procedural justice) on 7-point Likert-type scales.

Students' evaluations of the instructor were measured by asking them to rate the preparation of the instructor, course organization, subject matter presentation, knowledge of the subject matter, availability of the instructor, his or her attitude toward students, and an overall evaluation of the instructor. These items were based on scales used in empirical research by Chacko (1983) and Carkenord and Stephens (1994).

Distributive justice was measured by asking participants to rate the extent to which they felt that the actual distribution of grades was fair and what they deserved, and procedural justice was measured by asking participants to rate the extent to which they felt that the decision about the grade was made in a fair way and they were treated fairly; these scales were based on those used by Bies, Shapiro, and Cummings (1988) and Shapiro (1991). After completing the ratings, participants were debriefed about the purpose of the study.

RESULTS

Reliability Analyses and Manipulation Checks

Cronbach's reliability coefficients were calculated for the scales and were found to be greater than .75 for each condition; mean ratings were also computed for each scale. Next, I conducted manipulation checks to examine the participants' understanding of the distributive justice and procedural justice manipulations. I conducted separate t tests for the two manipulation checks. The results of the t tests indicated that the manipulations had the intended effects. Grade distributions influenced perceptions of distributive justice; participants who had been assigned expected grades gave higher ratings for distributive justice than those who had been assigned grades lower than expected, Ms = 4.81 and 3.59, respectively, $t(95)$ = 3.84, p <.05. Also, the instructor's grading procedures influenced perceptions of procedural justice; participants gave higher ratings of procedural justice for consistent procedures than for inconsistent procedures, Ms = 5.11 and 3.87, respectively, $t(95)$ = 4.06, p <.05.

Tests of Hypotheses

Of interest in this study was the relative influence of grade distributions (distributive fairness) and grading procedures (procedural fairness) on students' evaluations of the instructor. I conducted an analysis of variance (ANOVA) with grade distributions and grading procedures as independent variables and students' evaluations of the instructor as the dependent variable. The two main effects and the interaction effect were significant.

In support of Hypothesis 1, evaluations of the instructor were influenced by grade distributions. Participants who were assigned expected grades (fair distributions) gave higher evaluations of the instructor than participants who were assigned grades lower than expected (unfair distributions), Ms = 5.54 and 4.67, respectively, $t(95)$ = 2.42, p <.05. Hypothesis 2 was also supported. Students' evaluations of the instructor were influenced by grading procedures; when consistent (fair) procedures were used, participants gave higher evaluations of the instructor than when inconsistent (unfair) procedures were used, Ms = 5.52 and 4.69, respectively, $t(95)$ = 2.31, p <.05.

The interaction of grade distributions and grading procedures was also significant, and simple main effects were calculated using Gabriel's simultaneous test procedure (Kirk, 1982). Among participants who received expected grades (fair distributions), there were no significant differences in evaluations of the instructor between those who were provided with consistent procedures and those who were provided with inconsistent procedures, Ms = 5.61 and 5.47, respectively, $t(95)$ = 0.39, p >.05. Among the participants who received grades lower than expected (unfair distributions), however, respondents who were provided with consistent (fair) grading procedures gave the instructor higher evaluations than those who were provided with inconsistent (unfair) procedures, Ms = 5.42 and 3.91, respectively, $t(95)$ = 4.19, p <.05. Therefore, grading procedures appeared to influence evaluations of the instructor only when students received grades lower than expected.

To test Hypothesis 3, I calculated partial correlation coefficients. The partial correlation between procedural fairness and the students' evaluations of the instructor (controlling for distributive fairness) was compared with the partial correlation between distributive fairness and evaluations of the instructor (controlling for procedural fairness). The results suggest that the relationship between procedural fairness and evaluations of the instructor was no stronger than the relationship between distributive fairness and evaluations of the instructor. Thus, Hypothesis 3 was not supported.

DISCUSSION

The purpose of this study was to examine the influence of the fairness of grade distributions and grading procedures on students' evaluations of the instructors. Distributive fairness was manipulated by providing participants with grades that either met expectations or were lower than expected. Procedural fairness was manipulated by providing consistent or inconsistent grading procedures.

The results indicate that students' evaluations of an instructor are influenced by distributive fairness because participants who received expected grades gave higher evaluations than those receiving grades lower than expected. Procedural fairness also influenced evaluations of the instructor. Participants provided higher evaluations under consistent procedures than under inconsistent procedures. The fairness of grading procedures, however, influenced evaluations of the instructor only under unfair grade distributions. When students received expected (fair) grade distributions, grading procedures did not significantly influence evaluations of the instructor. This suggests that procedural fairness becomes more salient under conditions of distributive unfairness.

The fairness of grading procedures, however, did not influence students' evaluations of the instructor to a greater extent than the fairness of grade distributions; this finding is not consistent with previous research conducted in organizations but may be explained by examining the differences between organizational settings and the classroom context. Employees in organizations are likely to have a long-term perspective of their relationships with management and organizations. In contrast, students are more likely to have a short-term perspective of their relationships with instructors, as they generally interact with instructors for only the length of a semester.

These differences in time horizons can be connected to perceptions of fairness. Procedural fairness influences system variables (e.g., trust in management or evaluations of instructors) partly because fair procedures ensure that, over time, outcome distributions (e.g., pay or grades) will be favorable (Lind & Tyler, 1988). Employees who have long-term relationships with management may be influenced to a greater extent by procedural fairness than students who have short-term relationships with instructors and are not concerned about future outcomes distributed by the instructor. Thus, students may not emphasize grading procedures to a greater extent than grade distributions when evaluating instructors.

Before generalizing from the results of this study, certain limitations of the methodology should be kept in mind. Patterns obtained in a scenario-based study may not always be generalizable to other settings. Unfortunately, the sensitive nature of this line of research made it problematic to conduct in a classroom setting. Also, the subtle differences between the independent variables used in this study made it difficult to examine the independent and interaction effects under natural circumstances. The external validity of the study, however, was increased by using students as participants, because they could easily relate to the grading incidents. Future researchers can extend the generalizability of this study by replicating it using other methods in other settings.

Another potential limitation of the study is the use of only one manipulation of grade distributions and one of grading procedures. In actuality, students' perceptions of distributive fairness may be influenced not only by comparisons between their grades and expectations, but also by comparisons between their grades and others' grades. Similarly, procedural fairness may be perceived not only through the consistency of grading procedures but also through other factors such as lack of bias and the use of accurate information. Although the manipulation checks indicated that participants' perceptions of distributive and procedural justice were influenced by the manipulations used in the study, future researchers can use other techniques to examine connections between the perceived fairness of grades and students' evaluations of instructors.

When the results of this study are viewed along with past studies (Perkins et al., 1990; Snyder & Clair, 1976), grade distributions appear to be a consistent influence on evaluations of teaching. To the extent that students' evaluations of the instructor's performance reflect the instructor's evaluations of the students' performance (grades), teaching evaluations have the potential to be contaminated by factors unrelated to teaching behavior.

The influence of grade distributions, however, can be mitigated by the grading procedures used. The results suggest that the fairness of grading procedures has a significant influence on students' evaluations of instructors. As such, this study connects the research on procedural justice in organizational settings (Greenberg, 1990; Lind & Tyler, 1988; Tyler, 1986) to the classroom context; just as managers perceived as fair by employees are more likely to receive positive evaluations, instructors perceived as fair receive higher ratings. Instructors can ensure the fairness of their grading procedures by being consistent, using accurate information, and maintaining an impartial process.

The validity of students' evaluations of instructors is a complex issue. Although factors external to instructor performance (such as grade distributions) can influence evaluations, so can other factors intrinsic to performance such as the fairness of the grading process. The validity of students' evaluations of instructors can be strengthened by using other measures of teaching effectiveness along with student ratings, especially in making decisions about salary increases, promotions, and tenure.

REFERENCES

Abram. P. C., Dickens, W.J., Perry, R. P., & Leventhal, L. (1980). Do teacher standards for assigning grades affect student evaluations of instruction? *Journal of Educational Psychology, 72,* 107–111.

Adams, J. S. (1965). Inequity in social exchange. In L. Berkowitz (Ed.). *Advances in experimental social psychology* (Vol. 2, pp. 267–299). San Diego, CA: Academic Press.

Alexander, S., & Ruderman, M. (1987). The role of procedural and distributive justice in organizational behavior. *Social justice Research, 1,* 117–198.

Bies, R. J., Shapiro. D., & Cummings. L. L. (1988). Causal accounts and managing conflict. *Communication Research, 15,* 381–399.

Carkenord, D. M., & Stephens, M. G. (1994). Understanding student judgments of teaching effectiveness: A "policy capturing" approach. *The Journal of Psychology, 128,* 675–682.

Chacko, T. I. (1983). Student ratings of instruction: A function of grading standards. *Educational Research Quarterly, 8,* 19–25.

Crosby, F. (1984). Relative deprivation in organizational settings. *Research in organizational behavior* (Vol. 6, pp. 51–93). Greenwich, CT: JAI Press.

Folger, R. (1986). Rethinking equity theory: A referent cognitions model. In H. W. Bierhoff, R. L. Cohen, & J. Greenberg (Eds.), *Justice in social relations* (pp. 145–164). New York: Plenum Press.

Folger, R., & Konovsky, M. A. (1989). Effects of procedural and distributive justice on reactions to pay raise decisions. *Academy of Management Journal, 32,* 115–130.

Greenberg, J. (1987). Reactions to procedural justice in payment decisions: Do the means justify the ends? *Journal of Applied Psychology, 72,* 55–61.

Greenberg, J. (1990). Looking fair vs being fair: Managing impressions of organizational justice *Research in Organizational Behavior, 12,* 111–157.

Holmes, D. S. (1972). Effects of grades and discontinued grade expectancies on students evaluations of their instructor. *Journal of Educational Psychology, 63,* 130–133.

Kirk, R. E. (1982). *Experimental design: Procedures for the behavioral sciences.* Belmont, CA: Brooks/Cole.

Leventhal, G. S. (1980). What should be done with equity theory? In K.J. Gergen, M. S. Greenberg. & R. H. Willis (Eds.), *Social exchange: Advances in theory and research* (pp. 27–55). New York: Plenum Press.

Lind, E. A., & Tyler, T. R. (1988). *The social psychology of procedural justice.* New York: Plenum Press.

Marlin, J. W., & Gaynor, P. E. (1989). Do anticipated grades affect student evaluations? A discriminant analysis approach. *College Student Journal, 23,* 184–192.

Perkins, D., Guerin, D., & Sciileii, J. (1990). Effects of grading standards information, assigned grade, and grade discrepancies on students' evaluations. *Psychological Reports, 66,* 635–642.

Sampson, E. E. (1980). Justice and social character. In G. Mikula (Ed.), *Justice and social interaction* (pp. 285–314). New York: Springer-Verlag.

Shapiro, D. (1991). The effects of explanations on negative reactions to deceit. *Administrative Science Quarterly, 36,* 614–630.

Snyder, C., & Clair, M. (1976). Effects of expected and obtained grades on teacher evaluation and attribution of performance. *Journal of Educational Psychology, 68,* 76–82.

Sweeney, P. D., & McFarlin, D. B. (1993). Workers' evaluations of the "ends" and the "means": An examination of four models of distributive and procedural justice. *Organizational Behavior and Human Decision Processes, 55,* 23–40.

Thibaut, J., & Walker, L. (1975). *Procedural justice: A psychological analysis.* Hillsdale, NJ: Erlbaum.

Tyler, T. R. (1986). When does procedural justice matter in organizational settings? In R.J.Lewicki, B. H. Sheppard, & M. H. Bazerman (Eds.), *Research on negotiation in organizations* (Vol. 1, pp. 7–23). Greenwich, CT: JAI Press.

Received February 18, 1998

Evaluation Criteria

1. Is the general purpose of the study clear? Will the study provide a significant contribution?

The general purpose is clearly stated in the fifth paragraph, as well as in the abstract. The author makes a sound case for significance in the sixth paragraph.

2. Does the review of literature establish the relationship between previous studies and the current one? Is the review well organized and up-to-date?

The excellent review of literature is well organized with major headings. Previous research is clearly related to the study. There is extensive reference to theory, which provides a foundation for explaining the results. One wonders why there are no references published after 1994.

3. Is the specific research hypothesis or question clearly and concisely stated?

The three research hypotheses are clearly stated, indicating specific expected results.

4. Is the method of sampling clearly presented? Was there random assignment of subjects? If there was no random assignment, was there anything in the way the groups were formed that might have influenced the reaction of the group to the treatment?

The sampling is clear, but the description of the students is insufficient. There is indication of random assignment of students to the four conditions.

5. What was manipulated as the independent variable or variables?

There were two manipulated independent variables (grade distribution expectation and grading consistency), each with two levels.

6. Are the procedures for collecting information described fully?

The procedures are well described, though it is not clear if students responded to different scenarios together, in the same room, or individually. There is incomplete information about the dependent variables (evaluations of instructors and distributive justice).

Discussion Questions

1. Does the major contribution of this study focus on theory or on the more practical aspects of grading?

2. When does the introduction end and the review of literature begin? Examine the references. Which are most likely to be primary sources? Which are probably secondary sources? Which type seems to be stressed in the review?

3. Notice how the research hypotheses are formulated from theory. Why is this helpful when analyzing the results?

4. How might the nature of the sample affect the results? Is it likely that students from another university would respond in a similar way? Is there enough information about random assignment?

5. Would other independent variables possibly be significant in this study? Are two levels for each of the variables sufficient, or would three or four levels be better?

6. What further information about the dependent variables would be helpful in judging the credibility of the measures?

7. Are there any threats to internal validity that seem plausible?

There are no glaring or probable threats to internal validity. It is possible that the students would want to please the experimenter (subject effects), and the experimenter may have indicated some kind of bias or preference (experimenter effect). Instrumentation could be a threat because of lack of information.

8. Do the conclusions and interpretations follow logically from the results presented? Are limitations indicated?

The results are clearly and logically presented, though a graph of the significant interaction would be helpful. The conclusions are reasonable and accurate and well integrated with theory to explain results that were not as expected. Limitations, especially those related to a scenario approach, are appropriately noted.

9. Is the experiment so contrived and artificial that the findings have little generalizability?

Given that this study was conducted at one university and used scenarios rather than actual conditions, the results are fairly contrived and have limited generalizability.

7. Overall, how good is the internal validity of this study? How could the internal validity be strengthened?

8. Based on this study, what would a reasonable follow-up study look like? Could the results help college administrators make better decisions about salary increases and promotions?

9. What could be done to increase the generalizability of this kind of study?

Credibility Scorecard
Grade Distributions, Grading Procedures, and Students' Evaluations of Instructors: A Justice Perspective

	Excellent	Very Good	Adequate	Marginal	Poor
General purpose	5	4	3	2	1
Contribution/ significance	5	4	3	2	1
Review of literature	5	4	3	2	1
Research questions or hypotheses	5	4	3	2	1
Subjects or participants	5	4	3	2	1
Instrumentation	5	4	3	2	1
Procedures	5	4	3	2	1
Results	5	4	3	2	1
Practical significance	5	4	3	2	1
Graphics	5	4	3	2	1
Conclusions	5	4	3	2	1
Any fatal flaws?					

4 QUALITATIVE DESIGNS

Qualitative research encompasses both a philosophy of knowing and a number of approaches to collecting and analyzing information. As a philosophy of knowing, qualitative research focuses on understanding from the perspective of whoever and whatever is being studied. Rather than try to establish objective descriptions and relationships, as quantitative research does, qualitative studies are based on the assumption that reality is subjective and dependent on context. There are multiple realities that need to be described in detail to result in a complete and deep understanding of the phenomena being investigated.

As pointed out in Chapter 1, *qualitative* is a generic term that refers to a number of different approaches. These approaches or methods share some or all of the following characteristics:

Search for meaning—Qualitative studies are designed to better understand the interpretations and meanings people give to events, objects, other people, and environmental contexts.

Constructed reality—Reality is socially constructed and constantly changing.

Natural settings—Qualitative studies emphasize the understanding of behavior as it occurs naturally, without artificial constraints or controls.

Rich narrative description—Data are collected as words and/or pictures rather than as numbers. Rich or "thick" descriptions are made to enhance understanding.

Direct data collection—Qualitative researchers collect data directly from persons or documents. They establish close, trusting, and empathetic relationships with the individuals being studied.

Concern with process—An important goal of qualitative studies is to understand how and why behavior occurs, rather than to predict and control behavior.

Inductive data analysis—No deductive hypotheses are used in qualitative research. Data are gathered first and synthesized inductively for understanding. Conclusions are grounded from the bottom up.

Participant perspectives—Qualitative researchers take a phenomenological approach. They are interested in the sense people make of their lives, how people interpret experiences, define terms, and conceptualize their lives. The point of view of the individuals studied is critical to this understanding.

Emergent research design—The research procedures are flexible and evolving and change during the study.

As the previous characteristics indicate, a good qualitative study is a lot more than just collecting data about a topic through interviews or focus groups. A study of parental attitudes toward school choice, for example, which relies on data collected through telephone interviews, would not be a qualitative study unless the researchers spent considerable time with the parents or schools in question, collected a lot of other data, and reported their findings as in-depth narratives.

There are three major types of qualitative studies, as summarized in Chapter 1, though you may not find these specific terms when reading research articles. This is because different discipline traditions have contributed to our understanding about qualitative designs or methods (e.g., sociology, anthropology, and philosophy), and each discipline has used unique language. It is not unusual to see terms such as *field study, ethnography, ecological,* and *ethnomethodological* used interchangeably.

We have restricted the term *qualitative* in this text to those methods that involve some kind of data collection directly from people, either through observation or interviews. These can be thought of as interactive qualitative methods. Many qualitative studies include a noninteractive component, such as review of documents or pictures, along with interactive data collection.

An **ethnographic** study, or **ethnography,** is an in-depth description and interpretation of naturally occurring behavior within a culture or social group. It involves long and intense involvement in the culture to provide rich descriptions that lead to insights and a more complete understanding. Three modes of data collection are emphasized—interview, observation, and document review. The researcher engages in extensive involvement in the culture itself to study behavior as it occurs naturally.

The purpose of a **grounded theory** study is to discover or generate a theory, an abstract schema, or a set of propositions that pertains to a specific experience, situation, or setting. The theory is developed from, or "grounded in," the data collected from the field. The primary method of collecting data is the individual interview, which typically is open-ended, searching, and extensive. The theory is developed through a process of *constant comparison,* in which emerging ideas and themes are continually "tested" with new data. The context in which the entity has occurred is essential to the development of the theory.

As we noted in Chapter 1, **phenomenology** is the philosophical basis for all qualitative research, holding that subjective experience, rather than objective observation, is the key to deep understanding. The underlying assumption is that there are multiple ways of experiencing and interpreting the same event or situation, and that the meaning of the phenomena to each person is what constitutes reality. While a phenomenological perspective underlies all qualitative inquiry, phenomenology is also a branch of qualitative research. Purely phenomenological studies describe and interpret the experience of people in order to understand the essence of the experience as perceived by those studied. Thus, **participant perspectives** are the focus of the research. Individuals who become participants are selected on the basis of their experience with the phenomena being studied, and on their willingness to be interviewed and observed. Typically, a series of extensive, in-depth, unstructured interviews with the participants provides the data for the research. In summarizing phenomenological studies, the researchers are careful to suspend their way of describing and use the participant's language, terms, and phrases to illustrate shared meanings and consciousness.

RESEARCH PROBLEM

Qualitative researchers begin with what is called a **foreshadowed problem**. A foreshadowed problem is a general statement or question that communicates the broad purpose of the study. It provides a framework and a focus for beginning the study and is refined during the study. By stating such general problems, rather than a specific research question or hypothesis, the researcher stays open to all possible interpretations and meanings.

METHODOLOGY

Qualitative researchers use several **purposeful sampling** techniques to select participants (not subjects), documents, or settings. Purposeful sampling is done to select individuals, sites, or documents that will be most informative.

In interactive qualitative studies the mainstays of data collection are interviewing and observation. Interviews may be very open ended, with few predetermined questions, or the interview may have a more structured format, such as a focus group.

Observations vary in the extent to which the researcher is involved in the natural events of the setting. At one extreme is the **complete observer,** who remains detached from the participants. At the other extreme is the **full participant,** who is an actual participant, along with others, in the setting. A complete observer would view the events in a classroom from the back of the class, whereas a full participant would be a student or teacher. Most qualitative studies use observers between these two extremes (sometimes called a participant observer).

Observers write extensive, highly detailed **field notes** to record their observations. These field notes are analyzed by constructing codes that can be used to categorize the observations. The notes are coded and reorganized to illustrate important patterns or relationships that lead to generalizations and conclusions. Taped interviews are transcribed and analyzed in a similar fashion.

Like quantitative researchers, qualitative researchers consider the internal and external validity of a study, but the meaning of these terms is somewhat different for judging qualitative studies.

Typically, qualitative research is strong in internal validity and weak in external validity. This is because the primary purpose of the research is to obtain an understanding of the phenomenon under study rather than generalize the findings to a broader population, and because the methodology, which is labor and time intensive, uses a limited number of persons, situations, or events.

The internal validity of qualitative research typically revolves around the issue of credibility. **Credibility** is the extent to which the data, data analysis, and results are accurate and trustworthy. Threats especially troublesome to the credibility of a qualitative study are instrumentation and researcher bias.

Recall that the principal characteristics of a good data collection tool in quantitative studies are reliability and validity. **Reliability** in a qualitative study is the extent to which what is recorded is what actually occurred in the setting. Two qualitative researchers working in the same setting might well come up with different data, as they may have observed different things; the question is whether the data are accurate. Reliability is enhanced by using detailed field notes, audio and video recording, and teams of researchers; searching for negative cases or discrepant data; and having interview and observation notes reviewed by participants for accuracy. **Validity** is strong in these studies if there is a good fit between the intent of the research (foreshadowed questions) and what was actually studied. Validity is enhanced by establishing rapport with interviewees, unobtrusive observation (so that the participant is unaware of being observed), appropriate selection of participants, repeated patterns illustrated by the data, and sufficient detail in the data and depth of the analysis.

One of the most common techniques used to enhance credibility is triangulation. **Triangulation** refers to the use of different data sources, time periods, and data collection methods that result in similar findings. In other words, if the results of several different approaches to gathering data are similar, there is triangulation of the data. For example, if what is found in interviews coincides with what is observed and what is found in documents, then these three data sources triangulate. A second important way to increase credibility is **member checking,** submitting notes to informants to ensure that their perspectives have been recorded accurately. A third common technique (actually, set of techniques) is **cross-examination** of the evidence, wherein a researcher submits preliminary findings to a disinterested third party, who analyzes the logic behind any inferences drawn, much like an attorney who is cross-examining a witness in court.

External validity takes on a completely different meaning in qualitative research. Since there is no intent in this kind of research to generalize from a sample to a larger population, but rather to understand the phenomenon itself, external validity is usually discussed using such terms as *translatability* or *comparability.* The key issue is the extent to which the results provide insights useful in other comparable settings. The heart of the external validity question for a qualitative study is what the study can teach us—about our students, our organizations, or our lives. The best studies, therefore, are complete enough and rich enough that readers are able to engage in what can be called a vicarious experience. They identify sufficiently with the case that they are able to discern what might be most applicable to their own settings.

REPORTING OF RESULTS

As one would expect, qualitative studies are long on text and narrative and short on numbers and statistics. The most common, but by no means exclusive, way to report the results of qualitative inquiry is through a **case study**. Case studies are, in essence, stories about the phenomenon under study. They clearly define the boundaries of the subject and its contents. For example, in education the subject of a case study could be a classroom, school, the central office, or the school board. The key to a successful case study is the degree to which it is able to provide the reader with a vicarious experience, that is, a strong sense of being there. There are several types of case studies:

Historical/organizational—The focus is on a specific organization over time.

Observational—The researcher becomes a member of the group being studied to observe the realities from the inside out.

Life history—A first-person narrative is completed with a single person (also called an *oral history*).

Situation analysis—A specific event is studied from different perspectives.

Multi-case—Several different independent entities are studied.

Multi-site—Many sites or locations are used.

While a case study is the most common means of reporting the results of qualitative inquiry, other formats exist as well. In grounded theory, especially, while there may be extensive description and documentation of the study context, its purpose is not to tell a story but to generate theory. Thus, the results section of a grounded theory study is likely to be in the form of themes and constructs rather than extended narrative. This may be true of a strictly phenomenological study as well.

Criteria for Evaluating Qualitative Research

1. What is the foreshadowed problem and how clearly is it stated? Is it reformulated later on, after some initial data have been collected?

2. Is the conceptual and theoretical framework for the study clear? How well does the literature review argue for the importance of the current research?

3. What are the biases and preconceived ideas of the researcher? How are these dealt with in the study? Is the researcher well prepared to complete the study?

4. Is the method of selecting participants clear and appropriate to the foreshadowed problem? How well are the participants and sites described?

5. How involved was the researcher in the setting being observed? Could this involvement have affected the behavior of the participants?

6. If appropriate, were multiple methods of data collection used? What was the duration and intensity of data collection?

7. Are issues of credibility directly addressed by the researchers? How, and how effectively?

8. Are the findings presented clearly? Are the data sufficiently detailed to allow a rich description? Are results accompanied by illustrative quotes and specific instances?

9. Do conclusions and interpretations follow logically from the results presented?

10. Is sufficient detail provided to discern which parts of the study might be applicable to other settings? To which contexts is the study transferable?

Building Bridges to Student Engagement: Communicating Respect and Care for Students in Urban High Schools

Donetta J. Cothran
Indiana University

Catherine D. Ennis
University of Maryland

Student engagement is a prerequisite for student learning and retention. Unfortunately, the number of disengaged students may exceed two-thirds of the high school population. Although there are many reform efforts to increase engagement, participants' perspectives on the topic are often ignored. The purpose of this study was to investigate teachers' and students' perspectives on engagement. Four teachers and 51 students from three urban high schools were observed and interviewed. The data were analyzed via constant comparison. Teachers' discussions focused on barriers that they perceived restrained their ability to engage students. Although students also noted barriers, they reported that their own engagement levels were flexible and responsive to teachers' actions. From the students' perspectives, engaging teachers communicated, cared, and enthusiastically presented active learning opportunities.

Educational engagement is a prerequisite for academic success (Montgomery & Rossi, 1994). Even a quality curriculum guided by a knowledgeable teacher will not result in student learning unless students first are engaged in the learning process. Unfortunately, the number of disengaged students may exceed two-thirds of the student population in high schools (Sedlak, Wheeler, Pullin, & Cusick, 1986). Some of these students may be at risk for dropping out of school and most are at risk for minimal involvement and therefore minimal learning in school.

Engagement is defined as the willingness of students to make the "psychological investment required to comprehend and master knowledge and skills" (Wehlage, Rutter, Smith, Lesko, & Fernandez, 1989, p. 177). The importance of student engagement in learning is a common theme in the educational literature and is related, at least in part, to the current popularity of constructivist learning theories. For sociocultural theorists, student involvement in culturally organized activity is central to the educational process, while more individually focused constructivists focus on the sensory-motor and conceptual activity of the student (Cobb, 1994). From both theoretical perspectives, however, the student's active engagement is a key concept in the learning process.

In addition to its importance to learning, educational engagement is also a key component in student retention. Finn's (1989) review of the literature related to student withdrawal and disengagement from schools described two primary models posited to explain this phenomenon. The frustration self-esteem model was developed primarily from work with juvenile delinquents. The model's components involve student difficulty in attaining success in school and the resulting negative self-view that contributes to the student's rejection of and disengagement from achievement settings, such as school. In contrast, the participant-identification theory model stresses student engagement and sense of belonging in the school as key components to student success. As with the constructivist learning theories, these two models differ in focus, yet, both models place emphasis on the interaction of student engagement and retention.

Despite the widespread agreement on the value of student engagement in learning and retention, programs to promote student engagement often are based on good ideas and intentions, rather than on proven theory (Finn, 1989). We actually know very little about what students think about schooling and engagement. In particular, the perspective of urban and minority students has been largely ignored. As Stinson (1993) noted, "Educators blame students for their lack of engagement but have appeared to have little interest in understanding how students perceive school and how they assign (or fail to assign) meaning and value to their experiences there" (p. 216). Understanding the student perspective is important if educators are to conceptualize reform efforts that students will find meaningful, thereby increasing the likelihood of their engagement.

The purpose of this study was to investigate and compare teachers' and students' perspectives on educational engagement. Specifically, how does each group perceive current levels of student engagement? Additionally, how do teachers and students perceive their current context and its influence on student engagement? This investigation was part of a larger study to examine participants' perspectives in urban secondary schools.

This study is significant because the results provide insights into minority, urban students' perspectives on education. The information can be used by teachers to design more engaging classes that, in turn, may lead to increased student learning. Examining the specific barriers to engagement reported by participants may provide guidance for school reform efforts. Additionally, identifying similarities and differences in teachers' and students' perspectives can contribute to our knowledge of student-teacher relationships and interactions.

STUDENT ENGAGEMENT

Researchers have proposed several theories to explain the important role of engagement in learning and school retention (e.g., Finn, 1989; Wehlage et al., 1989). The theories place varying importance on the influence of personal and school factors that enhance or constrain engagement. Perhaps the most comprehensive theory proposed thus far is that by Wehlage et al. (1989). Within this framework (described in Figure 1), engagement is not an isolated construct but rather is connected to additional concepts that mediate the extent to which a student is actively involved in the educational process. The left side of the model describes personal characteristics of the student. The list of possible influences is long, and may include the characteristics, influence, and importance of the student's family, peers, jobs,

and home community. For example, previous research has suggested that disengagement is related to personal characteristics such as the education level of parents (Ekstrom, Goertz, Pollack, & Rock, 1986), peer group norms (Eckert, 1989), and socioeconomic status (Wehlage & Rutter, 1986).

In addition to these extraneous to school influences, there are school factors that may impact the student's willingness and ability to engage. The center section of the model describes learning and membership impediments within the school structure that can stand between the student and engagement. Learning impediments involve a lack of extrinsic and intrinsic rewards. Extrinsic rewards are related to the student's perceptions of the relationship between school and valued goals (e.g., college, jobs). Intrinsic rewards, such as student interest and competence, can be negatively impacted by educators' narrow conceptions of learning and obsession with coverage of the curriculum.

Impediments to membership influence student engagement because of the reciprocal relationship between engagement and school membership. In Wehlage et al.'s (1989) model, four characteristics of school may impact a student's sense of school membership: adjustment, difficulty, incongruence, and isolation. These four membership impediments were also described in Tinto's (1987) investigation of college students who left school.

Adjustment refers to the frequently cited problems some students face when transitioning from one type or level of school to another. For example, Eccles and Midgely (1990) documented the challenges many adolescents face during the transition

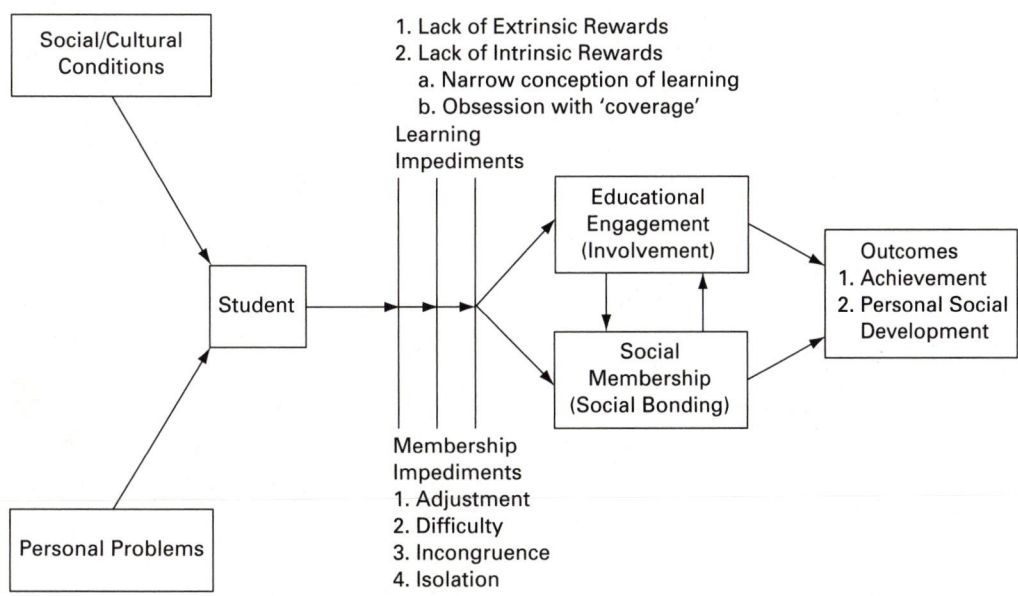

Figure 1.   Wehlage et al. (1989) model.

from elementary to junior high schools. The larger, less personal, and more formal nature of many junior high schools may not be a developmentally appropriate transition for adolescents. The second impediment to membership, the difficulty of the academic work, is often related to adjustment challenges. It is rare to find students who are academically unable to complete the work. It is common, however, for students who are most at risk for disengagement to need more time or intensive tutoring to complete the work, support that may not be available in many schools. The third impediment, incongruence, occurs when the student's perception of self and future does not involve the traditional goals and rewards of school. Cothran and Ennis (1999) described the lack of relevance and consequent disengagement many students find in their school experiences. The final membership impediment is isolation from meaningful interactions with adults or peers. For example, Schlosser (1992) found that personal connections between teachers and students were related to at-risk students' willingness to engage.

The personal and school characteristics interact to influence the student's sense of membership, engagement level, and ultimately the outcomes of the schooling process. As illustrated on the right side of the model, educational engagement and school membership are mutually influencing components that interactively determine the student's possible educational achievement as well as personal and social development.

From this perspective, changes in student engagement are only likely to result from large-scale and complex reform (school restructuring and social interventions). Wehlage et al. (1989) suggested that changing levels of student engagement is difficult and requires significant innovations in curriculum, instruction, and school structures. Although they provide evidence of successful changes in student engagement with at-risk students, most intervention examples are of alternative schools with relatively innovative curricula and unique school structures. Unfortunately, those reform options are not available to a vast majority of educators and students. We therefore must know more about how to alter engagement patterns in current school settings. This investigation explored teachers' and students' perspectives on engagement within the framework of traditional school structures and curricula.

METHODS

Participants and Setting

The participants in this study were four physical education teachers and their students at three urban high schools in the Highlands school district. (All names used in this paper are pseudonyms.) Madison and Longwood High both enrolled approximately 1500 students, while Georgetown High was smaller with just more than 950 students. The students at Madison High represented one of the more diverse schools in the district. The school's students were African American (67.2%), European American (29.6%), Hispanic (2.1%), and Asian (0.6%). The Longwood High student body was 92% African American, 4% European American, 2.6% Asian, and 1% Hispanic. Georgetown High's demographics were similar to Longwood High with 93% of the student body reporting African American heritage. The remainder of Georgetown's student body was 3.4% European American, 1.6% Hispanic, and 1.5% Asian. A majority of the students from all three schools were from lower to middle class socioeconomic backgrounds.

The Highlands district is a large urban school system on the East Coast that served more than 115,000 students. It was representative of the challenges facing many large, urban school systems. The district was under a court ordered desegregation plan to achieve racial balance. Yet declining nonminority enrollments resulted in African American students being bused many miles from home neighborhoods to attend schools that were already predominantly African American. Due to declining test scores, administrators and teachers faced pressure to increase student performance on standardized tests. School violence was an ever-present threat that required security funding from an already strained fiscal budget.

The four teachers in this study were European American and had from 18–29 years experience in the school district. Mr. Steel and Ms. Newman both taught at Madison High School. Ms. Rodman taught at Longwood High, and Ms. McKinney was employed at Georgetown High.

The 51 students who agreed to participate in this study were members of the 4 teachers' classes. Nineteen students, 10 boys and 9 girls, were from Longwood High. Fifteen Georgetown High students, 5 girls and 10 boys, participated as did 17 students, 7 boys and 10 girls, from Madison High. Students were selected to represent a range of demographic and class participation levels. The demographics of the 51 students were similar to the schools' combined demographics with 89% of the students reporting African American heritage and 11% non-African American.

DATA COLLECTION AND ANALYSIS

Data were collected via class observations and interviews. Each school was observed a minimum of 40 hours over the course of 15 weeks. The purpose of the observations was twofold. First, we wanted to select students with a wide range of student engagement levels for interviews and class observations helped in the identification of these students. Second, the observations provided us with actual records of student and teacher engagement rather than relying solely on self-reports. The focus of the observations was on teachers' selection and presentation of content, and interactions with students. Relatedly, the field notes included students' responses to the teacher's actions as well as student initiated activity. The field notes also included the content of informal conversations with class members, administrators, and other teachers. The class observations were hand recorded as field notes in a notebook during class. At the conclusion of the day the field notes were rewritten in a more detailed and complete manner.

A preliminary analysis of the field notes and a review of literature related to engagement provided a framework for developing the questions utilized in the general interview guide (Patton, 1990). The interview guide focused on students' descriptions of their own engagement, engaging classes, preferred class activities, and changes that students would like to make in their schools. Specific class examples of lessons that appeared to be successful and unsuccessful in engaging students were described by the investigator and participants reflected on those lessons. In addition, participants were asked to provide examples and nonexamples of instances when students and teachers worked well together in class. The teachers' interview guide focused on similar topics.

Interviews were conducted with students during two different semesters. The first group of 30 students was interviewed during the last week of the fall semester. The second group of 21 students was interviewed during the second month of the spring semester. Teachers were interviewed at the conclusion of the spring student interviews. Student interviews occurred during regularly scheduled class periods and teacher interviews were held during their planning periods. All interviews were audiotaped and later transcribed.

The constant comparison process outlined by LeCompte and Preissle (1993) served as the guide for data reduction and analysis. Initially each school's data was analyzed separately from the other schools. Common data categories were developed for each school via continuous and multiple reviews of the data. Tentative themes were then identified and compared to the original data. These themes were then retained for further examination or eliminated due to lack of significant data evidence. This cycle continued until major themes were developed for each school. The same cyclical process was then used to identify themes across school settings.

The methods undertaken to ensure the trustworthiness of the data included the use of a peer debriefer and a triangulation of data sources by interviewing two different groups of students at each school during different times of the school year and by interviewing students at different schools. Additionally, the data were carefully reviewed for negative cases that could serve to disprove an emerging theme or to provide alternative perspectives on key issues.

RESULTS AND DISCUSSION

Discussions with teachers and students supported Wehlage et al.'s (1989) suggestions that there are barriers to student engagement. Teachers' discussions focused on barriers that they perceived constrained their ability to engage students in the teaching-learning process. Although students also noted impediments to engagement, they reported that their own engagement levels were flexible and responsive to teachers' actions. From the students' perspectives, engaging teachers were those who communicated, cared, and enthusiastically presented active learning opportunities.

Barriers to Engagement

Student Attitude. All 4 teachers agreed that the single greatest impediment to student engagement was that students arrived in their classes with poor attitudes and low engagement. Ms. Newman described her students, "These kids don't want to do anything. They don't listen. They aren't responsible. They think they know everything so they don't want to learn." Similarly, one day after class Mr. Steel described a long list of activities and teaching strategies that he no longer used and concluded, "Students are different now. I don't know what to do with them."

Observations of and discussions with students supported the teachers' claims that many students entered classes with a low level of engagement. Many class members were slow to respond to teachers' requests and displayed minimal involvement in the planned class activities. Catrina described her general attitude toward school, "Why should I care about it? It's something I got to do, but it's like something that I probably don't like or need anyway." Terrance reported a similar disinterest in school, but commented that he would "do the minimum. I just do it to get the grade. You got to pass or end up in here again."

The teachers also believed that difficulties in student engagement were not isolated to physical education class. Mr. Steel suggested that in classes throughout the school a large percentage of students, "don't care at all. They're basically worthless in class. They're just here because they have to have a class. They think they're too cool to participate."

Although other classes were not formally observed, informal conversations with administrators and other subject matter area teachers supported the physical education teachers' reports of consistently low student engagement in a variety of classes. Mr. Stanton, one of the school's vice-principals, noted that, "The biggest problem, once you get them to class, is that most students don't want to be there. It's very tough to get them interested in most subjects."

Responsibility for Engagement. Perhaps related to the student attitude barrier was the issue of who should assume responsibility for student engagement. Students often began class with a low engagement level and waited for the teacher to provide some reason to engage. The teachers, however, did not believe they should, nor did they feel prepared to, fill the role of primary motivator and engager of students. Ms. Rodman suggested that to engage students, "Teachers have to be entertainers now to get the kids to pay attention." The teachers did not believe their role was to serve as the primary catalyst for student engagement. Rather, their role was to supply valuable information to receptive students.

The teachers' perceptions of the teacher-student roles were problematic, however, because students frequently failed to value the knowledge that teachers wanted to impart. Jarrod's response to a question about how school would help him after graduation was similar to many students' views, "I just don't see how this stuff is going to help me. I don't see these classes going with me from here." Rejection of the teachers' preferred subject matter can be difficult for teachers to accept (Ennis, 1996). Ms. Newman discussed the difference between her value for the subject matter and her students, "They just don't find much personally meaningful in there (the curriculum). I would have loved it, but they don't." When students fail to see connections between academic knowledge and their current and future lives, there is little reason to engage (Brantlinger, 1991; Erickson & Shultz, 1992).

Due to the low value that students frequently assigned to the subject matter, the teacher rather than the class content often became the reason for student engagement. The need for teachers to be the primary "energy source" in creating an educationally engaging environment, however, was an exhausting task. Ms. McKinney reported that she worked very hard to engage her Georgetown High students. She was, however, frustrated with the overwhelming needs of so many students, "Everyone seems so needy. At some point during the class I'm having to give individual encouragement and attention to every student. I'm exhausted by the end of the day from trying to motivate everyone."

School Violence. An additional constraint that interfered with the teachers' ability and willingness to engage students was the threat of school violence. Teachers were increasingly wary of becoming involved and intervening in students' lives and conduct. Ms. Rodman described her sixth-period class, "This is our worst class. We've got some hoodlums. There are three kids we don't even say anything to they're so dangerous." The threat of serious violence likely was small, but very real. Within the past 5 years, a teacher at another school in the Highlands district was shot by a student. Ms. McKinney discussed how the increasing threat of violence had changed how she interacted with students:

> If things break out, I'm in my office. In the old days I was there breaking up the fight. But now with guns, knives, and razor blades, I just don't get in it anymore the way I used to do. I have trouble accepting this new role. I think I should do whatever I need to do in my school without thinking about that stuff. The peer mediator counselor told me that my responsibility was to my family first to stay safe and then I am responsible for my students. I struggle with that.

At a time when students were perhaps most in need of personal involvement with their teachers, the teachers perceived barriers that created distance between themselves and their students. That distance, disagreement over the responsibility for engagement, and students' initially low engagement levels combined to create a largely negative teacher perception of student engagement and the teachers' ability to alter it.

Bridges to Engagement

Students also perceived impediments to educational engagement. In contrast to their teachers' perceptions, however, students reported that their engagement level was variable and the key factor in their engagement was the teacher. Consistent with Nicholls' (1992) conceptualization of students as educational theorists, these students offered clear and consistent reports of educational contexts that impeded or contributed to their engagement in class. From the students' perspectives, engaging teachers were those who communicated, cared, and enthusiastically presented active learning opportunities.

Communication. A key factor in the students' willingness to engage in class was their perception of the teacher's willingness to communicate with them. Although communication would seem to be a daily part of classroom interaction, students' perceptions of their classes were that a majority of their teachers did not talk with or listen to them. Sharonda summarized the effect when students did not believe there were open lines of communication, "Teachers never talk to students and then they be wondering why we don't work with them."

For students, communication involved talking with students about topics other than the subject matter. Robert's advice to a new teacher was, "You gotta get to know your kids. Conversate [sic] with them. Bond with them. Talk with them before class. Students like that." Michelle suggested that when teachers talk to students, "You'll [the teacher] know what they're thinking and then you'll do better at getting to know them. Then they'll open up to you and do what you want." Student comments suggest that the establishment of a personal dialogue can be a prerequisite to the development of an educational dialogue.

In addition to talking with students, engaging teachers listened to students and respected their ideas. When asked what advice she would like to give to her teachers, Alicia replied:

> I'd tell them [teachers] to listen to us. Just because we're teenagers doesn't mean we don't know things. We don't know everything, but we know things. We know what we want to do and how we want to do it, but they want us to do it their way. We might have an easier or a different way to do it but the teachers might not have thought of it. They think we're disrespectful because we're not listening to what they have to say, but teachers don't listen to what we have to say at all.

As Alicia noted, respect was a critical aspect of the teacher-student relationship. Rather than respect being an automatic right to which the teacher was entitled, a majority of students believed that teachers had to earn their respect. A teacher could earn respect by demonstrating respect to students first. Then in return, the teacher would receive respect from students. DeJuan described the relationship:

> You [the teacher] have to respect the students first. When somebody is talking then you don't interrupt. You don't yell at them. If you get an attitude, they'll get an attitude back. You give me respect and I'll respect you. You don't respect me and I won't respect you.

The idea that the teacher should initiate respect in the student-teacher relationship may be in contrast to many teachers' conceptions of respect in the student-teacher relationship. Delpit (1988) suggested that differing views of authority can contribute to teacher-student conflict over appropriate behavior. For teachers who often come from the dominant European-American culture, authority comes with the role that a person fills. Accordingly, these teachers expect students to respect them automatically due to the position they hold. As described by Delpit and supported by DeJuan's comment, however, students from many minority cultures may believe that authority is earned and not automatically given. Although these students are willing to respect the authority of those individuals who earn their respect, teachers from the dominant culture may not recognize this difference and continue to operate under the automatic moral authority rules of their culture.

Another aspect of communication mentioned by students was involvement in class decision making. Students did not believe that most of their teachers encouraged or allowed student involvement in class decisions and this lack of involvement contributed to their lack of engagement in those classes. Randy described Mr. Kitts, his English teacher, as the worst teacher at Georgetown High because, "He don't ask us what we want, like what we want to do or how we want to do it. I guess he figures it's his class and we just got to like it." Although a few students reported they should get to do whatever they wanted to in class, most students recognized the teacher's need to cover certain content and to evaluate students. While they recognized the teacher's constraints and responsibilities, students wanted to be involved in at least some of the class decisions. Joseph suggested that teachers sometimes should ask students for suggestions, "You'd be the teacher and you'd have the say-so, but to be a good teacher you need to know what they [students] think and want to do."

Consistent with Wehlage et al.'s (1989) model, isolation was an impediment to student engagement. When students felt isolated from teachers and the decision-making process, they were less likely to engage. Nevertheless, when teachers communicated with students and included them in the class decision-making process, student engagement was more likely. For example, Tonya described Ms. McKinney, her physical education teacher, "She's cool and kids respect her." When asked why students thought Ms. McKinney was "cool," Tonya replied, "Well, we know when we come into her class we're going to have to do something. She's cool because she gives us alternatives, like we sometimes decide how to do it or talk about it and stuff." By allowing and encouraging student involvement, and respecting their ability to make decisions, Ms. McKinney was rewarded with students who respected her and engaged in her class.

Care. In addition to communication, students reported that they were more willing to engage when they felt the teacher cared if they learned the subject matter and cared about them as a person. From the students' perspectives, teachers demonstrated caring in two ways: (a) a willingness to work with students, and (b) a concern for students' personal life and welfare.

Educators often assume that students care about the subject matter, or at least care about their grade, and therefore will engage in class. Many of these students, however, had little value for the subject matter content of their classes and their grades. There was little perceived congruence between their world outside of school and their courses. Consequently, they were unwilling to engage in a class for which they saw little value or meaning. When students perceived however, that the teacher cared if they learned, they were much more willing to engage despite the incongruence. Denise suggested that, "If you see a teacher cares if you learn, then you'll learn." Students reported, however, that many teachers did not care if they learned. Malcolm said that most "teachers in this school just don't care. They come to get paid. If you learn it or if you don't, it don't matter to them." Students recognized that they were responsible for doing the work, but Ann expressed a common belief that teachers made the difference, "The teacher's got to care about if they [students] learn it. I mean it's the child's responsibility for their grade, but you [the teacher] should help them too."

Students also described caring teachers as those who were willing to work with them until they mastered the content. Rob suggested his math teacher, Mr. Hill, was the best teacher at Longwood High because, "He comes around and he helps you. You don't have to just figure it out by yourself. He enjoys working with children. You know he's going to work with you until you learn it." Students, however, did not believe most teachers cared or were willing to work with them. When asked what she would change about school, Angela replied:

> More teachers need to help. They always tell you when you're a little kid that you can go to your teacher, but I mean, when you get to high school, you gotta ask what happened to that theory? What happened to teachers who are supposed to be there to help you and work with you?

Caring teachers were not easy teachers. They did, however, create environments where students felt they could be successful. For example, several students at Madison High nominated their math teacher as a very engaging teacher. Raymond described why, "Students will deny it, but they like challenging things. I had this one teacher, Mr. Carson, and everybody said he was the hardest teacher in the school. He was, but everyone ran to be in his class. He made you work really hard but he made sure you could do it." Caring teachers appeared to provide a safe, supportive environment in which the students did not feel alone when faced with challenging assignments.

In addition to working with students in class, students also reported that their most engaging teachers knew them and cared about what they did outside of class. Marla reported that, "Good teachers get involved with their students. They maybe come to social activities or sports and when they cheer you on it's really cool." Teachers also demonstrated caring by showing concern for students outside of school and extramural activities. Two students nominated Ms. Woodside, a government teacher at Georgetown High, as their best teacher. Carlos said that she always knew what students were doing and she would tell them not to do something if she thought it was dangerous:

> She'll take you off to the side and say, "I don't want you doing that, cause I'll worry about you." Like if we go out on weekends and whatever and if she doesn't see us on Monday she worries cause she doesn't know where we are. When we come back to school she'll ask where we were.

Kelly agreed that Ms. Woodside was the best because she cared about and trusted students, "Like if you put your head down on your desk she'll think you're sick and she'll ask you if you're okay or if you need something. She checks on us and she trusts us." In return for the personal attention and care Ms. Woodside gave her students, students respected her and reported engaging in her class.

The students' desire for communication and caring may have reflected a need for a personal relationship between teachers and students. As the importance of other social institutions have declined, the school may be the only student opportunity to have sustained, quality relationships with adults. Students wanted connections with their teachers. Yet, as Wehlage et al. (1989) noted, "Many teachers in comprehensive high schools believe it is important to create social distance between themselves and their students as a means of maintaining discipline and helping students to become independent, responsible, and mature" (p. 122). Instead of increased discipline and independent learners, however, isolation between teachers and students more often led to disengaged students.

Consistent with the students' reports of teacher caring to be a key factor in their engagement, a number of educators also promote a focus on caring in schools. Noddings (1984) called for the entire school curriculum to be built around the ethic of care. Within this framework, the key concept is the presence and continued development of a committed, caring, reciprocal relationship between the teacher and student. Through that caring relationship, the teacher develops a commitment to understanding the student's experiences and assumes personal responsibility for the student's learning and total school experience.

Enthusiastic, Active Learning. In addition to communication and caring, students also described certain class activities as enhancing their engagement, regardless of the subject matter. First, engaging teachers did not talk too much. Students preferred teachers who introduced a topic or assignment and then allowed the students to be involved actively in a learning task. Juanita described her history teacher at Madison High as a bad teacher, "All we do is just sit there and he talks to us. He wants us to learn what he's talking about, but I don't learn that well if he's just sitting there talking a hole in my head."

Instead of a teacher-centered, passive learning environment, students preferred an active learning context. Chris agreed that most teachers, "just talk on-and-on" and suggested that instead of talking so much, teachers "should tell us and then let us work on it and move around and help instead of keeping on talking. You be like, are we high school kids or what? Just let us do it."

Students also reported a desire to work together with other students, yet even their most engaging teachers rarely provided opportunities to do so. Kevin said that in all of his classes, "You just do one-on-one. It's you and the teacher and you're doing your work. You just sit there and you do your work." When asked why it was important to do group work he replied, "You need to learn how to deal with people with different attitudes. You can learn to adjust and deal with different things."

The one exception to this trend was physical education where students reported frequent opportunities to work with other students. As a result, some students described physical education as their favorite class. Ann reported physical education was best because, "You have to listen to the teacher, but you don't have to sit in the same spot and just stay there until the bell rings. You can move around and work with other people and stuff." Students reported that cooperative, group activities helped to engage them, possibly by alleviating isolation and lessening the risk of academic failure.

Finally, engaging classes were characterized by teachers who were enthusiastic about their subject matter. Roxanne reported that, "When the teacher gets into it, then we get into it." For many students, there was little intrinsic interest in and value for academic content, but if the teacher supplied the initial enthusiasm for the class, students reported "catching" the teacher's enthusiasm. Antoinette claimed, however, that none of her teachers "show any emotion or have fun with it." Terrance reported that most teachers were not enthusiastic, but that he did have one teacher who "is really into what she's doing. You

[the teacher] have to be into what you're doing. You can't be like this, 'Well, class we're going to do this, blah, blah, blah.' " He further explained that in this teacher's class he was more likely to stay awake, listen, and complete assignments.

TEACHERS AS BRIDGES TO ENGAGEMENT

In the educational interventions described by Wehlage et al. (1989), teachers were able to successfully engage students when school restructuring removed or lessened the engagement impediments. School and curricular reform are promising avenues for engaging students; however, it is unlikely that many students or teachers will experience significant reform efforts in their current settings. The students in this study describe a potential, alternate route to overcoming impediments to engagement. A few teachers in these schools were able to create an engaging environment for their students. They were able to do so not by removing the impediments to engagement, but rather by using their interpersonal skills to build a bridge over the learning and membership impediments that can keep students from educational engagement. Figure 2 illustrates the teachers' "tools" that helped them to build the bridge: communicating, caring, and presenting content with enthusiasm and active learning opportunities.

It is encouraging that alternatives are available to promote student engagement; however, students reported that while a few teachers were able to create engaging contexts, a majority of their teachers failed to do so. What kept the majority of teachers from building bridges to engagement for their students? It is likely the teachers perceived the same substantial impediments that these four teachers reported. It is also possible that the teachers did not recognize the need for the bridge or may not have had the skills to be bridge builders.

Providing a bridge for student engagement is a new role and responsibility for many teachers. Although teachers have always played an important role in student engagement, economic and social changes may have increased the teachers' importance in today's schools. Students always have faced engagement impediments, but students had the economic motivation to "push onward" through those impediments to achieve the economic success that was likely with completion of high school. Now, however, the opportunity for economic success is small for many urban students. For example, over half of all young adult black males are unemployed and those that do have jobs frequently hold lower-skilled entry level jobs (Wilson, 1987). Kantor and Brenzel (1992) detail the social and economic changes in urban areas

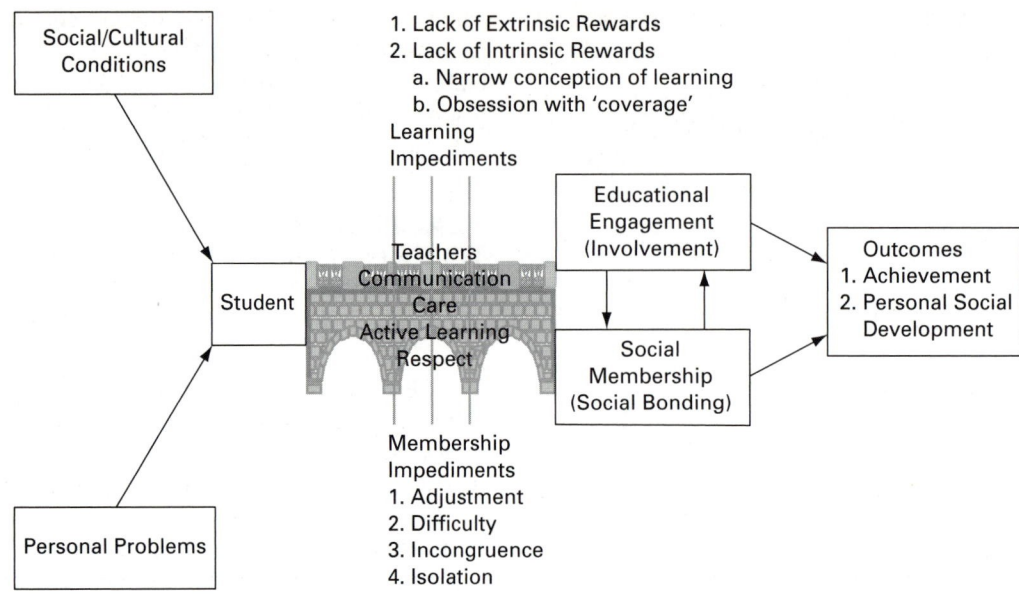

Figure 2.   Teachers as bridge builders.

that have created what they describe as the "contemporary crisis" facing urban youth and schools.

Additionally, the increasingly multi-cultural nature of today's schools may mean that more students disengage from school due to the incongruence between their home culture and the culture of school. Students may feel that their language (Nieto, 1994) is not valued, their culture and problems not discussed (Cummins, 1989), and that school information is unrelated to their lives outside of school (Sleeter & Grant, 1991). Farrell, Peguero, Lindsey, and White (1988) detail the external social pressures students also face that negatively impact school engagement. This lack of external support for engagement is further complicated in urban schools by the isolation (Weiner, 1993), limited funding (Fine, 1991), and diminished family and social networks (Nightingale & Wolverton, 1993) of urban school systems.

As a result of these external changes, schools are forced to rely more on internal resources within the school's control to engage students. Two critical, internal resources to promote student engagement are the curriculum and teachers. Ideally, the two work together to enhance student engagement. Although curricula can promote student engagement, the disjointed, frequently irrelevant, secondary school curriculum (e.g., Cusick, 1983; Nieto, 1994) has contributed more often to the problem of student disengagement, rather than to enhancing engagement. When students find little knowledge of worth in the curriculum, there is little reason to engage. If schools continue to operate with current curricular approaches, it appears that teachers must assume an even larger, more demanding role and become the primary resource to engage students.

Even if teachers acknowledge and accept the role of primary bridge builders, they may not have the skills nor be given the time to create bridges. Weiner persuasively argues that even teachers who are "talented, fresh, and idealistic, cannot sustain the effort" (1993, p. 77) to serve their students under the restrictive structural and systematic conditions in many urban school systems. The limited resources, mandated curriculum, and isolated nature of the school systems create conditions that subvert the teachers' ability to meet their students' needs (Weiner, 1993). Significant school reforms are likely necessary for more teachers to feel as if they can make a difference in their students' lives.

In addition to public school reforms, teacher education programs may need revision. The interpersonal and communication skills described by the students are not common components of teacher education programs. Teacher education and professional development programs more often focus on subject matter content knowledge. For example, many of the current school reform efforts are based on the assumption that public school education problems are based on teachers' inadequate professional preparation (Wade & Baker, 1995). Yet these students reported that teachers' knowledge was less important than their personal skills. Although subject matter expertise is no doubt important in the learning process, interpersonal skills may be critical to the initial phase of learning, student engagement. Teachers need to learn communication and caring skills that allow them to build a personal relationship with students for their professional expertise and the curriculum to be effective.

These results suggest that both teachers and students faced impediments that kept them from making the psychological investment necessary for engagement in the teaching-learning process. Students perceived few connections between school and life outside of school, and therefore engaged only when a personal connection was made with a teacher. Teachers, however, faced many challenges in creating environments where that personal connection was possible. It appears that reform at the curricular, school, and teacher preparation levels may be necessary in order to create widespread engaging environments in schools. Only when students and teachers are freed from the impediments that keep them from engagement are they able to engage meaningfully with one another and the subject matter content.

REFERENCES

Brantlinger, E. (1991). Low income adolescents' perceptions of social class related peer affiliations in school. *Interchange, 22,* 9-27.

Cobb, P. (1994). Where is the mind? Constructivist and sociocultural perspectives on mathematical development. *Educational Researcher, 23,* 13-20.

Cothran, D. J., & Ennis, C. D. (1999). Alone in a crowd: Meeting students' needs for relevance and connection in urban high school physical education. *Journal of Teaching in Physical Education, 18,* 234-247.

Cummins, N. L. (1989). Language and affect: Bilingual students at home and at school. *Language Arts, 66,* 29-43.

Cusick, P. A. (1983). *The egalitarian ideal and the American high school.* New York, NY: Longman.

Delpit, L. D. (1988). The silenced dialogue: Power and pedagogy in educating other peoples' children. *Harvard Educational Review, 58,* 280-298.

Eccles, J. S., & Midgley, C. (1990). Changes in academic motivation and self-perception during early adolescence. In R. Montemayor, G.R. Adams, & T.P. Gullotta (Eds.) *From childhood to adolescence* (pp. 134-155). Newbury Park, CA: Sage Publications.

Eckert, P. (1989). *Jocks & burnouts: Social categories and identity in the high school.* New York: Teachers College Press.

Ekstrom, R. B., Goertz, M. E., Pollack, J. M., & Rock, D.A. (1986). Who drops out of high school and why? Findings from a national study. *Teachers College Record, 87,* 356-373.

Ennis, C. D. (1996). When avoiding confrontation leads to avoiding content: Disruptive students' impact on curriculum. *Journal of Curriculum and Supervision, 11,* 145-162.

Erickson, F., & Shultz, J. (1992). Students' experience of the curriculum. In P. W. Jackson (Ed.), *Handbook of research on curriculum* (pp. 465-485). New York: Macmillan.

Farrell, E., Peguero G., Lindsey, R., & White, R. (1988). Giving voice to high school students: Pressure and boredom, ya know what I'm sayin'? *American Educational Research Journal, 25,* 489-502.

Fine, M. (1991). *Framing dropouts.* Albany, NY: State University of New York Press.

Finn, J. D. (1989). Withdrawing from school. *Review of Educational Research, 59,* 117-142.

Kantor, H., & Brenzel, B. (1992). Urban education and the "truly disadvantaged": The historical roots of the contemporary crisis. *Teachers College Record, 94,* 278-314.

LeCompte, M. D., & Preissle, J. (1993). *Ethnography and qualitative design in educational research* (2d ed). San Diego: Academic Press.

Montgomery, A., & Rossi, R. (1994). *Educational reforms and students at risk.* Washington, DC: Department of Education, Office of Educational Research and Improvement.

Nicholls, J. G. (1992). Students as educational theorists. In D. Schunk & J. Meece (Eds.) *Students' perceptions in the classroom* (pp. 267-286). Hillsdale, NJ: Erlbaum.

Nieto, S. (1994). Lessons from students on creating a chance to dream. *Harvard Educational Review, 64,* 392-426.

Nightingale, E.O., & Wolverton, L. (1993). Adolescent rolelessness in modern society. *Teachers College Record, 94,* 472-486.

Noddings, N. (1984). *Caring: A feminine approach to ethics and moral education.* Berkeley: University of California Press.

Patton, M.Q. (1990). *Qualitative evaluation and research methods* (2d ed.). Newbury Park, CA: Sage.

Schlosser, L. M. (1992). Teacher distance and student disengagement: School lives on the margin. *Journal of Teacher Education, 43,* 128-140.

Sedlak, M. W., Wheeler, C.W., Pullin, D.C., & Cusick, P. A. (1986). *Selling students short.* New York: Teachers College Press.

Sleeter, C. E., & Grant, C. A. (1991). Mapping terrains of power: Student cultural knowledge vs. classroom knowledge. In C. E. Sleeter (Ed.) *Empowerment through multicultural education* (pp. 49-67). Albany: State University of New York Press.

Stinson, S. W. (1993). Meaning and value: Reflections on what students say about school. *Journal of Curriculum and Supervision, 8,* 216-238.

Tinto, V. (1987). *Leaving college: Rethinking the causes and cures of student attrition.* Chicago: University of Chicago Press.

Wade, M. G., & Baker, J. A. (1995). *Introduction to kinesiology.* Dubuque: Brown and Bench mark.

Wehlage, G. G., & Rutter, R. A. (1986). Dropping out: How much do schools contribute to the problem? *Teachers College Record, 87,* 374-392.

Wehlage, G. G., Rutter, R. A., Smith, G. A., Lesko, N., & Fernandez, R. R. (1989). *Reducing the risk: Schools as communities of support.* New York: The Falmer Press.

Weiner, L. (1993). *Preparing teachers for urban schools.* New York: Teachers College Press.

Wilson, W. J. (1987). *The truly disadvantaged: The inner city, the underclass, and public policy.* Chicago: University of Chicago Press.

Evaluation Criteria	**Discussion Questions**
1. What is the foreshadowed problem and how clearly is it stated? Is it reformulated later on, after some initial data have been collected?	**1.** This study is part of a larger investigation of teacher and student perspectives of urban high schools. What influence, if any, would this have on the nature of the foreshadowed problem? Would it be helpful to know more about the larger study?
The foreshadowed problem in this grounded theory study is clearly stated in the fifth para-graph and repeated in the sentence just prior to the Methods Section. It is concerned with student and teacher perspectives about engagement, particularly beliefs about context and barriers. The problem is rather general, which is appropriate. Although not explicitly stated, the problem is somewhat reformulated as data are collected to focus more on what teachers can do and be like to encourage engagement.	
2. Is the conceptual and theoretical framework for the study clear? How well does the literature review argue for the importance of the current research?	**2.** Would you expect there to be more on teachers' "communicating respect and care" or "teachers as bridges" in this section of the article? If included, how might this bias the researchers?
The conceptual and theoretical framework is clearly stated in the Student Engagement section. This is essentially a review of literature and is fairly comprehensive for a qualitative study. It does help establish the importance of the study.	
3. What are the biases and preconceived ideas of the researcher? How are these dealt with in the study? Is the researcher well prepared to complete the study?	**3.** Where in this article would it be appropriate for the researchers to indicate their biases and preconceived ideas? How would such an addition possibly affect the interpretation and conclusions?
Potential biases and preconceived ideas are not explicitly stated. From the introduction and theoretical framework it can be concluded that the researchers feel strongly that engagement is critical and that high schools are not paying enough attention to this variable.	
4. Is the method of selecting participants clear and appropriate to the foreshadowed problem? How well are the participants and sites described?	**4.** How might the selection of the teachers and students have biased the results? Since students agreed to participate, how might this bias the results?
There is a good description of the sites (high schools), but it is not clear why physical education teachers were selected. The participants as a group are well described, but it would be helpful to know more about how students were selected to "represent a range of demographic and class participation levels," and, at the same time, represent "a wide range of student engagement levels."	

5. How involved was the researcher in the setting being observed? Could this involvement have affected the behavior of the participants?

The issue here is whether the researchers, by being in the classrooms, affected the students' and teachers' behavior. The longer the researchers' presence, the less effect they would have. Students are often less influenced than teachers by the presence of another adult in the class.

6. If appropriate, were multiple methods of data collection used? What was the duration and intensity of data collection?

Multiple methods were used (interviews and observations), and the number of hours time frame for the observations in each school are summarized. The duration and intensity are reasonable. It is not clear, however, how long the interviews lasted, and whether the student interviews were done individually or in groups.

7. Are issues of credibility directly addressed by the researchers? How, and how effectively?

While the term *credibility* was not used, several techniques were briefly summarized that enhance confidence in the methods and results. These include the constant comparison method, use of a peer debriefer (cross-examination), triangulation of data, and examination of data for negative cases.

8. Are the findings presented clearly? Are the data sufficiently detailed to allow a rich description? Are results accompanied by illustrative quotes and specific instances?

The results are clearly presented and well organized. Illustrative quotes and specific instances are used extensively. The results are appropriately integrated with engagement literature. The presentation of results is a strength of the study.

9. Do conclusions and interpretations follow logically from the results presented?

Yes, the conclusions and interpretations, in general, follow logically from the results. However, the implications about "a new role for teachers" and teacher preparation programs are not directly related to the results. The idea that teachers can serve as "bridges" is well supported and reasonable. A weakness is that few limitations are indicated.

5. What further information could the researchers provide to indicate their degree of involvement in the schools?

6. Two methods of data collection barely constitute multiple methods. Can you think of some additional methods of gathering data that could have been used to strengthen the study?

7. What further information about the methods used to enhance credibility would be helpful in making judgments about the overall quality of the research?

8. Could the findings have been organized in another way? Should results and discussion be presented together or separately?

9. What three or four main conclusions from this study would be appropriate? Is the last sentence of this article reasonable?

10. Is sufficient detail provided to discern which parts of the study might be applicable to other settings? To which contexts is the study transferable?

There is good detail to indicate translatability and comparability. Although the authors provide some data to show that the students are somewhat representative, this study can make no claims about generalizability either to other students or teachers. However, teachers reading the study will likely see similarities with their own situations and students.

10. What limitations to transferability could be indicated? Is it a problem that only physical education teachers were involved? Does this limit the findings to other physical education teachers?

Credibility Scorecard
Building Bridges to Student Engagement: Communicating Respect and Care for Students in Urban High Schools

	Excellent	Very Good	Adequate	Marginal	Poor
General purpose	5	4	3	2	1
Contribution/ significance	5	4	3	2	1
Review of literature	5	4	3	2	1
Research questions or hypotheses	5	4	3	2	1
Subjects or participants	5	4	3	2	1
Instrumentation	5	4	3	2	1
Procedures	5	4	3	2	1
Results	5	4	3	2	1
Practical significance	5	4	3	2	1
Graphics	5	4	3	2	1
Conclusions	5	4	3	2	1
Any fatal flaws?					

"A Fly in the Buttermilk": Descriptions of University Life by Successful Black Undergraduate Students at a Predominately White Southeastern University

Mitzi Davis   Yvonne Dias-Bowie   Katherine Greenberg   Gary Klukken
Howard R. Pollio   Sandra P. Thomas   Charles L. Thompson

> "And so a lot of times I felt out of place, because you see all white faces. You know I'm the only fly in the buttermilk, so that took some getting used to ..."

These words, shared by a Black student during an interview for the present study, poignantly reflect the essence of the experience of being a minority student on a predominately white university campus. The impetus for this study of that experience was our realization that the graduation rate for Black students was lower than the total rate for the university (four-year graduation rates are 19.6% versus 16.8%; five year rates are 36.1% versus 50.7). Available data provided no ready explanation for this discrepancy, although preliminary information from a research project concerning graduates of the university's nursing program indicated painful and alienating experiences among Black students (Thomas & Davis, 2000). These early results led to a decision to enlarge the research team and to broaden the study to include students in other undergraduate majors. The purpose of this study was to obtain the first-person perspective of the students themselves, a perspective missing from most of the literature about the academic experience of Black students.

REVIEW OF LITERATURE

Minority groups in the United States currently constitute 25% of the overall population, and it is projected that before the year 2015 one-third of the population will consist of individuals culturally and ethnically different from the white majority (American Council on Education, 1988; U.S. Census Bureau, 1993). This national pattern of cultural change is also reflected on college campuses where increasing numbers of minority students are enrolling and, far too often, dropping out. Predominantly white institutions of higher education, in fact, often devote intensive efforts to minority student recruitment but find that subsequent retention is a significant problem. In predominantly white institutions, 70% of Black students do not complete baccalaureate education compared to 20% of those from historically black institutions (National Center for Education Statistics, 1992; Steele, 1992). Throughout the 1990s the national college dropout rate for blacks was 20–25% higher than that for whites (Steele, 1999). This discrepancy is often explained by inferior academic preparation of Black students prior to college entry. Extant data, however, strongly suggest that academic concerns are not paramount in the high attrition of Black students (Echols, 1998) and certainly not the sole reason for their premature departure from campus (Steele, 1999). Given this possibility, attention must be given to nonacademic factors that influence attrition.

In a meta-analysis of 113 studies covering research on minority students from 1970 to 1997, a number of social, academic, family, and institutional factors were found to be linked to academic success (Echols, 1998). Over 1500 institutions and 46,000 minority students (Hispanic Americans and Native Americans as well as Black students) were represented in Echols' analysis. Supporting a theory proposed by Tinto (1975, 1987)—regarding the importance of social integration in promoting graduation—this analysis revealed that integrative experiences were a highly significant predictor variable. Negative or nonintegrative experiences (loneliness, alienation, and so forth) were positively correlated with voluntary withdrawal from college whereas positive or integrative experiences enhanced minority student persistence. Fostering educational attainment were factors such as an ability to be bicultural yet also maintain a cultural identity and to avoid becoming disheartened by racist events.

Several authors suggest that the predominately white university campus does not present a hospitable

The authors of this article are members of an interdisciplinary research team. Each of the team members contributed equally to the research and the writing of the article.

atmosphere for minority student learning. If educational offerings are Euro-centric, culturally different students may feel unappreciated or come to devalue their own cultural group (Sue, Bingham, Porche-Burke, & Vasquez, 1999). If faculty are operating on the basis of negative stereotypes in the classroom, whether consciously or not, minority students may become acutely uncomfortable, mistrustful, or demoralized. Dominant group members are known to have ambivalent attitudes toward minority groups (Fiske, Xu, Cuddy, & Glick, 1999) producing an increase in their positive or negative behaviors toward members of the minority group (Katz & Hass, 1988). Such inconsistent behaviors on the part of white faculty, at the very least, may be confusing to Black students. It is likely that Black students have negative or ambivalent attitudes toward whites based on race-related issues and personal experiences (Shelton, 2000). Thus, a number of factors may serve to complicate the establishment of good relationships between white university faculty and Black students.

Another significant aspect of campus climate with great relevance for the comfort level of African American students is the behavior of white students. Many Black students are not used to being in classes with the large numbers of white students they encounter on a predominantly white college campus. Many, in fact, are accustomed to attending schools where they comprised the majority: Despite national resolve to accomplish integration, more than 70% of Black students went to schools with more than 50% minority enrollment, and 36.5% of these students went to schools with a minority enrollment of 90–100% (Bjerklie, 2001).

All students, having absorbed years of indoctrination by families, peers, and mass media, come to the university with stereotypes about people different from themselves. As noted by Paul (1999), children already have definite stereotypes about other racial groups by the time they are five years of age, and Black children are aware early of the negative stereotypes that whites hold toward their racial group (Sigelman & Welch, 1991). Contemporary emphasis on "political correctness" also may serve as a confounding factor. For example, research by Judd, Park, Ryan, Brauer, and Kraus (1995) suggested that white college students are socialized to avoid stereotyping Blacks and thinking about racial differences whereas Black college students are socialized to emphasize racial group membership and to notice differences between themselves and whites. Commenting on these findings, Shelton (2000) observed that such socialization patterns are opposite to one another and may create conflict that could be exacerbated on a predominantly white college campus.

While the extant literature sheds light on several important aspects of the black college experience, conspicuously absent are the voices of Black students themselves. Most studies, with the exception of Steele's laboratory experiments, have used structured questionnaires to measure variables preselected by researchers. As Echols (1998) noted upon concluding her meta-analysis of 27 years of studies: "This field is ripe for phenomenological and other types of qualitative inquiry where intense, depthful exchange and evaluation of ideas can be achieved, adding texture and color to the portraits the numbers are helping us to paint" (p. 164). This reading of the research literature suggests that an optimum research strategy for enabling such voices to emerge must make the use of an open-ended interview procedure, a strategy implemented in the present study.

METHOD

Interview procedures have been found useful in enabling researchers to develop first-person descriptions of diverse human experiences (Polkinghorne, 1989; Kvale, 1996; Thomas & Pollio, 2002). Pollio, Henley, and Thompson (1997) have characterized the phenomenological interview as one in which a participant is enabled to describe his or her experiences of some phenomenon with as little direction from the interviewer as possible. Unconcerned with issues of causality or mechanism, phenomenological interviewing concerns the "what" of an experience and seeks to capture the specific meanings uniquely characterizing that experience. Once noted, these meanings are then named using either the language of the participant or the more conceptual language of the investigator's discipline.

After the initial question is asked, a phenomenological interview proceeds largely under the direction of the participant. Freedom is afforded the participant to locate frames of reference both for the interviewer and for him or herself. Because of its conversational tone, the researcher encourages dialogue to flow without a preformed agenda of items to be covered. Questions emerging within the flow of the dialogue are meant to provide clarity and understanding; additionally they may serve to promote more focused and intimate dialogues. Descriptions deriving from interviews of this type supply a rich and nuanced source of information concerning the personal meaning attributed by participants to the phenomenon under consideration (for a more extended discussion of phenomenological interviewing and interpretation, see Kvale, 1996; Pollio, Henley & Thompson, 1997; and Thomas & Pollio, 2002).

PARTICIPANTS

Participants in the present study were 11 Black undergraduate students at a large southeastern state university. This institution, which is a research-oriented land-grant university, has an overall enrollment of some 26.000 students. Of this number, some 1550 or so are Black and approximately 1400 are Asian or Hispanic. Of the 11 Black undergraduate students who were interviewed, seven were women whose ages varied from 21 to 24 and four were men whose ages varied between 22 and 26. Participants were purposefully selected because they had successfully completed all requirements for their degrees and were about to graduate. We chose to interview successful students (i.e., those who were about to graduate) because we felt they would be able to provide us with a description of their experiences uncontaminated by fear of academic difficulty or failure. We also chose graduating students because we felt they would enable us to track any significant changes in their experiences during the four- or five-year course of their under-graduate education. As may be noted in Table 1, participants majored in such diverse fields as engineering, psychology, accounting, education, and English.

PROCEDURE

Since the goal of phenomenological interviewing is to describe the meaning of some particular event(s) as experienced by the participant, a central concern is for the interviewer to hold in abeyance (as much as possible) his/her own presuppositions regarding the experience to be described—a process termed "bracketing" (Pollio, Henley, & Thompson, 1997). The purpose is to make the interviewer sensitive to her own issues. In preparation for the present set of interviews, the interviewer conducting all 11 interviews participated in a bracketing interview designed to highlight her presuppositions regarding having been a Black undergraduate student. The interviewer, who is currently a faculty member in the College of Nursing, was born in Jamaica and now lives in the United States. Her interview was conducted by another member of the research team skilled in phenomenological interviewing: the specific opening question to which she responded was: "Please describe some experiences that stand out to you from your own college experiences."

Once this interview was completed, it was transcribed verbatim and submitted to an interpretative group for an analysis of themes. The results of this analysis revealed that even though the interviewer reported little or no difficulty in identifying with Black colleagues and students, she is aware that she normally does not view the larger white society in as racially defined terms as do most Blacks. In fact, she believes that growing up in a predominately black society (Jamaica) seems to have given her more comfort in dealing with Caucasians. The construct of "outsider within," proposed by Collins (1986,1999), has relevance here. The Jamaican interviewer has "insider" knowledge of Southern American culture through a long period of residence here and commonality with study participants by virtue of dark skin, but she is also an "outsider" because her earlier life background differs from theirs. While she cannot fully grasp, initially, what "insiders" (participants) have experienced, she can be fully open to listening to them, continually seeking to understand their experiences. It is not necessary that the interviewer (or the other members of the research team) had the same life experience as the interviewees. For example, one does not have to have a history of depressive illness to conduct a phenomenological study of depression. In fact, naiveté regarding participants' experience may permit even closer attention to the nuances of their narratives. A Black interviewer was chosen to minimize the mistrust students may have felt toward a

Table 1 Demographic Characteristics of Study Participants

	Age	Sex	Major
#1	23	F	Psychology
#2	21	F	Social work
#3	24	F	Psychology
#4	22	F	Sports management
#5	21	F	Human ecology
#6	21	F	Education
#7	21	F	Logistics/transportation
#8	22	M	Accounting
#9	26	M	Electrical engineering
#10	23	M	Psychology
#11	22	M	History

white interviewer. We believe this aim was accomplished. The quality of the resultant interviews, rich with details of painful experiences, is evidence that interviewees did feel comfortable with their Jamaican interviewer despite her outsider status.

PARTICIPANT INTERVIEWS

Individual interviews for all 11 participants were scheduled at their convenience and were conducted in a comfortable and convenient environment for the participant. The initial question opening each interview was as follows: "Please describe what stands out to you about your college experiences here at University X." From audiotapes of these interviews, a verbatim text was transcribed for each participant. Each of these typed transcripts was interpreted with the help of the six-member, multidisciplinary, interpretive research group presently in place on our campus. Using hermeneutic techniques to be described in the following section, significant meaning units in each transcript were identified, carefully analyzed, and formulated into an overall pattern of themes.

The process of interpretation followed in this study is one in which one group member assumes the role of the interviewer and another takes the role of the participant. Given these assignments, the transcript is read aloud until a change in topic is perceived to occur, at which point the reading stops for a period of discussion concerning that passage. When this takes place, various group members highlight phrases that seem to stand out and/or to express significant meanings to them from the perspective of the participant. On the basis of tentative interpretations, meaning statements are formulated for use in developing themes for this, and ultimately all, transcripts. The present process of analysis proceeds in a circular fashion such that interpretation of later passages continually informs thematic meanings deriving from earlier passages. It is not atypical for the first interpretation of a single transcript to require as many as two to three hours.

Once an overall thematic analysis is developed, members of the research group evaluate it in terms of the joint criteria of plausibility and illumination (Pollio et al., 1997). Findings are considered plausible if the specific descriptive themes are supported by textual evidence; they are considered illuminating if they provide the reader with a new and revealing understanding of the phenomenon as lived/described by participants. Meeting both conditions implies that an interested reader will be able to read the results of an interpretative study, see connections between the interpretation and the text, and come away with an expanded view of the phenomenon. After continuously considering these two concerns against the

developing thematic structure, adjustments are made until agreement is reached concerning the thematic meaning of the experience: such meaning is then expressed by exemplary quotes for each theme.

RESULTS

An interpretive analysis of transcripts revealed that five major themes characterized undergraduate experiences described by participants. Each of the five major themes was labeled by a phrase actually used by one or more participants: this was done to preserve the student's own language in describing specific meanings. Themes, however, are not to be construed as independent of one another but as interrelated aspects of a single overall pattern or gestalt. The five themes, as derived from the present set of transcripts, are as follows:

1. "It Happens Every Day": Unfairness/Sabotage/Condescension.
2. "You Have to Initiate the Conversation": Isolation and Connection.
3. "They Seem the Same; I'm The One Who's Different."
4. "I Have to Prove I'm Worthy To Be Here."
5. "Sometimes I'm Not Even Here/Sometimes I Have to Represent All Black Students": Invisibility and Supervisibility.

Theme I. "It Happens Every Day": Unfairness/Sabotage/Condescension

All 11 participants reported incidents of unfairness, sabotage, and condescension. Wearily, they described incident after incident. Actions of faculty, classmates, and the larger community contributed to their perceptions that the university failed to offer "an environment that's healthy for black people." One participant described the situation in the following terms:

> "I call my mother like every other week. I have a new story for her every week: They had nooses hanging out of trees this week, and they said it was an art project and they didn't understand why we would be offended . . . Or somebody wrote 'nigger this, nigger that' and this white girl bumped into me and called me a 'nigger.' . . . She bumped into me and walked off." (P6)

Study participants were distressed by the presence on campus of graffiti and objects that symbolized or overtly conveyed racism:

> "I remember actually my first week here, my first day of class. I passed by (name of residence hall), and there was a great big Rebel flag hanging in a guy's window as curtains. I really didn't expect to see

anything like that . . . I didn't expect to see things like 'niggers go home' written in the men's room wall. And you know, KKK carved on the desk." (P8)

The university administration was not perceived as being particularly interested in investigating racist graffiti on campus buildings or other racial incidents that were occurring:

"With racial slurs written in the residence hall, it disturbed a lot of people because . . . the housing administration was not conducting interviews or anything trying to find out . . . who did this." (P4)

Many incidents related by participants involved professors or university staff who were perceived to be condescending and/or treating them unfairly on the basis of race. The following two examples from Participant 3 are illustrative:

"I went to class every day. I took notes every day. . . . I probably made a C because I was black. So what I did was I went to talk to him [the professor], and he was like very, very vague about it. . . . He couldn't give me any kind of evidence . . . any kind of rationale to why I should make a C. . . ."

One professor's behavior was so offensive to a female participant that she left some of the classes:

"A couple of times I just walked out of class because she would say things in her lecture that really upset me."

Later in this interview, the participant revealed that she went to talk to this professor about her feelings. The professor retaliated:

"She told me that she had been thinking about recommending [me] for a scholarship that's offered through the department for black students, but 'you have to have the grades for it.' And I was like. 'Actually I have a 4.0 in the department.' And she just laughed. 'Well, I don't know what your grade will be in this class'. . . . I came out with a C in her course. And I really did think it was unfair." (P6)

Classmates often were perceived to be sabotaging their efforts, as depicted in the following examples:

"They [classmates] wanted me to redo my part "[of a collective essay assignment involving four white girls, another black girl, and herself]. . . . "If I don't redo it, they're going to try to sabotage my grade. . . . And I don't see why I have to rewrite my part. I think that she should rewrite her part, the white girl, . . . I felt that . . . because I was black, they didn't think I knew what I was doing." (P3)

The words of Participant 5 aptly summarize this theme:

"It [racist treatment] happens every single day. It's real and racism is probably never going to go away,

not ever. . . . I can't even count on three hands how many times I've been discriminated against in food stores . . . on campus. in the university center. I mean just everywhere." (P5)

Theme 2: "You Have to Initiate the Conversation" Isolation and Connection

This theme emerged as participants described their experiences of seeking to make successful connections with various segments of the university community. These include students of the same race, students of different race, campus groups, faculty/staff, extracurricular activities, and campus employment.

The first two excerpts deal with the issue of needing to initiate any kind of activity on campus, whether it be getting notes or entering into a conversation.

"I mean for the, for most of my classes that I've been in I had to initiate the conversation to let them know that I am a black person and I can talk. And I have good sense . . . but mostly in my experience I find that I have to initiate it, and that's another obstacle that I think I have to get across, to create relationships with people so that I can fit in the classroom." (P3)

"When you're in a classroom full of white people and you have to initiate getting notes, you already have preconceived notions that they are not going to want to give them to you. I mean for me. I feel that, I mean if they don't talk to you, what makes you think they want to give you notes?" (P3)

Students also reported being disconnected specifically from white students.

"I mean there's been classes where I've sat in where I will be sitting in the middle of two white people who know each other or whatever. And they would be talking a group up and do group work and they would completely bypass me and go to each other. And I'm just like that's fine. I mean that's fine, if you don't want to sit with me then okay. I'm not going to go home and cry about it or anything, but bump you. So it's hard, it is hard." (P6)

Another student was taken aback by the attitude of one of her white peers. After making a comment about deficits in inner city schools, one of her classmates responded as follows:

"He got totally upset and he was saying. 'Well, if you wouldn't be so violent, you being black of course, if you wouldn't and stop scaring your teachers and cussing and fighting, hitting your teachers, you know they wouldn't be scared to teach. You know, it's your fault you don't have good teachers because you just act so bad that the teachers don't want to teach in your schools." (P7)

There also were some excerpts in which students even described alienation from other Black students:

> "I don't feel like other black students are ambitious enough, and I think some of them act very stereotypical and I really don't like that at all. I mean you know how white people say you act certain things, loud and everything like that, and they are like that … It's kind of annoying to me, kind of embarrassing for me to see them act like that, so I do not want to hang around them. But I just don't, haven't felt I just fit in with the black students here." (P1)

> "That's the way I feel, is just everybody has a chip on their shoulder and I get the vibes like the black female is my own worst enemy. And I'm not trying to, I don't give that off I don't think, but it's kind of like we can't, if somebody's doing something good then it's like, oh, they're trying to be this or they're trying to be that. It's not oh, they're really doing a good job." (P5)

In addition to experiences of disconnection and the need to initiate relationships, participants also described examples of connection. Some of these involved connection with other people—some students, some professors—still others, to one or another organization. All in all, however, the African American student reported that he or she had to be cautious and the one to initiate connection.

> "Yeah, I guess, as far as my fitting in and making friends at (University X) each year, I think it would be a lot better if people took initiative and did things they like to do. For example, like I said, this past year or two I've been involved definitely in poetry … doing stuff that you enjoy, and finding people with common interests and that kind of thing and doing stuff together I think that would make it a lot easier for a lot of blacks, because when they come up here they don't know." (P10)

> "As you break through your freshman level classes and you start going more into your major classes they're smaller more personalized, you get to interact with your professor one on one, and most of those professors I dealt with take it back, with all of the professors I dealt with, things have gone rather well." (P9)

> "I mean I've had some really good experiences here. I joined a sorority my freshman year, and my second semester there was really good. I've learned a lot of life lessons and working with black women. Got into some really wonderful honor societies, met some people, and got a chance to join some groups on campus. Black Cultural Program committee, I was part of that, I was part of Student Government Association for a year so I've touched a little bit around campus, just to get a feel for it." (P5)

Theme 3: "They All Seem The Same;. I'm The One Who's Different"

All 11 participants focused on experiences of being the same in some ways and different in other ways from those around them. Students were aware of how important it was to them to be the same as others in learning and social settings. Feeling different was seldom a positive experience and often made participants feel "mad," "frustrated," "isolated," or "bothered." Situations in which differences stood out were viewed as "crazy," "amazing," or "comical." Participant 4 stated, "I don't see a lot of (people) like me. And that bothers you."

Participant 2 described her experience of realizing that she was different:

> "It kind of dawned on me, you know. I am the only Black in this group. I guess I am different in a way.… I never just saw myself as being isolated or different from anybody else. Until she [the instructor] brought that up.…"

Some participants learned for the first time that being seen as different could mean being seen as inferior. One participant had learned this from his best friend, who is white.

> "And he's [my white friend] just like 'you'd be amazed at how backward some people can be.' He's known people that feel that way. Who really feel that just because you're black you're inferior, just not as good, not as capable as a white person. And I just can't believe those attitudes are still around, but it's not all bad I guess. It's still in knowing, to deal with, to know that still exists." (P8)

Some participants also described how they were different from other Black students:

> "And you know. I'd try to explain to them. 'We're all different, so I can't answer, you know, for all blacks or for minorities period as a whole," (P2)

Participant I focused at a more personal level:

> "I feel like sort of an outsider because I really don't … I never really fit in with other black students here.… I have a different way of thinking or something. I don't talk like the black slang and everything, and so they are like you know, 'You're trying to be white.' And you know. I'm just being me.… I mean they all seem the same. I'm the one who's different." (P1)

Another participant described the experience of intentionally being different from other Black students:

> "… you know how hard it is with black people without an education. You have a chance to get an

education to better yourself, you ought to make the best of it. And when people don't that really bothered me a lot, too. I didn't understand why, and so when I saw that I was like. I've got to do different . . . I've got to do the best that I can, and at least graduate." (P10)

Most participants thought they were, to some degree, the same as other students:

"But after you sit down and talk with them, actually you're not too much different than they are, you just come from a different place and you have a different skin color, but for the most part you have a lot of things in common." (P9)

"Just because you're not from the same area or have the same accent or language doesn't mean you don't have a common bond or goal, or you can't understand each other." (P4)

Participants talked about the need to help faculty and white students understand that Black students are able to learn the same as others. One participant described how she "plays the game":

"But I've held a 4.0 for two years in these [white] professors' classes, so they look at me as being kind of one of them. I'm accepted into their kind of, their culture, because I know how to play the game to get what I need." (P5)

Some participants indicated a need to connect to other Black students and faculty, even though they appreciated an opportunity to get to know others different from themselves.

"But it turned out to be a good experience, hanging out and finding out about the white kids and stuff. But then there was a certain level of degree where you still feel left out, if you're not really connected with people of your own race." (P3)

One participant deeply questioned her need to have only Black friends in college when this had not been her experience in high school:

"I honestly can say I don't know why . . . because I've never just had so many people of my same culture and same ideas and beliefs that I have, to be my friends all at one time." (P4)

Participants described their need to be in classes with Black instructors and, perhaps even more, to be in classes with a sizeable number of black students:

"I've had two black instructors since I've been at (University X). I never thought about that before, and that's sad. You know, the vibes in their class is totally different from any other classes I had, and I want to

say it was because there were a lot more black people in these classes. . . . I think out of all my classes I have taken here my best experiences have been in classes with black professors. And sadly to say that's just how it is. I felt at home in those classes. I felt like I learned more because I didn't have to spend time fighting somebody I guess and saying quit looking at me or having to pick my words very carefully, or there have been times when I felt like I hindered class discussions." (P6)

In summary, the experience of same/different for Black students in this study can best be described in the words of one student:

"It's crazy, it's crazy up here, but it's a learning experience. I think that is the positive thing that I can say about it. It's a learning experience for black people. You will come here and you will learn that you are black. And that it means something. And what it means to you depends on how you take it. It really does depend on how you take it." (P6)

Theme 4. "I Have to Prove I'm Worthy To Be Here"

A common theme in participant narratives was the idea that whites saw Blacks as a group and individually as less capable until proven otherwise. Participants described how they had to work harder to overcome such preconceived ideas and succeed in spite of the obstacles presented.

"I had the feeling then, and even still now, when I walk in a classroom that they're already . . . that everybody's eye is on me, that everybody is watching me, wanting to see what I am going to do. How is my performance going to be? And I feel like I have to work harder, study more, answer more questions, ask more questions, to prove to both my teachers and to my fellow classmates that, you know, I am worthy to be here. I'm deserving to be here. And, you know, don't automatically doubt my academic capabilities just because I am black." (P7)

"I'm always on my Ps and Qs and know that I've got to do better than anybody else. I have to. And I'm not sure that that's, you know, absolutely true in somebody else's eyes, but just the situations I've been in and the way people have treated me, it makes me feel like Oh. I have to do better than best for them to see what I'm really capable of doing, what I'm really, really capable of doing." (P5)

"And I'm proud that I'm black and that I'm doing it. But it's almost like I have to prove a point. Just like with Dr. Smith. She assumed that I didn't have the grades. I was like 'No baby, I have a 4.0 in the English department.' So why should I have to give you my credentials just because I'm black?" (P6)

In the classroom the need to prove oneself led to more effort and more stress on the part of Black students who saw classroom interaction as crucial for their success. Some participants identified specific strategies they employed.

> "In my history class I sit in the front row, and I sit in the front row of every class. I have to. And I do this because I feel . . . I want the professor to know that I am in the classroom, that I want to learn and that I'm paying attention." (P3)

> "I have to work ten times harder to make an A because, due definitely to the teacher's teaching techniques in the classroom. Most of my classroom I feel, like I said before, that the teacher tends to teach towards another area in the classroom. So what I have to do . . . I have to call upon the teacher, get her attention, and ask whatever problem that I have to see if she can help me solve it. I kind of feel neglected. So what you have to do is you have to let them know you have good sense. And that's one reason why I said I worked ten times as hard." (P2)

The need to prove themselves was not limited to interactions with faculty, but also occurred with peers in a variety of settings. Strategies and extra effort were needed there too:

> "And so I went with the mentality I could prove something to my professor and that sort of thing. But then what shocked me was having to prove it to my peers as well. Like I say, a lot of them assume that you're on some kind of minority scholarship and you're here because of affirmative action and that sort of stuff. No, just because I'm black doesn't mean I get special privileges you know, but they automatically assume that. It's like you really had to prove it, you really had to show them that hey, not all black folks are dumb or lazy or apathetic or whatever." (P10)

Group work in particular was problematic for participants who felt they had to prove themselves to other group members.

> "Sometimes it feels like I have to prove myself, not so much now that I'm a senior. I guess that's why. I don't know. But a lot of times when I'm in classes I'm working in a group, but there's not that many black people in (College X), and when we're just forming ideas and working on something. It's kind of like for the first 30 minutes I'm ignored until I prove to them that yes, I know what I'm talking about." (P8)

In the experience of one participant there were clear expectations, even anticipations, of failure:

> "So it's like when you come here and if you're in one of their groups, they're looking at you. Once you've been assigned to their group, sort of sneering up their nose sometimes, some people, not all. And you know, they're just standing back to wait and see what you're going to do. You know, it's almost like they're

waiting for you to mess up. They're waiting for you to miss their one group meeting and say, 'Oh, well, she doesn't contribute.' (P7)

One participant did not see the need to prove oneself as limited to the university but as a more ubiquitous experience she expected to encounter in the workplace.

> "And you know, you may not think, that I'm good enough but I know I'm good enough. But sometimes I get really frustrated when I continuously have to prove myself. I have to prove myself all the time, but I think we have to continuously do that throughout society anyway. When I get my first job. I'm going to have to prove that I can do this, just to do the work that I do. But sometimes I feel like blacks have to prove themselves just a tad bit more because people look at our color as a discrepancy and not as a difference and just a uniqueness about ourselves. So I think that we have to go that extra mile to say hey. I'm actually prepared and I'm qualified to do this job." (P5)

In addition to the need to prove themselves individually with faculty and peers, some participants described efforts to prove themselves collectively.

> "It shouldn't take all of that to prove to the whites on campus and to the president and the student newspaper. We shouldn't have to have walks and send in letters every week just to say hey, we're doing what we're supposed to. That's what we're supposed to do. I mean we're here to get an education, to do our best, to get a degree, that's what we're supposed to do." (P6)

Theme 5: "Sometimes I'm Not Even Here/Sometimes I Have to Represent Every Black Student in Here": Invisibility/Supervisibility:

A final theme described in the present set of interviews was that of relative visibility. This theme expressed the participants' experiences of being noticed or not being noticed, wholly as a result of being Black. This experience took many forms which led to a feeling of being uncomfortable because of standing out. This was illustrated by the young man in this paper's opening quote who said:

> "And so a lot of times I felt out of place, because you see all white faces. You know I'm the only fly in the buttermilk, so that took some getting used to . . ." (P10)

This was clearly an experience of being hypervisible and of feeling out of place. The image of "a fly in the buttermilk" is not only about hypervisibility, but also has a potentially self-derogatory tone. One young woman commented on such experiences as intimidating and, ultimately, hindering.

> "…but when there's like two black people in a classroom and a hundred white people in the classroom, to me it made me feel kind of intimidated. And definitely if I felt that they didn't want to help me, for example if I had to miss class and I had to get notes. I didn't have that relationship with somebody to where I could call them up and say 'Hey can I get those notes?' And so for me it hindered my education experience and made me have to work harder." (P3)

A different student noted that she experiences both invisibility and hypervisibility. Since there are few Black students visible to her, she feels even more alone:

> "And I feel like when I go to classes and if I walk in and I see that there are no other black faces, I automatically sit down and I say: 'Lord, it's going to be one of those semesters. And I don't think that I should have to feel like that in school." (P6)

Hypervisibility was not only a personal inconvenience, it also had overt negative consequences in classes where professors were perceived as having difficulty with Black students:

> "(Professor X had) been picking on me all semester because I'm the only black person. I mean she asked me to sing the Black National Anthem. And I was like. 'No, I can't sing, I'm sorry? I mean, she would use words like 'you people' and (it was) just horrible. She was horrible … I found that they would have a hard time talking about blacks, slavery, and when we would get to history, they would have a hard time talking about that when I was in class. …" (P6)

One side effect to hypervisibility is that the student is sometimes treated as a representative of all Blacks. This became a significant sub-theme in itself.

> "Because in most of my classes when we talk about an issue that deals with black people I become like the black representative of the United States of America. I become that. I really do. And I'm like. I don't represent the black population of the U.S. … It's like I know what I think but I don't know what the rest of the black people in the world think." (P5)

> "I guess they would just ask questions about black people in general you know, and expect you to have the answers. Whether, you know, do all black people like chicken? You know. I don't know. I've never met all black people, you know." (P10)

The reverse experience to hypervisibility is invisibility. In these incidents, the students reported being deliberately ignored.

> "In like asking for their help with something, or like, they were just like, some of them, like if you were waiting in line for snacks or something, they would like, go around you. You'd be standing there and they'd be like picking the next person in line." (P1)

> "And I can remember some of my classes, going into some of my classes, not really being recognized because I would raise my hand and it would be like I wasn't there. I didn't really understand that, because I know people see me. I know I'm not invisible." (P5)

> "I would be standing here and there was a white girl beside me and people would come up to ask a question and they would look right at her. I was like 'I'm right here.' And that's happened in every job I've had at University X." (P8)

While the issue of visibility has a range of manifestations, one woman summarized its consequences quite succinctly.

> "I mean, just college itself is already intense. I just don't think that anybody needs any added pressures. But you come to (University X) and you're black, it automatically is there." (P6)

DISCUSSION

When we want to understand what stands out for people in a given situation, phenomenological research gives voice to their experiences in a singularly powerful way. The descriptions shared by our participants can help us understand what being "a fly in the buttermilk" is really like. Only through such understanding can we begin to experience some of the challenges faced by Black students at predominately white institutions.

All of the experiences reported by our participants as figural events in their college careers were superimposed on the backdrop of a white dominated world. After careful analyses of the transcripts, the essence of our participants' experiences might read as follows:

> Unfairness, sabotage, and condescension are everyday occurrences in the white world in which I live at the university. In order to connect with students, faculty, administrators, and others on and around campus I must be the one to initiate interaction, and I must also prove I am worthy as a student or friend. I am continuously made aware of how different I am, especially when I am the only black student in a class. Life is full of opposites: I feel as if I am seen as the same as other blacks by many whites, yet I often feel different from other black students. Perhaps the most common experience I have is one of extremes: Either I am invisible or I am its opposite—I am supervisible.

All participants reported positive experiences when they were students in a predominantly white university. They also reported negative experiences that might have overwhelmed students with lesser strength and/or resolve to succeed. As discussed earlier, other studies have pointed to numerous factors connected to higher dropout rates for Black students in predominantly white universities. Four of the five themes capturing participant experiences offer support to prior findings although one potentially important theme (invisible/supervisible) has rarely been discussed in the research literature. All five themes, however, may help university faculty and administrators come to understand prior research in a way that leads to a better environment for all students.

The unfairness/sabotage/condescension theme was an especially crucial element of our participants' hurtful experiences at their university. It was voiced clearly in the statement of one participant who said, "It happens everyday." Numerous prior studies echo our participant's reactions to insensitive and sometimes racist acts. Participants in survey studies completed by Smith (1980) and Allen, Nunley, & Scott-Warner (1988) reported that 55–78% of students, staff, and faculty described their institutions as hostile and unwelcoming to Black students. Kirkland (1998) found that Black students reported insensitive attitudes of Caucasian faculty and students, along with lack of support, as the most frequently reported stressors they faced. A study by Fischer and Shaw (1999) found more than 50% of their participants reported feeling unfairly treated by faculty, and a large proportion noted racist treatment and subsequent feelings of anger. It was clear that most of the hurt our participants experienced came from the unfairness, sabotage, and condescension they perceived as happening every day. While the perception of generalized injustice such as that reported by our participants is undoubtedly important in their affective response to life on campus, it also has a potential adverse effect on academic performance. Members of socially stigmatized groups may protect their self-esteem by adopting coping strategies such as de-emphasizing the value of academic success or discounting academic feedback, either positive or negative, as a valid indicator of their performance and ability (Schmader, Major, & Gramzow, 2002). Either behavior may result in poorer academic achievement. The pervasive nature of the unfairness/sabotage/condescension mandates a coordinated institutional and faculty response if efforts to increase success of Black students are effective.

The themes of isolation/connection and same/different are also supported by previous research. The first of these themes is represented by the statement. "You have to initiate the connection," Whereas the second is embodied in the words of one student who said, "They seem all the same. I am the one who is different." Taken in combination, these themes illustrate the complexity of interpersonal relationships described by participants as they worked to survive in a predominately white university.

The theme of isolation/connection denotes a perceived barrier participants needed to overcome to achieve academic success. It is well documented that the inability to develop a connection with some aspect of the university will generally result in failure. Tinto (1975, 1987) noted that nonintegrative experiences of loneliness and alienation were positively correlated with withdrawal from college whereas positive or integrative experiences enhanced minority student persistence. D'Souza (1991) cited institutional alienation as the most significant characteristic experience of Black students attending predominately white universities. The perception expressed by participants—that they always had to initiate a connection—is complicated by feelings of alienation and of being different from other students.

Participants reported that when they arrived on campus they felt isolated as though no one was reaching out to them. University-sponsored programs to help students make successful connections were not always perceived as helpful or effective but instead cliquish and divisive. Connection with white students appeared to be easier for participants who had previously attended a white high school, supporting the idea that preparation for racist treatment enhances the possibilities of coping (Nghe & Mahalik, 2001). It was clear, however, that connecting with other students, white or black, was quite difficult for some participants. Tinto (1975, 1987) pointed out that the ability to be bicultural while maintaining a cultural identity was significant in fostering educational attainment. Unfortunately, individuals who are marginalized on the basis of race often internalize stereotypic images of themselves in addition to their own more differentiated identities—a splitting of self image (Hall, Stevens, & Meleis, 1994). When this occurs connection with others will be more difficult and the difficulty is compounded by a feeling of being different.

"A fly in the buttermilk" was one participant's way of describing his perception of an experience that stood out for all participants: being alone in a class with many white students. All participants reported how comforting it was to have other Black students in their classes and what a pleasure (albeit a rare one) it was to have a Black professor. This feeling of being different also reflects a more general feeling of alienation from white students and the overall university community. This is not surprising in light of Judd et al.'s (1995) contention that while whites may be socialized to avoid stereotyping and thinking about racial differences, Blacks are socialized to emphasize racial group differences between themselves and whites. In addition, however, some participants felt they were different from other Black students and reported being criticized for being too serious about grades and for not talking Black slang. In turn, some of them were critical of other Black students whom they saw as too loud and boisterous and lacking a commitment to academic success. It seemed that many of our participants saw other Blacks as the same and themselves as the one who was different. While the themes of isolation and difference are perhaps reflective of the ambivalent attitudes reported by Blacks regarding whites (Shelton, 2000) and by dominant groups towards minority groups (Fiske et al., 1999), it is clear that the "I am different" theme relates to an obstacle salient to our participants' university experience.

Having to prove one's worthiness represents a potentially serious barrier to success for Black students in a predominately white university. Unique to minority or marginalized groups, the assumption of unworthiness is associated with a particularly detrimental factor—stereotype threat—that seems to impair performance of even the most skilled achievement-oriented and confident Black students (Steele, 1999). In a series of experiments Steele found that "stereotype threat" tends to depress test scores and that dramatic improvement occurs when such threat is lifted. What impairs student performance is the threat of doing something they feel may inadvertently confirm a negative stereotype. Mistrustful of the faculty, Black students often try too hard, rather than not hard enough. Steele likens this to "John Henryism." a phenomenon observed in Blacks who seem to be emulating that legendary figure whose superhuman work efforts led to his death. The sense of being seen through the lens of a negative stereotype as unworthy leads to fear of doing something to confirm that stereotype, decreased class participation, increased anxiety, and often poor academic performance in spite of ample ability and preparation.

It also appeared that while our participants perceived the need to prove their academic worth and engaged in behaviors to do so, they also had the goal of invalidating negative prejudices about the academic ability of Black students. Although, in one sense, they did not want to be spokespersons for the Black race, they did want to do all they could to improve negative impressions the university community might hold concerning the ability of Black students to succeed.

In terms of visibility/invisibility the participants in our study perceived themselves as being at both ends of a continuum. One participant stated it this way: "Sometimes I'm not even here. And sometimes I have to represent every black student here." Reading participant transcripts gives one the impression that there is some truth in the sweet bliss of finding a pleasant middle ground between the extremes of being cast in the spotlight and of being totally ignored.

For major time periods in their college careers, participants reported themselves swinging from one extreme to the other. They reported that professors often called on them in classes to speak for the entire Black race when racial issues were broached. This supervisibility left them feeling out of place and uncomfortable in a majority of their classes. Conversely, when not in the spotlight, they often experienced themselves as invisible to the white university community. Participants reported that they were almost never invited to join white students in a study group and often were ignored when assigned to a project group. When participants were employed at campus stores, they noticed that whites sought assistance from less competent white personnel if there was a choice between Black and white clerks.

Our participants, however, were not the first African Americans to describe interrelationships between personal identity and the larger white community in terms of visibility. In the classic novel by Ralph Ellison, *The Invisible Man* (1952), the metaphoric play of light and shadow describing interactions between the narrator and his social setting was used to capture the complexities (and situatedness) of Black identity itself. Equating identity with visibility in this way suggests there is an optimal level of visibility in which the person, in conjunction with others, decides how—or even whether—to seek visibility in some setting. In the present case, the theme of invisibility captures student experiences of an absence of validation for who they experience themselves to be whereas the theme of supervisibility expresses student experiences of having one's identity defined by other, usually more powerful, persons in the present setting. In neither case does the student feel primary authorship for the identity attained, and this is precisely what participants were trying to describe when they noted that "sometimes I'm invisible and sometimes I have to represent every African American in the class."

As transcripts were analyzed, it became clear that there were some differences among participants on what has come to be called cultural identity. A conceptual understanding of these differences might help us better integrate the perceptions of our participants and the behaviors they reported for others in the predominately white university setting. The five stages of cultural identity as described by (Atkinson, Morton, & Sue, 1989; Sue et al., 1999; and Sue & Sue, 1999) include the following: Conformity, Dissonance, Resistance and Immersion, Introspective, and Integrative Awareness. These stages, as discussed by Sue and Sue (1999) and Atkinson et al. (1989), relate to the experiences of oppressed people as they struggle to understand their own culture, the dominant culture, and oppressive relationships between the two.

For the dominant white group, the conformity stage is marked by a generalized belief that white is right. For such individuals there is no personal responsibility taken for perpetuating racism, and there is a general lack of awareness about racial issues. The dissonance stage begins when a white person is forced to deal with contradictions in his/her attitudes and behavior. For example, a person in this stage may feel some guilt from being afraid to speak out or take action on racial issues. The resistance and immersion stage is characterized by an overreaction or a severe shift in personal values on racism. Individuals suddenly see racism everywhere. This new awareness often leads to anger toward others for their intolerance. A "White Liberal" syndrome may develop and be manifested in two complementary styles: the paternalistic, condescending, protector or an overidentification with minority group members. Whites soon discover that neither of these roles is appreciated by minority groups and often results in rejection by minority group members. The introspective stage seems to mediate between the two extremes of white identity and the rejection of whiteness. Feelings of guilt or anger that have motivated the person to identify with one or the other group are realized as dysfunctional, and individuals in this stage develop rational beliefs about who they are and what their responsibilities are in developing personal identities. The integrative awareness stage occurs when whites realize that race does not define any specific person. There is a sense of self-fulfillment as the person comes to terms with what his/her role in racism might be and what are effective ways of dealing with the eradication of racism.

It would appear that our participants encountered some students and faculty in the first stage (conformity) of identity development. Stealing Black History Month posters would be a stage one activity as would asking participants to speak for their entire race. Participants also reported encountering some resistance and immersion behaviors in the university community. One professor cried because of the guilt she felt about "her responsibility for slavery", another thought it would be nice if our participant sang the Black national anthem for the class. It seems clear the participants enjoyed several meaningful interactions with students and faculty where they were treated as individuals rather than members of a group. In this context, they responded by being able to form connections with other individuals based on common interests that crossed skin-color boundaries. Despite these experiences, it seems clear that most of the hurt our participants described came from experiences expressed by Theme I: "It Happens Everyday": unfairness/sabotage/condescension.

For minority group members the stages of cultural identity are described in a slightly different way (Atkinson et al., 1989 and Sue & Sue (1999). Movement from one stage to another for minority-group members is characterized by changes in attitude toward self, toward others of the same minority, toward others of a different minority, and toward members of the dominant group. For example, minority-group members move from an appreciation of the dominant culture, to depreciating the dominant culture, and then to a selective appreciation of people regardless of race. In other words, in the final stage of cultural-identity development, individuals withhold judgment of other individuals based on the groups to which they belong. That is, some white individuals and some Black individuals are good and some are bad, and not all members of the oppressed and dominant classes act and behave in the same way. Minority-group members move from rejecting their own culture and group (Stage One) to rejecting the dominant culture and group (Stage Three), to selective appreciation of individuals from both groups (Stage Five).

Some participants reported difficulty in connecting with their fellow Black students because attempts to connect with white students were viewed as "trying to be like them." It would appear that some black students tended to reject the dominant culture whereas others were able to appreciate individuals regardless of race. It may also be the case that some black students viewed participants who were appreciative of white students as attempting to reject their own culture.

RECOMMENDATIONS

We believe the understanding we gained from listening to the voices of our participants will help inform actions of students, faculty, and any predominately white university that wants to improve the learning environment for all students. Our participants shared strategies that led to successful graduation. The common thread running through the stories was a perceived ability to move beyond unfairness, sabotage, and condescension and to find common ground on which to build relationships. They felt that it was important to be the one to initiate connection, deal with being different and with being either invisible or supervisible, and to accept the perceived need to "prove I am worthy."

The students reported incidents and feelings emanating from classroom content, from assignments, from faculty comments, and from nonverbal communication. Faculty members must realize that academic achievement in their courses is influenced as much by intangibles as by pedagogy and just as pedagogy can be improved, the environment can be enhanced if the willingness is there. Faculty members need to examine what they do to promote an atmosphere that contributes to Black students' perceptions that they need to prove they are worthy to be in college. Why did student participants feel they faced unfairness, sabotage, and condescension every day? What can faculty members do to help these students be seen, not as representatives of all Blacks, but as individuals with unique goals and needs? How can faculty members help students connect with one another? Would it be possible to set aside a part of class time for students to work collaboratively in a safe and trusting environment? Would it be possible for students, in smaller classes or in small groups, to "check in" for a few moments at the beginning of class where they share something going on in their lives?

Several recommendations resulting from this study concern ways in which faculty and the university can improve the learning environment for minority students. University personnel need to develop and constantly evaluate ways to help Black students connect with various segments of the university. Faculty members should be encouraged to learn about cultural identity development, examine their own behavior to assess where they are in this regard, and set goals for further development. Much of the negative faculty behavior reported by our participants was described as being done out of ignorance. Cultural competency is not only possible but should be mandatory for administration and faculty alike.

We recommend that faculty members find ways to hear the stories of their Black (and other) students. While phenomenological research can be most helpful, it seems more feasible for departments to devise ways to encourage as many students as possible to share personal stories with faculty. If interviews are conducted, faculty members need to learn how to ask questions that do not interfere with students' perceptions and descriptions of their experiences.

Having looked at the experiences of successful Black students just before graduation, we think it is also necessary to study the experiences of students who lack confidence about their ability to graduate. The nature of their experiences may lead to different recommendations than those found in this study. In addition, we need to study the experiences of both Black and white faculty members in regard to the education of black students. We also need to study other minority groups to determine differences and similarities, as well as groups of students at various levels of undergraduate and graduate school. The more we can enable the life experiences of all students to be heard, the more we can develop an understanding capable of leading to a healthy environment for all students and all faculty.

REFERENCES

Atkinson, D. R., Morten, G., and Sue. D. W. (1989). A minority identity development model. In D. R. Atkinson, G. Morten, and D. W. Sue (Eds.), *Counseling American Minorities* (pp. 35-52). Dubuque. IA: W. C. Brown.

Allen, M. E., Nunley, J. C., & Scott-Warner, M. (1988). Recruitment and retention of black nursing students in baccalaureate nursing programs. *Journal of Nursing Education, 27* (3). 107-116.

American Council on Education (1988). *One-third of a nation*. Washington, DC: Author.

Bjerklie, D. (2001, July 30). In brief: Separate and unequal. *Time*, p. 58.

Collins, P. H. (1986). Learning from the outsider within. *Social Problems, 33*, 14-32.

Collins, P. H. (1999). Reflections on the outsider within. *Journal of Career Development, 26*(1), 85-88.

D'Souza, D. (1991). *Illiberal Education: The policies of race and sex on campus*. New York: The Free Press.

Echols, L. (1998). *Factors related to the recruitment and retention of minority students in Higher education: A meta-analysis*. Unpublished doctoral dissertation. University of Pennsylvania.

Ellison, R. (1952). *The invisible man*. New York: Random House.

Feagin, J. (1992). The continuing significance of racism: Discrimination against black students in white colleges. *Journal of Black Studies, 22*, 546-578.

Fischer, A., & Shaw, C. M. (1999). African Americans' mental health and perceptions of racist discrimination: The moderating effects of racial socialization experiences and self esteem. *Journal of Counseling Psychology, 46*, 395-407.

Fiske, S., Xu, J., Cuddy, A., & Glick, P. (1999). (Dis)respecting versus (dis)liking: Status and interdependence predict ambivalent stereotypes of competence and warmth. *Journal of Social Issues, 55*, 473-489.

Hall, J., Stevens, P., & Meleis, A. (1994). Marginalization; A guiding concept for valuing diversity in nursing knowledge development. *Advances in Nursing Science, 16*(4), 23-41.

Judd, C. M., Park. B., Ryan. C., Brauer, M., & Kraus, S. (1995). Stereotypes and ethnocentrism: Diverging interethnic perceptions of African American and white American youth. *Journal of Personality and Social Psychology, 69*, 460-481.

Katz, I., & Hass, R. G. (1988). Racial ambivalence and American value conflict: Correlation and priming studies of dual cognitive structures. *Journal of Personality and Social Psychology, 55*, 893-905.

Kirkland, M. L. S. (1998). Stressors and coping strategies among successful female African American baccalaureate nursing students. *Journal of Nursing Education, 27*, 5-12.

Kvale, S. (1996). *Inter views: Introduction to qualitative research interviewing*, Thousand Oaks, CA: Sage.

National Center for Education Statistics (1992). *Historically black colleges and universities: 1976-1990*. Washington, DC: Author.

Nghe, L. T., & Malhalik, J. R. (2001). Examining racial identity statuses as predictors of psychological defenses in African American college students. *Journal of Counseling Psychology, 48*, 10-16.

Paul, A. M. (1999). Where bias begins: The truth about stereotypes. *Psychology Today 31*(3), 52-55, 82.

Polkinghorne, D. E. (1989). Phenomenological research methods. In R. S. Valle & S. Halling (Eds.) *Existential phenomenological perspectives in psychology* (pp. 41–60). New York: Plenum Press.

Pollio, H. R., Henley, T. B., & Thompson, C. J. (1997). *The phenomenology of everyday life*. MA? Cambridge: University Press.

Schmader, T., Major., B. & Gramzow, R. (2002). How African American college students protect their self esteem. *Journal of Blacks in Higher Education*, Spring, 116–119.

Shelton, J. N. (2000). A reconceptualization of how we study issues of racial prejudice. *Personality and Social Psychology Review, 4*, 374–390.

Sigelman, L., & Welch, S. (1991). *Black Americans' views of racial inequality: The dream deferred*. New York: Cambridge University Press.

Smith, D. H., (1980). *Admissions and retention problems of black students at seven predominantly white universities*. National Advisory Committee on Black Higher Education. Washington. DC: U.S. Department of Education.

Steele, C. M. (1992). Race and the schooling of black American. *Atlantic Monthly, 4*, 68–78.

Steele, C. M. (1999, August). Thin ice: "Stereotype threat" and black college students. *Atlantic Monthly*, 44–54.

Sue, D. W., and Sue, D. (1999). *Counseling the Culturally Different: Theory and Practice*, New York: John Wiley and Sons.

Sue, D. W., Bingham, R. P., Porche-Burke, L., & Vasquez, M. (1999). The diversification of psychology: A multicultural revolution. *American Psychologist, 54*, 1061–1069.

Thomas, S. P., & Davis, M. (2000, November). *Enhancing success of block nursing students: Project SUCCESS*. Paper presented at the American Academy of Nursing 2000 Conference, San Diego.

Thomas, S. P., & Pollio, H. R. (2002). *Listening to patients: A phenomenological approach to nursing research and practice*. New York: Springer.

Tinto, V. (1975). Dropout from higher education: A theoretical synthesis of recent research. *Review of Educational Research, 45* (1), 89–125.

Tinto, V. (1987). *Leaving college*. Chicago: The University of Chicago Press.

U. S. Census Bureau (1993). *Statistical abstract of the United States*. Washington, DC: Author.

Evaluation Criteria

1. What is the foreshadowed problem and how clearly is it stated? Is it reformulated later on after some initial data have been collected?

The foreshadowed problem is implied by the study's stated purpose at the end of the first paragraph: "to obtain the first-person perspective of the [Black] students themselves . . . " Since the intent of the research was to provide an expansive account of Black student experiences, the foreshadowed problem was not reformulated later on.

2. Is the conceptual and theoretical framework for the study clear? How well does the literature review argue for the importance of the current research?

This is an example of purely phenomenological research. The authors do an impressive job of describing previous research, including a large meta-analysis (a quantitative analysis of the results of a group of studies addressing the same general research question). They point out that despite the size of the existing literature on the topic, none had approached it from the point of view of Black students themselves.

3. What are the biases and preconceived ideas of the researcher? How are these dealt with in the study? Is the researcher well prepared to complete the study?

The researchers selected a Black woman to conduct all of the interviews, someone who not only would likely engender strong rapport with participants but also, because she was Jamaican, would be able to maintain some distance from the participants. They addressed the question of potential interviewer bias in a creative manner by submitting her to a bracketing exercise designed to reveal her own preconceptions.

4. Is the method of selecting participants clear and appropriate to the foreshadowed problem? How well are the participants and sites described?

The criteria for selection of the 11 participants are clear (African American students about to graduate), but the method of selection is not described. No indication is given either about the number of students who may have been approached to participate but declined. Information about participants is limited to age, gender, and college major. The only information about the research site was that it was a "large southeastern state university."

Discussion Questions

1. What are the advantages and disadvantages of conducting a study with such an open-ended question?

2. It isn't enough to argue that a study should be done just because one like it hasn't been done before. What else should the argument contain?

3. Questions of researcher bias are always an issue in qualitative research. What else could the researchers have done in this study to address the bias problem?

4. Does the sketchy information given about the study participants and the research context hinder the study's credibility? Why or why not?

5. How involved was the researcher in the setting being observed? Could this involvement have affected the behavior of the participants?

The researchers were totally uninvolved in the setting, although it is unclear how many of the authors were faculty members or staff at the study site. Interviews were conducted by a faculty member from an academic program different from any of the students' majors.

6. If appropriate, were multiple methods of data collection used? What was the duration and intensity of data collection?

Methods of data collection were limited to a single interview of unknown length.

7. Are issues of credibility directly addressed by the researchers? How, and how effectively?

Issues of credibility are addressed at length. Each interview was recorded and transcribed, and themes were identified by a six-member team; each theme was subjected to scrutiny by the team for "plausibility" and "illumination." There is, however, no evidence that the researchers engaged in any member checking or cross-examination of the data beyond their initial analysis.

8. Are the findings presented clearly? Are the data sufficiently detailed to allow a rich description? Are results accompanied by illustrative quotes and specific instances?

This is the real strength of the study. The researchers identified five major themes and titled each one with an illustrative quote. They described each theme in detail, using quotes liberally throughout to illustrate key points. The reader finishes each section with a clear sense of what the participants meant, and this is the principal goal of phenomenological research. As the authors note at the beginning of their Discussion section, "When we want to understand what stands out for people in a given situation, phenomenological research gives voice to their experiences in a singularly powerful way."

9. Do conclusions and interpretations follow logically from the results presented?

The study is strong here as well. The five themes are summarized together, and each is addressed for connections to existing research literature (four of the five were).

5. Since there was no direct observation this criterion is, at first glance, not applicable. Still, how do you think the study setting and the characteristics of the interviewer might have affected the participants' responses to the interview questions?

6. Can you imagine any other methods of data collection in this study that would serve to triangulate the interviews?

7. Would member checking and cross-examination of the data have been feasible in this study? If so, what could the researchers have done?

8. A liberal use of quotes adds spice and a strong personal context to a qualitative study. In what ways are extensive quotations problematic, however?

9. Ideally any piece of research should both support the existing knowledge base and challenge or extend parts of it. To what extent did these researchers do this successfully?

10. Is sufficient detail provided to discern which parts of the study might be applicable to other settings? To which contexts is the study transferable?

Since little is known about the study context, transferability of the findings depends on the extent to which the reader is able to give credence to the five key themes. The authors suggest that the study should help inform students, faculty, and others at predominately white universities about ways to improve the learning environment for Black students; and they propose a number of practical intervention strategies suggested by their research.

10. A skeptic could ask, "Why should I trust a study based on 11 students from a single university, regardless of how well those students' experiences are captured?" How would you respond?

Credibility Scorecard
"A Fly in the Buttermilk": Descriptions of University Life by Successful Black Undergraduate Students at a Predominately White Southeastern University

	Excellent	Very Good	Adequate	Marginal	Poor
General purpose	5	4	3	2	1
Contribution/ significance	5	4	3	2	1
Review of literature	5	4	3	2	1
Research questions or hypotheses	5	4	3	2	1
Subjects or participants	5	4	3	2	1
Instrumentation	5	4	3	2	1
Procedures	5	4	3	2	1
Results	5	4	3	2	1
Practical significance	5	4	3	2	1
Graphics	5	4	3	2	1
Conclusions	5	4	3	2	1
Any fatal flaws?					

5 | MIXED-METHOD DESIGNS

Research combining both quantitative and qualitative approaches has become more and more common in educational research. So-called *mixed-method* studies have a sort of irrefutable logic: why not design a study that combines the best features of both approaches? But as we pointed out in Chapter 1, doing this is considerably more challenging than simply combining numbers and narratives. Quantitative and qualitative approaches to research have distinctly different philosophical roots. Quantitative designs are based on the traditional scientific method, which holds that knowledge is built by a strict adherence to certain rules: hypotheses drawn from an existing theory base and stated in terms of relationships between prespecified independent and dependent variables; control of extraneous variation, that is, isolating the variables of interest by holding constant all variables not under study; sampling procedures intended to represent a broader population; operational definitions of all variables in quantitative terms, allowing for statistical analysis of results; and, the assumption that observed relationships among variables are generalizable to other contexts.

Contrast these modes of scientific conduct with qualitative approaches, which are based upon a completely different set of assumptions. There is no single set of truths out there, but rather multiple realities, depending on both the setting and one's individual perspective. The world cannot be understood by analyzing its components, but rather as a whole, with all of its messy interactions. Knowledge is built not by a rigid protocol but rather by a spirit of inquisitiveness and openness to surprises. While a few general questions can help guide the research, formal hypotheses cannot begin to capture the complexity. Not all phenomena are measurable. Most important, what is observed in a given research context is to be understood on its own terms and is not assumed to be true anywhere else. Qualitative inquiry requires that research consumers decide for themselves what may or may not be transferable to their own settings.

These are substantial differences! It's no wonder that the educational research community has had such a spirited debate over the past quarter-century about which approach is correct or better.

Our view is that both quantitative and qualitative approaches to research in education are meritorious. Each has something important to offer. Quantitative research, with its structure and no-nonsense measurement, can cut through a tangle of competing claims and anecdotes; qualitative research, with its focus on description and understanding, can lend meaning and insight to what otherwise would be a sterile display of statistics. Both approaches, when done well, meet the three principal features of educational research: both are systematic, rigorous, and empirical.

So where, then, do mixed-methods studies fit in? As we noted in Chapter 1, the vastly different philosophical bases of the two dominant approaches are very difficult to integrate in practice, unless they're done sequentially. Far more common are studies which either operate from a mostly quantitative perspective and employ qualitative data to flesh out the numbers, or operate from a mostly qualitative perspective with some additional statistical displays and analysis. The criteria for evaluating mixed-methods research therefore depends on what the dominant perspective is judged to be, based upon the questions given in Chapter 1. Again, these include the following:

- Do the researchers begin the study with some clear hypotheses they want to test?
- Do they set up comparison groups?
- Do they express concern about the representativeness of samples, or the generalizability of results?

If the answer to any of the above questions is "yes," then you should evaluate the study according to the criteria given in Chapter 2 or 3. If the answer to all of the above is "no," then you should evaluate the study according to the criteria given in Chapter 4. Here are some additional questions to ask of research employing mixed methods follow:

1. Is the research question phrased in such a way that suggests that both quantitative and qualitative data are appropriate?
2. Are the multiple approaches employed sequentially (first one, then the other), or concurrently? If the former, are the results of the first step used to inform the second step? If the latter, how are the results triangulated? How do the authors deal with discrepant findings?
3. What are the key quality criteria appropriate for the study's secondary approach? When applied, how do they enhance or hinder the study's overall credibility?
4. What, if anything, do the multiple approaches add to the richness of the study? Do they contribute significantly to understanding, or do they appear to be mostly window dressing?

The Artistic and Professional Development of Teachers

A Study of Teachers' Attitudes Toward and Use of the Arts in Teaching

Barry Oreck
University of Connecticut

During the past decade, the arts have been increasingly included in professional development programs for general education teachers in the United States. Little is known, however, about teachers' attitudes toward the arts in education or the applications of arts processes in their teaching practice. In this mixed-methods study, data collected from 423 K–12 teachers indicated that teachers believe the arts are important in education, but use them rarely. They are hindered by a lack of professional development and intense pressure to teach the mandated curriculum. Awareness of student diversity and the need for improved motivation and enjoyment in learning were the most frequently cited motivations for using the arts. Teachers' self-efficacy and self-image relating to creativity and artistry influenced arts use more than any other personal characteristic. Surprisingly, neither prior arts instruction, current artistic practice, nor years of teaching experience were significant predictors of arts use in the classroom.

KEYWORDS:
arts in teaching; arts-based professional development; arts in the classroom; teacher attitudes; teacher education; arts in education partnerships

The arts have played a role in general teacher education since Dewey and the beginning of the progressive education movement. During the past 80 years, the status of the arts in the curriculum has ebbed and flowed, increasing in eras of progressive reform and decreasing during back-to-basics movements and when funding is tight (Goodlad, 1992). In the past decade, national school reform efforts based on educational research (Gardner, 1983, 1993; Renzulli, 1994; Sizer, 1984), public/private partnerships between schools and cultural institutions (Remer, 1996), and new national standards in the arts (Consortium of National Arts Education Organizations, 1994) have fueled a significant increase in the arts as part of in-service professional development programs for classroom and academic subject-area teachers (Fowler, 1996). In addition to courses specifically focused on the arts, artistic processes and related teaching methods are often included in pre-service and in-service programs on multiple intelligences theory (Gardner, 1993), literacy education (Calkins, 1994; Crafton, 1996), and performance-based assessment (Wiggins, 1998; Wolf & Reardon, 1996). The primary purpose of most arts-based teacher education programs is not to transform academic classroom teachers into arts specialists. Rather, the general aims are to increase teachers' understanding of and efficacy in using the arts as part of an expanded repertoire of teaching techniques and to promote active, creative, teaching and learning (Fowler, 1996; Torrance & Myers, 1970).

Despite the presence of the arts in professional development initiatives across the country, little data exists about the use of the arts by regular classroom teachers. One obstacle to such a study is the sheer breadth of the subject. The arts exist as distinct subjects and disciplines and as intrinsic parts of culture, history, and literature, with potent links to math and science. Students may be exposed to works of art through field trips, visiting artists, or media including videotape, computers, or books. They may create their own works of art or participate in exploratory activities using movement, dramatic play, music, or art materials. Discussion, reflection, and analyses may be part of any of these activities. In the continuum of arts activities in the classroom—from playing background music, to discussing a painting or a play, to mounting a full-fledged student-created opera complete with costumes and sets—there is no absolute way to classify what is and what is not "art." We cannot simply look at how often students sing a song or draw a picture to gauge the frequency of students' arts experiences. Dewey (1934) placed art in the realm of experience rather than product. In this view, almost any classroom activity can potentially provide an artistic experience if it involves attention to aesthetic qualities and the intentional application of artistic skills interacting with a symbolic object or idea (Eisner, 1985; Gardner, 1973; May, 1993). When teachers are aware of and can engage their students in appreciation and exploration of the aesthetic characteristics of experience in the world around us—the form and shape, dynamics and color, feelings and communication in many symbol systems—they can find artistic experiences in virtually any topic or subject area.

To design effective professional development programs using the arts, it is essential to understand the personal and institutional factors that enhance or undermine teachers' efforts to use the arts in their own practice and to look at the characteristics and attitudes of teachers who have been able to successfully implement the arts in various ways in their classrooms. Does one need a strong arts background to learn to employ the arts in the classroom? What attitudes seem to promote creative and artistic methods in teaching, and can those attitudes be developed through professional development? How can teachers be encouraged to attend professional development workshops and make use of the methods they learn there in a time of increased pressure for test score results and standardized curriculum?

This study gathered data on teachers' attitudes and practices to investigate the factors that support or inhibit arts use. The objective was not to evaluate the effectiveness of any specific professional development program but to better understand the subject from teachers' points of view. By examining the perspectives of teachers who have had access to arts-based professional development programs, this study can offer empirical data to strengthen the link between professional development and teaching practices in the arts.

BACKGROUND

Learning to use any new, creative teaching approach requires a level of personal motivation and willingness to take risks. However, the arts, more than most other activities, demand a significant shift in attitude toward the students and toward the curricular objectives (Fuller, 1969; Smith, 1966; Torrance, 1970). Creative arts experiences involve open-ended discovery and encourage unique, personal responses, as opposed to predetermined objectives and right or wrong answers (Eisner, 1994; Gardner, 1973). For a teacher to make the commitment to use a new approach, particularly in a discretionary area of the curriculum such as the arts, he or she must understand the instructional purpose, recognize the benefits, and feel confident in the skills required to teach it (Clark & Joyce, 1981; Hord, Rutherford,

Hurling-Austin, & Hall, 1998). As Torrance (1970) and many others have demonstrated, creativity and creative self-image can be developed and nurtured to a great extent through professional development (Smith, 1966; Starko, 1995). The ability to facilitate arts activities and adapt curriculum to include the arts, however, are more specific skill sets, which may require more specialized instruction to adopt into one's own teaching practice (ArtsConnection, 1996; Sarason, 1999; Spolin, 1986).

The messages that teachers receive about the educational priorities and value of the arts in their schools come from many sources—from direct supervisors to state and national politicians. The effectiveness of arts-based professional development must thus be evaluated in light of the current national movement for high-stakes testing and centralized control of curriculum. The arts remain largely outside of the core curriculum despite their inclusion as a core subject in the current No Child Left Behind Act (2000). Even in schools with a strong commitment to the arts, pressures to raise test scores and adhere to a standardized curriculum can undermine teachers' creativity and autonomy (Amabile, 1996; Gordon, 1999). Limits on space and time and lack of ongoing training and support can further inhibit teachers' efforts to use artistic methods in classroom practice (Baum, Owen, & Oreck, 1997; McKean, 1998; Stake, Bresler, & Mabry, 1991). A teacher may feel that the arts are enjoyable and recognize potential cognitive and social benefits for students but still be unconvinced that learning and enjoyment in the arts is a judicious use of time.

Despite the adoption of national and state arts standards (Consortium of National Arts Education Organizations, 1994), few schools have increased the number of arts specialists (National Center for Education Statistics, 1998). The burden for reaching the standards falls primarily (as is so often the case) to the classroom teacher. Given the time pressures that most teachers face, it is unlikely that the arts will be added as separate subjects in the regular classroom. Clearly, for the arts to be used they must fit into the existing curriculum in an integrated way. The term *arts integration* (Fowler, 1996; Remer, 1996) can encompass a range of objectives and purposes, summarized by Goldberg (1997) as teaching about, with, or through the arts. Teaching about the arts focuses on the discipline and history of the art forms themselves. Teaching with the arts uses artistic processes to teach other academic subjects (Cecil & Lauritzen, 1994), and teaching through the arts focuses on the development of basic learning and communication skills (Gallas, 1994). In the simplest sense, arts activities can be separated into two categories: creating/producing activities (e.g., singing, painting, dancing, or acting) and observation/exposure activities (e.g., listening to music, visiting an art exhibition, or watching a videotape). Verbal response, discussion, analysis, and reflection are a natural part of producing and exposure experiences and are given equal weight in the National Standards for Arts Education (Consortium of National Arts Education Organizations, 1994).

METHOD

Data were collected from 423 urban, suburban, and rural K-12 teachers with a newly developed 48-item survey (Teaching with the Arts Survey, TWAS; Oreck, 2000). TWAS provided information on teacher demographics (15 items), frequency of use of the arts in the classroom (8 items), and attitudes toward the arts that may be related to arts use in teaching (25 items). TWAS was developed based on an extensive review of literature and a prior survey instrument, the Arts in the Classroom Survey (Oreck, Baum, & Owen, 1999), and tested over the course of two 2-year U.S. Department of Education projects (U.S. Department of Education Grant #R206A00148). The current version of TWAS was pilot tested with teachers in schools similar to the study sites and revised after review by content experts.

Research Questions

Three major research questions guided the study:

1. What attitudes related to arts use in teaching can be identified and interpreted from teachers' responses on the Teaching With the Arts Survey (TWAS)?

2. To what extent can variance in teachers' self-reported frequency of use of the arts in their teaching be explained by demographic characteristics (i.e., gender, ethnicity, years of teaching experience, grade level taught), personal experience with the arts (i.e., past and current involvement in the arts, attendance at arts-based professional development), and their scores on attitude measures on the TWAS?

3. What do teachers consider to be the primary issues related to the use of the arts in their teaching?

Question 1 identified and clarified the dimensions of the constructs involved through the development and testing of a new survey instrument. Question 2 looked at the relevance and relationships of those attitudes and experiences to teachers' frequency of use of the arts, and Question 3 explored and described the issues in context, in the teachers' own words.

Data Sources

Schools were solicited to participate in the study through the arts-based professional development providers with which they worked. This guaranteed that teachers in the sample had access to arts workshops whether they actually attended or not. The 11 service providers included five arts-in-education organizations—ArtsConnection, Lincoln Center Institute, and City Center in New York City; Higher Order Thinking Schools (HOTS) in Connecticut; and Arts Resources in Teaching (A.R.T.) in Chicago, five school districts in Arizona, Colorado, Minnesota, and New York (2); and one university education program at the College of New Rochelle. Of the respondents, 56% ($n = 235$) of respondents had attended arts-based staff development in the previous year.

The sample ($N = 423$) consisted of public school classroom teachers ($n = 250$) and specialists ($n = 173$) in gifted arts, and special education, representing 97 schools in six states. The demographic makeup of the sample in terms of age ($M = 39$), gender (86.8% women), ethnic group percentages (73% White), years of teaching experience (12), and average class size (23) closely resembles the national averages for teachers (National Center for Education Statistics, 1995). The sample was primarily made up of elementary school teachers (Grade K to 3: 47%, Grade 4 to 6: 24%, Grade K to 6 specialists: 14.7%) that generally reflects the grade levels of the schools in which the arts-based professional development programs were offered.

Teaching with the Arts Surveys were distributed to all teachers in the participating schools but were completed and returned voluntarily, so the sample of teachers is a purposive or non-probability sample (Babbie, 1990; Rae & Parker, 1997), which limits the generalizability of the results. The relatively low overall response rate (43%) caused concern that the respondents were not representative of the faculty as a whole. To test this external validity threat, a variable (SchlN) was used in multiple regression analysis to compare schools with high-and low-response rates. Response rate was not found to be a statistically significant variable.

Data Analysis

Principal components analysis (PCA) (SPSS, 1998) was employed to provide validity evidence for the TWAS and to identify interpretable components that explain significant variation among the responses. PCA was selected to identify components that account for the greatest portion of total variance in the data for later use in a regression analysis (Hair, Anderson, Tatham, & Black, 1998). Two separate analyses were conducted: one with the 23 attitude items and another with the 8 frequency-of-use items.

After initial component extraction (oblique rotation, oblimin with Kaiser normalization), alpha reliability estimates were obtained for the derived components.

Question 2 was investigated using stepwise hierarchical multiple-regression analysis to ascertain the degree to which the demographic and attitude variables contributed to variance in the level of self-reported use of the arts in the classroom. Selection and order of independent variables entered into the model were determined by the researcher prior to the analysis based on theoretical grounds (Tabachnick & Fidell, 1996). Demographic variables (gender, years teaching), teaching characteristics (grade level taught, attendance at arts-based staff development), and personal arts experiences (length of past arts instruction, frequency of current arts involvement) were entered first. The attitude components were entered in the last step of the model. Ethnicity was not included in the regression analysis because the extreme differences in group sizes (White = 309, Latino = 63, African American = 36, Asian = 9) would make the variable unstable as a predictor. All categorical variables were dummy coded. Potential interaction effects (gender/grade level, years of teaching experience/attendance at arts workshops) hypothesized to have a relationship to the dependent variable were tested along with main effects. Sample size was more than adequate for principal components and multiple-regression analysis (Gable & Wolf, 1991). There were no significant violations of the multivariate assumptions for principal components and multiple regression. Tolerance levels for all predictor variables were greater than .75 indicating low multicollinearity. Six outliers (Mahalonobis D^2_{30} = 59.703, p <.05) were identified but retained in the analysis after examination to ensure that they were valid and reflected an intentional response pattern.

To address Question 3, data from two openended short answer questions (n = 389) were coded with an open-coded, emergent classification system (Erlandson, Harris, Skipper, & Allen, 1993), analyzed for patterns and themes using QSR Nudist 4.0 (SCOLARI, 1996) software, and combined into patterns with an axial coding schema (Strauss & Corbin, 1990).

RESULTS

Questions 1: Investigation of Teachers' Attitudes and Uses of the Arts

The first research question sought to identify and define psychological constructs that have a bearing on teachers' use of the arts and quantify the frequency of their self-reported arts use in the classroom. The analyses were conducted in two separate stages—first with the 23 attitude items and subsequently with the 8 frequency-of-use items.

In the initial principal components solution for the 23 attitude items (using the Kaiser eigenvalue > 1 criterion), six components were obtained. Two of those components, #4 and #5, were loaded on by only three and two variables, respectively, and had a clear conceptual relationship to other obtained components. Inspection of the scree plot suggested the restructuring of components for a final four-component solution. When the analysis was rerun forcing four factors and using an oblique rotation (direct oblimin method), the total variance explained decreased from 60% in the six-component solution to 51% in the four. The improved interpretability of the results, however, supports the more parsimonious solution. The values of the squared multiple correlations (SMC) for most of the items were in the moderate range (.30 to .50) with a few high (.70) and low (.06) SMCs. Table 1 presents the loadings for the 23 attitude items after rotation.

Alpha reliability estimates for three of the four derived components were between .74 and .92. Lower reliability for the constraints component (.55) appeared to reflect significant differences in school environments and the specific circumstances encountered by the teachers in the study. Scales means and reliability estimates for the four components are presented in Table 2.

The teachers' sense of importance of the arts in the curriculum was the first derived component. The importance component included nine items concerning the four art forms and art-making (doing) and exposure-type activities that reflects a high level of consistency in teachers' value for all of the arts and various instructional purposes. The high average scores for importance (M = 4.28 out of 5) demonstrates that the arts are valued by teachers as part of the educational experience of students, regardless of other constraints, concerns, or external pressures that limit their use. It should be noted that these teachers say art is important, not necessarily that they should be the ones teaching it.

The items concerning self-image and self-efficacy combined to form a second component with loadings of .65 to .75 (alpha reliability = .79). Similar to the importance component, responses seem to be clearly based not on a specific art form or type of activity but on a more general sense of artistic self-efficacy. The results of the TWAS suggest that although the teachers regard themselves as slightly more creative than artistic, these are correlated constructs (r = .574). In the short answer responses, teachers tended to use the terms *artistic* and *creative* interchangeably.

The support component derived from the TWAS involved three distinct issues—general school support, specific supervisor support, and sense of autonomy. These three aspects of support loaded on a

Table 1   Structure Matrix for Attitude Items

Item Stem	Component			
	1	2	3	4
14. (I feel it is) important for students to read or attend a play	.789			
16. Important for students to look at works of art	.779			
17. Important for students to engage in theater activities	.759			
12. Important for students to listen to a piece of music	.749			
16. Important for students to engage in music activities	.732			
18. Important for students to engage in visual arts activities	.696	−.309		
13. Important for students to engage in dance activities	.655			
11. Important for students to view a videotape of a dance	.621			
128. I feel that there are many students in my class who would especially benefit from more arts activities in the curriculum.	.485		−.342	
130. I consider myself a highly creative person.		−.747		
119. I consider myself an artist.		−.747		
126. I feel confident in my ability to facilitate theater activities.	.312	−.696		
121. I feel confident in my ability to facilitate music activities.		−.695		
124. I feel confident in my ability to facilitate visual arts activities.		−.681		
117. I feel confident in my ability to facilitate dance activities.		−.651		
127. In general, my school is supportive of innovative teaching approaches.			−.885	
129. I am free to use new teaching approaches in my classroom as I see fit.			−.865	
122. My supervisor encourages teacher creativity.			−.766	
131. I feel constrained by the demands of the curriculum I have to teach.				.701
118. I feel that I don't have enough time to teach the arts along with the rest of the curriculum.				.641
123. I don't have enough space to use movement effectively in the classroom.				.603
125. My students have trouble concentrating on other work after an arts activity.				.556
120. I am concerned that music, dance, and theater activities are too noisy or disruptive for the classroom.	.332			.425

Note: Extraction method: Principal component analysis. Rotation method: oblimin with Kaiser normalization.

Table 2   Alpha Reliability Results for Four Component Solution for Attitude Items

Component	Name	No. of Items	Alpha Reliability	Scale Mean	SD
1	Importance of Arts	9	.87	4.29	.58
2	Self (efficacy and image)	6	.79	3.12	.86
3	Support	3	.83	3.99	.92
4	Constraints	5	.55	2.75	.74

single component with alpha reliability of .83, quite high for a three-item component. The responses to these items suggest that teachers perceived that they have a relatively high level of support and autonomy to try new, innovative, and creative approaches in their classrooms (mean support score = 3.98 out of 5).

The constraints component had a wide spread of loadings (.42 to .71) and lower alpha reliability estimates than the other components but did emerge as a distinct construct. Responses concerning major issues—such as demands on time, pressure for test results, and expectations to teach a mandated curriculum—varied greatly among teachers from different schools and districts. A number of specific issues, such as the physical layout of classrooms, noise problems, and the availability of materials and resources, appeared to be of high concern only in certain schools and were not consistent across the sample.

In the second principal components analysis, the eight frequency-of-use items loaded on a single frequency component, encompassed the exposure and art-making activities in dance, music, theater, and visual arts. High alpha reliability of .83 for the eight frequency items reflects overall consistency in teachers' use (or nonuse) of the arts in their teaching. This consistency supports the use of the single frequency component (scale mean = 2.63) as the dependent variable in the regression analysis. Figure 1 shows the teachers' self-reported frequency of use of the arts.

As reported in prior studies (Oreck, Baum, & Owen, 1999), visual arts was the most frequently used participatory arts activity. Whether this reflects actual instruction or simply an enjoyable use of free time, teachers seem more comfortable with the visual, as opposed to the performing, arts. Music was rated highest in the exposure mode. Again, it is unclear if self-reported use reflects focused, active listening activities to live or recorded music, or more passive activities, such as playing background music at various times during the school day.

Question 2: Personal Characteristics and Experience That Influence Arts Use in Teaching

Question 2 investigated the relationship of teachers' personal characteristics and attitudes to their self-reported arts usage. Of the 13 variables in the multiple regression analysis, 7 were found to be statistically significant (adj-Bonferroni alpha < .005). Demographic and personal experience variables were entered first and accounted for 20.2% of the variation in the dependent variable (frequency of arts use). The four derived attitude components accounted for an additional 18.4% of variance. Overall, the model explained 38.6% of the variation in self-reported arts usage, which represents a large multivariate effect size (Cohen, 1992) ($F = 18.113$, $p < .001$, $R^2 = .386$, Adj. $R^2 = .364$). The four-step regression model is presented in Table 3.

Two of the attitude components—self-efficacy/self-image and constraints—made the greatest unique contributions to overall variance. Not surprisingly, the other most significant contributor was grade level taught, with early childhood teachers (Grades K to 3) using the arts most frequently and middle and high school teachers least. As expected, participants in arts workshops in the last 12 months used the arts more frequently; however, because attendance tended to be voluntary, no causal inference can be made. It is likely that teachers who were already most inclined toward the arts participated in arts workshops. The difference in frequency of use between workshop participants ($M = 2.8$) and non-participants ($M = 2.4$ out of 5) was statistically significant ($t = 5.3$, $p = .001$) but still placed workshop participants between "rarely" and "monthly" in the frequency-of-use scale. Coefficients for the variables entered in the final model are presented in Table 4.

Gender initially appeared to be a significant predictor with women in the sample using the arts more frequently than men, however this difference was not significant when the other predictors were entered into the regression model. Lack of significant interaction effects between gender and grade level showed that the differences between genders could not be explained by the higher percentage of women teaching in the early grades. The extreme inequality in group sizes in this study (86.8% women) makes any conclusions speculative, at best.

Surprisingly, neither prior formal arts instruction nor current artistic practice outside of school were found to be significant predictors of arts use in teaching. Years of teaching experience (highly correlated with age) and subject-area specialties were also not significant in the model. Some age differences might have been expected, given that teachers currently in their 20 were elementary school students in the 1980s, after the severe cutbacks in many school arts programs across the country.

Question 3: Motivations and Constraints to Using the Arts in the Classroom

The two open-ended, short answer responses allowed the teachers to respond in their own words about their primary motivations to arts use (Q.31: "What do you feel is the strongest current motivation for you to use the arts in your teaching?," Q.32: "What do you feel would motivate you to use the arts

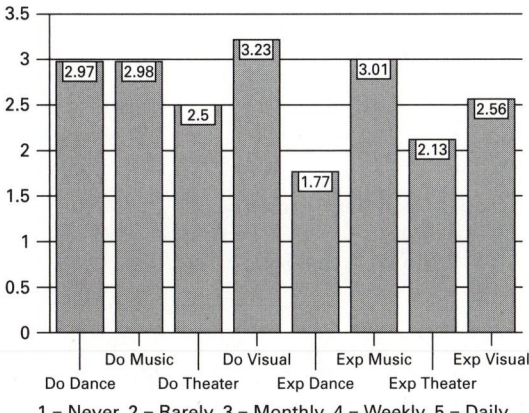

Figure 1. Frequency of Use of the Four Art Forms in Doing and Exposure Modes.

Table 3 Hierarchical Regression Analysis Model Summary

	Incremental Validity Statistics				Change Statistics				
Model	R	R^2	Adl. R^2	SE Estimate	R^2	F	df 1	df 2	Significant F
Step 1[a]	.275	.075	.066	.7485	.075	7.836	4	384	.000"
Step 2[b]	.318	.101	.087	.7400	.026	5.430	2	382	.005"
Step 3[c]	.450	.202	.183	.6999	.101	16.018	3	379	.000"
Step 4[d]	.621	.386	.364	.6174	.184	28.012	4	375	.000"

[a]Predictors: (constant), grade level, SchIN (school response rate).
[b]New predictors: gender, years teaching.
[c]New predictors: Level of past instruction, attendance at art workshop, level of current practice.
[d]New predictors: Support Component, Constraints Component, Importance Component, Self-Efficacy-Self-Image Component
**significant at alpha = .005.

Table 4 Summary of Coefficients for the Hierarchical Regression Analysis (_n_ = 389)

	Unstandardized Coefficients		Standardized Coefficients	Significance of the Slope		Correlations		Collinearity Statistics	
	B	SE	β	t	Sig	Zero Order	Part	Tolerance	VIF
1. Grade level (4 to 6)[a]	−.121	.080	−.068	−1.509	.132	−.048	−.061	.812	1.232
2. Grade level (K to 6)	−.371	.099	−.165	_−3.732_	.000	−.088	−.151	.843	1.186
3. Grade level (7 to 12)	−.449	.103	−.191	_−4.367_	.000	−.181	−.177	.857	1.167
4. School N[b]	−.044	.066	−.028	−.664	.507	−.131	−.027	.943	1.061
5. Gender[c]	−.265	.098	−.116	−2.719	.007	−.171	−.110	.905	1.105
6. Years teaching	.064	.004	.082	1.941	.053	.083	.079	.917	1.090
7. Level of current practice[d]	.064	.032	.096	2.037	.042	.216	.082	.754	1.325
8. Level of past instruction[e]	−.014	.029	−.024	−.510	.610	.162	−.021	.755	1.324
9. Art workshop Y/N?	.228	.067	.147	_3.391_	.001	.273	.137	.873	1.145
10. Component 1— importance[f]	.118	.033	.152	_3.578_	.000	.173	.145	.907	1.103
11. Component 2— Self	.260	.034	.337	_7.678_	.000	.373	.311	.851	1.175
12. Component 3— Support	.098	.032	.127	_3.055_	.002	.149	.124	.949	1.054
13. Component 4— Constraints	−.203	.033	−.260	_−6.231_	.000	−.290	−.252	.940	1.063
Constant	2.611	.087		29.886	.000				

Note: VIF = variance inflation factor.
Italic = statistically significant at Bonferroni alpha = .0005.
Dependent variable (average of 8 frequency-of-use items).
[a]Dummy coded (kindergarten to third grade = reference group).
[b]Dummy coded (schools with n > 10 = reference group).
[c]Dummy coded (females = reference group).
[d]An interval variable representing current arts involvement (4 levels: rarely, never; occasionally; weekly, monthly; daily).
[e]An interval variable representing past arts instruction (4 levels; none; 1 year or less; 2 to 4 years; more than 4 years).
[f]Continuous variables: Mean scale scores calculated for each of four factors on the Teaching with the Arts Survey (TWAS).

more often?"). Analysis of responses to these questions revealed four major themes related to: (a) self, (b) students, (c) curriculum and pedagogy, and (d) external factors. Each of the four themes contained 8 to 15 specific categories of responses. Responses were also coded along a positive (motivation)/ negative (concerns or constraints) axis. The relative importance and power of each issue was analyzed by (a) frequency of the response, (b) context and intersections between the issue in question and other major issues, and (c) the issue in question in relation to the respondents' frequency-of-use scores and other grouping variables (demographics, personal experience, teaching experience).

Self issues. The most frequently mentioned issue in the open-ended responses was the need for more training to gain skills and build self-efficacy in using the arts ($n = 114$). Teachers specifically expressed the need for additional techniques and knowledge to make connections with other areas of the academic curriculum. The responses concerning oneself frequently combined specific self concerns (e.g., self-image, self-efficacy) with more general statements about personal experience, interests, and background. The two constructs of attitudes toward the self, personal characteristics, and background, handled separately in the statistical analyses, were frequently linked in the teachers' own words and are clearly interrelated. Teachers' lack of confidence, for example, was most often explained by their lack of specific training or prior arts instruction.

Teachers were motivated to use the arts by a desire to increase their enjoyment in teaching ($n = 25$), and to enhance their own creativity ($n = 18$).

Their motivation also reflected their personal values about art and education ($n = 30$). High arts users were most likely to mention educational philosophy as a motivation, particularly multiple intelligences theory (Gardner, 1983), aesthetic education (Schubart, 1996), and a general philosophy of teaching the whole child. The existence of national, state, or local standards in the arts was not mentioned as a rationale for arts use. Examples of responses about self are shown in Table 5.

Student issues. The teachers' comments about students overwhelmingly focused on the positive value of the arts, citing a wide variety of instructional and social benefits. Their awareness of the diversity of student strengths, learning styles, and intelligences ($n = 85$) was the strongest motivation mentioned. They also discussed the benefits of the arts for students who speak English as a second language ($n = 30$), those with various special therapeutic needs ($n = 16$), and artistically talented students ($n = 16$). They expressed the belief that the arts increase intrinsic motivation ($n = 78$) and enjoyment ($n = 50$) in learning and observed increased thinking and problem-solving skills ($n = 18$), memory ($n = 8$), and

Table 5   Sample Responses Concerning Self-Issues, Student Issues, Curricular Issues, External Issues

Motivation	Concern
"My strongest current motivation is …"	"I would be motivated more often if …"
Self-issues	
Q32: For myself, the arts are the most stimulating activities that I undertake. Approaching life through movement and new ways of seeing expand me and allow me to be a more creative and effective person and teacher.	Q33: I need training in how to integrate the arts, since I was never taught how to teach/use music/art/ movement in the classroom.
Student issues	
Q32: My strongest past and current motivation for using the arts in teaching is twofold: It taps into one of those multiple intelligences (other than academic), and it helps students who have different learning styles.	Q33: Having a class where arts would not interfere with basic math, reading, and writing time. Having a class that was not so academically needy in fundamental areas.
Curricular issues	
Q32: It is fun! We learn so much about cultures, time periods, ourselves, and curriculum through the arts. We open our creative channels, add to our learning strengths.	Q33: I would use arts more often if it was directly tied into my curriculum I don't want to (or can't) design projects to go along with my curriculum.
External issues	
Q32: The fact that our principal is very supportive of the arts.	Q33: I would need fewer curricular requirements and unnecessary paperwork, as well as more time to plan and complete activities with the inclusion of the arts.

discipline (n = 14). Students' need to express their feelings (n = 35) and physical needs (n = 19) were also mentioned. Only five teachers in the survey expressed concerns about arts activities acting as possible distraction or conflict with other academic work. Table 5 also presents examples of teachers' comments concerning student issues.

Curricular and pedagogical issues. Most teachers who mentioned curriculum said the arts enhanced the academic curriculum (n = 68), particularly in the areas of literacy (n = 30) and cultural awareness (n = 13). The most common concerns mentioned were lack of materials (n = 53) and lesson plans (n = 24), and lack of opportunities to collaborate with colleagues (n = 47) and visiting artists (n = 32). The demands to cover the curriculum (related to time issues) were another common concern.

Teachers' comments related to curriculum and pedagogy often encompassed other themes—self-issues (involving the need for more training to integrate the arts into the curriculum), student issues (regarding motivation and diversity of learning styles), and external issues (reflecting the pressure to cover the mandated curriculum). The teachers emphasized the need to fit the arts into the existing curriculum rather than teach it as a separate curricular area. Table 5 also presents an example of responses concerning the curriculum.

External issues. Time was the most frequently mentioned external source of concern. Comments about time were most often made in the context of pressure to teach the mandated curriculum (65 of 105 responses) and were also related to issues of autonomy and perceived support for creative teaching methods.

External support was mentioned in relation to direct supervisors, school and district administrators, and colleagues. The responses to the items on the TWAS concerning support from supervisors for creative and artistic teaching methods were positive and relatively high, however the short-answer responses revealed teachers' concerns that they lacked support from supervisors to use the arts more frequently (n = 43). After time and support, lack of space was mentioned most frequently as a limitation to arts use (n = 29). The space problem may partially explain why teachers used the visual arts most often. Teachers also mentioned lack of arts supplies and money for additional supplies and field trips (n = 46) as current and increasing obstacles. Table 5 also presents sample responses about external issues.

DISCUSSION

Staff developers and arts educators may find the results of this study encouraging and troubling. Although the majority of the teachers in this sample

report having had 1 year or less of formal arts instruction in their lifetime, they value the arts in education. They believe in its importance in the curriculum and recognize its potential benefits for students. They also express the desire for more artistic and creative experiences in their own lives. Despite these values and attitudes, however, and despite the fact that the arts are offered by their schools or districts as part of professional development, these teachers rarely use the arts in the classroom. There are many reasons for this. Teachers report being hindered by lack of time and by pressures to cover the prescribed curriculum and to prepare students for standardized tests. They express a lack of confidence in their facilitation skills in the arts. Space and materials are in short supply, and support from and collaboration with arts specialists, teaching artists, and experienced colleagues is often absent. Teachers have conflicting perceptions about their own autonomy and the support they have from supervisors to use the arts in the classroom. Responses on the survey reflected generally positive support for innovation and creative teaching methods, whereas many answers to the open-ended questions focused on the pressure to conform. This apparent contradiction can be interpreted in a number of ways. Despite external pressures, teachers may actually have more freedom to innovate than most take advantage of. Or, the opposite may be just as likely—that teachers' perceptions of support from supervisors and principals would evaporate if they tested the limits by employing the arts in the classroom more frequently.

High-use teachers did not share a common, specific profile in this survey. Women were slightly higher arts users than men, however the differences were small. The attitude components, particularly those related to self-image and self-efficacy, had the strongest relationship to frequency of arts use in teaching. This can be seen as highly encouraging to those interested in developing greater arts use among classroom teachers. If artistic attitudes and self-confidence—rather than arts-rich backgrounds or previously developed sets of skills—are the critical elements for arts use in teaching, then professional development can make a difference in promoting arts-inclusive pedagogy.

The surprising finding that prior arts instruction was not a significant predictor of current arts use might appear to contradict the intuitive assumption that a person's value for and skills in the arts would have been established, to a great extent, through formal arts experiences in childhood or young adulthood. The statistical result is more understandable in light of the fact that with so many teachers (53%) in the lowest level of involvement (less than 1 year), there was relatively little diversity in the sample to explain significant variation in art use.

In the open-ended question segment of the survey, the need for more training to gain skills in teaching the arts ($n = 114$) was the most frequently cited concern. Pressure to teach the mandated curriculum ($n = 105$) was the second most frequently mentioned hindrance to arts use. Despite their belief in the importance of the arts for all students and a sense that many students could especially benefit from artistic approaches, teachers appear to lack the confidence and/or the autonomy to include the arts in their teaching. Teachers' ability to overcome these impediments is likely tied to Huberman's (1992) concept of "personal teaching efficacy" and Ashton and Webb's (1986) ideas of "general teaching efficacy." Teaching efficacy links the self-perception of competence with the situation-specific expectation that the teacher can successfully influence student learning. Teachers may comprehend the general importance of the arts for students but must have evidence that their own successful inclusion of arts processes will have a positive impact on student performance. They must attempt some aspect of artistic processes or methods on a regular basis (certainly more frequently than the "monthly to rarely" average in this sample) to gain the confidence and gather the evidence of student learning needed to achieve teaching efficacy.

The teachers' personal/self-motivations and concerns are difficult to separate from the curricular and institutional priorities of the schools in which they work and in which they themselves were educated. Concerns about lack of training, for example, appear to reflect the low priority given to the arts in preservice and inservice teacher education. Instructional time in the school day is always a central issue for teachers. The arts take time, however, even more critically, they require a change of pacing, expectations, and methods on the part of teachers. The nature of learning through the arts is fundamentally contrary to the single-right-answer mentality of a test-driven curriculum. Teachers need the motivation and the pedagogical skills to make the transitions within the school day from more didactic processes to the more open-ended approaches found in arts teaching and learning. They also need the autonomy and encouragement from supervisors to alter and adapt their curriculum to include the arts.

Clearly, the constraints of time, space, curricular demands, and testing will not disappear anytime soon. A teacher's ability to change gears, to take risks, to encourage artistic explorations and expression, and to employ openended, creative curriculum and pedagogy is an individual endeavor driven by personal commitment. Despite obstacles, some teachers find ways to integrate the arts on a regular basis. Teachers who have evidence that artistic approaches aid student learning are more able to justify the time spent on the arts and to articulate the benefits to supervisors and parents. In a follow-up interview to the TWAS, one of the high-use teachers in the study explained why her students did improvisational theater games in the week leading up to the state reading exams, whereas the other fifth grades were in intensive test preparation:

> It was like an ice-breaker. How can you cram something into a week's period? You just say, "Since we worked so hard since September, let's have some fun expressing ourselves." And [my students] did extremely well in both English Language Arts and in the math. So [the principal] can't really complain. I show them the results (Oreck, 2001, p. 126).

Although each art form requires certain unique facilitation skills, effective teaching of the arts shares many basic features with good teaching in other subjects. Many current approaches to literacy, science, social studies, and math promote active, student-centered, differentiated, discovery-oriented approaches and involve many of the same specific facilitation skills. A number of teachers referred in the short-answer responses to their training in the Teachers College Reading and Writing Project (Calkins, 1994), hands-on science curricula (Kendall & Marzano, 1997; Saul & Reardon, 1996), and the development of classroom learning and interest centers (Renzulli & Reis, 1997), as preparation for using the arts in their classrooms. These approaches require teachers to act more as facilitators and coaches than purveyors of information, to assist small groups working at different speeds and on different topics, to create flexible and changeable classroom configurations, and to encourage student problem solving and problem finding. Furthermore, the processes used to develop concept-based curricula that encourage higher-order thinking skills (Wiggins & McTighe, 1998) ask teachers to think of curriculum in more integrated, holistic ways. A high-use teacher in the survey referred to her use of the arts in teaching as "finding an alternative way to deliver the same concept using different ideas and methods." She continued:

> Everything's connected. . . . I like this concept of teaching not subject by subject but teaching by concept. If we're talking about patterns, let's talk about patterns in all subject areas. If we're talking about the concept of before and after, let's talk about it in all subject areas. . . . If I have a strong handle on the concept, I could basically link to any subject matter and that's where I get the creativeness out (Oreck, 2001. p. 134).

Ultimately, the ability and motivation of teachers to use the arts as a tool in their practice is related to their complete education—from childhood arts experiences, to preparation in preservice courses, to in-service experiences in the arts and in other subjects. It is difficult to generalize from these results to the larger teacher population because we do not know how many schools include the arts in their professional development program for teachers. This sample was chosen specifically because they worked in a diverse group of urban, suburban, and rural schools where the arts were at least offered. The results suggest some general recommendations for the design of and recruitment for in-service and preservice staff development in the arts.

Recommendations for Professional Development

1. Teachers need ongoing support for their own creative and artistic development. The predominance of self and personal issues throughout the study strongly supports a concentration on teachers' own creative and artistic skills, attitudes, and behaviors. Most arts workshops share this goal to a greater or lesser extent; they tend to include active participation with the teacher's role primarily as the learner. However, the excitement, creativity, and supportive environment generated in an arts workshop is difficult to maintain amid the pressures of the school day. Ongoing support for teacher creativity can take many forms—regular professional development workshops, arts classes for teachers, meetings with colleagues, observations of arts classes and arts-infused lessons, sharing and celebrations of teachers' artistic accomplishments, reading and study groups, and direct encouragement from supervisors.

2. Professional development should help teachers recognize and articulate the impact of the arts on students. The impact of the arts on students was identified as the most powerful motivator for arts use.

   Unfortunately, empirical evidence of this impact is scarce and often does not address the primary issues that concern teachers. The oft-cited observation that the arts build self-esteem, although undoubtedly true in many cases, is difficult to measure and does not directly address academic performance issues that concern teachers on a daily basis. Teachers who have seen specific academic and behavioral improvement appear to have the strongest commitment to using the arts on a regular basis.

3. School and district administrators should make in-service arts workshops a higher priority for teachers. Even in schools involved in ongoing partnerships with arts organizations such as ArtsConnection and Lincoln Center Institute,

attendance at arts workshops tends to be voluntary (ArtsConnection, 1996). Joyce and Showers (1995) directly linked faculty participation rates with successful implementation of new approaches. The closer a school is to 100% faculty involvement, the higher the level of transfer to the classroom. The low participation rates in arts workshops reported for the schools in this study thus pose a serious obstacle to implementation of the arts.

CONCLUSION

The arts exemplify the conflict between active, open-ended, constructivist approaches and prescribed, narrowly defined objectives of a test-based educational culture described by Dewey 80 years ago. The current educational climate only deepens the rift and raises the stakes for teachers who dare to try new, creative, and artistic teaching methods and approaches. The findings of this study indicate three critical challenges for teachers in using the arts: (a) to nurture and maintain their own creativity and artistic skills, (b) to develop facilitation skills in the arts, and (c) to find a balance between their artistic values and the pressures of their jobs.

As in any professional development initiative, learning to use the arts in teaching has personal and pedagogical components. In the arts, the personal aspect is magnified. To teach artistically, whether engaging in specific arts activities or attending to the aesthetic qualities of experience, a teacher must trust his or her intuition and respond to the individuality of students. He or she must also be able to facilitate confidently, creating an atmosphere in which artistic attitudes, behaviors, and expression can flourish.

The inner resources of teachers; their attitudes toward art, creativity, and innovation; their commitment to personal growth; and their educational and life values all need nurturing within the school and in professional development programs. The arts, Dewey (1934) contended, can be a model of the kind of experiences we most value in education. Now, more than ever, teachers need support and training to make all teaching more artistic.

REFERENCES

Amabile, T. M. (1996). *Creativity in context.* Boulder, CO: Westview.

Arts Connection. (1996). *New horizons* (Report to the Jacob Javits Gifted and Talented Students Education Program, U.S. Department of Education. Office of Education Research and Improvement, #R206A30046). New York: Author.

Ashton, P., & Webb, R. (1986). *Making a difference; Teachers' sense of efficacy and students achievement.* New York: Longman.

Babbie, E. (1990). *Survey research methods.* Belmont, CA: Wadsworth.

Baum, S., Owen, S., & Oreck, B. (1997). Transferring individual self-regulation processes from arts to academics. *Arts Education Policy review, 98*(4), 32-39.

Calkins, L. M. (1994). *The art of teaching writing.* Portsmouth, NH: Heinemann.

Cecil, N. L., & Lauritzen, P. (1994). *Literacy and the arts for the integrated classroom.* White Plains, NY: Longman.

Clark, C., & Joyce. B. R. (1981). Teacher decision making and teaching effectiveness. In B. R. Joyce, C. C. Brown, & L. Peck (Eds.), *Flexibility in teaching* (pp. 228-235). New York: Longman.

Cohen, J. (1992). A power primer. *Psychological Bulletin, 112,* 155-159.

Consortium of National Arts Education Organizations. (1994). *National standards for arts education.* Reston, VA: Music Educators National Conference.

Crafton, L. (1996). *Standards in practice.* Urbana, IL: National Council of Teachers of English.

Dewey, J. (1934). *Arts as experience.* New York: Minton, Balch & Co.

Eisner, E. W. (1985). *The art of educational evaluation: A personal view.* London: Falmer Press.

Eisner, E. W. (1994). *Cognition and curriculum reconsidered* (2nd ed.). New York: Teachers College Press.

Erlandson, D. A., Harris, E. L., Skipper, B. L., & Allen, S. D. (1993). *Doing naturalistic inquiry.* Newbury Park, CA: Sage.

Fowler, C. (1996). *Strong arts, strong schools.* New York: Oxford University Press.

Fuller, E. F. (1969). Concerns of teachers: A developmental conceptualization. *American Educational Research Journal, 6*(2), 207-226.

Gable, R. K., & Wolf, M. (1991). *Instrument development in the affective domain: Measuring attitudes and values in corporate and school settings* (2nd ed.). Norwell, MA: Kluwer Academic.

Gallas, K. (1994). *The languages of learning.* New York: Teachers College Press.

Gardner, H. (1973). *The arts and human development.* New York: John Wiley.

Gardner, H. (1983). *Frames of mind.* New York: Basic Books.

Gardner, H. (1990). *Art education and human development.* Los Angeles: Getty Education Institute for the Arts.

Gardner, H. (1993). *Multiple intelligences: Theory into practice.* New York: Basic Books.

Goldberg, M. (1997). *Arts and learning.* New York: Longman.

Goodlad, J. I. (1992). Toward a place in the curriculum for the arts. In B. Reimer & R. A. Smith (Eds.), *The arts, education and aesthetic knowing: 91st yearbook of the National Society for the Study of Education* (pp. 192-212). Chicago: University of Chicago Press.

Gordon, E. W. (1999). Toward an equitable system of educational assessment. In E. W. Gordon (Ed.), *Education and justice* (pp. 119-136). New York: Teachers College Press.

Hair, J. E., Anderson, R. E., Tatham, R. L., & Black, W. C. (1998). *Multivariate data analysis* (5th ed.). Upper Saddle River, NJ: Prentice Hall.

Hord, S. M., Rutherford, W. L., Hurling-Austin, L., & Hall, G. E. (1998). *Taking charge of change.* Austin, TX: Southwest Educational Development Laboratory.

Huberman, M. (1992). Teacher development and instructional mastery. In A. Hargreaves & M. G. Fullan (Eds.), *Understanding teacher development* (pp. 122-142). New York: Teachers College Press.

Joyce, B. R., & Showers, B. (1995). *Student achievement through staff development: Fundamentals of school renewal* (2nd ed.). New York: Longman.

Kendall, J. S., & Marzano, R. J. (1997). *Content knowledge: A compendium of standards and benchmarks for K-12 education,* Aurora, CO: McRel.

May, W. T. (1993). Teaching as a work of art in the medium of curriculum. *Theory Into Practice, 32*(4), 210-218. Columbus: Ohio State University.

McKean, B. (1998, April). *Teachers conceptions of arts education: Fostering personal, social and cultural development through the arts.* Paper presented at the annual meeting of the American Educational Research Association, New York.

National Center for Education Statistics, (1995). *Degrees and other formal awards, conferred surveys, and integrated postsecondary education data system (IPEDS).* Washington, DC: U.S. Department of Education.

National Center for Education Statistics. (1998). *The NAEP 1997 arts report card* (NCES 1999-486). Washington, DC: U.S. Department of Education.

No Child Left Behind Act of 2000, Pub. L. No. 107-110. § 5551 (2000). Retrieved January 4, 2003, from www.ed.gov/policy/eseq02/pg80.html

Oreck, B. (2000). *The arts in teaching: An investigation of factors influencing teachers' use of the arts in the classroom.* Doctoral dissertation, University of Connecticut, Storrs. ProQuest Cat. #9999695.

Oreck, B. (2001). *Teaching with the arts survey.* Unpublished survey instrument. University of Connecticut at Storrs.

Oreck, B., Baum, S., & Owen, S. (1999, April). *The development of teachers' skills and confidence in using the arts in the classroom.* Paper presented at the annual meeting of the American Educational Research Association, Montreal, Quebec, Canada.

Rae, L. M., & Parker, R. A. (1997). *Designing and conducting survey research: A comprehensive guide* (2nd ed). San Francisco: Jossey-Bass.

Remer, J. (1996). *Beyond enrichment: Building effective arts partnerships with schools and your community.* New York: ACA Books.

Renzulli, J. S. (1994). *Schools for talent development.* Mansfield Center, CT: Creative Learning Press.

Renzulli, J. S., & Reis, S. M. (1997). *The schoolwide enrichment model* (2nd ed.). Mansfield Center, CT: Creative Learning Press.

Sarason, S. B. (1999). *Teaching as a performing art.* New York: Teachers College Press.

Saul, W., & Reardon, J. (Eds.). (1996). *Beyond the science kit: Inquiry in action.* Portsmouth, NH: Heinemann.

Schubart, M. (1996). Teaching kids to listen: A conversation with Mark Schubart. In J. Remer (Ed.), *Beyond enrichment: Building effective arts partnerships with schools and your community* (pp. 155–162). New York: ACA Books.

SCOLARI. (1996). QSR Nudist software (Version 4.0). Thousand Oaks, CA: Sage.

Sizer, T. R. (1984). *Horace's compromise.* Boston: Houghton Mifflin.

Smith, J. A. (1966). *Setting conditions for creative teaching in the elementary school.* Boston: Allyn & Bacon.

SPSS. (1998). SPSS 9.0 [computer software]. Chicago: Author.

Spolin, V. (1986). *Theater games for the classroom.* Evanston, IL: Northwestern University Press.

Stake, R., Bresler, L., & Mabry, L. (1991). *Custom and cherishing: The arts in elementary schools.* Urbana, IL: National Arts Education Research Center at the University of Illinois.

Starko, A. J. (1995). *Creativity in the classroom.* New York: Longman.

Strauss, A. L., & Corbin, J. (1990). *Basics of qualitative research: Grounded theory procedures and techniques.* Newbury Park, CA: Sage.

Tabachnick, B. G., & Fidell, L. S. (1996). *Using multivariate statistics* (3rd ed.). New York: Harper-Collins.

Torrance, E. P. (1970). *Encouraging creativity in the classroom.* Dubuque, IA: Wm, Brown.

Torrance, E. P., & Myers, R. E. (1970). *Creative learning and teaching.* New York: Dodd, Mead.

Wiggins, G. (1998). *Educative assessment: Designing assessments to inform and improve student performance.* San Francisco: Jossey-Bass.

Wiggins, G., & McTighe, J. (1998). *Understanding by design.* Upper Saddle River, NJ: Merrill/Prentice Hall.

Wolf, D. P., & Reardon, S. F. (1996). Access to excellence through new forms of students' assessment. In J. B. Baron & D. P. Wolf (Eds.). *Performance-based student assessment: Challenges and possibilities: 95th yearbook of the National Society of Education* (part 1, pp. 1–31). Chicago: University of Chicago Press.

Dr. Barry Oreck *has worked in arts education since 1974 as a teaching artist, program director, staff developer, curriculum specialist, evaluator, researcher, and consultant. He directed arts in education programs in more than 150 New York City public schools with ArtsConnection including research projects in talent identification, curriculum design, and student achievement funded by the U.S. Department of Education and the U.S. Department of Juvenile Justice. He received his doctorate in Educational Psychology from the University of Connecticut and served as assessment chair for the 1997 National Assessment of Educational Progress (NAEP) in dance. He is a consultant for school districts and departments of education in New York, Ohio, Colorado, and Mississippi and teaches at the University of Connecticut and Long Island University. His monograph,* Artistic Talent Development for Urban Youth: The Promise and the Challenge, *was published by the National Research Center for the Gifted and Talented and was honored as the best research paper of the year by the National Association for Gifted Children in 2000.*

Evaluation Criteria	**Discussion Questions**

1. Which is the dominant perspective in this study: quantitative or qualitative?

Clearly quantitative. Even though the author calls this a mixed-methods study the focus is on samples, numbers, and generalizability. The only qualitative contribution consists of two open-ended questions appended to the survey. The design is primarily quantitative nonexperimental. (from Chapter 2):

1. What would this study have to look like in order for it to be predominately qualitative?

2. Is the general purpose of the study clear? Will it provide a significant contribution?

The author's problem statement is clear and compelling. His statement of purpose has widespread significance for educational practice: "to understand the personal and institutional factors that enhance or undermine teachers' efforts to use the arts in their own practice and to look at the characteristics and attitudes of teachers who have been able to successfully implement the arts in various ways in their classrooms."

2. Whether a study provides a significant contribution is a matter of professional judgment. What considerations should be part of this judgment?

3. Does the review of literature establish the relationship between previous studies and the current one? Is the review well organized and up to date?

The literature review, while brief, is well-written, and communicates well the research context for the study.

3. Can you think of any areas the literature review should have covered but did not?

4. Is the specific research hypothesis or question clearly and concisely stated?

Three research questions are specified, all clearly related to the author's statement of purpose.

4. Read the first research question carefully. What about it is problematic?

5. Is the method of sampling clearly presented? Could the way the sample was obtained influence the results?

Schools were selected based upon their connection with one or more providers of professional development in the arts. Whether all schools meeting this criterion were selected is not specified. Still, the sample is large, covering several regions of the country, and is demographically representative.

5. How do you think the sampling strategy may have limited the study's generalizability?

6. Is there anything in the procedures for collecting the information, or in the instruments themselves, that could bias the results or weaken the study?

One weakness of the study is the low response rate to the survey (43%). The author does not indicate that he did any follow-up mailings or undertook any other strategies to increase the rate of return, so we have to assume that he did not. It's likely that more surveys would be returned by teachers with particular interests in or concern for the arts, which would make them not representative of the faculty as a whole.

7. Do graphic presentations of the data distort the findings?

Results are presented in a straight-forward manner, and they both support and challenge conventional wisdom. Still, the complexity of the presentation is likely to be lost on all but the most statistically-sophisticated reader. Table 4 especially seems unnecessary.

8. Do the conclusions and interpretations follow logically from the results presented? Are unwarranted causal conclusions made from correlations or comparisons? Are limitations indicated?

The author discusses his results carefully, is candid about the study's limitations, doesn't overreach with his conclusions, and includes specific suggestions for practice.

9. Are the research questions phrased in such a way that suggests that both quantitative and qualitative data are appropriate?

Two of the three research questions suggest quantitative analysis, the third, qualitative.

10. Are the multiple approaches employed sequentially or concurrently? How are they triangulated?

The integration of quantitative and qualitative data is effective. After a comprehensive analysis of the survey data the author analyses the qualitative responses to the open-ended questions. He then uses the qualitative analysis both to help explain the survey findings and to point out areas of apparent contradiction. The net effect is to reveal the complexity of teachers' attitudes on the subject.

6. What could have been done to increase the rate of survey returns?

7. The author undertook a factor analysis as the principal means of analyzing his survey data. What would have been lost if the author had just calculated means for each of the items?

8. Review the author's recommendations. How well, in your opinion, do they follow from his data?

9. How would you rephrase Research Question 2 to make it suitable for qualitative inquiry?

10. In what ways do the qualitative findings appear to contradict the quantitative survey results?

11. What are the key quality criteria appropriate for the study's secondary approach? When applied, how do they enhance or hinder the study's overall credibility?

While the author specifies the method of analysis of the qualitative data, he provides no evidence about the quality of these data. Since the qualitative and quantitative data were compared extensively in the discussion, this is a significant omission.

12. What do multiple approaches add to the richness of the study?

As noted above, the qualitative data, while clearly secondary, contributed significantly to understanding the issues involved in the use of the arts in teaching, in ways that could not have been possible with a quantitative analysis alone.

11. What could the author have done to establish the credibility of the qualitative data?

12. How could the qualitative component of this study been enlarged? What would have been accomplished thereby?

Credibility Scorecard
The Artistic and Professional Development of Teachers

	Excellent	Very Good	Adequate	Marginal	Poor
General purpose	5	4	3	2	1
Contribution/ significance	5	4	3	2	1
Review of literature	5	4	3	2	1
Research questions or hypotheses	5	4	3	2	1
Subjects or participants	5	4	3	2	1
Instrumentation	5	4	3	2	1
Procedures	5	4	3	2	1
Results	5	4	3	2	1
Practical significance	5	4	3	2	1
Graphics	5	4	3	2	1
Conclusions	5	4	3	2	1
Any fatal flaws?					

Preservice Teachers' Educational Beliefs and Their Perceptions of Characteristics of Effective Teachers

Lynn C. Minor
Valdosta State University

Anthony J. Onwuegbuzie
Howard University

Ann E. Witcher
Terry L. James
University of Central Arkansas

ABSTRACT

The purpose of this study was to examine preservice teachers' perceptions of characteristics of effective teachers, as well as to investigate whether these perceptions are related to educational beliefs (i.e., progressive vs. transmissive). Data for this study were collected from 134 preservice teachers enrolled in several sections of an introductory-level education class for education majors at a large university in southern Georgia. During the 1st week of classes, the authors gave students (a) a questionnaire asking them to identify, rank, and define characteristics that they believed excellent teachers possess or demonstrate and (b) a published survey that identified participants' educational beliefs as either progressive or transmissive. A phenomenological analysis of responses revealed several characteristics that many of the preservice teachers considered to reflect effective teaching. In order of endorsement level, the following 7 themes emerged from these characteristics: (a) student centered (55.2%), (b) effective classroom and behavior manager (33.6%), (c) competent instructor (33.6%), (d) ethical (29.9%), (e) enthusiastic about teaching (23.9%), (f) knowledgeable about subject (19.4%), and (g) professional (15.7%). With the Bonferroni adjustment, a series of chi-square analyses revealed no relationship between the 7 perception categories of effective teachers and preservice teachers' year of study, preferred grade level for teaching, and educational belief. However, significantly more men than women endorsed teacher characteristics that were associated with being an effective classroom and behavior manager.

KEYWORDS:

multistage mixed-methods analysis, perceptions of effective teacher characteristics, preservice teacher beliefs

For at least 20 years, teacher education researchers and program designers have given attention to the issue of how preservice candidates learn to teach, broadly defined to include a host of topics from how students learn to what constitutes good teaching. Emerging from this research are strong data that support the position that the characteristics that preservice teachers bring with them (e.g., experiences, knowledge, dispositions, beliefs, attitudes, perceptions) upon entry into formal preparation programs greatly influence their subsequent development as both students and practitioners of teaching (Carter, 1990; Day, Calderhead, & Denicolo, 1993; Witherell & Noddings, 1991). This research study and line of inquiry represent a starting point for engaging preservice candidates in self-reflection for purposes of examining and confronting entering beliefs and values they hold regarding various aspects of the practice of teaching.

Doyle (1997) investigated the influence of education programs on preservice teachers' beliefs. Doyle found that preservice teachers' beliefs changed from viewing teaching and learning as passive acts of teachers giving the information to students to a belief that teaching and learning are active processes in which teachers should act as facilitators. Two important influences on the changes in preservice teachers' beliefs were experiences gained while teaching in the field and the preservice teachers' abilities to reflect on and analyze their experiences. Length of time in a teacher education program and the amount of field experience were identified as important factors in assisting preservice teachers in the development of their beliefs as they progress through the teacher education program. Doyle suggested the need for teacher educators to encourage preservice teachers to challenge their own beliefs when these beliefs contradict what they experience in the field. Similarly, according to So (1997), reflective teaching has emerged as an approach to teacher

The Journal of Educational Research, Vol. 96, No. 2, 116–127, 2002. Reprinted with the permission of the Helen Dwight Reid Educational Foundation. Published by Heldref Publications, 1319 Eighteenth St., N.W., Washington, DC 20036-1802. Copyright © 2002. Address correspondence to Anthony J. Onwuegbuzie, Department of Human Development and Psychoeducational Studies, School of Education, Howard University, 2441 Fourth Street, NW, Washington, DC 20059. (E-mail: tonyonwuegbuzie@aol.com) education whereby preservice teachers are asked to think about their attitudes, beliefs, and assumptions, and to use reflection as a means to promote self-evaluation and change.

Having students identify characteristics of effective teachers is often an early goal in teacher preparation programs. In some cases, students examine textbook definitions of effective teachers and then discuss the characteristics as exemplified by teachers in their own K–12 schooling experience. In other cases, students are asked to think about past teachers, name qualities they believe reflect effectiveness, and then examine how well the qualities they identified match textbook definitions. These textbook definitions generally describe effective teachers as knowledgeable, self-confident, and enthusiastic, with strong communication and management skills, clear instructional focus, and high expectations of self and students (e.g., Reed & Bergemann, 1992; Segall & Wilson, 1998). One need not look far into the literature to find further characteristics of effective teachers as identified through research.

Effective teachers are profiled as having strong cognitive skills (Cotton, 1995; Demmon-Berger, 1986; Educational Testing Service [ETS], 1997; Finn, 1993; Good & Brophy, 1994; National Board for Professional Teaching Standards [NBPTS], 1987; Redfield & Rousseau, 1981; Rosenshine & Stevens, 1986; Tobin, 1987; Wortruba & Wright, 1975; Wubbels, Levy, & Brekelmans, 1997). They are subject specialists who are able to select, organize, and deliver content; are efficient and effective in the use of instructional time; and are able to vary their teaching strategies according to student needs. Effective teachers are creative, encourage active student participation, make relevant assignments, arrange for plenty of successful engaged time, are skillful in using questions, promote critical and creative thinking, and use wait time when seeking student response. In addition, they provide feedback, monitor programs and student progress, use both traditional and alternative assessment, and are fair in assessment and grading procedures. Finally, these teachers reflect on their practice and learn from their experiences, and they are members of learning communities, interested in continuing their own professional development.

Effective teachers also are described as caring (Cotton, 1995; Demmon-Berger, 1986; ETS, 1997; Norton, 1997; Roueche, Baker, Mullin, & Boy, 1986; Wubbels et al., 1997). Furthermore, they are motivators who provide incentives through recognition and rewards, flexible in their abilities to be dominant and cooperative, and empathetic yet in control. They have strong interpersonal skills, handle discipline through prevention, and promote a classroom climate of respect and rapport that reflects their commitment to students and their learning.

The American Association of School Administrators (AASA) investigated characteristics of effective teachers and concluded that qualities tend to fall into two categories: (a) management and instructional techniques and (b) personal characteristics (Demmon-Berger, 1986). In general, the AASA describes effective teachers as good managers who (a) handle discipline through prevention; (b) use systematic, yet varied, instructional techniques; (c) are knowledgeable of subject matter and task oriented while tailoring teaching to student needs; (d) are highly flexible, enthusiastic, and imaginative and emphasize perceptual meanings more than facts and events; (e) believe in their own abilities and have high expectations; (f) are democratic in their approach and display warmth, care, and concern when interacting with students; and (g) are readily accessible outside of class.

Of the investigations undertaken in the area of teacher effectiveness, most have examined actual characteristics of effective teachers or have asked inservice teachers and educational theorists about their beliefs regarding effective teaching: that is, few researchers have studied the perceptions of preservice teachers concerning the attributes of effective teachers. Moreover, most of the investigations have used qualitative techniques (e.g., interview) with small samples. A paucity of studies has incorporated qualitative and quantitative analyses within the same framework.

Knowing preservice teachers' perceptions of effective teachers and teaching is a necessary precondition for identifying program experiences that require candidates to confront their own beliefs and to consider the appropriateness of those beliefs in the context of the research, promising practice, psychological theories, and philosophical beliefs that underpin professional goals and practice. Indeed, the ability to reflect on entering beliefs and to change ill-founded beliefs is consistent with the expectations of the Interstate New Teacher Assessment and Support Consortium (INTASC, 1992) and the National Council for the Accreditation of Teacher Education (NCATE, 2002).

The role of beliefs as a determinant of teacher change has received increasing attention among researchers over the last several years, and a substantial body of evidence has emerged during this time suggesting that teacher beliefs drive instructional pedagogy (e.g., Pajares, 1992; Richardson, 1996; Thompson, 1992). To change teaching practices, teachers' beliefs should be taken into consideration (Hart, 2002). According to Pajares (1992), beliefs about teaching, which include perceptions about what it takes to be an effective teacher, are formed before a student enters college. These beliefs are then either challenged or nurtured during what

Lortie (1975) termed as a period of apprenticeship of observation, which occurs throughout the teacher training program. Thus, as recommended by Hart (p. 4), "It seems imperative that teacher education programs assess their effectiveness, at least in part, on how well they nurture beliefs that are consistent with the program's philosophy of learning and teaching."

Recently, Witcher, Onwuegbuzie, and Minor (2001), using mixed-methodological approaches, found that preservice teachers' perceptions of effective teachers fell into the following six categories, in order of endorsement level: (a) student centeredness (79.5%), (b) enthusiasm for teaching (40.2%), (c) ethicalness (38.8%), (d) classroom and behavior management (33.3%), (e) teaching methodology (32.4%), and (f) knowledge of subject (31.5%). Also, these authors noted that women, college-level juniors, and minority students tended to endorse teacher characteristics that were associated with ethical behavior and teaching methodology to a greater extent than did the other participants in the study (e.g., White men and nonjuniors). In addition, they tended to rate attributes that were associated with knowledge of subject and classroom and behavior management to a lesser degree than other researchers did.

Thus, the objective of the present inquiry was to replicate and extend the work of Witcher et al. (2001). Specifically, our purpose was to investigate what preservice teachers view as important characteristics of effective teachers, with the intent of comparing their responses with descriptions provided in the literature. We also wanted to investigate factors (e.g., educational beliefs, gender, ethnicity, and year of study) that may influence their responses. We hoped that results from the present inquiry would allow teacher education faculty and candidates to design experiences (e.g., readings, practica, case studies) that help candidates to develop conceptual models of effective teaching that will guide their decision making once they assume responsibilities as practitioners.

METHOD

Participants

Participants were 134 preservice teachers who were enrolled in several sections of an introductory-level education class for education majors at a large university in southern Georgia. The majority of the sample was female (78.4%) and White (72.4%). With regard to year of study, participants were either freshman (10.4%), sophomore (59%), junior (23.1%), senior (2.2%), or graduate (1.5%) students. Nearly all participants (94%) were full-time students. Approximately one half (i.e., 40%) of the preservice teachers intended to teach at the kindergarten and

elementary school levels, 32.3% desired to teach at the secondary school level, 12.3% desired to teach at the middle school level, and the remaining 15.4% wanted to work as special educators. Approximately one third (34.3%) of the participants preferred to teach in a public school in a rural area, one fourth (24.6%) wanted to teach in a public school in a suburban area, and 20.1% expressed a desire to teach in an urban public school. The remainder preferred to teach in either a church-sponsored private school (12.7%) or a non-denominational private school (5.2%).

Instruments and Procedures

During the 1st week of the class, participants were administered the Preservice Teachers' Perceptions of Characteristics of Effective Teachers Survey (PTPCETS) and the Witcher-Travers (1999) Survey of Educational Beliefs (WTSEB). The PTPCETS asks participants to identify, rank, and define between three and six characteristics that they believe effective teachers possess or demonstrate in general. Because responses to the PTPCETS are open ended, information about reliability was not appropriate. The WTSEB, developed by Witcher and Travers, contains two parts. The first part elicits demographic information (e.g., gender, age) from the respondents, and the second section contains a 40-item, 5-point Likert-type scale. Respondents are requested to react to statements by making one of five possible choices: *SA = strongly agree, A = agree, U = undecided, D = disagree,* or *SD = strongly disagree.* Of the 40 items, 20 statements indicate a transmissive view and 20 statements reflect a progressive view of education. These two labels, transmissive and progressive, are used only to organize statements that reflect the dichotomy faced in education over the last century. This dichotomy is represented in the works of such persons as Hyman Rickover, Arthur Bestor, and E. D. Hirsh for the transmissive models and John Dewey, Jerome Bruner, and Lev Vygotsky for progressive models. Sample items that represent a transmissive viewpoint are (a) "Effective teachers dispense content knowledge in a sequenced, systematic, and efficient manner" and (b) "Since life is competitive, students should be evaluated on standardized tests according to how they compare with others in most subjects." Conversely, sample items that indicate a progressive orientation are (a) "Vocational education and the study of liberal arts are equally important" and (b) "The basic purpose of formal education is to assist in the complete development of the total personality."

According to the instrument developers, the WTSEB can be completed in approximately 15 minutes (Witchers & Travers, 1999). Responses are scored by computer. Possible scores range from 0 to 40, with higher scores (i.e., greater than 23) indicating interest in progressivism and lower scores (i.e., less than 17) indicating a transmissive orientation. Scores occurring in the range of 17 to 23 indicate an eclectic viewpoint. Witcher and Travers further noted that the terms *higher* and *lower* do not denote values of superiority or inferiority.

Originally, the WTSEB was mailed to a random sample of 70 Arkansas public school superintendents in January 1996. Superintendents were requested to complete and return the survey within 2 weeks. In April 1996, a second copy of the survey was mailed to those superintendents who responded to the initial mailing. Again, superintendents were asked to complete and return the survey within 2 weeks. Sixty-five superintendents completed both the pre- and posttests. These paired responses were recorded and compared to establish test-retest reliability. The authors (Witcher & Travers, 1999) noted a coefficient of 63.

As recommended by many researchers (e.g., Onwuegbuzie, in press; Onwuegbuzie & Daniel, 2000; Thompson & Vacha-Haase, 2000), reliability coefficients always should be reported for the data at hand. Unfortunately, no reliability information was available for the WTSEB for the present study because participants were not scored as a group; rather, each sample member's responses were scored individually.

Analysis

We used a multistage qualitative-quantitative analysis (Onwuegbuzie, in press; Onwuegbuzie & Teddlie, 2002) to analyze the data. Specifically, a sequential mixed analysis was undertaken in which data were analyzed sequentially (Onwuegbuzie & Teddlie, 2002). This form of analysis involved four stages. The first stage consisted of a phenomenological mode of inquiry (inductive, generative, and constructive) to examine the responses of students regarding their perceptions of characteristics of effective teachers (Goetz & Lecompte, 1984). To determine the percentage of students who cited each attribute, these data were unitized; that is, units of information served as the basis for defining a significant statement (Glaser & Strauss, 1967). Each unit corresponded to a unique characteristic (Lincoln & Guba, 1985).

We used the method of constant comparison (Glaser & Strauss, 1967) to categorize units that appeared similar in content. Each one of the categories represented a distinct theme. This method of analysis revealed a number of themes relating to students' perceptions of characteristics of effective teachers.

In the second stage of the analysis, we used descriptive statistics to analyze the hierarchical structure of the emergent themes (Onwuegbuzie, in press). In particular, each theme was quantitized (Tashakkori & Teddlie, 1998). Specifically, for each participant, a score of 1 was given for a theme if that theme was represented in at least one of the stated characteristics that the student listed; otherwise, a score of 0 was given for that theme. That is, for each sample member, each theme was quantitized either to a 1 or 0 depending on whether it was represented by that individual. Such quantitizing allowed the frequency of each theme to be calculated. From these frequencies, we computed percentages to determine the prevalence rates of each theme. These prevalence rates served as effect-size measures (Onwuegbuzie, in press; Onwuegbuzie & Teddlie, 2002).

The third stage of the analysis involved a series of chi-square analyses to determine which background variables were related to each of the themes. We used a Bonferroni adjustment to maintain the error rate at the 5% level of significance. The fourth and final stage involved an exploratory factor analysis to ascertain the underlying structure of these themes. This factor analysis determined the number of factor underlying the themes. These factors, or latent constructs, represented metathemes (Onwuegbuzie, in press; Onwuegbuzie & Teddlie, 2002) such that each metatheme contained one or more of the emergent themes. The trace, or proportion of variance explained by each factor after rotation, served as a latent effect size for each metatheme (Onwuegbuzie, in press). In addition, we computed a manifest effect size for each metatheme by determining the combined frequency effect size for themes within each metatheme (Onwuegbuzie, in press).

RESULTS

Using cut-off scores for the WTSEB advocated by Witcher and Travers (1999), we found that the participants distributed themselves as follows: 28.4% transmissive, 12.7% progressive, and 59.0% eclectic. Table 1 contains the themes that emerged from students' responses. It can be seen that the following seven themes surfaced from these responses student centered, effective classroom and behavior manager, competent instructor, ethical, enthusiastic about teaching, knowledgeable about subject, and professional.

Verbatim examples of student-centered themes include "love of students," "optimism," "supportive," "kind," "caring," and "patient"; descriptors of effective classroom and behavior manager are "authoritative," "leadership skills," and "alert"; examples of competent instructor are "creativity," "open to new teaching styles," "clarity in teaching subject," and "ability to spark child's interest"; words that describe ethical are "fairness," "honest," "trustworthy," "impartial," "dependable," and "reliable"; examples that characterize enthusiastic about teaching are "love of subject," "passion for teaching," "eager to teach," and "dedicated"; descriptors of knowledge about subject

Table 1 Themes Emerging From Preservice Teachers'
Perceptions of Characteristics of Effective Teachers

Theme	Endorsement Rate (%)
Student centered	55.2
Effective classroom and behavior manager	33.6
Competent instructor	33.6
Ethical	29.9
Enthusiastic about teaching	23.9
Knowledgeable about subject	19.4
Professional	15.7

include "efficiently teach and know material" and "knowledge of subject"; and examples of professional are "disciplined" and "good communicator."

Student-centered descriptors received the greatest endorsement. Specifically, more than one half of preservice teachers noted one or more characteristics representing this theme. Effective classroom and behavior manager and competent instructor each were endorsed by one-third of the participants as being characteristic of effective teachers. Ethical was the next most common category, with slightly less than one-third of students subscribing to this characteristic. Approximately one-fourth of the sample identified characteristics pertaining to being enthusiastic about teaching. One-fifth of the preservice teachers cited traits relating to being knowledgeable about subject matter. Finally, professional was the theme that received the lowest endorsements—with only 15% of participants referring to characteristics in this area.

A series of chi-square analyses, using the Bonferroni adjustment to control for Type 1 error (p <.05), indicated no relationship between the seven perception categories of effective teachers and preservice teachers' race, year of study, and preferred grade level for teaching. Similarly, no gender differences were found with respect to student centered, competent instructor, ethical, enthusiastic about teaching, knowledgeable about subject, and professional. However, statistically significantly more men than women endorsed teacher characteristics that were associated with being an effective classroom and behavior manager. A series of independent samples t tests, adjusting for Type I error (i.e., Bonferroni adjustment), revealed no statistically significant relationship between students' levels of educational beliefs and each of the seven perception categories.

We used an exploratory factor analysis to determine the number of factors underlying the seven themes. Specifically, we used a maximum likelihood (ML) factor analysis with a varimax rotation. This technique, which gives better estimates than does principal factor analysis (Bickel & Doksum, 1977;

Onwuegbuzie & Daniel, in press), is perhaps the most frequently used method of common factor analysis (Lawley & Maxwell, 1971). We implemented the eigenvalue-greater-than-one rule, also known as K1 (Kaiser, 1958), to ascertain an appropriate number of factors to retain. This technique resulted in three factors (i.e., metathemes). The scree test (Cattell, 1966; Zwick & Velicer, 1986) also suggested that three factors be retained.

The ML factor analyses revealed a three-factor solution, which explained 55.5% of the total variance. Loadings of items on each factor are presented in Table 2. With a cutoff correlation of .3 (i.e., factor loading criterion) recommended by Lambert and Durand (1975) as an acceptable minimum loading value, the competent instructor, student centered, and effective classroom and behavior manager themes loaded significantly on the first factor; ethical and professional themes loaded on the second factor, and the enthusiastic about teaching and knowledgeable about subject themes loaded on the third factor. The first factor can be labeled instructional and management skills. The second factor can be termed ethical and well-tempered behavior, and the third factor can be termed knowledge and enthusiasm of/for subject and student. With respect to the third factor, the factor loading pertaining to the enthusiastic-about-teaching theme was positive, whereas the loading for the knowledgeable-about-subject theme was negative. This finding suggests that enthusiastic about teaching and knowledgeable about subject were inversely related. That is, preservice teachers who were the most likely to endorse enthusiasm as a characteristic of effective teaching tended to be the least likely to endorse subject knowledge as an effective trait. The thematic structure is presented in Figure 1. This figure illustrates the hierarchical structure among the themes and metathemes arising from preservice teachers' perceptions of the characteristics of effective teachers.

An examination of the *trace* (i.e., the proportion of variance explained, or eigenvalue, after rotation; Hetzel, 1996) revealed that the instructional

Table 2   Summary of Themes and Factor Loadings From Maximum Likelihood Varimax Factor Analysis: Three-Factor Solution

Theme	Factor Loading			
	1	2	3	C
Competent instructor	.75			.58
Student centered	.59			.40
Effective classroom and behavior manager	.56			.40
Ethical		.84		.72
Professional		.71		.56
Enthusiastic about teaching			.78	.67
Knowledgeable about subject			−.68	.55
Trace	1.44	1.28	1.17	3.88
% of variance explained	22.51	17.93	15.07	55.51

Note: Only loadings with large effect sizes are displayed. We used a cutoff loading of .3 recommended by Lambert and Durand (1975). C = Countability coefficient.

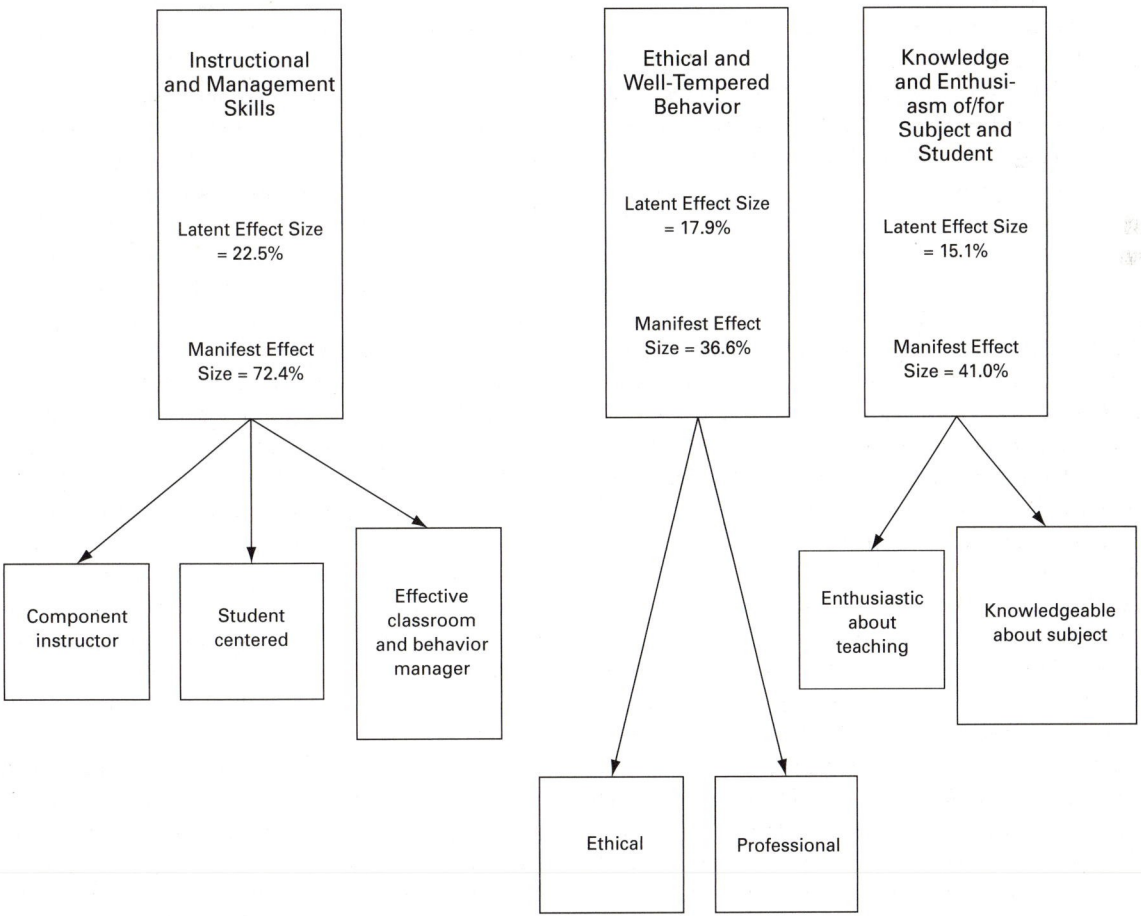

Figure 1.   Thematic structure pertaining to preservice teachers' perceptions of characteristics of effective teachers.

Note. The two themes representing the knowledge enthusiasm of/for subject and student metatheme were inversely related.

and management skills metatheme (i.e., Factor 1) explained 22.51% of the total variance; the ethical and well-tempered behavior metatheme (i.e., Factor 2) accounted for 17.93% of the variance; and the knowledge-and-enthusiasm of/for subject and student metatheme (i.e., Factor 3) explained 15.07% of the variance. These three metathemes combined explained 55.51% of the total variance. This total proportion of variance represents a very large latent effect size. Latent effect sizes represent effect sizes that pertain to nonobservable, underlying aspects of the phenomenon being studied (i.e., preservice teachers' perceptions of characteristics of effective teachers; Onwuegbuzie & Teddlie, 2002). Onwuegbuzie and Teddlie also defined *manifest effect sizes* as effect sizes pertaining to observable content (i.e., preservice teachers' perceptions). The manifest effect sizes associated with the three metathemes (i.e., proportion of characteristics identified per metathemes) were as follows: instructional and management skills (72.4%), ethical and well-tempered behavior (36.6%), and knowledge and enthusiasm of/for subject and student (41%).

DISCUSSION

The purpose of the present study was to determine preservice teachers' perceptions about the characteristics of effective teachers, as well as to investigate factors that may have influenced their responses. A multistage qualitative-quantitative analysis (Onwuegbuzie, in press) revealed that the perceptions held by preservice teachers represent a multidimensional construct. This multidimensionality is consistent with that found by Witcher et al. (2001). Specifically, in the current investigation, perceptions were identified that led to the following seven themes: student centered, effective classroom and behavior manager, competent instructor, ethical, enthusiastic about teaching, knowledgeable about subject, and professional.

Student-centered descriptors received the greatest endorsement, with more than one-half of preservice teachers noting one or more characteristics representing this theme. This finding suggests that the current sample, in general, rated being student centered as the most common characteristic of effective teachers. This finding is consistent with Witcher et al. (2001), who found that this theme was endorsed by 79.5% of the sample that comprised preservice teachers in Arkansas. Thus, preservice teachers, in general, regard the interpersonal context as the most important aspect of teaching.

The seven themes, which loaded on three factors, dealt with instructional and management skills, ethical and well-tempered behavior, and knowledge and enthusiasm of/for subject and student. These factors suggest that the perceptions of preservice teachers represent a complex phenomenon. The themes that emerged from the preservice teachers' responses are more informative than the AASA's two-element conceptualization of effective teachers, namely, (a) management and instructional techniques and (b) personal characteristics (Demmon-Berger, 1986). The management and instructional techniques dimension of the AASA is similar to the instructional and management skills component that emerged in the present investigation. However, whereas the AASA conceptualized a personal characteristics element, the responses of the present sample suggest that this dimension could be broken down into (a) ethical and well-tempered behavior and (b) knowledge and enthusiasm of/for subject and student.

One finding was the fact that endorsements to the enthusiastic-about-teaching and knowledgeable-about-subject themes were inversely related. In other words, preservice teachers who were most likely to endorse enthusiasm as a characteristic of effective teaching were least likely to endorse subject knowledge as an effective trait. This result is consistent with the findings of Witcher et al. (2001). Several characteristics of the present sample could have induced this finding. In particular, it is possible that the difference in preservice teachers' priority between being enthusiastic about teaching and knowledgeable about subject could have reflected the grade level they were intending to teach. On the one hand, it is possible that prospective elementary school teachers are more likely to rate enthusiasm than knowledge as an essential instructional trait because the level of information imparted to elementary students is much lower than that disseminated to students in higher grades. Consequently, elementary school preservice candidates may perceive that subject matter expertise is not as important as is the ability to motivate students to learn by being enthusiastic. On the other hand, it is possible that preservice candidates intending to teach at the middle and/or high school levels are more likely to endorse knowledge over enthusiasm. However, a reexamination of the data did not entirely support this prediction. A greater proportion of elementary, middle, and high school candidates rated enthusiasm more favorably than knowledge. Although the difference in proportions was marginal for both elementary school (22.8% vs. 19.3%) and high school (26.1% vs. 23.9%) candidates, twice as many middle school preservice teachers endorsed enthusiasm (23.5%) over knowledge (11.8%). Thus, middle school candidates' differential response to the enthusiasm and knowledge themes may have contributed, albeit in a small way, to the inverse relationship between these two themes. In any case, more research is needed to compare perceptions of preservice teachers as a function of their chosen grade level.

A much clearer picture emerges when responses to these two themes are compared as a function of gender. Whereas men and women were equally as likely to endorse enthusiasm about teaching (odds ratio [OR] = 1.12), men were more than $2\frac{1}{2}$ times more likely to endorse knowledge of subject (OR = 2.59) than were women. Thus, gender likely explains the inverse relationship between responses to the enthusiasm and knowledge themes. This result again implicates gender as being important in forming the perceptions of preservice teachers.

That women rated enthusiasm about teaching higher than they rated knowledge of subject matter may reflect the historical lack of gender consideration in the schools. A substantial literature base exists that documents differential treatment of students based on gender (e.g., Altermatt, Jovanovic, & Perry, 1998; American Association of University Women, 1992, 1998; Sadker, Sadker, & Klien, 1991), and this base illustrates the imbalance in curricular organization, curricular content, and verbal interaction between teacher and student faced by students as they progress through school. For instance, as early as elementary school, instructional methods reflect male preferences in that the entire curriculum is organized to meet the needs of young male students who typically mature more slowly than do female students (Stevens, Wood, & Sheehan, 2002). An examination of textbooks from history to music to science reveals only a small percentage of information addressing the contributions, experiences, and challenges of women (Zittleman & Sadker, 2002). Investigations of teacher-student verbal interaction show that teachers call upon male students more often than female students, allow male students more often than female students to call out answers, and provide a greater quantity of verbal interactions to male than to female students (M. Sadker, Sadker, Fox, & Salata, 1993/1994). The cumulative result of the research in this area is that the differential treatment of male and female students in the schools is gender specific.

Psychological studies have helped broaden the understanding of female moral and emotional development. Findings (e.g., Gilligan, 1982) reveal that females stress interdependence, connectiveness, and attachment as important concepts compared with values of independence and separation held in high regard by males, and these values are nurtured in a gender-specific manner from early years, in society and school. The fact that female respondents in this study rated enthusiasm higher than knowledge may be indicative of their desire to create a more caring schooling environment to replace the "male model that emphasizes rationality, order, detachment, and the pursuit of profit/power above personal and emotional attachment" (Stevens et al., 2002, p. 83). As already documented, candidates enter into teacher preparation with powerful views of teacher roles

and general purposes of education that come from a myriad of personal experiences and general beliefs. One of the purposes of a teacher education program is to have candidates confront their beliefs and begin moderating these beliefs on the basis of research, theory, exemplary practices, and philosophical approaches to education (Schwartz, Slate, & Onwuegbuzie, 1999).

Teacher educators should be aware that some progress has been made over the last 20 years in the fair treatment of gender in teacher education textbooks, but the progress has been minimal. Even in teacher education, sexism persists (Zittleman & Sadker, 2002). Although the tone is supportive for gender issues, text coverage is minimal and specific strategies for promoting gender fairness and justice are lacking. In this study, it is impossible to know why female respondents rated enthusiasm higher than knowledge; however, this rating, coupled with a growing body of literature, suggests that teacher education must be cognizant of possible gender differences in perceptions.

Similarly, race and culture may have contributed to the relationship between the enthusiasm and knowledge themes. Racial comparisons revealed that an equal proportion of minority and White candidates (OR = 1.17) endorsed enthusiasm. White preservice teachers were $2\frac{1}{2}$ times more likely to endorse knowledge of subject (OR = 2.67) than were their minority counterparts. The fact that minority candidates endorsed enthusiasm for teaching over knowledge of subject to a significantly relatively higher degree (i.e., 2.32:1 ratio) than did White candidates highlights the difference between these two populations. First and foremost, minority teachers are more likely to begin their teaching careers in large urban school districts in which teaching conditions are uniquely difficult, characterized by large proportions of minority students, high student failure rates, and low academic motivation and self-esteem (Gay, 1997; Murname, Singer, Willett, Kemple, & Olsen, 1991). Many teachers in such districts develop low teacher morale, which may be transmitted to their students, leading to a downward cycle of underachievement and low ebullience. In such schools, teacher enthusiasm likely is more crucial than in schools typified by high student achievement, more resources, and highly educated parents. Thus, it is likely that minority candidates, many of whom had poor or negative experiences as primary and secondary students (Ford & Grantham, 1997), deem enthusiasm for teaching to be more important than knowledge of subject.

As noted by Ladson-Billings (1994), the academic success and resilience among Black students at risk for educational failure has been attributed to African American teachers who provided moral support by taking an interest in their students and exhibiting enthusiasm toward teaching them (Ford & Grantham, 1997; Onwuegbuzie, 1999). According to Foster (1990), Black teachers tend to hold a philosophy that attempts to instill values associated with pride, equity, wealth, power, and cultural continuity among Black children. Black teachers accomplish these goals by going beyond the subject matter. Specifically, Black teachers strive to help Black students value achievement, as well as to understand the personal value, collective power, and political ramifications of academic success (Foster, 1990; King, 1993). Enthusiasm for teaching clearly plays a role here.

Findings suggest that Black teachers are more in a position than are White teachers to integrate the realities of the Black students' backgrounds and cultures, while, at the same time, acknowledging, validating, and affirming their identities (Ladson-Billings, 1994). Moreover, in addition to being a teacher and role model, Black teachers routinely assume the roles of surrogate parents, mentors, motivators, counselors, and disciplinarians. Thus, the minority preservice teachers' greater propensity for enthusiasm as a characteristic of effective teaching may be indicative of a proclivity toward an "emancipatory pedagogy," namely, a pedagogy that is culturally affirming and responsive to the needs of minority students (King, 1993). Such a pedagogy requires tremendous enthusiasm for teaching.

Studies have indicated that negative teacher–student relationships decrease teachers' motivation and expectations and, consequently, students' motivation and achievement (Ford & Grantham, 1997). White teachers have been found to hold lower expectations for Black students than for White students (Good & Brophy, 1985), to give preferential treatment to White students, to exhibit less enthusiasm for teaching Black students, and to exert less academic encouragement for Black students (Irvine, 1991). Thus, the extent to which White teachers hold knowledge of subject matter more important than enthusiasm, as was found in the present investigation, suggests that a cultural mismatch or incongruence may take place between minority students and many White teachers (Boykin, 1994; Ogbu, 1990). This, in turn, helps to justify the importance of preparation for multicultural education in teacher education programs. At many schools of education with predominantly White students, multicultural education is not emphasized to the extent that it typically is in historically Black colleges and universities (Darling-Hammond, 1994, 1995). As such, few White preservice teachers receive adequate training in multicultural education, and few White teacher candidates are trained to examine their biases and stereotypes regarding Black students, which can culminate in a lack of understanding of or appreciation among White teachers for cultural differences (Darling-Hammond, 1994; Ladson-Billings, 1994).

Furthermore, once admitted to teacher education programs, minority candidates often find little emphasis on multicultural education and, thus, are underprepared to teach in urban schools (Banks, 1993). Feelings of under-preparedness may lead minority preservice teachers to lose interest in teaching, and, consequently, not complete their teaching certification, turning their backs on the profession in favor of other college majors and careers (Ford & Grantham, 1997), thereby exacerbating further the dire shortage of minority teachers and administrators (Onwuegbuzie, 1999). Thus, an implication of the current findings may be that schools and colleges should prepare all teachers to work more effectively with minority students, including helping them to appreciate more the importance of displaying enthusiasm for teaching.

The fact that the minority sample members have a relatively lower regard for knowledge of subject as a characteristic of effective teachers also can be counterproductive. Specifically, the perception that enthusiasm is more important than is subject knowledge may lead minority candidates to prepare less well for standardized examinations than do their White counterparts. Minority students tend to perform insufficiently on standardized tests, including the National Teachers' Examination (NTE), thereby making licensure impossible (Bianchini, Kimble, Pitcher, Sullivan, & Wright, 1995). Thus, in addition to multicultural education, preservice candidates should be encouraged and helped to maximize knowledge of their discipline, as well as be prepared for standardized tests such as the NTE.

As accomplished professionals, teacher educators are cognizant that effective teachers do not embody characteristics that represent a dichotomy; in fact, effective teachers possess a complex blend of attributes, including enthusiasm and knowledge of content. With regard to gender and race, the present findings provide evidence that candidates enter teacher preparation programs with different views about what constitutes effective teaching. Because of the many experiences that candidates bring into the setting, their views likely reflect differences rather than biases. Regardless of these initial views, teacher candidates need to learn when and how to balance expressions of enthusiasm and the commitment to seeing that students learn appropriate content at an acceptable level. Therefore, teacher educators should hold themselves responsible for being aware of the entering beliefs of their teacher candidates and should help them develop the knowledge, skills, and dispositions necessary to perform competently in their classrooms (NCATE, 2002).

No relationship was found between the seven perception categories of effective teachers and many of the demographic variables. These findings indicate that members of the present sample were relatively homogeneous with respect to their perceptions. These nonsignificant findings emerged despite the fact that students completed the surveys during the 1st week of class, that is, before the instructors or course readings could begin to shape the majority of preservice teachers toward a unitary educational belief system. Thus, replications are needed to determine the reliability of these nonsignificant results.

The fact that men tended to place more weight on being an effective classroom and behavior manager than did women suggests that issues pertaining to classroom discipline may have a gender context. This finding of a gender difference is consistent with Witcher et al. (2001). It is likely that this gender difference stemmed, at least in part, from the fact that a statistically significantly larger proportion of men (84%) than women (43%) were training to be either middle school or high school teachers, χ^2 (3, N = 134) = 18.10, p < .001; Cramer's V = .39). Onwuegbuzie, Witcher, Filer, Collins, and Downing (in press) and Martin and Baldwin (1996) found that inservice and preservice secondary school teachers were more likely to have an interventionist orientation than were elementary school teachers. Interventionists are teachers who ascribe to a rules/rewards–punishment viewpoint and who believe that children and adolescents are conditioned by their environment; therefore, the teacher must take control of the environment to prevent or address inappropriate behavior (Wolfgang, 1995; Wolfgang & Glickman, 1986). Furthermore, Onwuegbuzie et al. (in press) noted that elementary school inservice and preservice teachers were more likely to have an inter-actionalist orientation. *Interactionalists* are teachers who take a confronting–contracting point of view and who believe that teachers should continually interact with students who behave inappropriately (Wolfgang, 1995; Wolfgang & Glickman, 1986). Consequently, the extent to which the male preservice teachers in the present investigation were more interventionist than were the female preservice teachers likely explains their propensity to endorse effective classroom and behavior management as an important characteristic of a teacher. As noted by Witcher et al. (in press), disciplinary problems that occur in the middle and secondary school setting typically are more complex and severe than those at the elementary level. Thus, it is likely that secondary school teachers believe that they should maintain the maximum amount of power over their students in order to secure control over the learning environment. Future researchers should investigate this gender bias found in the current inquiry. In any case, teacher educators should be cognizant of possible gender differences when exposing their students to different discipline styles.

Gender differences likely are reflected in the notion that female teachers reprimand by showing supportive behavior through their physical and verbal interactions with students by moving closer to the student when correcting her and using supportive language (Stevens et al., 2002). This is in contrast to the notion that male teachers are direct and somewhat aloof in their behavior management styles. Teacher educators may want to spend time on discipline approaches and help their candidates analyze approaches in terms of gender differences and classroom settings. It is only through analyzing and evaluating different orientations to behavior management that teacher educators can expect candidates to acknowledge, and perhaps abandon, biases that may interfere with effective discipline practice.

Another finding of this study revealed that the educational beliefs of only a minority (i.e., 12.7%) of preservice teachers were classified as progressive. Progressive teachers are referred to as being modern or experiential. According to Witcher and Travers (1999), this group of educators tends to view school as a social institution and seeks to align school programming with contemporary needs in order to make education meaningful and relevant to the knowledge, abilities, and interests of their students. That is, these individuals tend to base curricula on their students' personal, familial, and social experiences, with a goal of providing a continuous link between students' school-based learning and their lives outside the school context. As such, progressive teachers tend to view themselves as facilitators, guides, or motivators. Moreover, these teachers tend to present curricula holistically and in an open-ended manner to help students develop problem-solving skills. Using more student-centered teaching techniques, students of progressive educators tend to engage in active learning, both independently and cooperatively, which focuses on solving learner-generated problems. Examples of progressive philosophies, theories, and tenets include constructivism, experimentalism, and naturalism.

On the other hand, slightly more than one-fourth (28.4%) of the sample could be considered as having transmissive beliefs. Transmissive educators are often referred to as being traditional or conservative (Witcher & Travers, 1999). This group of professionals views the needs of the community and student as essentially stable. As such, they are reluctant to revise, modify, or redesign the schooling process in any dramatic way. Transmissive teachers believe that the purpose of school is to develop the intellect. Thus, they view their role as one of dispensing important knowledge to students, and they prefer lecture, demonstration, and recitation as teaching methods. Teachers who represent this paradigm tend to advocate curricula that are subject-centered, organized and sequenced, and focused on mastery of specific skills and content. Consequently, their classrooms tend to have a business-like atmosphere in which students are passive learners who generally work independently. As noted by Witcher and Travers, examples of transmissive philosophies, theories, and tenets include idealism, realism, perennialism, and essentialism.

A very high percentage of preservice teachers (59%) appeared to have eclectic educational beliefs. It is likely that this large number of "eclectics" attenuated the relationship between educational beliefs and their perceptions of the characteristics of effective teachers. It is also possible that as preservice teachers become more aware of various teaching philosophies through their educational classes and their field experiences, many of these eclectics will lean more toward either a progressive or transmissive tendency. According to Witchers and Travers (1999), educators possessing an eclectic philosophical orientation sometimes are referred to as persons holding a central or moderate position on educational views. Apparently, this position is valid only if educators holding such a position first seriously consider transmissive and progressive educational viewpoints about the purposes of education and ideal types of curricula to achieve these purposes. In other words, an individual must understand well both transmissive and progressive positions before an eclectic educational position is genuine; otherwise, this view indicates that a future teacher or practitioner has not thought through the ends and means of schooling (Witchers and Travers). This suggests that once a preservice teacher begins to reflect more about her or his future teaching, a dominant educational belief system typically should emerge that reflects consistency of belief about the purpose and process of schooling.

The larger number of participants scoring in the eclectic range suggests that the majority of the sample members may have not yet been exposed adequately to the various educational approaches taught at the institution where the study took place. Thus, they have not yet adopted either a transmissive or progressive orientation. Furthermore, the small percentage of respondent scores falling within the progressive range and larger percentage falling within the transmissive range might reflect the background of the sample. Participants were from a university in southern Georgia. A significant proportion of individuals representing this geographic area likely are conservative in their social views. As such, the study participants may well have received a transmissive education in their own K–12 experience and were reflecting that philosophy. It is possible that other explanations exist for the relatively small number of progressive sample members; however, it is beyond the scope of this investigation to identify these reasons. Consequently, this should be a subject of future inquiries.

Future research also should investigate how stable preservice teachers' perceptions and educational beliefs are over time. Currently, we plan to track the attitudes and beliefs of the members of the present sample throughout their preservice training, with the next measurement of attitudes taking place after they have completed their introductory-level education course. Such information should help to assess the impact that teacher education institutions have on educational beliefs and perceptions, which, in turn, should facilitate assessment of the extent to which these education programs are meeting the INTASC (1992) standards of developing teachers as reflective practitioners.

In summary, findings from the present study and that of Witcher et al. (2001) yield several implications. First and foremost, the result that teacher candidates express perceptions of characteristics of effective teachers that fall into as many as six (i.e., Witcher et al., 2001) or seven (i.e., current findings) categories highlights the diversity in beliefs that exists among this population. However, because candidates were not asked to discuss their beliefs, the extent of this diversity was not determined. Even so, the current investigation and its predecessor demonstrate the importance for preservice teachers to examine their educational beliefs and perceptions. The ability to reflect on entering beliefs and to change ill-founded beliefs is consistent with the recommendations of the Interstate New Teacher Assessment and Support Consortium (INTASC, 1992) and the National Council for the Accreditation of Teacher Education (NCATE, 2002).

By demonstrating that teacher candidates' beliefs may have a gender and cultural context, findings from this study suggest that teacher educators should develop and use activities that deal specifically with gender issues and multicultural education. Such activities include encouraging preservice teachers to identify their beliefs, as was undertaken in this study, and to link these beliefs to curricula and pedagogy in their respective disciplines while considering gender and cultural issues. Furthermore, students could be asked to align their thoughts, opinions, and convictions with the INTASC principles in an attempt to ascertain areas of consistency, as well as gaps in their belief systems. With respect to the latter recommendation, the findings of Witcher and colleagues (2001) and the present inquiry suggest that preservice teachers do not consider several of the standards that have been recognized by INTASC (1992). For instance, no teacher candidate mentioned that an effective teacher should use a variety of instructional techniques to foster students' development of critical thinking, problem solving, and performance skills (Principle 4). Similarly, no preservice teacher identified the importance of using media communication strategies to promote active inquiry, collaboration, and supportive interaction in the classroom (Principle 6). Also, no preservice teacher deemed important the understanding and use of formal and informal assessment strategies to evaluate the continuous intellectual, social, and physical development of the learner (Principle 8). When teacher candidates are asked to reflect on their beliefs in the context of the NCATE and INTASC standards, they are more likely to realize the knowledge, skills, dispositions, and performances that are considered essential for all teachers, regardless of their specialty areas.

As early as possible in their programs, teacher candidates could be asked to explore their own dispositions through expository writings that outline why they want to be teachers. Both they and those responsible for their professional development could then compare these reasons with their educational beliefs and their perceptions of characteristics of effective teachers. Moreover, candidates should be expected continually to reflect on and compare their belief systems as they progress through their teacher education program. Teacher educators also should monitor the evolution of these beliefs to determine the extent to which they are becoming more aligned with the INTASC and NCATE standards, as well as other pedagogical and curricular tenets and frameworks. To facilitate such monitoring, candidates could be asked to maintain a detailed record of their knowledge, skills, dispositions, and performances via such techniques as traditional and electronic portfolios.

Case studies and readings also can play a useful role in maximizing preservice teachers' awareness of the characteristics of effective teachers. As suggested by the present findings, case studies could be selected that provide candidates with the opportunity to examine the importance of gender and culture in the teaching and learning process. Also, while they are undertaking their field experiences, teacher candidates should be encouraged to observe and examine the gender and cultural milieux.

The findings from the present study also have implications for future research. A significant proportion of teacher candidates identify enthusiasm as an important characteristic of effective teachers. The extent to which this characteristic is endorsed represents a function of both gender and race/culture; however, it is not clear what students actually mean by the term *enthusiasm*. This could be the subject of future investigations. Also of interest is how teacher candidates' beliefs translate to teaching practices in the classroom during their field experiences, Finally, researchers might investigate how candidate beliefs change or modify as a result of field experiences and knowledge gained in the teacher preparation program.

We are currently designing an instrument that is based on the seven themes that emerged from this study. This instrument, titled Beliefs about Characteristics of Effective Teachers Scale, will contain 5-point Likert-type format items that assess the extent to which each preservice candidate endorses each of the seven categories of characteristics found in the present research. We hope that such a scale will help to determine the extent to which candidate beliefs predict a myriad of future outcomes, such as whether a preservice teacher becomes licensed, the type of school a teacher candidate ends up teaching in, whether a teacher becomes an administrator, and whether and how much time elapses before a teacher leaves the profession for another career.

Finally, Principle 9 of the INTASC Standards states that teachers should be reflective practitioners who continually assess the impact of their choices and actions on others (e.g., students, parents/guardians, colleagues, and members of the community) and who actively identify and seek out opportunities to grow as professionals. It is only by finding ways to maximize preservice candidates' capacity to reflect that this principle can be fully realized. The present study is a step in this direction.

REFERENCES

Altermatt, E., Jovanovic, J., & Perry, M. (1998). Bias or responsivity? Sex and achievement-level effects on teachers' classroom questioning practices. *Journal of Educational Psychology, 90,* 516-527.

American Association of University Women. (1992). *How schools short-change girls.* Annapolis Junction, MD: Author.

American Association of University Women. (1998). *Gender gap: Where schools still fail our children.* Annapolis Junction, MD: Author.

Banks, J. A. (1993). Multicultural education: Historical development, dimensions, and practice. In L. Darling-Hammond (Ed.), *Review of research in education* (pp. 3-50). Washington, DC: American Educational Research Association.

Bianchini, J. C., Kimble, K., Pitcher, B., Sullivan, T. L., & Wright, W. L. (1995). *NTE programs annual report: October 1992-September 1993.* Princeton, NJ: Educational Testing Service.

Bickel, P. J., & Doksum, K. A. (1977). *Mathematical statistics.* San Francisco: Holden-Day.

Boykin, A. W. (1994). Afrocultural expression and its implications for schooling. In E. R. Hollins, J. E. King, & W. C. Hayman (Eds.), *Teaching diverse populations: Formulating a knowledge base* (pp. 225-273). New York: State University of New York Press.

Carter, K. (1990). Teachers' knowledge and learning to teach. In W. R. Houston (Ed.), *Handbook of research on teacher education* (pp. 291-310). New York: Macmillan.

Cattell, R. B. (1966). The scree test for the number of factors. *Multivariate Behavioral Research, 1,* 245-276.

Cotton, K. (1995). *Effective student practices: A research synthesis—1995 update.* [On-line]. Available http://www.nwrel.org/scpd/esp/esp95.html#1

Darling-Hammond, L. (Ed.) (1994). *Review of research in education.* Washington, DC: American Educational Research Association.

Darling-Hammond, L. (1995). Inequality and access to knowledge. In J. A. Banks & C. A. M. Banks (Eds.), *Handbook of research on multicultural education* (pp. 465–483). New York: Macmillan.

Day, C., Calderhead, J., & Denicolo, O. P. (Eds.) (1993). *Research an teacher thinking: Understanding professional development.* Washington, DC: The Falmer Press.

Demmon-Berger, D. (1986). *Effective teaching: Observations from research.* Arlington, VA: American Association of School Administrators, (ERIC Document Reproduction Service No. ED274087)

Doyle, M. (1997). Beyond life history as a student: Preservice teachers' beliefs about teaching and learning. *College Student Journal, 31,* 519–532.

Educational Testing Service. (1997). Pathwise: A framework for teaching. Retrieved December 1, 1999 from http://www.teachingandlearning.org

Firm, J. D. (1993). *School engagement and students at risk.* Washington, DC: National Center for Education Statistics, U.S. Department of Education.

Ford, D. Y., & Grantham, T. C. (1997). The recruitment and retention of minority teachers in gifted education. *Roeper Review, 19,* 213–219.

Foster, M. (1990). The politics of race: Through the eyes of African-American teachers. *Journal of Education, 172,* 123–141.

Gay, G. (1997). Educational equity for students of color. In J. A. Banks & C. A. M. Banks (Eds.), *Multicultural education: Issues and perspectives* (3rd ed., pp. 195–228). Needham Heights, MA: Allyn & Bacon.

Gilligan, C. (1982). *In a different voice: Psychological theory and women's development.* Cambridge, MA: Harvard University Press.

Glaser, B. G., & Strauss, A. L. (1967). *The discovery of grounded theory: Strategies for qualitative research.* Chicago: Aldino.

Goetz, J. P., & Lecompte, M. D. (1984). *Ethnography and the qualitative design in educational research,* New York: Academic Press.

Good, T. L., & Brophy, I. E. (1985). *Looking in classrooms.* New York: HarperCollins.

Good, T. L., & Brophy, J. E. (1994). *Looking in classrooms* (6th ed.). New York: HarperCollins.

Hart, L. (2002). Preservice teachers' beliefs and practice after participating in an integrated content/methods courses. *School Science & Mathematics, 102,* 4–14.

Hetzel, R. D. (1996). A primer on factor analysis with comments on patterns of practice and reporting. In B. Thompson (Ed.), *Advances in social science methodology* (Vol. 4, pp. 175–206). Greenwich, CT: JAI Press.

Interstate New Teacher Assessment and Support Consortium. (1992). *Model standards for beginning teacher licensing and development: A resource for state dialogue.* Washington, DC: The Council of Chief State School Officers.

Irvine, J. J. (1991). *Black students and school failure. Policies, practices, and prescriptions.* New York: Greenwood Press.

Kaiser, H. F. (1958). The varimax criterion for analytic rotation in factor analysis. *Psychametrika, 23,* 187–200.

King, S. H. (1993). The limited presence of African-American teachers. *Review of Educational Research, 63,* 115–149.

Ladson-Billings, G. (1994). *The dreamkeepers. Successful teachers for African-American children.* San Francisco: Jessey-Bass.

Lambert, Z. V., & Durand, R. M. (1975). Some precautions in using canonical analysis. *Journal of Market Research, XII,* 468–475.

Lawley, D. N., & Maxwell, A. E. (1971). *Factor analysis as a statistical method.* New York: Macmillan.

Lincoln, Y. S., & Guba, E. G. (1985). *Naturalistic inquiry.* Beverly Hills, CA: Sage.

Lortie, D. (1975). *Schoolteacher: A sociological study.* Chicago: University of Chicago Press.

Martin, N. K., & Baldwin, B. (1996, January). *Perspectives regarding classroom management style: Differences between elementary and secondary level teachers.* Paper presented at the annual meeting of the Southwest Educational Research Association, New Orleans, LA. (ERIC Document Reproduction Service No. ED393835)

Murname, R. J., Singer, J. D., Willett, J. B., Kemple, J. J., & Olsen, R. J. (1991). *Who will teach? Policies that matter.* Cambridge, MA: Harvard University Press.

National Board for Professional Teaching Standards. (1987). *Policy Position.* [On-Line]. Available http://www.nbpts.org/nbpts/standards/policy.htm.

National Council for Accreditation of Teacher Education. (2002). *Professional standards for the accreditation of schools, colleges, and departments of education.* Washington, DC: Author.

Norton, J. L. (1997, November). *Learning from first year teachers: Characteristics of the effective practitioner.* Paper presented at the annual meeting of the Mid-South Educational Research Association, Memphis, TN. (ERIC Document Reproduction Service No. ED418050)

Ogbu, J. U. (1990). Literacy and schooling in subordinate cultures: The case of Black Americans. In K. Lomotey (Ed.), *Going to school: The African-American experience* (pp. 113–131). Albany: State University of New York Press.

Onwuegbuzie, A. J. (1999). Underachievement of African-American graduate students in research methodology classes: Possible implications for the supply of school administrators. *The Journal of Negro Education, 67,* 67–78.

Onwuegbuzie, A. J. (in press). *Effect sizes in qualitative research: A prolegomenon. Quality & Quantity: International Journal of Methodology.*

Onwuegbuzie, A. J. (in press). Common analytical and interpretational errors in educational research: An analysis of the 1998 volume of the *British Journal of Educational Psychology. Research for Educational Reform.*

Onwuegbuzie, A. J., & Daniel, L. G. (2002). Uses and misuses of the correlation coefficient. *Research in the Schools, 9,* 73–90.

Onwuegbuzie, A. J., & Daniel, L. G. (in press). Typology of analytical and interpretational errors in quantitative and qualitative educational research. *Current Issues in Education.*

Onwuegbuzie, A. J., & Teddlie, C. (2002). A framework for analyzing data in mixed methods research. In A. Tashakkori & C. Teddlie (Eds.), *Handbook of mixed methods in social and behavioral research* (pp. 351–383). Thousand Oaks, CA: Sage.

Onwuegbuzie, A. J., Witcher, A. E., Filer, J., Collins, K. M. T., & Downing, J. (in press). Factors associated with teachers' beliefs about discipline in the context of practice. *Research in the Schools.*

Pajares, M. F. (1992). Teachers' beliefs and educational research: Cleaning up a messy construct. *Review of Educational Research, 62,* 307-332.

Redfield, D., & Rousseau, E. (1981). A meta-analysis of experimental research on teacher questioning behavior. *Review of Educational Research, 18,* 237-245.

Reed, A. J., & Bergemann, V. E. (1992). *In the classroom: An introduction to education.* Guilford, CT: Dushkin.

Richardson, V. (1996). The role of attitudes and beliefs in learning to teach. In J. Sikula (Ed.), *Handbook of research on teacher education* (pp. 102-119). New York: Simon & Schuster.

Rosenshine, B., & Stevens, R. (1986). Teaching functions. In M. Wittrock (Ed.), *Handbook of research on teaching* (3rd ed., pp. 376-391). New York: Macmillan.

Roueche, J. E., Baker, G. A., Mullin, P. I., & Boy, N. H. O. (1986). Excellent teachers. In J. F. Roucche & G. A. Baker (Eds.), *Profiling excellence in schools* (pp. 87-133). Arlington, VA: American Association of School Administrators.

Sadker, M., Sadker, D., Fox, L., & Salata, M. (1993/1994). Gender equity in the classroom: The unfinished agenda. *The College Board Review, 170,* 14-21.

Sadker, M., Sadker, D., & Klien, S. (1991). The issue of gender in elementary and secondary education. In G. Grant (Ed.), *Review of research in education* (Vol. 17, pp. 269-334). Washington, DC: American Educational Research Association.

Schwartz, R., Slate, J., & Onwuegbuzie, A. J. (1999). Empowering teachers: Acting upon action research, *GATEways to Teacher Education, 11*(2), 44-59.

Segall, W. E., & Wilson, A. V. (1998). *Introduction to education: Teaching in a diverse society.* Upper Saddle River, NJ: Merrill.

So, S. (1997). To be a reflective teacher. *Canadian Modern Language Review, 53,* 581-587.

Stevens, E. Jr., Wood, G. H., & Sheehan, J. J. (2002). *Justice, ideology education: An introduction to the social foundations of education* (4th ed.). Boston: McGraw-Hill.

Tashakkori, A., & Teddlie, C. (1998). *Mixed methodology: Combining qualitative and quantitative approaches. Applied social research methods series, Vol. 46.* Thousand Oaks, CA: Sage.

Thompson, A. G. (1992). Teachers' beliefs and conceptions: A synthesis of the research. In D. Grouws (Ed.), *Handbook of research on mathematics teaching and learning.* New York: Macmillan.

Thompson, B., & Vacha-Haase, T. (2000). Psychometrics is datametrics: The test is not reliable. *Educational and Psychological Measurement, 60,* 174-195.

Tobin, K. (1987). The role of wait-time is higher cognitive learning. *Review of Educational Research, 24*(1), 69-95.

Witcher, A. E., Onwuegbuzie, A. J., & Minor, L. C. (2001). Characteristics of effective teachers: Perceptions of preservice teachers. *Research in the Schools, 8,* 45-57.

Witcher, A., & Travers, P. (1999). Witcher-Travers Survey of Educational Beliefs. [On-line]. Available http://www.abacon.com/witcher-travers

Witherell, C., & Noddings, N. (1991). *Stories lives tell: Narrative and dialogue in education.* New York: Teachers College Press.

Wolfgang, C. H. (1995). *Solving discipline problems: Strategies for classroom teachers* (3rd ed.). Boston: Allyn & Bacon.

Wolfgang, C. H., & Glickman, C. D. (1986). *Solving discipline problems: Strategies for classroom teachers* (2nd ed.). Boston: Allyn & Bacon.

Wortruba, T. R., & Wright, P. L. (1975). How to develop a teacher-rating instrument: A research approach. *Journal of Higher Education, 46,* 653-663.

Wubbels, T., Levy, J., & Brekelmans, M. (1997, April). Paying attention to relationships. *Educational Leadership, 54*(7), 82-86.

Zittleman, K., & Sadker, D. (2002). Gender bias in teacher education texts: New and old lessons. *Journal of Teacher Education, 53,* 168-180.

Zwick, W. R., & Velicer, W. F. (1986). Comparison of five rules for determining the number of components to retain. *Psychological Bulletin, 99,* 432-442.

Evaluation Criteria	Discussion Questions

Evaluation Criteria

1. Which is the dominant perspective in this study: quantitative or qualitative?

Unlike the previous article, this one is a tough call. The authors used a sequential form of mixed-method inquiry, conducting a qualitative study to identify themes and then undertaking a quantitative analysis to study relationships between these themes and student characteristics. The nod goes to quantitative, however, because the intent of the study is clearly to generalize: "our purpose was to investigate what preservice teachers view as important characteristics of effective teachers, with the intent of comparing their responses with descriptions provided in the literature." Furthermore, no attempt is made in the article to provide a detailed contextual description of the study context, a necessary step in qualitative research.

2. Is the general purpose of the study clear? Will it provide a significant contribution?

Yes. See above. The authors do a nice job of showing the potential impact of attitudes held by students on their later professional practice.

3. Does the review of literature establish the relationship between previous studies and the current one? Is the review well organized and up to date?

The review focuses on the literature on effective teaching and mostly just reports it, with minimal integration. The authors use this literature to show that few studies have concentrated on the beliefs of preservice teachers. They do cite an earlier study by the same authors that appears to have examined the same question; how the current study is similar to and different from that one is not explained.

4. Is the specific research hypothesis or question clearly and concisely stated?

Research questions are implied rather than explicitly stated (in the paragraph immediately preceding the Method section); even so, what the researchers are looking for is reasonably clear.

Discussion Questions

1. Does the logic of this answer suggest that most if not all sequential mixed-method studies are predominately quantitative in perspective? Why or why not?

2. The authors indicate that they want to replicate an earlier study of theirs. How much detail about that earlier study should be given? Is the authors' description sufficient?

3. How well did the literature review persuade you of the importance of this study?

4. Was enough detail presented? Would you have preferred more specific research questions?

5. Is the method of sampling clearly presented? Could the way the sample was obtained influence the results?

The researchers used a convenience sample of preservice teachers in a single university program. Given the size of the sample, it probably includes nearly all students enrolled in the program. The question then becomes the extent to which the sample represents preservice students generally, and that would require a substantial inferential leap.

6. Is there anything in the procedures for collecting the information, or in the instruments themselves, that could bias the results or weaken the study?

Subjects were given two instruments, one qualitative and one quantitative. No information about the qualitative instrument, its origin, validity or reliability, is given, and thus the reader has no evidence upon which to judge its quality. The authors do provide reliability data on the quantitative instrument, although these data were collected from an entirely different population (school superintendents), and thus are of questionable usefulness.

7. Do graphic presentations of the data distort the findings?

Figure 1 purports to represent the key themes of student perceptions. Seven themes were originally identified from the qualitative analysis, and then boiled down to three after a factor analysis. These three factors however explained only slightly more than half of the variance, suggesting that students were responding in ways not well captured by the three metathemes. The presentation would have been enhanced by a table showing the correlations between the seven original themes and student characteristics. Results of the quantitative survey are presented strictly as a frequency distribution and then not mentioned again until the Discussion; no attempt is made to connect these findings with those from the qualitative survey.

5. Note the sample demographics, and the overwhelming majorities of White and female students. Do these numbers make it more difficult to interpret findings by race and gender? Why or why not?

6. What would be reasonable evidence of instrument quality in this case?

7. What do you suppose led the researchers to focus on the factor analysis as the centerpiece of their analysis?

8. Do the conclusions and interpretations follow logically from the results presented? Are unwarranted causal conclusions made from correlations or comparisons? Are limitations indicated?

The authors spend most of the Discussion section on an apparent inverse relationship between valuing "knowledge of subject matter" and "enthusiasm for teaching." (They demonstrate that gender, and perhaps race, may account for this.) This conclusion follows logically from the results. Despite the fact that the study's original purpose was to "replicate and extend" the researchers' earlier study, no attempt is made to compare and contrast the two sets of findings. No causal conclusions are made; no study limitations are discussed.

9. Are the research questions phrased in such a way which suggests that both quantitative and qualitative data are appropriate?

Yes. They imply both exploratory questions, suggesting qualitative, and comparison questions, suggesting quantitative.

10. Are the multiple approaches employed sequentially or concurrently? If concurrently, how are they triangulated?

Sequentially. The researchers used qualitative data to derive categories which they then submitted to quantitative analysis.

11. What are the key quality criteria appropriate for the study's secondary approach? When applied, how do they enhance or hinder the study's overall credibility?

No evidence is presented pertaining to the accuracy or credibility of the qualitative data, thus hurting the study's overall credibility.

12. What do multiple approaches add to the richness of the study?

Creating categories for later statistical analysis based entirely on created responses to open-ended questions is an attractive and logical means of representing participants' real beliefs and attitudes, and has higher credibility than items and categories created by the researchers themselves.

8. Why do you think the researchers spent so much on the "subject matter vs. enthusiasm" issue? What do you think of their implications for preservice teacher education? Do they follow from the data presented?

9. Can you imagine this study being conducted in a totally qualitative manner? What would such a study look like?

10. A sequential qualitative-quantitative study like this one will generally fall into the quantitative camp. What might be an example of a study having the reverse sequence?

11. What would you like to have known about the qualitative survey?

12. Go back to the purely qualitative study from Chapter 4, "Fly in the Buttermilk." How could that study have been turned into one with a sequential mixed-method design?

Credibility Scorecard
Preservice Teachers' Educational Beliefs and Their Perceptions of Characteristics of
Effective Teachers

	Excellent	Very Good	Adequate	Marginal	Poor
General purpose	5	4	3	2	1
Contribution/ significance	5	4	3	2	1
Review of literature	5	4	3	2	1
Research questions or hypotheses	5	4	3	2	1
Subjects or participants	5	4	3	2	1
Instrumentation	5	4	3	2	1
Procedures	5	4	3	2	1
Results	5	4	3	2	1
Practical significance	5	4	3	2	1
Graphics	5	4	3	2	1
Conclusions	5	4	3	2	1
Any fatal flaws?					

6 | ACTION/PRACTITIONER RESEARCH

All of the studies reviewed in the previous chapters, both quantitative and qualitative, have a common goal: to expand the existing knowledge base about an educational problem or issue. Their intention is to generate insights that may be useful in other settings.

Sometimes, however, research has another purpose entirely. An empirical study may be undertaken in order to help make decisions about specific problems in specific settings. Generalizing beyond the setting is at best a secondary consideration. This kind of study is called **action/practitioner research** (also called *practice-based research, teacher research, teacher-as-researcher* or *classroom research*). The study is undertaken by educational professionals in their own practice settings for the purpose of better understanding their work and how to improve it. What distinguishes action research is not how the study is done, but why. It can take on any of the designs previously reviewed (e.g., experimental, nonexperimental, qualitative), though it may not be as methodologically sophisticated as research intended to be generalized to the broader field of study. Some specific action in the form of changes in policy or practice is expected to occur as a result of the inquiry. The basic differences between action/practitioner research and more traditional research are summarized below:

	Traditional Research	Action/Practitioner Research
Purpose	Conclusion	Decision
Focus	Theory	Practice
Standard	Truth	Usefulness

The purpose of traditional research is to draw conclusions about the nature of the world; the purpose of action/practitioner research is to go a step further and ask, What, if anything, should change? Whereas in a traditional study researchers might examine the correlation between class size and pupil achievement in order to draw conclusions about the relationship between these two variables, in an action/practitioner research study investigators might assess the effects of class size on school achievement to help a local school board develop appropriate policies on the maximum number of students allowable per classroom.

The focus of traditional research is theory. In most quantitative research, specific research questions follow from more general theoretical propositions, and in most qualitative research theory is built inductively. In action/practitioner research, however, theory plays a distinctly secondary role. Key research questions derive from practice: How effective is a local Head Start program in increasing school readiness among disadvantaged children? How can a teacher modify her behavior so as to motivate underachieving students in her third-grade classroom? While the results of action/practitioner research may often have theoretical implications, the focus is on the tangible and the here-and-now.

The principal standard by which traditional research is evaluated is the extent to which it helps reveal generalized truth. The standard for action/practitioner research, on the other hand, is much more practical: Does it provide information that helps informed decision making? For example, a traditional study of the impacts of modular scheduling on student achievement would be most concerned with the credibility of the data and the internal and external validity of the design. An action/practitioner research study, while not discounting the importance of scientific credibility, would be more concerned with the extent to which these data help lead to optimal scheduling policies in the school.

One might conclude from this discussion that action/practitioner research is less academically rigorous than the kinds of research presented in previous chapters. Not necessarily. It is true that designs with strong internal validity are hard to find in action/practitioner research simply because the opportunities for experimental control are few or unavailable. This may be why a lot of action/practitioner research uses qualitative designs, which are flexible, emergent, and better able to capture complexity and contextual nuance. In fact, in many ways the criteria for good action/practitioner research pose greater challenges. Not only do action/practitioner researchers need to pay attention to the general criteria governing all educational research, but they also need to consider the consequences of their findings. As action/practitioner research is intended to facilitate change, researchers in this realm cannot afford simply to conduct their study, write up their results, and move on. They also need to consider the implications of their data for the policy or practice context. It is not enough, for example, for the evaluator of an adult literacy program to find that certain groups appear to benefit from the program while others do not. The researcher must also be sensitive to the ways in which the data from the study will be used; information that is used to help make value judgments—about what is and is not effective—has both political and ethical overtones.

Thus, one of the best ways to identify action/practitioner research in the literature is to look for value-laden terms in the title and/or research question. For example, instead of Did the educational intervention raise standardized test scores? an action/practitioner research question would be, Was this technique effective in improving educational performance for students in a particular classroom?

CRITERIA FOR EVALUATING ACTION/PRACTITIONER RESEARCH[1]

1. Does the research provide accurate information about the practices studied? (This is similar to the credibility criterion in traditional research.)
2. Does the research serve the needs of a given audience?
3. Is the research realistic, frugal, and diplomatic?
4. Was the research conducted legally and ethically?

---

[1]Adapted from *Standards for Evaluations of Educational Programs, Projects, and Materials,* by the Joint Committee on Standards for Educational Evaluation, New York: McGraw Hill, 1991.

When Do They Choose the Reading Center? Promoting Literacy in a Kindergarten Classroom

Susan K. Green
Winthrop University

Clair Britt
Winthrop University

Patsy Parker
Cotton Belt Elementary School

This action research project investigated activities designed to encourage children to visit the reading center in a kindergarten classroom. Three interventions were implemented on alternating days. Analyses suggested that these interventions led to increased voluntary use of the reading center. The days the intern read a story produced the most visits. This process of systematic data collection also increased monitoring of the children with the lowest literacy skills and provided opportunities to tailor literacy activities to their interests.

The Recent Shift away from viewing teachers solely as consumers of research to viewing them as producers and mediators of knowledge has fueled the popularity of action research as part of educational practice (Richardson, 1994). Reflecting this trend, a recent survey of institutions affiliated with the American Association of Colleges for Teacher Education found that almost half of the respondents require their teacher education candidates to participate in action research (Henderson, Hunt, & Wester, 1999).

Perhaps the most frequently stated goal for action research is to provide candidates with skills and the opportunity to improve professional practice (e.g., Auger & Wideman, 2000; Brown & Macatangay, 2002; Lytle & Cochran-Smith, 1994; Noffke, 1997). By answering a question or solving a problem that arises in specific classroom circumstances, teachers analyze and modify their practice to become more effective.

The three of us, a classroom teacher, university intern, and the university liaison to the school, decided to initiate an action research project in a kindergarten classroom. We undertook this project to see if action research could viably be completed during a one-semester internship at the school. Both the school administrators and the university liaison had recently learned about benefits of action research, and we hoped to reap such benefits at our school.

Cotton Belt Elementary School is a rural pre-K–5 professional development school associated with Winthrop University in South Carolina. The student body is 75 percent European American, 23 percent African American and 2 percent other ethnicities, with 47 percent eligible for free or reduced fee lunch. Our kindergarten class had 21 students, including 16 European Americans (8 boys and 8 girls) and 5 African Americans (3 girls and 2 boys). Twelve of these students qualified for free or reduced fee lunch. The classroom teacher was a European American female with Bachelor's and Master's degrees in elementary education and 30 hours above the Master's level in early childhood education. At the time of this study, she had been teaching 28 years, including six in kindergarten.

We decided to explore the question of how to entice children to visit the reading center more frequently. The reading center is always a part of the kindergarten classroom, but is often the least-used center. In our experience, many children prefer the more active play of the block center and housekeeping. Many children in our rural area are not exposed to literature, nor do they see their parents reading; consequently, they do not understand the importance or enjoyment of reading. As lifelong readers, the three of us consider getting children and books together as most important.

The reading center is one of six centers that children can choose each morning after large group time. It is in a relatively quiet area of the room near the computer center and the art center. It consists of a two-sided bookcase and two inflatable chairs, with wall art in the area that changes from time to time and may include environmental print, posters of poems, or the children's writings. There is a basket with pointers and eyeglass frames that children can incorporate into literacy activities.

We had noticed that some children willingly go to the reading center and happily spend their time reading, looking at pictures, and sharing books with friends. Other children never choose to pick up a book. We wanted to try different ways of encouraging children to spend time in the reading center. We agreed that participating in reading center activities could be thought of as a good, concrete indicator of children's motivation to read. Watching patterns of attendance at the reading center could yield important insights that we could use to encourage more reading.

ACTIVITIES TO ENCOURAGE READING

Next, we decided to think about putting activities in place that might promote visits to the reading center. We wanted to test three approaches to get books into the hands of children. One of these activities would be presented each day, and every day we would start again with the first activity.

On the first day, Ms. B, the teacher intern, would introduce a book during early morning group time, telling the children about the book and that she would be in the reading center later to read it to them. During center time, the children could first listen to the story if they chose the reading center, and then move to another center or stay and look at other books. We called this "Read To" day.

On the second day, baskets of books would be placed on the tables when the children came into the classroom in the morning. At the beginning of the day, children could sit at the tables and talk quietly or look at books. Some of the books in the baskets were easy to read, some were small copies of the big books used in guided reading with the whole class, some were good picture books, and some were specially chosen based on students' interests at that table. We called this "On Tables" day.

The third day the book baskets would be in the centers during center time, available to the children if they wished to stop and read or to incorporate the books into their center activities. For example, the children might read a book to a doll in the housekeeping center. Children in the writing center might choose to copy words and sentences from the books in the basket. In both the writing center and the art center, the children might use tracing paper to trace words and illustrations from books. The basket in the building center included books about construction and vehicles. The only center in which we did not place a book basket during this intervention was the computer center. We called this intervention "In Centers" day. We implemented this three-day alternating pattern for 13 weeks.

INDICATORS OF PARTICIPATION AT THE READING CENTER

We decided that a handy way to keep track of children's use of books and attendance at the reading center would be a chart listing all students' names with dates and the alternating daily activities across the top. Ms. B would note with a check when each student used books to meet the objective of each of the three daily activities (e.g., listening to the story

on "Read To" Day, reading at the tables on "On Tables" day, or incorporating books into center activities on "In Centers" day). She entered a star whenever students visited the reading center and read books in addition to the daily activities (or sometimes instead of them). This system proved simple to keep daily track and did not require modification over the course of the project.

FIRST ANALYSIS OF THE READING CENTER ATTENDANCE DATA

The three of us decided to meet on the average of every two weeks to look at the data Ms. B collected and to see what patterns emerged. The first time we met, we noticed that, of the three activities, children met the reading objective for the day most frequently on "On Tables" days when books were on the tables in the early morning. We thought this was the case because they had only one other choice at this time—quiet talking in their seats.

In looking at which of the three activities generated more stars (visits to the reading center) after the first two weeks, "Read To" day stood out as the clear favorite (9 stars vs. 4 and 5). The children seemed to be spending more free time at the reading center on the days that Ms. B read to them.

We also checked which children had no stars. After two weeks of the project, three of the four students judged to be lowest in literacy skills had no stars. Our discovery led Ms. B to focus on the interests of these children, handpicking books for "Read To" days that suited their interests. For example, she learned that one student had a strong interest in NASCAR, so she found a book to read about auto racing. Several students showed interest in dogs, so she chose *The Most Obedient Dog in the World* (Jeram, 1993) for another session. She also found an interactive book about pizza (Pelam, 1996) for a child who loves pizza. Books with an unusual characteristic were a real draw. For example, children found the shiny scales of *Rainbow Fish* (Pfister, 1992) or the raised web of *The Very Busy Spider* (Carle, 1984) fascinating. Books with wonderful rhythm or literary devices like *17 Kings and 42 Elephants* (Mahy, 1987) or *Chicka Chicka Boom Boom* (Martin & Archambault, 1989) were also favorites and encouraged children to go to the reading center for a closer look and to read their favorite passages. We have developed a list of titles that we have found pique the interest of reluctant kindergarten students, which is displayed in Table 1.

LATER ANALYSES

We continued to meet three more times during the semester to examine the children's patterns of

Table 1.   Books for Reluctant Kindergarten Readers

Art
Purple, Green, and Yellow by Robert N. Munsch
My Crayon Talk by G. Patricia Hubbard
Elmer by David McKee

Housekeeping
Dress-up by Anne Geddes

Math Center
Number Munch! by Chuck Reasoner
Bear In A Square by Stella Blackston
Ten, Nine, Eight by Molly Bang

Writing Center
The Jungle ABC by Michael Roberts
Clifford's ABC by Norman Bridwell

Reading Center/Reading with the Teacher
I Love to Eat Bugs! by John Strejan (Pop-up)
Alpha Bugs by David A. Carter (Interactive/pop-up)
Monster's Lunch Box by Marc Brown
    (Interactive/pop-up)
Five Little Ducks Raffi Songs to Read
I Can Read by Rozanne Lanczak Williams
ABC and You by Eugine Fernandes
Where the Wild Things Are by Maurice Sendak
What Makes a Rainbow? by Betty Ann Schwartz
Joseph Had a Little Overcoat by Simms Taback
I Can Read With My Eyes Shut! by Dr. Seuss
The Wheels on the Bus by Maryann Kovalski
Rain by Manya Stojic
The Ants Go Marching (Traditional) Illustrated by
Jeffrey Scherer
Sunflower House by Eve Bunting
The Grouchy Ladybug by Eric Carle
The Hungry Caterpillar by Eric Carle

Table 2.   Patterns of Book Use and Reading Center Participation at the Beginning and End of the Project

	First 9 days		Last 9 days	
	✓	*	✓	*
Read To	15	5	20	12
On Tables	43	4	36	19
In Centers	18	5	7	3
Total	76	14	63	34

Note: ✓ = Met reading objective for that day
* = Looked at books in the Reading Center

reading activities. We found that voluntary use of the reading center increased over time, with 34 students visiting the reading center on the last nine days of the project compared to 14 during the first nine days (See Table 2). Children tended to visit most consistently on the "Read To" days, with a median of three children per day. On "On Tables" days and on the "In Centers" days, a median of one student per day visited the reading center.

We also continued to focus on the three students with the lowest literacy skills (the fourth had moved away three weeks into this project). We quizzed them about their interests and helped them find books that related to these interests. One boy seemed enthralled with trains, so we kept an eye out for any interesting train books. We also encouraged these children to reread books and not to give up after one try, even urging them to take their favorite books home. Our focus on them paid off because we found that by the end of the project these students visited the reading center voluntarily a total of 16 times. We even noted that their visits to the reading center occurred on "In Centers" and "On Tables" days, not just on "Read To" days. For comparison purposes, we found that three other randomly chosen boys (who had stronger literacy skills) visited the reading center a total of ten times during the project.

Other issues arose in later meetings. Our data helped us discover that changing books in the baskets and in the reading center helped keep students' interest. We started changing books in the baskets and in the reading center every two weeks. We wanted to make sure that, as visits increased, we would have fresh books available that children had not seen. When using the baskets less frequently, we only changed them every seven weeks.

Ms. P voiced concern about how to maintain the "Read To" days when Ms. B finished the internship. We brainstormed ideas about having parent volunteers or fourth and fifth graders take turns at reading a story in the reading center. This year we have a fifth-grade child who visits twice a week to read to children in the reading center during center time. We also thought about ways the children could keep track of their own visits to the reading center with a specially designed sign-up sheet they could initial.

CONCLUSIONS AND IMPLICATIONS

This project helped us take a fresh look at our efforts to encourage children to enjoy books and to see them as an important part of life. Our three different interventions seemed overall to make a difference. As the year progressed, children visited the reading center more often, as verified by the increasing numbers of stars on our charts. We also saw children staying longer at the reading center and asking for more books to be read to them.

Collecting data made us conscious everyday of our goal of encouraging literacy, and as such other ideas came to us about that goal. We put books we read to the whole group in the reading center and told children they could look at them again. We found children going to the baskets to get books to use in the housekeeping center for their pretend play even on the days when we did not place books in centers. We found ourselves saying, "When you go to the reading center. . ." more often. Articulating our assumption that they would go helped them to understand that a visit to the reading center could be as much a part of the day as going to lunch. We made our higher expectations clear, and the children eagerly met them. We realized again the power of teacher expectations on children's behavior, a phenomenon that has been clearly and broadly established in educational research over the last 30 years (e.g., Brophy, 1983; Jussim, Smith, Madon, & Palumbo, 1998; Rosenthal, 1994).

We found that the more time children spent with books, the more they enjoyed and noticed similarities and differences between them. For example, after reading *Have You Seen My Duckling?* (Tafuri, 1984), the children asked that more books where you have to look for something hiding in the picture be in the reading center. Ms. P then suggested children to look for the little deer hiding in every picture in *Anansi and the Moss Covered Rock* (Kimmel, 1988) when they went to the reading center. Sometimes she put two versions of the same book in the center and asked the children to compare the two and tell her what they discovered when the class next got back together again. The children also started comparing Caldecott award winners. They were amazed that *Make Way for Ducklings* (McCloskey, 1941) won because the pictures were not colorful. Upon further discussion about the details in the pictures, they agreed that the sepia tones actually enhanced the pictures.

For us, one implication of doing this project is the importance of collecting data and using it to make some decisions about what goes on in a classroom. We so often get caught up in the day-to-day management of the classroom that we do not have time for reflection, to think about how we can do things better. Collecting the data forced us to reflect. We found it made us think about ways to encourage children to enjoy reading and books. Both Ms. B and Ms. P intend to incorporate data collection and the reflection it engenders into other aspects of their classroom practices next year.

More important, perhaps, the project made us think about individual children and their needs and interests. We could see in black and white that some kids were "falling through the cracks," and we had to do something about it. One of the most important applications of this project for us will be our future effort to conduct action research with the more reluctant learners in the forefront of our minds and our data collection. Our state has placed a good deal of emphasis on teaching the standards, and doing this kind of action research helps us integrate teaching children with teaching standards.

REFERENCES

Auger, W., & Wideman, R. (2000). Using action research to open the door to life-long professional learning. *Education, 121,* 120–128.

Brown, M., & Macatangay, A. (2002). The impact of action research for professional development: Case studies in two Manchester schools. *Westminster Studies in Education, 25* (1), 35–45.

Brophy, J. (1983). Research on the self-fulfilling prophecy and teacher expectations. *Journal of Educational Psychology, 75*(5), 631–661.

Carle, E. (1984). *The very busy spider.* New York: Scholastic Books.

Henderson, M. V., Hunt, S.N., & Wester, C. (1999). Action Research: A survey of AACTE-Member Institutions. *Education, 119,* 663–669.

Jeram, A. (1993). *The most obedient dog in the world.* London: Walker Books, Ltd.

Jussim, L., Smith, A., Madon, S., & Palumbo, P. (1998). Teacher expectations. In J. Brophy (Ed.) *Advances in research on teaching, 7.* 1–47.

Kimmel, E. (1988). *Anansi and the moss covered rock.* New York: Scholastic Books.

Lytle, S., & Cochran-Smith, M. (1994). Inquiry, knowledge and practice, in S. Hollingsworth & H. Sockett (Eds.) *Teacher research and educational reform.* Chicago: University of Chicago Press.

Mahy, M. (1987). *17 kings and 42 elephants.* New York: Dial Books for Young Readers.

Martin, B., & Archambault, J. (1989). *Chicka chicka boom boom.* New York: Simon and Schuster.

McCloskey, R. (1941). *Make way for ducklings.* New York: Viking Press.

Noffke, S. E. (1997). Professional, personal, and political dimensions of action research. *Review of Research in Education, 22,* 305–343.

Pelam, D. (1996). *Sam's pizza.* New York: Dutton Children's Books.

Pfister, M. (1992). *Rainbow fish.* New York: North-South Books.

Richardson, V. (1994). Conducting research on practice. *Educational Researcher, 23* (5), 5–10.

Rosenthal, R. (1994). Interpersonal expectancy effects: A 30-year perspective. *Current Directions in Psychological Science, 3,* 176–179.

Tafuri, N. (1984). *Have you seen my duckling?* New York: Scholastic.

Susan Green is a faculty member at Winthrop University. Clair Britt is an Intern for Cotton Belt Elementary School and Winthrop University. Patsy Parker is a faculty member at Cotton Belt Elementary School.

Evaluation Criteria

1. Does the research provide accurate information about the practices studied?

The authors nicely capture the essence of *classroom research,* a concept based on the notion that, as professionals, teachers can and should also be inquirers into their professional practice. In a brief but informative introduction the authors describe the school context and the rationale for the study, an investigation of strategies for enticing children to use the reading center. They decided on three intervention strategies based in part on their observations of the children's behavior. Each of the three strategies, and the method of introducing them, was clearly described.

2. Does the research cover the needs of a given audience?

Clearly, yes. Action research allows the investigator to inquire into new leads, based upon preliminary findings. Note, for example, how the researchers were drawn to focus on the needs of slow readers. Note also how the authors made specific changes in their teaching practice on the basis of these data, and how the exercise itself changed the way they looked at their teaching.

3. Is the research realistic, frugal, and diplomatic?

It was certainly realistic and frugal. Note how spare Table 2 is: these simple data told the researchers all they needed to know to make an informed decision. As the research was conducted by the participants themselves, "diplomatic" does not apply.

4. Was the research conducted legally and ethically?

Yes. All data were based on observation only.

Discussion Questions

1. Classroom research has risen considerably in popularity as a form of action research. What do you think about this technique? Should all teachers be encouraged to engage in classroom research? Why or why not?

2. Classroom research, by definition, exists to serve the needs of those who are conducting it, and so is completely context-bound. Who, then, is served by reporting studies like these in professional journals?

3. Put yourself in the place of these researchers. Would you have taken the same steps as they did, based upon the results of Table 2? Why or why not?

4. What forms of classroom research would lead to stronger concerns about legal and/or ethical issues?

Credibility Scorecard
When do They Choose the Reading Center? Promoting Literacy in a Kindergarten Classroom

	Excellent	Very Good	Adequate	Marginal	Poor
General purpose	5	4	3	2	1
Contribution/ significance	5	4	3	2	1
Review of literature	5	4	3	2	1
Research questions or hypotheses	5	4	3	2	1
Subjects or participants	5	4	3	2	1
Instrumentation	5	4	3	2	1
Procedures	5	4	3	2	1
Results	5	4	3	2	1
Practical significance	5	4	3	2	1
Graphics	5	4	3	2	1
Conclusions	5	4	3	2	1
Any fatal flaws?					

Doing Research That Makes a Difference

Estela Mara Bensimon   Donald E. Polkinghorne
Georgia L. Bauman   Edlyn Vallejo

Over the past several years, the chasms between research and practice as well as research and policy have been the topic of commentaries (Keller, 1985; Layzell, 1990) of several addresses given by presidents of the Association for the Study of Higher Education (e.g., Terenzini, 1996; Conrad, 1989; Nettles, 1995), and books (Kezar & Eckel, 2000). A prevalent theme in these publications is the disconnect between higher education research and policymakers and practitioners. The solutions that have been offered to close these gaps include writing in a more user-friendly style, publishing research results in outlets that are practitioner-oriented, presenting research results at practitioner-oriented meetings, and studying problems that are high on policy-makers and practitioners' lists of priorities. Essentially, solutions for closing the gap between research and practice involve two issues. These are the need to study problems that are of greater relevance to policy-makers and practitioners (whoever they are) and the need to broaden the ways in which research findings are disseminated.

We do not believe that the gap between research and practice will be closed by researchers choosing more relevant and/or bigger problems to study nor by their developing more user-friendly forms of dissemination. Instead, we believe that the problem lies in the traditional methodology of knowledge production. As members of the educational research community we have been socialized to believe that the purpose of research is to produce scientific-like knowledge that practitioners can apply at the local level to improve educational outcomes, student success, leadership, and so on.

In this article we describe an alternative methodology for conducting research that is intended to bring about institutional change. This process involves developing deeper awareness among faculty members, administrators, or counselors, of a problem that exists in their local context. In some instances these individuals may be unaware that the problem exists; in others, they may be aware of the problem but not of its magnitude; or they may perceive its broad outline but not the details.

To differentiate between this alternative methodology and the traditional way of conducting research, we call the former the "practitioner-as-researcher" model. The principal distinction between the two models is in their approach to knowledge production. In the traditional model the individual identified as the researcher controls the production of knowledge; in the practitioner-as-researcher model, stakeholders produce knowledge within a local context in order to identify local problems and take action to solve them.

This article contains four parts that serve to delineate the distinctiveness and utility of the practioner-as-researcher model. In the first section we contrast the traditional model of research with the practitioner-as-researcher model. Second, we provide details about a project in which we have utilized the practitioner-as-researcher approach, the Diversity Scorecard project. Next, we discuss the outcomes that the practitioners who engaged in research experienced. Finally, we provide our concluding thoughts and reflections on the process.

PART I: THE METHODOLOGIES OF THE TRADITIONAL AND THE PRACTITIONER-AS-RESEARCHER MODEL

The Traditional Model

The traditional model of research production calls for a division of labor between the manufacturers of

The study upon which this paper is based, "Designing and Implementing a Diversity Scorecard to Improve Institutional Effectiveness for Underserved Minority Students," is funded by The James Irvine Foundation. The findings and opinions written here are solely those of the authors and do not reflect the position or priorities of the foundation. We wish to thank Adrianna Kezar and Susan Talburt for their many good suggestions.

Estela Mara Bensimon is director, Center for Urban Education and professor of higher education, Rossier School of Education. Donald E. Polkinghorne is Fahmy Attallah and Donna Attallah Chair in humanistic psychology, Rossier School of Education. Georgia L. Bauman is associate director and postdoctoral Fellow, Center for Urban Education, Rossier School of Education, Edlyn Vallejo is a PhD candidate, Center for Urban Education, Rossier School of Education, University of Southern California.

research findings (researcher) and the consumers of those findings (practitioner). In the traditional research model, the researcher defines the problem to be studied, selects the appropriate methods, collects the data, interprets them, and reports the findings. The role of the research subject is to provide the information the researcher is seeking. The researcher is the expert on the problem to be studied, which gives him or her the authority to provide solutions. The results of the research are reported in journal articles that are generally read by other researchers. Most of these articles have no influence whatsoever on the actions of higher education practitioners. Consequently, the knowledge obtained through research tends to remain unnoticed and unused by those for whom it is intended. If research is to have a real impact on higher education, it will take more than making the research producers' reports more user-friendly for practitioners. What is needed is another model for research production in higher education—a model that will at least supplement the traditional model if not replace it.

The norms that characterize the traditional model of conducting educational research place a premium on the production of representational knowledge. Representational knowledge is acquired by converting the characteristics of individuals, organizations, or phenomena into variables that are connected to one another in a functional manner (Park, 1999). An example of this is the analysis of student success in college as a function of the number of mathematics courses completed in high school. Park writes, "The instrumental power of representational knowledge in this functional form lies in its capacity to make predictions by showing antecedent events leading to probable consequences, which makes it possible, in theory, to produce desired events or to prevent undesirable ones" (p. 82). In the scholarship of higher education, much of the published research on student retention, institutional change, and leadership effectiveness is characteristic of representational knowledge.

Proponents of "decolonizing" or "emancipatory" methodologies describe traditional research as looking at indigenous people through "imperial eyes" (Smith, 1999, p. 42). In higher education, one might say that traditional research is looking at students, faculty, or institutions through "researcher eyes." Drawing on the work of Stuart Hall (1992), Smith describes traditional research as the "West," a model of research that has the following characteristics:

> It (1) allows 'us' to characterize and *classify* societies into categories, (2) condense complex images of other societies through a *system of representation,* (3) provide a standard *model of comparison,* and (4) provide

criteria of evaluation against which other societies can be ranked. (pp. 42–43; emphasis in the original).

We see the traditional model of knowledge production as being far more to blame for the gap between research and practice than the irrelevance of the problems studied, the colorless writing of researchers, or their overreliance on specialized journals as the accepted vehicle for the dissemination. The traditional model's methods, such as classification, measurement, and the creation of ideal models, even though they are remarkably effective in reducing complexity and chaos into manageable concepts, rarely provide a picture that reflects the reality of a particular place and particular people.

In the traditional model, research production is held to be a highly sophisticated and skilled enterprise. In addition to requiring years of graduate training to understand its intricacies, it demands extensive knowledge of procedures for eliminating biases and proficiency in ever more complex statistical techniques. Because of the difficulties involved, an individual's research production serves not only to create new knowledge but also to demonstrate his or her skill and worthiness for academic promotions. The focal audience for research reports consists of journal reviewers and editors. Thus, the reports display the care with which the study adheres to the requirements of an accepted methodology.

Traditional research methodology has a stronger association with quantitative studies that mimic the scientific approach. However, even though the methods of data gathering are different, qualitative studies constitute traditional research in that the roles assumed by the researcher and researched are based on the traditional model of knowledge production.

The kind of knowledge valued in the quantitative-based traditional model is independent of context. It states what, in general, is so. It is not focused on the individual differences at local institutions (Huberman, 1999). In its applied form, it asserts that certain programmatic interventions bring about better results than others. When the consumers of higher education research are confronted with a problem, they consult the journals to find out which programs the researchers have determined will provide effective solutions. Then they can implement such programs with confidence that they will solve the local problem. In traditional qualitative studies, even though knowledge is treated as context dependent and emphasis is placed on individual differences, the researcher does not involve the subjects in decisions about research approaches and research design (Heron, 1996). Research, whether in the tradition of positivism or interpretivism is still conducted at a distance and "largely fails to penetrate the experienced reality" (Stringer, 1996, p. 6) of the everyday life of the researched.

Practitioner-as-Researcher

Our motivation to create a practitioner-as-researcher model stems from our affiliation with the Center for Urban Education (CUE), the mission of which is to conduct research that will result in the creation of enabling institutional environments for children, youth, and adults from socially and economically disenfranchised groups residing in urban settings. Realizing that the data collection practices used in the past would not enable us to attain our goal, we decided to adopt a practitioner-as-researcher model that was more closely aligned with the Center's mission. Our opportunity to develop this approach came two years ago, when CUE received a grant from the James Irvine Foundation to work with 14 urban colleges in Southern California on improving educational outcomes for African-American and Latino students. The model for conducting research introduced in this article evolved from our work with these institutions over a two-year period on the Diversity Scorecard project. We call this model "practitioner-as-researcher" to emphasize that in it the roles of the researched and researcher are reversed to some extent. That is, practitioners take the role of researchers, and researchers assume the role of facilitators and consultants.

The practitioner-as-researcher model has elements of community (Smith, 1999), collaborative, and participatory action research (Bray et al., 2000; Stringer, 1996) in that the purpose of inquiry is to bring about change at individual, organizational, and societal levels. The methodology consists of outsider researchers working as facilitators engaged with insider teams of practitioners in a process of collecting data and creating knowledge about local problems as seen from a local perspective.

Reason and Bradbury (2001) write that action research "is a participatory, democratic process concerned with developing practical knowing in the pursuit of worthwhile human purposes" and that its primary purpose "is to produce practical knowledge that is useful to people in the everyday function of their lives" (pp. 1–2). In the practitioner-as-researcher model, individuals conduct research about their own institutions, and by doing so they acquire knowledge that they can use to bring about change in these institutions.

Because institutional insiders conduct the actual research, the role of the professional researcher shifts from research producer to consultant and facilitator for the practitioner researchers. The practitioner-as-researcher model requires that the professional researcher be skilled in building and maintaining

personal relationships as well as in research design. Above all, it is important for the insiders to assume ownership of their findings. The outcome is knowledge that heightens the members' awareness of what is occurring within their institutions and increases their motivation to effect change. Thus, the knowledge produced in this model is practical and effective in directing changes.

To more clearly define what we mean by the practitioner-as-researcher model, we will distinguish it from other forms of action-oriented research which prioritize participation as a key feature. Reason (1994) describes three approaches to participative inquiry: cooperative inquiry, participatory action research, and action science or action inquiry. In the first phase of cooperative inquiry, the core-searchers agree upon the proposed area for research and methods for carrying out the research. In utilizing the practitioner-as-researcher model, we did not collaborate with the practitioners on the identification of the problem. We, the outsiders, identified a suspected problem area—inequities in educational outcomes for African-American and Latino students in postsecondary education—and in that sense set the agenda for the research. We also chose the method for conducting this research—examining institutional data disaggregated by race and ethnicity. So while we feel that the practitioners' involvement in the research is, in fact, the key feature that produced the outcomes we sought, the practitioners were not involved in the development of the research question or method. In this sense, the practitioner-as-researcher process is not a faithful application of action-oriented research.

Participatory action research operates in the political realm and is concerned with producing knowledge and empowering people and communities through genuine collaboration. This model may have been more applicable to our project had we worked directly with students of color on participating campuses who were experiencing inequities in educational outcomes. Instead we worked with faculty, administrators, and staff to conduct research on this problem. When comparing the political power of these two groups, the students appear to be those in need of empowerment in terms of making institutional change. We chose to work with faculty, administrators, and staff because we felt they were closer to and could have more direct effects on the decision-making systems of the institutions.

Our model belongs to that category of research known generally as *action science* or *action inquiry,* which is a "form of inquiry into practice" (Reason, 1994, p. 330). There are differences among researchers who operate within these categories. Research conducted in these areas is concerned with transforming organizations and communities to act self-reflectively and collaboratively within everyday practice. However, this reflection among community members often operates at a more theoretical and abstract level, focusing on "the collective dream and mission" (p. 331). Reflections such as these are secondary to those engaged in by the practitioners-as-researchers in our current project. The target for our collaborative inquiry was more concrete and specific—to raise awareness of the existence of inequities in educational outcomes by involving members of 14 campuses in a data-driven project. Hence, our model fills a distinct space in the realm of action research because of the questions and methods it employs, as well as the focused nature of the study.

PART II: THE DIVERSITY SCORECARD: A PRACTITIONER-AS-RESEARCHER PROJECT

The purpose of this section is to illustrate the practitioner-as-researcher model by discussing a particular case of the use of the model as well as the choice to use this model by describing the Diversity Scorecard project in depth. The Diversity Scorecard project is concerned with equity in educational outcomes for African-American and Latino students. The stated goal was to work in partnership with 14 urban two-and four-year colleges, public as well as independent, to improve educational outcomes for undergraduate students who are African-American, Latino, or members of other groups with a history of underrepresentation in and underpreparation for higher education. We proposed to accomplish this by involving participants from the 14 institutions in the identification of indicators that would enable them to assess and improve institutional effectiveness in terms of equity in access, retention, institutional receptivity, and excellence for students of color. The focus was specifically on African Americans and Latinos because they typically experience the greatest inequities in educational outcomes. Equity is defined as the point at which a particular ethnic group's representation across all majors, programs, honors, and so on at the institution is equal to the group's representation in the student body. Therefore, if Latino students make up 25% of the student body, they should also make up 25% of the Dean's List. To achieve this, the activities of the project were aimed at developing leadership for change among the research team members in the 14 participating institutions.

Why use the Practitioner-as-Researcher Model to Explore Equity?

Our interest in conducting research that will make a difference arose from the predicted consequences of the demographic and educational changes in

California, the state in which we live and work. California is known for its ethnic diversity and growing minority population. Steady influxes of immigrants continue to intensify this trend. Not only is California the most ethnically diverse state with an expediently growing immigrant population, it is often seen as a prime example of an economy experiencing the polarizing effects of globalization (Sassen. 1994). Increasingly, the scenario being written for California is one of economic polarization because a growing sector of the population, primarily Latino, is not reaching the educational level that will be a prerequisite for the jobs in the future. Demographers have painted a bleak future showing that the gap between the haves and have-nots is widening, with an increasing likelihood of social breakdown as low-skilled immigrant and ethnic minorities proliferate at the bottom of the labor market and highly skilled workers are imported from other states or countries (Myers, Park, & Hacegaba 2000).

The primary approach used to address these concerns has been the development of a system for enhancing diversity in higher education. Termed the *pipeline* model, this system focuses on providing minority students with greater access to higher education. It is based on the view that the normal channels are blocked for minorities and barriers must be removed and new pipelines of access laid. Ibarra (2001) described the four-fold mission of the pipeline model: (1) to increase the number of minority students enrolled in higher education; (2) to offer remedial courses and tutorial support for underprepared minority students; (3) to assist in meeting the financial, academic, and sociocultural needs of minority students, and (4) to offer academic advice and counseling on issues related to culture (pp. 236–237). The pipeline model has been extended into the primary and secondary schools with programs designed to help minority students in preparation for college and eventually for graduate school admission and academic positions.

In spite of long involvement with diversity initiatives, institutions of higher education do not appear to have made much headway in reversing these troubling trends (the California Citizens Commission on Higher Education. 1998). Presently, only 4% of California's Latino and 3% of African American high-school graduates have the grades and test scores to qualify for admission to the University of California. This compares most unfavorably with the 13% of white and 30% of Asian American high-school graduates who qualify for the University of California. Furthermore, in *Shape of the River,* a study intended to show how ethnic minorities benefit from the pipeline model, Bowen and Bok (1998) found a performance gap or academic differential between the GPA ranking of graduating minority and majority students.

This being the case, the project described in this article was motivated by a concern that in spite of increased access to higher education for students of color, there continue to be major inequities in educational out-comes, particularly among African-American and Latino students. Had we chosen to use the traditional model of research, our team of outsiders would have collected data from the 14 institutions, taken it back to our offices at the University of Southern California for analysis, and written a report emphasizing the technical sophistication of our work. The report would then have been submitted for publication and a copy forwarded to the presidents of the participating institutions. These presidents might or might not have read it and might or might not have shared it with the faculty who might or might not have found it useful.

However, rather than conducting research that would culminate with papers and articles in which we would reveal patterns of inequity in educational outcomes and make general recommendations about how they might be reduced, we wanted our work to make differences at the very sites where inequities in educational outcomes exist. That is, rather than trying to reach an unspecified audience in the hope that our findings would influence their practices, we wanted to find a way of conducting research that would be situated in and shaped by local conditions and local individuals. We wanted the participating institutions to learn whether the pipeline approach was working in terms of achieving equity in educational outcomes for African-American and Latino students. We wanted the institutions to incorporate the knowledge they had acquired into the local systems of decision making. To put it simply, we wanted to be able to facilitate research by local participants that would improve their understanding of diversity on their respective campuses and influence their actions to achieve equity in educational outcomes among their students. The vehicle for accomplishing this was the Diversity Scorecard project, which is described in greater detail in the following section.

The Diversity Scorecard Project

As mentioned above, most efforts related to diversity and achievement in higher education have focused on access to postsecondary institutions and on the dynamics of interracial and intercultural human relations, most often on predominantly white campuses.

Our interest was quite different. We wanted to focus attention on the accountability side of diversity—the missing link between access to institutions and evidence of results in educational outcomes in the diversity agenda in general. We sought to do this among those institutions that have successfully achieved diversity in their student body but who have a long way to go in duplicating the same degree of diversity in those educational outcomes that indicate students of color have an opportunity to gain access to opportunity and power.

The scorecard tool. The strategy used in the Diversity Scorecard project was the examination of institutional data disaggregated by race/ethnicity that reflected educational outcomes by teams of institutional actors in the local context. The Diversity Scorecard was derived from Kaplan and Norton's (1992) balanced scorecard for business and the academic scorecard (O'Neil et al., 1999). The Diversity Scorecard provides four concurrent perspectives on institutional performance in terms of equity in educational outcomes; access, retention, institutional receptivity, and excellence. It is basically an accountability framework that is appealing to institutional leaders who have to respond to external calls for creating "cultures of evidence." It has been observed that administrators act when things go wrong and that one of the ways that administrators sense that things are going wrong is through data analysis (Birnbaum, 1988). It is also true that what gets measured is what gets attended to by campus leaders. A serious shortcoming of the diversity agenda thus far has been the absence of baseline data and benchmarks that would make it possible for institutions to engage in a systematic and continuous self-appraisal and improvement of their diversity efforts.

The scorecard process. The Diversity Scorecard provided the means to involve campus members in the production of knowledge about student outcomes disaggregated by race and ethnicity. The involvement of campus teams in gathering and analyzing data in order to create the measures and benchmarks for their institution's Diversity Scorecard was the strategy that we used to develop or intensify their awareness and consciousness about the fact that inequity in educational outcomes is widespread on their campuses.

The evidence teams' first order of business was to identify inequities in educational outcomes: this is a cognitive process.[1] Recognition requires learning, something that was not known before or that was

---

[1]Susan Talburt (personal communication) has pointed out that if addressing inequity was only a matter of cognition it would be easier to deal with. We agree that inequities are the product of institutionalized and societal forms of racism and power asymmetries that affect the quality of education for students of color from kindergarten through higher education. However, we felt it would be more productive in the long run to use the strategy of knowledge production as the starting place for the recognition of inequities.

suspected but never confirmed with evidence. As learning is more likely to happen through conversation, proponents of communities of practice recommend that professionals who have something in common learn by participating in activities in which they interact with one another (Wenger, 1998). However, participation in a community of practice is not simply a matter of attending meetings or events. According to Wenger, it is a "more encompassing process of being active participants in the practices of social communities and constructing identities in relation to these communities" (p. 4). Thus, a community of practice provides the situation and establishes the conditions associated with effective learning, which can bring about important changes in an individual's beliefs, values, and actions of individuals. The opportunity for institutional change lies in the possibility that individual participants will transfer their learning to other contexts within the institution, and by doing so, enable others to learn and to change.

Although we "outsiders" identified the problem and the framework to be used for research, each evidence team selected the educational outcomes to focus on. Their choices reflected the unique concerns of each type of institution. The ability of each team to concentrate on institutional priorities indicates a major advantage of the practitioner-as-researcher model. Institutions of higher education are very different from one another, but their differences are not clearly revealed in much of the research, particularly when viewed through the interpretive lens of the "research university." The fact that the evidence teams of 14 institutions developed 58 fine-grained measures[2] of educational outcomes indicates why it is so difficult to translate generalized research findings into practice. According to one participant.

> The DS could be the antidote to anti-affirmative action. When you make the institutions choose the indicators and show whether they are succeeding or failing on them.... It's more meaningful than if others [external agents] construct measures.

Our expectation was that through the process of developing the Diversity Scorecard and writing up a report on their findings, the members of the campus teams would become experts on the state of equity on their respective campuses. By involving team members in the actual gathering of information on student outcomes and disaggregating it by race and ethnicity, some of the participants might feel more empowered to assume the role of change agents. That is, "The knowledge production itself may become a form of mobilization" that induces individuals to take action (Gaventa & Cornwall. 2001, p. 76).

PART III: OUTCOMES FOR PRACTITIONERS-AS-RESEARCHERS

Action research is a valuable strategy because the production of knowledge by members of an inquiry group has the potential to be transformational. Participating in an inquiry group can increase members' awareness of a problem, make them more conscious of their capacities for action, and empower them to use their newly acquired expertise to influence others (Gaventa & Cornwall, 2001: Park, 1999; Smith, 1999). According to Stringer (1996). "If an action research project does not *make a difference,* in a very specific way, for practitioners and/or their clients, then it has failed to achieve its objectives" (p. 11; emphasis in the original). The effectiveness of the Diversity Scorecard project depends on two kinds of changes. The first kind has to do with the teams and their individual members. At the team level, one might ask these questions: "Is there evidence that mutual involvement in the production of knowledge has made a difference for the group as a whole? Has the team acquired new awareness about inequities, and if so, has this awareness led to collective action?" At the individual level, one might ask: "Is there evidence that individuals have developed new awareness, that they feel empowered, that they have initiated changes in their own practices as faculty members, academic administrators, institutional researchers, or counselors?"

The second kind of change is the ultimate indication of the effectiveness of this project. At some point, one must ask, "Is there evidence that educational outcomes for African-American and Latino students reflect progress toward equity?" When this question can be answered affirmatively, then change is occurring. In our view, change of this nature requires that the individuals who are responsible for decisions affecting the education of African-American and Latino students must, themselves, go through a process of change. At this stage of the project it is too soon to evaluate changes in student outcomes. Moreover, it would not be possible to do so without initiating longitudinal cohort studies.[3]

In order to determine the effects of the inquiry process on members of the evidence teams, we maintained field notes and also conducted interviews with a subset of the participants. This aspect of the project is in progress, and the quotations provided are only for the purposes of illustration. A more rigorous analysis of the kinds of changes experienced by individuals is currently underway. In the following sections we provide examples of individual changes as well as examples of individuals for whom the project made no difference.

---

[2] The measures are available at http://www.use.edu/dept/education/CUE/projects/ds/diversityscorecard.html

[3] Phase II of the project, which started on January 1, 2003, will involve cohort studies and ethnographic interviews with students.

New Awareness about Inequities in Educational Outcomes

Considering the limited awareness of inequities in educational outcomes for African Americans and Latinos, the inquiry process proved to be a revelation for the evidence teams. To realize the seriousness and enormity of the problem, they had to find the evidence and draw their own conclusions. While some had initially been dubious, data disaggregated by race and ethnicity convinced them that inequities did indeed exist on their own campuses. Team members usually reacted with surprise when they saw what the data revealed. For example, in one institution, it was generally known that about 41% of the first-time students needed remediation in mathematics. Compared to other institutions, this was a low percentage. However, when the data on remediation were disaggregated by race and ethnicity, they indicated that within the first-time student population, 78% of the African Americans and 52% of the Latinos experienced this need. The following comment from a team member reflects the group's overall response.

> This is the first time that I'm aware of that anyone is looking at this problem by ethnicity and to this level of detail. [Now that the data have been disaggregated] we can look more deeply and systematically at remediation rather than just the 59/41 split (between Math and English). This is central on everyone's mind. We can really raise conversation around this.

On another campus, as the evidence team was reviewing data tables that had been prepared for them by the institutional research office, a dean was particularly struck by what they disclosed about students' performance in several mathematics courses:

> It was presented in such a way that it was very overwhelming. I think everybody who saw the data said. "Wow, we have a real serious problem." All of a sudden, seeing the data provided in that way, everybody stepped back and gasped and said. "Boy, there's something going on." We shared it with the Provost. He was in awe of it. We talked about it in several committee meetings and people were in awe of it . . . and the President was made aware of this information and he was in awe of it.

One of the reasons why these data inspired such awe was that they were displayed on a table with five columns, each of which represented an ethnic group. The rows listed about 27 "gateway" courses—e.g., Introduction to Economics, various mathematics courses. The last column showed what percentage of all the students who had taken a particular course completed it with a grade of C or higher. The other columns showed the pass rates for students from each ethnic group. For example, in Introduction to Economics 70% of the students may have completed it with a grade of C or higher. The other columns showed the pass rates for each ethnic group. If the percentage of, say, Latinos who earned a C or higher grade was equal to (70%) or higher than the pass rate for the total, the percentage was shown in the color blue, but if the percentage was below the total (<70%), it would be shown in red. This color coding made inequities in educational outcomes of minority students startlingly obvious.[4]

> The columns for Latinos. African Americans, and Native Americans were almost virtually all in red . . . they were below the average in all the remedial courses. They were below the average in all of the college-level math courses. They were below the average in the business quantitative courses. And when you look at this, you're thinking "These students aren't going to be around."

According to Huberman (1999). "Mindshifts are invariably self-initiated" (p. 311). This may account for the limited impact of traditional research on everyday practice, because research knowledge alone is not sufficient to bring about conceptual shifts among practitioners. On the other hand, when practitioners are the researchers, the knowledge they generate is more likely to produce a conceptual shift. The following excerpt from one of our interviews describes such an occurrence:

> We've known for some time that the highest graduation rates are among the Latinos, and we've always been very proud of that. Then somebody said, "Do they graduate with GPAs as high as everybody else? Do they graduate in majors across the campus or are they congregated in a few places? Are those places preparing them for careers?" And I'm going "I don't know. I never thought about that." But then not only do we need to think about those questions but to realize that the numbers can start toward giving you answers to them. And in some cases watching the numbers gets you closer and closer to the causes . . . When somebody went. "Oh God, the culture of assessment again!" I'd say "But look at what I learned." And you know, you figure if it changed my attitude I might be able to change somebody else's attitude.

Another individual experienced a conceptual shift and discussed how working on the Diversity Scorecard affected how she and other team members developed a different way of thinking about data.

---

[4]If this table had been presented in black and white, as is the customary way of presenting institutional data, it would not have had much of an impact.

[The Diversity Scorecard] really changed our way of thinking, and it changed the way in which we talked with others on campus about data and information ... it has been frustrating because we're clearly thinking in a different way than a lot of our peers or colleagues ... They haven't had the opportunity to really think in the same way or to question or probe.

Evidence Supersedes Anecdotes

Participation is a learning process as well as a research process (Green & Levin, 1998). In addition to raised awareness about inequities in educational outcomes, another outcome of the use of the practitioner-as-researcher model in the Diversity Scorecard project was that participants developed a commitment to data-informed knowledge that extended beyond the immediate project and into other aspects of their professional work. Through their work as researchers, they came to recognize the superiority of knowledge derived from data over that which is based on anecdotal evidence. One team member expressed that the data confirmed what he knew and validated his work as a dean. He reported that the Diversity Scorecard

> has provided the opportunity for me, as the dean of undergraduate studies, not just as a concerned individual, to focus on something. And what it did is, it validated I think what I was feeling intuitively, and I had heard it anecdotally for a number of years ... it presented data in a way that was just over-whelming.

Another team member from a private institution told us that we had taken away his innocence, because he now sees everything in terms of outcomes and benchmarks. He said,

> You have tainted my vision ... I now think differently.

Two other members of the same team had similar responses. One commented.

> On this campus when we talk about issues and problems we often talk about mythologies. Evidence-based practices provide [information] about where we are and where we need to improve. This project is training me to think critically. I now look at some of the mythologies and ask about supportive data.

The second member said,

> There are a lot of mythologies. Doing this project I've found many ways of thinking about data. I've even learned new techniques as an Institutional Research person.

A member of another team admitted having changed from being skeptical about the project to becoming an advocate for it.

I want it understood that at first I was very skeptical about this project. However I have found the approaches to data very useful. This makes it easy when tying it into other things I'm doing or committees I'm on. The evidence-based practices have allowed for a lot of spillover. This pushing to look at data is spilling over to other areas such as when we ask. "Is the curriculum working?

Participants indicated that the project provided an important learning experience. Comments such as these were typical: "We can make arguments supported with numbers"; "something we've learned from this project is to ask questions about how we can do things better"; "I had never thought about gateway courses—ever"; "I'm learning lots about how I can look at data"; "I have learned different ways of perceiving"; "I'm trying out ways I can apply the knowledge more this semester."

Self-Change and Empowerment

It is too early in the project to determine whether new awareness has led to self-change and empowerment among the participants. However, at this point we can provide brief examples from Diversity Scorecard team reports and from a few individuals who have been interviewed. One Diversity Scorecard team from a public institution wrote a report to their president noting that in learning more about their students, they attained a new perspective by looking at the data. They then reported:

> With the information gained from this exercise and a sustained effort, we believe that [our institution] can make an even greater difference in the level of success that our students achieve while at [our institution] and beyond.

Another report written by a team from a small, private institution to the president of the college stated they had

> ... found the Scorecard approach and process—of evidentiary inquiry into the state of equity in student outcomes and potentially enabling or inhibiting practices that contribute to these outcomes—a "high" learning experience, transformational, and likely to bring about or has already resulted in changes in practices.

These excerpts exemplify empowerment as a result of participating in the Diversity Scorecard process at the team level. The teams highlighted felt compelled to improve the conditions at their institutions to ensure the academic success of Latino and African-American students.

Empowerment also occurred at the individual level. One individual spoke expansively about the project having intensified his commitment to issues of equity.

It reinforces your feelings about wanting to continue to try to bring about change, it helps me kind of get a little fired up . . . it is like when you go to a concert, a good concert and you come back and you're fired up because you're ready to go again.

This individual made other comments about the project that were very consistent with our view of ways in which the practitioner-as-researcher model might make a difference.

As a result of this project, you kind of become a bit more interested in wanting to become change agents. Not just merely people who facilitate the flow of work and the implementation of procedures and policies, but that we kind of take a conscious interest in trying to bring about change. I always try to be a change agent, but I also remind myself that given where I am. I know that I become complacent, and I know that there are certain things that I start taking for granted.

In another example of feeling empowered, a woman at a private college spoke about feeling more appreciated by the president and being seen as someone who has valuable information.

I think the project has transformed my role. The president will often call upon me or my colleagues on the team to brief her prior to meeting with an outside agency or about certain diversity issues and that has been an interesting learning experience for me.

This woman also discussed how the Scorecard inspired her and her team to actively make changes on campus to address students' needs. In her interview, she said.

I mean [the Diversity Scorecard project] even caused us at that point to do something we never had really sat down and done. And that was to create what for us became the Intercultural Vision Statement. You know, a kind of mission statement for the intercultural initiative . . . It was almost going back to ground zero and starting over, and it was. I think, an altogether positive thing that happened, and it wouldn't have happened without the Scorecard.

A woman from another team spoke of the Scorecard affecting her professional career in that it has provided her with resources that have motivated her.

Personally, it [the Diversity Scorecard Project] has opened my eyes . . . This process has really given me new energy, a new life for my professional work. It has opened up resources and access to information and to knowledge that I didn't have and its really . . .

it's made me excited again about my work and motivated me to pursue further studies for myself.

Individuals Who Did Not Experience Change

There were a few individuals who reported that the project had no effect on them. We feel it is important to be frank that not all members of the Diversity Scorecard project experienced a deepening of awareness of inequities, or a motivation to address inequities. For example, a woman faculty member told us.

It [the project] felt like an exercise. We did come up with a few things, but it wasn't as much as we would've liked. And one of the reasons . . . well, our team kept changing. I'm not sure it was worth all the time that was put into it on our part. We never did our homework as much as we should've because we had so much else going on, and I think had people gotten stipends[5] from the beginning it might have been taken a little more seriously. It might have been more useful. I really do. I think that would've made the difference. It didn't even have to be a lot but a kind of acknowledgment that we were adding to USC's project.

Another individual who was an institutional researcher, reported that the project had no effect on him and that he had learned nothing new. Toward the end of the interview, the USC interviewer summarized what he was hearing from this individual as follows.

I've gotten from you . . . that your eyes were open to start with in terms of these issues and they remained open. The program didn't close them and it didn't open them any wider basically.

To which the participant responded.

I think that's fair to say.

This individual had been resistant to the project from the outset, and in his interview he expressed considerable frustration with the design of the project as well as with the USC project staff members who were working with his team. He said.

I've been doing this kind of work for eighteen years, and when individuals come in and begin to dictate the scope, course, and direction of your work it was very difficult for me personally to indicate that your approach is simply not mine. There was no sense that we were partnering in this kind of investigation. It was "We have work to do. Let's get busy."

---

[5]The project does not provide stipends for the campus participants; however, there have been very few complaints about the lack of remuneration.

He also resented the time he and his colleagues had to spend in preparing the research report for the president.

> We're making this an elaborate twenty-page document, and there is no payoff for us in the sense of all the effort we've put in.

This individual had come into the project late, having inherited it from his predecessor. Soon after his appointment to the team, two other individuals joined the team, both of them senior faculty members who also had administrative responsibilities. The two of them were enthusiastic about the project and found it very useful. One, in particular, played a major role in the writing of the research report.

Not long after the institutional researcher had responded so negatively in his interview, the team met to rehearse the presentation of the report to the president. Much to our surprise this session turned out to be a moment of revelation. As the group was about to start going through their PowerPoint presentation of the data on student outcomes, the institutional researcher indicated that he was uncomfortable with the format being used to present the data as it was not the way that it is normally done. When he reiterated that there was nothing new in either the data or the report, one of the faculty members mentioned above interrupted and said.

> You may not have learned anything, but the rest of the team did. You get to see the data all the time because it's your job, but this was pretty much all new to me.

In the field notes the USC researcher wrote.

> It was like a light bulb had gone off over [the institutional researcher's] head. He reflected for a few moments and then said that the Diversity Scorecard could be used to 'raise consciousness' about these issues around campus. He said, "I don't know how else to phrase it." he admitted, adding a little hesitantly. "In fact that's what my office should be doing and we're not doing a very good job of it right now." To make sure that this point would not be lost in the meeting with the president, he added a bullet to the PowerPoint presentation, stating that the Diversity Scorecard can be used to 'raise consciousness among campus community members.

Since the institutional researcher came to this realization, his attitude toward the project and his involvement has changed dramatically, and he is now an advocate of the Scorecard approach.

PART IV: REFLECTIONS ON THE PRACTITIONER-AS-RESEARCHER MODEL

This article provides an account of the first two years of a four-year project. The manner in which it is presented may create the impression that the process was smooth and uneventful. Traditional research generally tends to follow a detailed plan with regard to what kind of instruments will be used to gather data, how the data will be analyzed, and how and where the findings will be reported. The practitioner-as-researcher model is quite different in many respects, one of which has to do with control over the implementation of the project.

Different Teams, Different Experiences

In this study we had to depend on the teams to meet and engage in the research process, and there were major differences in the number of times teams met and the number of team members who participated consistently. For example, a three-person team at a small private institution that stayed intact throughout the project had 29 two-hour on-campus meetings in a 24-month period. In contrast, a team whose report was found not to be of value by the president of the institution met only nine times during the same period. In retrospect, frequent meetings were crucial for building trusting and respectful relationships within teams. The relationship that developed between the USC staff and members of the teams that met regularly is more collegial and partner like; there is a sense that we are all in this together. On the other hand, our relationship with the teams that met less frequently is more formal and distant. In another article we have distinguished teams that demonstrated high levels of learning from those that did not on the basis of the former groups' new recognitions of inequity in educational outcomes (Bauman & Bensimon, 2002; Bauman 2002). To some extent those who demonstrated high levels of learning possessed some of the characteristics associated with "real teams" (Bensimon & Neumann, 1993)—e.g., there was a strong sense of connectedness among the members, they viewed data from different perspectives, asked questions, and engaged in extended conversations, and they accomplished the task. In contrast, the teams we perceived as not achieving a high level of learning exhibited some of the characteristics of "illusory teams,"—e.g., they approached the project as a chore to get out of the way rather than as something they were constructing. The members of these teams lacked connectedness, they met less often, and they did not engage in extended conversations about the data.

Rethinking Our Approaches with Team Members

Perhaps the greatest and most unsettling difference between this project and traditional research is that it has required us to rethink approaches constantly. Time and again we have changed our course in order to respond to emerging situations or incorporate our new learning. In the first 18 months, our work was as much about gaining the teams' trust and making them comfortable with us as it was about doing what we said we would do in our proposal. Never having worked with this kind of research model, we had to learn how to do it by trial and error, and at times this was frustrating. In particular, we had to adjust to the reality that working with people rather than working with subjects and data demanded that we be willing to be flexible and be more open to the teams' preferences and needs. Needless to say, it is very difficult to convey effectively the emotional energy that nurturing these teams required of us. Obviously, we are not consultants who come to the campuses a couple of times a year, advise faculty and staff on a particular topic or problem, and then go away. Having a much greater stake in the relationship, we worked to create a level of trust that would prevent the institutional teams from feeling constrained. While our efforts succeeded on most of the campuses, they achieved limited results or failed completely at three institutions.

Admittedly, the USC staff had to work through differences with certain members of the evidence teams. In some instances points of contention were not resolved but swept under the carpet in order to proceed with the task at hand. Another mistake we made was that we did not give sufficient consideration to how institutional researchers might react to this project—specifically that they might regard us as intruders in their domain. Fortunately, most of the resistance was eventually overcome. When institutional researchers began to see that others on the campus were interested in examining data and working cooperatively, they too usually became more enthusiastic. Some have commented that because the evidence teams' reports are simple and display data visually, they have received much more attention than is given to the institutional research reports they normally prepare.

Our decision to focus the project primarily on the educational outcomes for African Americans and Latinos caused some initial discomfort among some of the teams. In one institution, the president informed us that this was not acceptable to her and let it be known that she was apprehensive about the appearance that Black students were being flagged as underperforming.

Learning from the Practioner-as-Researcher Process

Robert Moses and Charles E. Cobb capture the difference we perceived between this project and the way we had conducted research previously in their description of research as community organizing.

The organizer does not have the complete answer in advance—the researcher's detailed comprehensive plans for remedying a perceived problem. The organizer wants to construct a solution with the community . . . This is a long journey and not a linear progression. It is a journey with zigs and zags, a process of pushes and pulls (Moses & Cobb. 2001, pp. 111–112).

The project did not evolve in a straight line. As we learned by doing and gained a better understanding of what the project was about, we reinvented it continuously. Our teamwork made it possible to do this without destabilizing the project. Throughout the duration of the project the Center for Urban Education research team came together once a week to strategize, plan, brainstorm, and think out loud. To a great extent the success of the project has depended on our capacity and willingness to dedicate time and effort to the process of working as a team ourselves.

Perhaps the most important advantage of the practitioner-as-researcher model is the knowledge it yields about local conditions. Colleges and universities cannot be treated as if they are all identical. They differ in mission, structures, student bodies, funding sources, resources, etc. They also change over time so that what was true of an institution in the past may not necessarily be so in the present. Neither are generalizations about institutions or interventions always applicable. The knowledge about a particular institution developed by its own members is usually more relevant than knowledge about higher education in general developed by experts.

To obtain findings through the practitioner-as-researcher model requires more time and involvement than traditional research. Transferring the role of researcher from the expert outsider to a team of institutional insiders can be a very complex undertaking. Furthermore traditional researchers involved in the project must adjust to the unfamiliar roles of facilitators and consultants. In spite of challenges the implementation of this approach may present, the CUE staff and the majority of the evidence team members agree that the practitioner-as-researcher model is uniquely effective. Its foremost advantage is that it yields findings that can actually make a difference in the understandings and actions of faculty and staff members within a particular institution of higher education.

REFERENCES

Bauman, G. L. (2002). *Developing a culture of evidence: Using institutional data to identify inequitable educational outcomes.* Unpublished doctoral dissertation. University of Southern California, Los Angeles.

Bauman, G. L., & Bensimon, E. M. (2002). *The promotion of organizational learning through the use of routine data.* Paper presented at the Association for the Study of Higher Education conference. November, Sacramento, CA.

Bensimon, E. M., & Neumann, A. (1993). *Redesigning collegiate leadership: Teams and teamwork in higher education.* Baltimore, MD: The Johns Hopkins University Press.

Birnbaum R. (1988). *How colleges work: The cybernetics of academic organization and leadership.* San Francisco: Jossey-Bass.

Bowen, W. G., & Bok, D. (1998). *The shape of the river: Long-term consequences of considering race in college and university admissions.* Princeton, NJ: Princeton University Press.

Bray, J. N., Lee, J., Smith, L. L., & Yorks, L. (2000). *Collaborative inquiry in practice: Action, reflection, and making meaning.* Thousand Oaks, CA: Sage.

California Citizens Commission on Higher Education. (1998). *A State of learning: California higher education in the twenty-first century* (June), Blueprint for implementing the report of the California Citizens Commission on Higher Education. Los Angeles, CA.

Conrad, C. F. (1989). Meditations on the ideology of inquiry in higher education: Exposition, critique, and conjecture. *Review of Higher Education, 12*(3), 199–200.

Gaventa, J., & Cornwall, A. (2001). Power and knowledge. In P. Reason & H. Bradbury (Eds.). *Handbook of action research.* Thousand Oaks, CA: Sage.

Green, D. J., & Levin, M. (1998). *An introduction to action research.* Thousand Oaks, CA: Sage.

Hall, S. (1992). The West and the rest: Discourse and power. In S. Hall & B. Gielben (Eds.), *Formations of modernity* (pp. 276–320). Cambridge: Polity Press and Open University.

Heron, J. (1996). *Co-operative inquiry: Research into the human condition.* Thousand Oaks, CA: Sage.

Huberman, M. (1999). The mind is its own place: The influence of sustained interactivity with practitioners on educational researchers. *Harvard Educational Review, 69*(3), 289–319.

Ibarra, R. A. (2001). *Beyond affirmative action: Reframing the contest of higher education.* Madison: University of Wisconsin Press.

Kaplan, R., & Norton, D. (1992). The Balanced Scorecard— Measures that drive performance. *Harvard Business Review, 70*(1), 71–79.

Keller, G. (1985). Trees without fruit: The problem with research about higher education, *Change, 17*(1), 7–10.

Kezar, A., & Eckel, P. (2000). Moving beyond the gap between research and practice in higher education. *New Directions for Higher Education,* no. 110. San Francisco: Jossey-Bass.

Layzell, D. T. (1990). Most research on higher education is stale, irrelevant, and of little use to policymakers. *Chronicle of Higher Education, 37*(8), pp. B1, B3.

Moses, R. P., & Cobb, C. E., Jr. (2001). *Radical equations: Math literacy and civil rights.* Boston: Beacon Press.

Myers, D., Park, J., & Hacegaba. N. (2000) *Reversing the shrinking middle and polarization in California's labor force: Report of a pilot investigation.* Center for Urban Education and Population Research Laboratory, University of Southern California. Available at: http://www.use.edu/dept/education/CUE/documents/ MyersShrinking-MiddlePaper.CUE.pdf

Nettles, M. T. (1995). The emerging national policy agenda on higher education assessment: A wake-up call. *Review of Higher Education, 18*(3), 293–313.

O'Neil, H. F., Jr., Bensimon, E. M., Diamond, M. A., & Moore, M. R. (1999). Designing and implementing an academic scorecard. *Change, 31*(6). 32–41.

Park, P. (1999). People, knowledge, and change in participatory research. *Management Learning 30*(2). 141–157.

Reason, P. (1994). Three approaches to participative inquiry. In N. K. Denzin & Y. Lincoln (Eds.) *Handbook of qualitative research.* Thousand Oaks, CA: Sage.

Reason, P., & Bradbury, H. (2001). Introduction: Inquiry and participation in search of a world worthy of human aspiration. In P. Reason & H. Bradbury (Eds.), *Handbook of action research: Participative inquiry and practice* (pp. 1–14). Thousand Oaks, CA: Sage.

Sassen, S. (1994). The urban complex in a world economy. *International Social Science Journal, 46*(1). 43–62.

Smith, L. T. (1999). *Decolonizing methodologies: Research and indigenous peoples.* New York and London: Zed Books Ltd, and Dunedin: Otago Press. (5th ed., 2000).

Stringer, E. T. (1996). *Action research: A handbook for practitioners.* Thousand Oaks: Sage.

Terenzini, P. T. (1996). Rediscovering roots: Public policy and higher education research. *Review of Higher Education, 20*(1). 5–13.

Wenger, E. (1998). *Communities of practice: Learning, meaning and identity.* Cambridge: Cambridge University Press.

Evaluation Criteria

1. Does the research provide accurate information about the practices studied?

The article describes an approach to action research which the authors call practitioner-as-researcher. They contrast this model not only with traditional academic research but also with other forms of participatory action research. They provide a detailed account of the Diversity Scorecard, its development and use. They describe how the Scorecard varied from campus to campus, depending on indicators developed by participants at each institution.

2. Does the research cover the needs of a given audience?

This seems to have been the major strength of the method: the authors describe how the development of local indicators, upon which data were collected and analyzed by the authors and then presented to campus participants for meaning-making, led to changes in orientation about the issues under study.

3. Is the research realistic, frugal, and diplomatic?

Because the study was grounded in what campus leaders wanted to know, and the data were presented to them with minimal interpretation, the research meets both the realistic and diplomatic criteria. No information is given about the cost of the research, although one must assume the costs to be substantial, as the approach is labor-intensive.

4. Was the research conducted legally and ethically?

There appear to be no legal issues at stake here; and since the researchers and their campus partners used only aggregate archival data, ethical issues would appear to be minimal as well.

Discussion Questions

1. The practitioner-as-researcher approach described in this article relies solely on numbers. Yet, unlike the quantitative perspective, there is no attempt to generalize beyond the campus context—in fact, the research is designed so as not to allow for such generalization. How then would you classify this study according to the criteria given in Chapter 1?

2. The authors suggest that having campus leaders define the key indicators, and having them generate their own interpretations, was what led to "research that makes a difference." Do you agree?

3. Imagine yourself as a member of the research team. What are the key diplomatic issues to address in campus meetings with project participants?

4. What do you see as the key ethical issues surrounding the disaggregation of data by ethnicity?

Credibility Scorecard
Doing Research that Makes a Difference

	Excellent	Very Good	Adequate	Marginal	Poor
General purpose	5	4	3	2	1
Contribution/ significance	5	4	3	2	1
Review of literature	5	4	3	2	1
Research questions or hypotheses	5	4	3	2	1
Subjects or participants	5	4	3	2	1
Instrumentation	5	4	3	2	1
Procedures	5	4	3	2	1
Results	5	4	3	2	1
Practical significance	5	4	3	2	1
Graphics	5	4	3	2	1
Conclusions	5	4	3	2	1
Any fatal flaws?					

INDEX